THE BIRDS OF VASHON ISLAND

A Natural History of Habitat & Population Transformation

Second Edition

by Ed Swan

Constancy Press, LLC   Seattle, Washington

The Birds of Vashon Island:
A Natural History of Habitat & Population Transformation
by Ed Swan

Second Edition

Copyright © 2013 Ed Swan

All rights reserved. No part of this book may be reproduced in any form or by any electronic or mechanical means incuding information storage and retrieval systems without permission in writing from Ed Swan, except by a reviewer, who may quote brief passages in a review.

Note: All photographs and maps are used with permission from the photographers and mapmakers, who shall retain their copyright.

Front Cover: Horned Grebe © Tim Kuhn
Back Cover (clockwise from upper left): Downy Woodpecker © Gregg Thompson; Rhinoceros Auklet © Steve Caldwell; Spotted Towhee © Gregg Thompson; Ed Swan © Linda Barnes

Published & distributed by Constancy Press, LLC, and Ed Swan
Copy-editing and production by Constancy Press, LLC
Printed in Nansha, China, by Everbest Printing Company, through Four Colour Print Group

November 2013

To obtain more copies of this book, write or call:
Ed Swan   (206)463-7976
11230 SW 212th Place
Vashon, WA 98070
www.theswancompany.com

Library of Congress Control Number: 2013953734

ISBN 978-0-9842002-3-8 $28.95

Dedication

To Linda for her hard work, help, and thoughtfulness.

Western Sandpiper. © Ed Swan

Acknowledgements

I would like to thank the many people who did so much to help create this book on Vashon birds.

My wife, Linda Barnes, and parents, Ed and Shirley Swan, made the time to wade through early and final drafts, spending countless hours bringing vital editing insights to the book. Linda encouraged and supported me every step of the way toward creating this revised edition.

Constance Sidles, owner of Constancy Press, brought her enthusiasm and expertise to the project. Her attention to detail and her many years of experience in print production carried the book to a higher level of professionalism and artistic creativity.

Many people shared their observations of birds and the environment of Vashon. In particular, Sue Trevathan and Gary Shugart always made themselves available to answer bird identification and general bird questions. Over a hundred others, too many to name, regularly shared sightings. The following contributed vital background and history and/or scores of records for both editions: Dan Willsie, John Friars, Ed Babcock, Dave Beaudette, Sue Trevathan, Rich Siegrist, Carole Elder, Steve Caldwell, Ron Simons, Rayna Holtz, Rick Sanders, Peter Murray, Bob Hawkins, Harsi and Ezra Parker, Emma Amiad, Brenda Sestrap, Alice Bloch, Sharon Helmick, Pam and Jack Dawdy, Marie Blichfeldt, Sherry Bottoms, and Gary Shugart. Susie Kalhorn and Bianca Perla helped fact-check and review many general habitat questions and particularly helped with water and stream issues.

I am very indebted to Derek Churchill for his help updating information on Vashon habitats types. Derek created the new habitat maps for this edition and assisted with their interpretation, making this revised edition much more accurate in its depiction of where each habitat occurs on the Island, how much of it exists, and what vegetation relationships pertain to every type. Derek contributed his forestry knowledge, enabling the descriptions of the forest habitats in particular to more precisely reflect their current status.

Many other people assisted with spectacular and informative illustrations throughout the book. For a complete list, see the Photographs and Maps credits beginning on page vi.

My heartfelt thanks to all these people, who generously gave their time, energy, expertise, and support. This book would not have been possible without you.

Contents

Acknowledgements iv

I. Introduction 1

II. The Natural History of Vashon Island 7

III. Habitats and Conservation 32

IV. Site Guide to Vashon Birding Hot Spots 89

V. The Vashon Year from a Birding Perspective 117

VI. Avian Seasonal Abundance 124

VII. Annotated List of Species 133

References 312

Index 323

Photographs & Maps

The author would like to extend a special thanks to all the photographers and mapmakers listed below who so generously offered their talent, expertise, and art to help make this book both beautiful and informative.

Linda Barnes
  Dry Douglas-fir/Madrone habitat at Maury Island Marine Park....59
  Ed Swan..Back Cover
  Mud Flat Shoreline habitat at Fern Cove........................50
  Shrubby Thicket habitat at Raab's Lagoon.......................66

Steve Caldwell
  Rhinoceros Auklet.....................................Back Cover

Michael Elenko
  Cedar Waxwings..278
  Common Loon..99
  Hardwood Forest habitat at Shinglemill Creek...................62
  Northern Flicker..234

Tim Kuhn
  Bald Eagle..180
  Bonaparte's Gull..105
  Horned Grebe..Front Cover

Kevin Lickfelt
  Townsend's Solitaire..271

Kathrine Lloyd
  Killdeer and baby..88
  Spotted Sandpiper...191

Peter Murray
  Anna's Hummingbird..226
  Barred Owl chicks..98
  Farm and Field habitat on Westside Highway.....................67
  Great Horned Owls...222
  Lewis's Woodpecker..231
  Pileated Woodpecker..95
  Saltwater habitat at Quartermaster Harbor......................41
  Wet Coniferous Forest habitat at Shinglemill Creek.............56

Doug Parrott
　　American Crow 246
　　American Goldfinch 310
　　Black-capped Chickadees 256
　　Brown-headed Cowbird 303
　　Cackling Goose 138
　　Great Blue Heron 132
　　Greater Yellowlegs 113
　　House Finches 306
　　Mallard adults 123
　　Mallard duckling 145
　　Pied-billed Grebe chick viii
　　Savannah Sparrow 288
　　Song Sparrow 291
　　Spotted Towhee 286
　　Tree Swallows 252
　　Western Grebe 110
　　Western Meadowlark 300
　　White-crowned Sparrow 294

Gary Shugart
　　Thayer's Gull with Glaucous-winged 101

Ed Swan
　　Black Turnstone 108
　　Douglas-fir Forest habitat on Old Mill Road 58
　　Osprey nest 71
　　Palm Warbler 282
　　Pelagic Cormorant 176
　　Pond and Wetlands habitat at Mukai Pond 53
　　Say's Phoebe 118
　　Sharp-shinned Hawk 184
　　Western Sandpiper iii

Gregg Thompson
　　American Robin 275
　　Band-tailed Pigeons 218
　　Brown Pelican 173
　　Dark-eyed Junco 297
　　Downy Woodpecker .... Back Cover
　　Golden-crowned Kinglet 266
　　Red Crossbill 308
　　Ruby-crowned Kinglet 267

Snow Bunting 279
Spotted Towhee...................................... Back Cover
Wilson's Warbler 102

Univerity of Washington Special Collections
Couple and old-growth tree 2
Ellisport 1892 7
Native American woman 9
Loggers 10
Old Mace Mill 11
C. Wright farm 15
Harvesters 17
Vashon Lake 21
Dead Cougar 27

Vashon Maury Island Heritage Association
Quail release 23

Maps

Derek Churchill
Vashon Island Habitat Types, North Section 42-43
Vashon Island Habitat Types, South Section 44-45
Vashon Island Habitat Types, Maury Section 46-47

King County Department of Natural Resources and Parks, Water and Land Resources Division, prepared by Todd Klinka
Vashon Island Protected Lands Map 90-91

Pied-billed Grebe chick. © Doug Parrott

Chapter I

Introduction

The Birds of Vashon Island first came out in 2005. In the eight years following, a great deal of change occurred in the birding world and the environmental scene as a whole on Vashon. The publishing industry continues to transform itself as well, lowering the price of color photos and allowing inclusion of color graphics, which makes illustrations much more interesting. As the first edition sold out essentially within eight months, the need for more copies as well as the wealth of new information appear to call for a second, extensively expanded and revised edition.

The same elements of the nature of Vashon Island and the same goals as the first edition continue to make a book on birds and Vashon habitats interesting and useful to Vashon residents and to some extent anyone concerned about the environment in the Puget Sound region. Birds provide a highly visible and often entertaining entry into understanding our environment. They are also a good indicator of the health of our local ecosystem. Vashon's history of habitat change mirrors the experience of the whole lowland region. Knowing how the alterations in habitats here affected bird species offers a viewpoint into similar population rises and falls for birds around Puget Sound.

Vashon Island forms a rural outpost in the center of the increasingly industrialized, urbanized, and sprawling Puget Sound region. It lies in King County, a fifteen-minute ferry ride from three points: Seattle in King County, Tacoma in Pierce County, and Southworth in Kitsap County. Maury Island, off Vashon's southeast quarter, connects to Vashon via a narrow isthmus. This book refers to the two together as "the Island" or simply Vashon.

The 150-year history of environmental change on Vashon Island created a wide variety of habitats that attract a great diversity of bird species to a small area. The mix of forest types, fields, residential areas, wetlands, and saltwater provides a habitat mosaic in which 251 species of birds are listed for the Island.

The second edition of *The Birds of Vashon Island* continues, as in the original, to aim at assisting Islanders and visitors to further enjoy the abundant bird life as a means toward illuminating the connectedness of the birds to the condition of the land and water on which we all depend. The history of modern culture's impact on the ecology of the Island clearly demonstrates again and again that the land-use decisions made by humans determine what other life remains to share Vashon with us. This book takes a change-by-change look at how habitat transformations resulted in elimination and introduction of whole populations and species of birds in the Island's ecosystem.

A couple sits in front of an old-growth tree. © University of Washington Special Collections (UW19419)

The final goal of this book centers on encouraging Islanders and residents of the remaining rural areas of the Puget lowlands to ask themselves: What will happen as development continues? Vashon and the rural areas of the Puget lowlands have now reached a crossroads where decisions or even the lack of a conscious choice of action will decide what happens to our local ecosystems. Ultimately, increased human population directly displaces or indirectly spreads disruption to every habitat type on the Island. Will Vashon remain truly rural, or will residential development spread throughout, even if the pace remains slower than that taking place in the region as a whole? Will the growing number of people living on Vashon threaten individual habitat types whose loss would mean the elimination of species from the Island? Which habitats face the most challenges, and which should have the highest priority for protection? The Vashon-Maury Island Land Trust, the Vashon-Maury Island Audubon Society, Sound Action (formerly Preserve Our Islands), the Vashon-Maury Island Groundwater Protection Committee, and the Vashon-Maury Island

Community Council, among others, have raised and acted on many of these issues. Vashon's environmental challenges require continued discussion as development advances and penetrates Island habitats.

Conservation Progress Since the First Edition

Sound Action and many other Vashon organizations met one major challenge and scored a significant victory since the first edition: stopping Glacier Northwest's gravel pit expansion. The Glacier Northwest project potentially threatened the sole source aquifer, its barge traffic likely would have affected Orcas already under serious pressure in the Sound, and work might have destroyed eelgrass and other key habitat in the Maury Island Aquatic Reserve. Vashon organizations and public officials successfully negotiated public purchase of the land such that now, with other adjacent preserved land, it forms the 350+ acre Dockton Forest and Natural Area. The Vashon-Maury Island Land Trust also continued its focus on conserving the Island's major watersheds. With a sustained effort over the last decade, it now has preserved roughly 200 acres along the Shinglemill Creek and Judd Creek drainages, and many more acres have been protected with conservation easements and other protections. Finally, the Groundwater Protection Committee worked closely with King County Groundwater Protection Program to further refine models to understand Vashon's water supply. While water supply and quality concerns require more research, these agencies now possess a much stronger knowledge base on which to make development decisions connected to water.

Expanded Knowledge over the Last Decade

The second edition of *The Birds of Vashon Island* provides a solid baseline for looking at potential changes coming to Vashon and their possible effects on wildlife. Much more data on the seasonal occurrence and population status of Vashon birds has been collected over the last decade. One of the goals of the first edition, "to assist Islanders and visitors to further enjoy the abundant bird life," succeeded, with the book encouraging more people to find out about birds on Vashon. Also, for a span of several years, Dan Willsie, Alan Huggins, Gary Shugart, Richard Rogers, Steve Caldwell, and others created and put on an "Enjoyment of Birds" and "Birding by Ear" series of classes attended altogether by at least 30 to 40 people each year. The author's bird alert email list and the Vashon Birders email list encouraged the sometimes almost instantaneous sharing of sightings and other information.* In the intervening time, seven additional

---

* Email the author at edswan@centurytel.net to report a sighting and/or go to Yahoo groups online to join the Vashon Birders list.

Christmas Bird Counts, organized by Sue Trevathan, brought the number of counts up to fifteen, doubling the existing data for that season.

The increase in the number of observers, the rise in the abilities of watchers to correctly identify species and know what birds to report, and the surge in sharing of sightings directly resulted in changes in the status of 21 Vashon species. Visitors or observers new to the Island found six of the fifteen new species. Altogether, increased observer effort and ability uncovered more than a third of the changes in species status noted since the first edition. Further literature research, increased sharing of observations, and more observer effort documented changes in status for 68 of the 251 species found on Vashon, a little over a quarter of the species list (see Table 1 below.) Over the last eight years, Vashon's bird species list grew from 239 to 251, a net gain of twelve species. Of the fifteen new additions, nine consisted of birds never before noted on Vashon. Three of these came from further review of ornithological literature. Two more showed up in historical ornithological literature, and also recent observers spotted them for a modern record. One more new to the list resulted from an Islander sharing an old sighting. Of the four deletions, three represent "paper losses," not population declines. Redheads, for example, originally included on the species list on the basis of several sightings over the years in two to three places near Vashon Center, turned out to be almost certainly escapees from a local breeder.

Overall, the change in status findings appears mostly good for Vashon. Increases in sightings from a real rise in numbers or presence (as opposed to just better observer coverage) totaled at least eight species. Six species spent more of a season or added one or more seasons to their time on the Island, and two first confirmed breeding records occurred. Of the fifteen new species added to the list, however, only one (Eurasian Collared-Dove)

Table 1: Change in Status of Vashon Bird Species 2005-2013	
Increased sightings from observer effort	21
Increased sightings from actual increase in numbers	8
Expanded season on Vashon	6
First breeding record for Vashon	2
New addition to the species list	15
Decline in sightings for Vashon	9
Deletion from the species list	4
Deletion from breeding species list	1
Incorrect status listing in first edition rectified	3

can be seen regularly; all the rest will be seen at most once every few years and represent species that visit Vashon only as passing visitors. When more good observers exist and share information, then all the missed rarities and accidental visitors get noticed and fill out any given location's list.

The declines also reflect species that for the most part visit the Island only rarely. Of the nine species with decreasing sightings, only the Common Tern formerly appeared regularly in good numbers. The deletion numbers include one species now extinct for Vashon. The California Quail must be removed from the list after experiencing habitat loss over the past 50 to 60 years. In addition, over the same period of time, pressure on the quail increased from introduced predators such as unmanaged cats and dogs and artificially enhanced populations of predators such as Raccoons. One species no longer successfully breeds on Vashon, the Great Blue Heron. As the Bald Eagle recovers from persecution and pesticides, a new ecological balance continues to develop that currently includes the eagles' heavy predation of herons at rookeries across the Puget Sound region. On Vashon, after the rookeries died out, eagles pursued and ended every known attempt by herons to build even solitary nests.

Our understanding of Vashon's habitat mix has also improved over the last decade. The first edition utilized data and GIS software from the late 1980s. This second edition uses satellite imagery from 2006 to 2008 and GIS software that has been much upgraded. In addition, Derek Churchill, Ph.D., a forestry consultant from the University of Washington's College of Forest Resources and a resident of Vashon for the past decade, provided mapping, analysis, and long-term firsthand knowledge of Island forests. The mapping covered not only forest habitats but also better described all of Vashon's terrestrial habitat types. In addition, the increase in color printing capability makes possible the inclusion of larger and more detailed habitat maps for this edition.

Enjoying Birding on Vashon

Several factors make Vashon attractive to those excited about birds and birding. First, the Island represents a beautiful, largely natural setting easily accessible to the highly developed areas of Puget Sound. A day's serious birding should find 60 to 70 species in any season. With luck and planning, more than 100 species might be possible from mid-November to mid-May. From winter to mid-spring, more than 60 species of loons, grebes, cormorants, waterfowl, shorebirds, gulls, terns, and alcids winter and migrate around Vashon. In April and May, neotropical songbirds join the spring water bird and shorebird migration, creating a period of great avian species diversity.

Second, a wide range of habitats provides the opportunity to see a large number of species in a relatively minute section of the Puget Sound region. Vashon habitats reflect a wide range of possibilities: open saltwater, sandy/cobble shore, ponds and wetlands, hardwood-dominated mixed forest, wet coniferous forest (Western Hemlock, Western Red Cedar, and Douglas-fir co-dominant), Douglas-fir forest, dry Douglas-fir/Pacific Madrone forest, shrubby thickets, developed area, and farmland.

Third, a good infrastructure exists supporting birding around Vashon. Public parks, privately owned land open to the public, and public right-of-way now cover well the important habitat and good birding spots. The Vashon-Maury Island Audubon Society (VMIAS) keeps a good, up-to-date website (www.vashonaudubon.org) that includes recent sightings and descriptions of birding hot spots. VMIAS also sponsors a second Saturday of the month field trip to Island birding locations open to the public. The author also maintains a website at www.theswancompany.com offering guiding services. Please report interesting bird observations to VMIAS or the author at edswan@centurytel.net.

Overview of Chapters

The following chapters frame the background for the above questions concerning the effects of habitat change and provide comparative data for measuring future alterations. Chapters II and III look closely at Island history and habitats in order to identify some of the challenges and solutions to problems facing the Island's ecosystems. Chapter II examines the history of changes in bird species on Vashon as human actions transformed the local environment. Chapter III focuses on the physical environment that provides the foundation for the various habitats of the Island. It examines each habitat in turn, with an eye toward describing which bird species utilize each particular habitat.

The remaining chapters look more closely at the bird species themselves. Chapter IV provides a site guide as a companion to the discussion of habitat types. It describes the best birding locations on the Island, what to expect there, and how to reach them. Chapter V consists of an overview of the year from the point of view of the changes occurring in bird populations and activity as the seasons turn. Chapter VI complements the annual overview with a species checklist and seasonal occurrence chart. Chapter VII constitutes an annotated list of each species with its current population status, history, and habitat preferences.

Chapter II

The Natural History of Vashon Island

Before the 1850s, coniferous old-growth forest formed the terrestrial habitat of Vashon Island, dominated by Western Hemlock, Western Red Cedar, and Douglas-fir. Creek mouths and a few open areas hosted deciduous woods and thickets. Spotted Owl and Northern Goshawk almost certainly bred, and Sooty Grouse abounded on the Island.

Native Americans arrived first and over several thousand years built a number of villages. They left the old-growth forest largely intact, subsisting on the bountiful food sources harvested from the creeks and saltwater.

Ellisport 1892. © University of Washington Special Collections, Oliver S. Van Olinda Photograph Collection, UW 19139

They likely intentionally burned some areas to create hunting and berry-picking grounds. European explorers with the Vancouver Expedition first appeared on May 28, 1792, naming the Island for Captain James Vashon of the British Royal Navy (Carey 1985). Some logging for ships' masts and spars occurred from the 1850s through the 1860s. The first survey of the Island took place in 1857. The European-American settlers began arriving in the late 1870s. The settlers lived in temporary shacks along the shoreline, where they cleared timber and loaded it onto ships. Gradually, over the last decade of the 19th century and the first few decades of the 20th, the settlers moved inland and cleared all of the old-growth forest (Carey 1985, Cole 1941). The amount of change that European-American-style settlement unleashed created a series of alterations to the Island ecosystem. Available documentation fails to completely describe all the effects on wildlife. Yet it is certain that more than half of the Vashon bird species experienced significant change in their population.

The following sections examine the various causes for the changes in species population. The species accounts later in the book investigate in more detail the changes in population for each bird species.

Native American Presence

For around 3,000 years, Native Americans occupied Vashon, at least in a seasonal manner. Arrow/spear points, probably from nomadic hunters, dating to 9000 BCE showed up on Vashon (Haulman in press). Indigenous peoples utilized other nearby sites such as West Point in Seattle longer than 4,000 years. Prior to European-American settlement, the S'Homamish people of the Puyallup Nation inhabited Vashon. They built several small villages scattered around the Island, especially in the Quartermaster Harbor area, including a fort at the mouth of the harbor (Stein et al. 2002). At the time of Vancouver's contact in 1792, five permanent village sites with about 650 inhabitants existed (Haulman in press). Clams and other shellfish provided much of the local diet, as well as salmon returning to Judd Creek. Salmon obtained easier access to the creek because at that time a passage existed between Maury and Vashon Islands at Portage.

Native Americans likely made a small impact on avian populations. Their diet focused on seafood and included some hunting of mammals and birds (Stein et al. 2002). A net was suspended across the passage at Portage to catch birds moving back and forth between Tramp and Quartermaster Harbors. "Immense nets, woven of grass, were stretched between the islands, and waterfowl flying at low altitude between the Sound (sic) and Quartermaster Harbor were snared by this net" (Carey 1985).

The S'Homamish made some changes to the forest that created a few open areas, probably introducing more habitat for sparrows and neotropical migrants. Buerge's (1994) search of survey records indicates several sections with fire damage to trees, possibly from natural causes such as lightning or Native American burning to allow clear spaces for berrying and hunting. Surveyors noted several large burned areas on the Island, possibly indicating that the S'Homamish were unable to contain some fires. White (1980) states in an extensive study of Whidbey and Camano Island ecological history that Salish Indian groups considerably shaped their island ecology by using a consistent burn regime on the prairies to encourage Bracken Fern, camas, and nettles. It appears that this occurred as well on a smaller scale for Vashon. Some open-area birds may have

Native American woman cutting driftwood, ca 1895. © University of Washington Special Collections, Oliver S. Van Olinda Photograph Collection, UW 19124

been able to use the clearings on Vashon. Unfortunately, no written or oral record of these birds, such as the Western Bluebird, surfaces until after extensive cutting of the forest took place in the late 1800s.

Elimination of Old-Growth Forest

Before the coming of westward-moving settlers, coniferous forest dominated Vashon. General Land Office surveyors platted Vashon into one-mile-square blocks in 1857. Survey posts marked each corner, and the surveyors were required to pick the closest tree at each cardinal compass point (N, S, E, and W) as witness trees (Schroeder 2013). They also chose one tree at the midpoint on the side of each block such that altogether, each square mile had eight witness trees, one in each corner and one in the middle of each side. The very rough look that this very small but random sample provides gives a glimpse of what tree species definitely grew on Vashon (Schroeder 2013): Douglas-fir made up 50 percent of the witness trees, Western Red Cedar 20 percent, Red Alder and Western Hemlock each about 13 percent, and Pacific Madrone about 2 percent. Other species at smaller amounts consisted of willow, Bigleaf Maple, Grand Fir, and Pacific Yew. Douglas-fir showed up more in central Vashon and to the south, Western Red Cedar scattered throughout, Western Hemlock mostly in the wetter north, and Red Alder along shorelines.

Loggers with cross-cut saw seated next to skid road (on left). © University of Washington Special Collections, Oliver S. Van Olinda Photograph Collection, UW 19392

Huge, thousand-year-old trees did not necessarily completely cover the Island. The average diameter of the Douglas-fir at chest height came out at 22.3 inches and Western Red Cedar at 26.3 inches (Schroeder 2013). The range of all the trees went from 2 inches to 84 inches, so some very large trees grew but likely did not dominate. Some open areas existed as a result of fire. A very large section all the way across the Island around the area of Bank Road lacked suitable witness trees because of fire. A smaller section showing fire damage appeared along Paradise Valley. These fires might have been natural, lightning-caused fires or fire from Native American practices. The existence of a large fire-affected area suggests a landscape that appears more dynamic, with trees of different ages and some open areas rather than a static age-old forest.

Around the mid-1800s, some logging occurred along the outer shorelines and Quartermaster Harbor, as water provided easier transportation for local use or shipping elsewhere. After permanent settlement began in 1877, the pace of logging accelerated (Carey 1985). By the beginning of World War I, one could walk from one side of the Island to the other without seeing a mature tree. Pope & Talbott logged off one-third of Vashon in a mere three years, from 1907 to 1910 (Haulman in press).

While logging turned many areas of Vashon into a vast wasteland of slash, large sections of the rest of the Island supported a variety of agri-

The Old Mace Mill with old-growth logs. © University of Washington Special Collections, Oliver S. Van Olinda Photograph Collection, UW 19323

cultural fields (Cole 1941). As farmers attempted a myriad of agricultural methods and crops with varying degrees of success and failure, forests began to regenerate. Currently, most of the mature woods on Vashon consist of stands anywhere from 50 to 100 years old, reflecting waves of logging on the Island. The last major wave of logging and also large forest fires came in the late 1940s, just after World War II. After the last of the major logging and fires and the decline of farming, forests regenerated naturally over these areas or in some cases, grew as part of plantations intended for later logging. By the beginning of the 21st century, wooded areas spread to cover 71 percent of Vashon (Churchill 2013b, Ohmann and Gregory 2002).

Of all of the human alterations to date, the clearing of Vashon caused the most dramatic changes in avian populations. The hardest-hit species consisted of those that formed the majority of the original terrestrial bird population, forest birds. At least 40 resident species would have been affected, mostly facing major population declines. Conversely, a handful of already resident species such as sparrows and Wilson's Warblers undoubtedly increased in population.

Seven species eventually became rare or extirpated entirely as a result of the old-growth forest elimination. Four of these birds, Northern Goshawk, Marbled Murrelet, Spotted Owl, and Vaux's Swift, rely heavily on

Table 2: Species Affected Most by the Elimination of Old-Growth Forest		
Species	**Historic Status**	**Current Status**
Northern Goshawk	If present, eliminated as possible breeder	Very rare visitor
Sooty Grouse	Originally fairly common	Extirpated by 1955
Marbled Murrelet	Eliminated as possible breeder	Rare visitor
Spotted Owl	If present, extirpated by 1900.	Extirpated
Vaux's Swift	Abundance unknown, possible breeder	Rare migrant
Lewis's Woodpecker	Known to be present in 1900s, likely colonized after initial cutting	Very rare visitor
Hairy Woodpecker	Likely once fairly common	Very rare visitor

old-growth forest for foraging and breeding habitat. They formerly bred to the shoreline in the Puget Sound area (Jewett et al. 1953, Smith et al. 1997, Wahl et al. 2005). Northern Goshawk and Spotted Owl no longer exist on Vashon because they require thousands of acres for their breeding territory. They probably vanished by the end of the 19th century, coincident with the disappearance of the old forest. Marbled Murrelet and Vaux's Swift either visit in migration or loosely forage around Vashon. They would have been eliminated as possible breeders by the end of the 19th century. Marbled Murrelet and Spotted Owl so closely depend on old-growth forest that they may actually become extinct in Western Washington as that habitat disappears on a region-wide basis.

The other three species, Hairy Woodpecker, Sooty Grouse, and Lewis's Woodpecker, don't require old-growth forest. Their needs revolve around the tree species composition of the woods and their management. Ornithologists consider Hairy Woodpecker fairly common in Western Washington (Wahl et al. 2005). These woodpeckers prefer conifers, utilizing mixed forests to a lesser extent (Smith et al. 1997, Wahl et al. 2005). Given the forest makeup, they would have presumably occurred in healthy numbers on the Island prior to European-American settlement. When loggers cut the original conifer forest, their numbers would have declined. Because of a lack of observers keeping records, no known sightings are available for Vashon prior to the last two decades. Forest again covers much of the Island and most of it conifer-dominated. But all of the forest, whether conifer- or hardwood-dominated, represents a mix of tree species. Hairy Woodpeckers now persist only as rare residents or visitors. Recent sightings could either be from residual populations or from re-colonization efforts.

The probable reasons for the extirpation of the last two, Sooty Grouse and Lewis's Woodpecker, relate to forest management practices. Observers historically found these birds in disturbed, second-growth Douglas-fir or burnt-over forests in the Puget Sound area (Ed Babcock pers. comm. 2005, Campbell et al. 1990, Jewett et al. 1953, Rathbun 1902). The amount of logging on Vashon tapered down extensively by World War II, creating fewer disturbed areas. Fire prevention disrupted the natural fire regime that provided snags and semi-open areas in the woods. It's interesting to note that after the last major wave of fires and logging on the Island immediately after World War II, both the Sooty Grouse and the Lewis's Woodpecker fell into decline and disappeared on Vashon. For the Lewis's Woodpecker, this mirrored a region-wide phenomenon west of the Cascades. A more thorough discussion of the population changes of these two species is found in the Annotated List.

In a study examining the effects of logging Douglas-fir forests on bird species in northwestern California, Raphael et al. (1988) predicted that no extirpations of bird species would occur. The study looked at 60 breeding bird species utilizing mature Douglas-fir forests, a fairly comprehensive sample. The researchers looked at the effects on bird populations following standard logging practices at the time and extrapolated results of a total harvest of old-growth woods. They felt that all species would survive even a complete elimination of old-growth forest. Because Vashon experienced just such a complete cut of its mature forest, the study appears to describe much of the change Vashon bird species experienced. Limits to the study's accuracy include the deliberate exclusion of the Spotted Owl because of the amount of study that species already received. The study also left out the Marbled Murrelet and Northern Goshawk. The Marbled Murrelet appears to require old-growth forest to the same degree as the Spotted Owl, and Northern Goshawks prefer mature forests of many types. Raphael et al. (1988) expected no extirpations because most of the forest species partially utilize multiple habitats. Bole-foraging species such as Hairy Woodpecker and Pileated Woodpecker—the species most dependent on trees—declined the most, followed by canopy/air foragers including Golden-crowned Kinglet.

Raphael et al. found that the most significant effect of the clearing of forests centered on the increase in populations of ground- and bush-foraging birds utilizing the early stage, re-growing forest habitats. While a few ground-dwelling residents such as Pacific Wren and Hermit Thrush would have been hit very hard, losing more than half their numbers, most species would grow in numbers to a great extent. In Table 3, Rapheal et al. predicted that the ground/bush-foraging cohort of birds would be expected to have thirteen species increasing in numbers, only four decreasing, and four remaining about the same. As follows in the discussion of the creation of farm and field habitat and of large hardwood mixed forest tracts, Vashon experienced the immigration of many open-area birds that loved thicket and deciduous vegetation. Forest clearing eliminated some species on Vashon and in Rapheal et al.'s study severely decreased a few species's populations, but most forest species survived and recovered as they used younger and more diverse forest types.

Askins (2000) notes in *Restoring North America's Birds* that most of the birds of western forests often shift among different forest habitat types. Western forests consist of a mosaic of wood patches in different successional stages. Bird species adapted to the use of multiple forest habitat types. One cause of extinction and population decline in the eastern forests possibly results from the nature of those woods as fairly uniform habitats. Askins indicates that species threatened by the elimination of old-growth woods and current forest practices may be divided into three groups:

1. Species requiring a regular fire regime rather than simply the creation of open areas such as clear-cuts (Lewis's Woodpecker).
2. Species needing large and greater than 200-year-old forests (Spotted Owl and Marbled Murrelet).
3. Species specializing in a particular food source that is available in large quantities in scattered locations on a region-wide basis (Red Crossbill).

Without an exact history of the logging of the area and the pace of the following forest succession, it is impossible to chart the fluctuations over time of most of the Island's forest bird species. Raphael et al. (1988) present a chart showing the estimated status of species after 100 percent of the

Table 3: Predicted Species Response to 100 Percent Clearing of Old-Growth Forest						
Response	Ground/ Bush Foraging	Bole Foraging	Migrant Canopy/ Air Foraging	Resident Canopy/ Air Foraging	Other	Total
Increase	13	1	11	2	3	30
Decrease	4	4	5	3	1	17
Same	4	2	4	2	1	13

C. Wright farm about 1891. © University of Washington Special Collections, Oliver S. Van Olinda Photograph Collection, UW 19104

old-growth was removed. Seventeen species showed declines, while 30 had increases. Only the Bole Foraging and Resident Canopy/Air Foraging groups of birds had a majority of species in decline. Western species' ability to survive in other habitat types or to utilize surviving stands of trees cut at different periods may mean that the Island percentages were similar. Only the species that were mentioned as not having been covered in the study would have been eliminated.

The Introduction of Farms and Fields

As previously discussed, the first major impact on the environment began with the clearing of forests, resulting in the elimination and decline of forest species. Within a relatively short time, birds that prefer open areas colonized Vashon in the new farms, fields, thickets, and brushy clear-cuts. Anywhere from a third to half of the Island's acreage may have been devoted to agriculture by the early 20th century, with the rest of the Island consisting of stump fields (Cole 1941).

The vast areas of new agricultural fields, shrubby thickets, and gardens created opportunities for several species that were either not present on the Island historically or would have been in existence only in small numbers. Yards and thickets along the fields provided additional habitat. The 20 species in Table 4 grew in population, most probably spreading from nearby prairies, such as those in what is now Joint Base Lewis-McChord, Pierce County. The species accounts in the Annotated List document in greater detail the habitat preferences and historical status for each bird. Of these twenty species, Red-tailed Hawk, Bewick's Wren, Common Yellowthroat, and Savannah Sparrow were undoubtedly already present as small breeding populations. They expanded to their present-day population with the new habitat available. While farm habitat declined by the end of the 20th century, sufficient wet fields still exist such that

Table 4: Species Attracted by Farms and Open Space

Species	Historic Status	Current Status
Red-tailed Hawk	Originally uncommon	Fairly common
Northern Harrier	Probably rare migrant, then used new open area and become possible breeder	Uncommon migrant
American Kestrel	Originally not present, became breeder	Rare migrant and winter resident
Mourning Dove	Originally not present, became breeder	Uncommon; rare breeder
Barn Owl	Originally not present, became breeder	Uncommon; breeds
Bewick's Wren	Originally uncommon	Fairly common
House Wren	Originally not present, became uncommon to fairly common breeder	Rare breeder and migrant
Western Bluebird	Originally not present, became breeder	Extirpated
MacGillivray's Warbler	Originally probably only migrant, became fairly common and probable breeder	Rare visitor
Common Yellow-throat	Rare to uncommon breeder	Fairly common breeder
Lazuli Bunting	Originally not present, became breeder	Rare visitor
Chipping Sparrow	Originally not present, became possible breeder	Very rare visitor
Vesper Sparrow	Originally not present, became possible breeder	Very rare visitor
Savannah Sparrow	Fairly common migrant	Fairly common migrant and breeder
White-crowned Sparrow	Originally probably rare visitor	Became common breeder
Golden-crowned Sparrow	Originally probably rare visitor	Became fairly common winter resident
White-throated Sparrow	At most very rare visitor	Uncommon winter resident
Harris's Sparrow	At most very rare visitor	Very rare visitor
Western Meadowlark	Originally probably rare visitor, became possible breeder	Rare visitor
Brewer's Blackbird	Originally not present, became breeder	Rare spring and summer visitor

Harvesters at the John Cage Gorsuch farm 1893. © University of Washington Special Collections, Oliver S. Van Olinda Photograph Collection, UW 19154

the numbers of Common Yellowthroat and Savannah Sparrow must be higher than before. White-crowned Sparrows, Golden-crowned Sparrows, White-throated Sparrows, Harris's Sparrows, harriers, and meadowlarks were probably rare or very rare migrants along the shorelines. Later, they expanded into the agricultural fields and pastures, adjacent shrubby thickets, and residential yards. The other species consisted of new colonizers, most of which, like the Western Bluebird, grew in population to become fairly common breeders. Many old-timers remember, as children, the colorful bluebirds and the singing of meadowlarks. Several of the new colonizers, such as House Wrens, Lazuli Buntings, and Chipping Sparrows, would have utilized fields, newly successional thickets growing up alongside the fields, and clear-cuts not yet transformed into fields.

Farming in logged-off areas can be difficult, as a 1924 USDA Bulletin discusses, using Vashon and other Puget Sound lowland areas as examples (Johnson 1924). The bulletin found that the cost of clearing the stumps added up to more than the value of the land. Most farms were small, five to 20 acres, and included both farm animals and crops. Poultry, followed by dairy and small berry crops, formed the main moneymakers.

By 1941, a land utilization study of Vashon indicated that far fewer poultry farmers and only one dairy still operated (Cole 1941). Over the previous decade, strawberry prices declined considerably. Labor was intensive and expensive, shrinking or eliminating the profit on berry crops. Most farmers had to hold down outside jobs as well as work their own fields. Farmers discontinued cultivation of several areas on the Island, including Paradise Valley, as they sought other employment in order to earn a living. Those trends continued steadily throughout the remainder of the century, making farm and field habitat presently only around fifteen percent of the land area (Churchill 2013b, Ohmann and Gregory 2002). As agriculture declined, residential areas spread. Forest succession brought woods of different types back to two-thirds of the Island's land area. Many of the open-area species declined in population to rare or casual visitors as a result. Some, including the Red-tailed Hawk, Bewick's Wren, Common Yellowthroat, and thicket-loving sparrows, find enough habitat with the remaining open areas or adapted to using residential area as well.

Increase of Hardwood Forest and Mixed Forest Communities

The early successional growth created an expansion opportunity for many more species. Originally, the Island's deciduous habitat consisted of some

Table 5: Species Attracted by Successional/Hardwood Forests

Species	Historic Status	Current Status
Downy Woodpecker	Originally uncommon	Fairly common
Northern Flicker	Originally uncommon	Fairly common
Hutton's Vireo	Originally rare to uncommon	Fairly common
Warbling Vireo	Originally probably only migrant	Fairly common breeder
Black-capped Chickadee	Originally uncommon	Fairly common
Swainson's Thrush	Originally uncommon	Common
American Robin	Originally uncommon	Common
Orange-crowned Warbler	Originally uncommon	Fairly common
Yellow Warbler	Originally probably only rare migrant	Fairly common migrant and probable breeder
Black-throated Gray Warbler	Originally probably only migrant	Uncommon to fairly common breeder
Black-headed Grosbeak	Originally uncommon	Fairly common breeder
Lazuli Bunting	Originally not present, became breeder	Rare visitor
Bullock's Oriole	Either not present or very rare	Very rare breeder
American Goldfinch	Originally not present	Fairly common breeder

thickets around a few burns and wetlands. A few hardwood trees grew along the bigger streams, and some Bigleaf Maple and Red Alder grew mixed in with conifer-dominated woods. The clearing of the old-growth coniferous woods provided the opportunity for a wider mix of species as the eventual regrowth of forest began. Early successional species, such as Red Alder and Bigleaf Maple, grew in significant patches and mixed in with early returning conifers. Also, large thickets and hedgerows grew up on the edges of farms. Northern Flicker, Hutton's Vireo, Black-capped Chickadee, Swainson's Thrush, American Robin, and Orange-crowned Warbler, already present in some numbers, almost certainly increased, since they use a variety of habitats. Hutton's Vireo, in particular, enjoys mixed coniferous and deciduous woods (Wahl et al. 2005), which increased considerably throughout the 1900s. Most of the rest of the species in Table 5 probably came through in small numbers as migrants but lacked breeding habitat. Once the hardwood forest and thickets grew, birds preferring deciduous and mixed woods colonized and became breeders. The challenges these species face in the future will be due, at least in part, to the slow maturing of the forests back to dominant conifers and the growth of residential development on the Island.

Creation of Freshwater Ponds

Emma Amiad, local conservationist and realtor, asserts that nothing on Vashon is pristine. That certainly rings true for the freshwater ponds on the Island. Human action created or re-developed all of the big ponds on Vashon. Wetland areas certainly occurred prior to European-American settlement, though few freshwater ponds appear to have been present. The only consistent mentioning of a pre-existing pond is Lost Lake (Carey 1985), created in the back-gap left by a bluff sliding down into Quartermaster Harbor. Lost Lake increasingly resembles more of a wetland than a pond, as vegetation rapidly fills it in through plant succession.

Van Olinda photographed another pond situated just north and west of the Mukai place in the Island Center Forest area. Titled Vashon Lake in the picture, it might have first naturally existed at least as a seasonal pond. The photo may be of Smart's Pond, the precursor to the modern-day Fisher Pond. A picture in 1891 (see page 21) shows it larger than the current size of Fisher Pond. Even if it started as a natural pond, many artificial alterations were made by farmers over the years. Prior to Bill Fisher's stewardship, farmers drained the pond and converted the rich soil to agriculture. Fisher recreated the pond named after him by building a dike with donations of fill over the years (Rayna Holtz pers. comm. 2005). In a year with heavy rainfall, the pond almost floods Bank Road. At least some part of the current pond area consisted of sphagnum bog in the 1800s. Settlers mined the sphagnum here and at a number of other bogs in the Island Center area for use as organic material in the greenhouse industry. That industry got its start on Vashon in the late 1800s supplying the Klondike Gold Rush (Woodruffe 2002). Whispering Firs Bog remains as the sole surviving sphagnum bog on the Island.

Settlers constructed many ponds during the agricultural boom on Vashon. Farmers created or redeveloped from existing wetlands Singer Pond, Ernst Pond along Old Mill Road, Mukai Pond, Meadowlake, the string of ponds along Westside Highway, and those in the Lisabeula area. Many of these ponds range up to 100 years old. Several ponds were constructed for flood control and others for aesthetics. Ernst Pond and the various Island Center ponds support thriving ecosystems and provide extremely valuable habitat for ducks, herons, and rails because of their largely undisturbed nature over the last few decades. However, off-road vehicles regularly exploited the Island Center Forest ponds, though that's now rare.

Wood Ducks and Ring-necked Ducks would not have been on Vashon before the creation of ponds by settlers. Northern Shoveler and Lesser Scaup would have been only brief visitors to the saltwater shoreline. Wood Ducks and Ring-necked Ducks are seen exclusively on freshwater ponds. Observers rarely note Northern Shoveler, Lesser Scaup, and

Table 6: Species Attracted by Freshwater Ponds		
Species	**Historic Status**	**Current Status**
Pied-billed Grebe	Formerly saltwater only	Now rare freshwater breeder, uncommon in winter on freshwater
Greater White-fronted Goose	Rare migrant along saltwater shoreline	Seen also at freshwater ponds
Wood Duck	Probably not present	Common breeder
Northern Shoveler	Probably at most rare on saltwater shoreline	Fairly common winter resident on freshwater ponds
Ring-necked Duck	Probably not present	Fairly common in winter
Lesser Scaup	Probably at most rare on saltwater shoreline	Very rare winter resident on freshwater ponds
Hooded Merganser	Formerly saltwater only	Uncommon breeder on freshwater ponds as well
Marsh Wren	Probably not present	Rare visitor
Red-winged Blackbird	Uncertain abundance	Fairly common breeder

Vashon Lake 1891. © University of Washington Special Collections, Oliver S. Van Olinda Photograph Collection, UW VAN003

Greater White-fronted Geese on saltwater here. The vast majority of recent records for these birds center on freshwater ponds. Hooded Mergansers and Pied-billed Grebes breed on the ponds and likely only foraged in winter on saltwater prior to the creation of the current habitat. Marsh Wrens, at present rare to very rare around Island ponds and wetlands, probably made only brief visits before settlers built the ponds. Red-winged Blackbirds probably lacked enough wetlands with emergent vegetation prior to the new pond creation to support a breeding population.

Introduced Species

The avifauna population of the Island includes many introduced species. A total of nine species exotic to North America lived on Vashon for varying periods of time, and one form of Canada Goose from east of the Cascades was introduced (Ed Babcock pers. comm. 2005, John Friars pers. comm. 2005, Smith et al. 1997). Some birds were released directly on Vashon. European immigrants brought others from Europe and set them free elsewhere in North America. These birds subsequently colonized Vashon.

Hunters brought several game birds to Vashon over the last century: Chinese Bamboo-Partridge (failed), Gray Partridge (failed), Ring-necked Pheasant, Northern Bobwhite (failed), and California Quail (failed; Ed Babcock pers. comm. 2005). Sportsmen released Gray Partridge, Northern Bobwhite, California Quail, and Ring-necked Pheasant early in the 20th century (Ed Babcock pers. comm. 2005, John Friars pers. comm. 2005, Kitchin 1925, Smith et al. 1997). Chinese Bamboo-Partridge were let loose in the mid-1950s (Ed Babcock pers. comm. 2005). Various groups and enthusiasts repeatedly liberated pheasants and California Quail throughout the 20th century. These game birds often survived quite well during the agricultural period. However, habitat changes combined with domestic and feral cat and dog predation eliminated nearly all of these birds.

The three European urban species, Rock Pigeon, European Starling, and House Sparrow, all successfully self-introduced in this area following westward range expansion coincident with the North American arrival of European settlers on the east coast (Smith et al. 1997). European Starling and House Sparrow aggressively take over cavity nesting sites and possibly had secondary roles in the decline of Lewis's Woodpecker, Purple Martin, and Tree Swallow. Eurasian Collared-Doves, introduced as aviary birds in the Bahamas, escaped in a storm and survived on their own. They later flew to Florida and then spread across the continent to eventually reach Vashon.

Historically, several subspecies of Canada Geese migrated through the Western Washington area. After the 1950s, the Great Basin form of Canada

Table 7: Introduced Species

Species	Historic Status	Current Status
Canada Goose	Formerly only a migrant	Common breeder
Gray Partridge	Introduced	Failed with habitat change, more predators
Chinese Bamboo-Partridge	Introduced	Failed with habitat change, more predators
Ring-necked Pheasant	Introduced	Fairly common breeder
Northern Bobwhite	Introduced	Failed with habitat change, more predators
California Quail	Introduced, became common breeder	Failed with habitat change, more predators
Rock Pigeon	Introduced in eastern U.S., spread across country	Common breeder
Eurasian Collared-Dove	Introduced in Bahamas, spread across country	New resident, likely to become breeder
European Starling	Introduced in eastern U.S., spread across country	Common breeder
House Sparrow	Introduced in eastern U.S., spread across country	Common breeder

Quail release on Vashon in 1964. Courtesy Vashon Maury Island Heritage Association

Goose was introduced to the Puget Sound area in a number of locations (Hunn 1982, Paulson 1992, Wahl 1995). Concurrent habitat changes transformed the Canada Goose from an uncommon migrant to a common resident and breeder.

Regional and Continent-wide Habitat Change

Human-caused habitat change on a regional and continent-wide scale encouraged ten species from outside the Pacific Northwest to expand their range to Vashon. Green Herons first appeared in southwest Washington in the 1930s (Jewett et al. 1953) and slowly spread through Western Washington. Caspian Terns, facing habitat disruption back east, took advantage of new nesting sites created by dredging in harbors and rivers in Washington (Wahl et al. 2005). Barred Owls followed logging west over the Rockies up in Canada and then spread southward to Washington State through British Columbia (Smith et al. 1997). The Brown-headed Cowbird spread with the westward expansion of agriculture from its original home in the Great Plains (Smith et al. 1997). Anna's Hummingbirds, Western Scrub-Jays, and House Finches form another California contingent that moved north to the Seattle area and flourished (Smith et al. 1997). The proliferation of "suburb"-like habitat and open areas proved advantageous to these birds.

European-American settlers assisted three other species: American Crow, Barn Swallow, and Cliff Swallow. American Crows expanded throughout the West, shadowing the movement of settlers (Marzluff et al. 2001b). In Washington, they bred mostly east of the Cascades. They expanded into the Puget Sound region by following major river valleys and

Table 8: Species Arriving in Regional and Continent-Wide Range Expansions

Species	Historic Status	Current Status
Green Heron	Not present in Washington State	Very rare visitor
Caspian Tern	Not present on Vashon, rare in Washington State	Fairly common in summer
Barred Owl	Not present in Washington State	Fairly common breeder
Anna's Hummingbird	Not present in Washington State	Fairly common breeder
Northwestern Crow	Resident	Extirpated or hybridized out
American Crow	Not present on Vashon	Common breeder
Cliff Swallow	Rare in Puget Sound region	Fairly common in region, rare on Vashon
Barn Swallow	Rare in Puget Sound region	Common breeder
Western Scrub-Jay	Not present in Washington State	Rare visitor
Brown-headed Cowbird	Not present in Washington State	Fairly common breeder
House Finch	Not present in Washington State	Common breeder

moving into newly cut forested and urban areas (Wahl et al. 2005). Crows took advantage of increased food supplies and limitations on predators created by settlers. The American Crow out-competed the Northwestern Crow, the shoreline crow of the outer coast and Puget Sound area. It's possible that the American Crow hybridized so extensively with the Northwestern Crow in the Puget Sound area that by the late 1800s, the Northwestern Crow maintained a distinct population only on the outer coast. Gulls increased regionally for similar reasons (Wahl et al. 2005), but aren't listed in the chart. Vashon gull populations may have fluctuated somewhat in response to agricultural, fishing, and garbage dump activity on the Island. Current numbers don't appear to be much different than what they would have been prior to European-American settlement, with the exception of the recent decline of Bonaparte's Gull (see pages 28 to 29).

Settlers assisted with Barn and Cliff Swallow expansion by providing more nesting habitat (Dawson and Bowles 1909, Jewett et al. 1953, Smith et al. 1997). Both swallow species existed in small numbers in Western

Washington using a limited number of natural cliff sites. All of the new buildings constructed over the last century provided ample nest sites for these two species. Barn Swallows now nest exclusively on artificial structures on Vashon and throughout other regions of Puget Sound.

Pesticides and Persecution

At least thirteen species present on the Island declined and then recovered from the effects of DDT in the late 1900s and/or over hunting and persecution that occurred on a continent-wide basis throughout the 1800s. Table 9 represents only a brief list, probably underestimating by many species the number of species persecuted by different types of hunting. For the continent as a whole, the list would be much greater. By 1935, the Trumpeter Swan's population fell to 73 birds left in the entire United States (Matthiessen 1959). John James Audubon once witnessed about 48,000 American Golden-Plover shot in New Orleans in one day (Stout 1967). Until the enforcement of migratory bird protection treaties, hunting seasons, and game regulations created in the late 1800s and early 1900s, many game species and raptors were shot without regard to species survival. Many species, such as the Trumpeter Swan, Wood Duck, Western Sandpiper, and Band-tailed Pigeon, were considered to be close to joining the Passenger Pigeon in extinction by early Washington ornithologists such as W. L. Dawson (1909), S. F. Rathbun (1902), and S. G. Jewett (1953). Rathbun, a Seattle area birder at the turn of the 20th century, commented about the Western Sandpiper:

> But large as the numbers of the Western Sandpiper still appear to be, they are not comparable to those of fifteen or twenty years ago, and the cause of this decrease in their numbers is the same old story. It seems hardly possible that a bird so small could have been regarded as game and its hunting come under the name of sport, but such was the case and it brought about the logical results (Bent 1927).

The Migratory Bird Treaty signed with Mexico and Great Britain (acting for Canada) protected game birds, insectivorous birds, and other non-game birds. The treaty developed hunting seasons for game birds not to exceed three and a half months, and outlawed egg collecting except for scientific purposes. The enforcement of this treaty resulted in the recovery of many shorebird populations (Matthiessen 1959).

The hunters of the last 50 years bear no resemblance to the "sportsmen" of the late 1800s, who shot anything and everything that moved, limited only by their ammunition. Others convinced themselves that every raptor was preying upon their chickens when in fact most raptors

Table 9: Species Affected by Pesticides and Persecution

Species	Historic Status	Current Status
Brown Pelican	Probably very rare, pesticides eliminated for decades	Rare, recovered with DDT regulation
Double-crested Cormorant	Probably common, population dip late 1800s, early 1900s	Common, recovery after egg collecting regulation
Trumpeter Swan	Probable winter visitor, nearly extirpated across continent	Rare winter visitor, recovered after hunting regulation
Wood Duck	Probably not present because of lack of ponds	Fairly common breeder, recovery with hunting regulation, nest box programs
American Wigeon	Population dip with hunting pressure	Common, recovery with hunting regulation
Osprey	Population dips with hunting and pesticides	Fairly common, recovery with DDT regulation
Bald Eagle	Population dips with hunting and pesticides	Fairly common, recovery with DDT regulation
Cooper's Hawk	Population dip with hunting pressure	Fairly common, recovery with hunting regulation
Sharp-shinned Hawk	Population dip with hunting pressure	Fairly common, recovery with hunting regulation
Peregrine Falcon	Probably rare, DDT eliminated it from Vashon for decades	Rare, recovered after DDT regulation
Western Sandpiper	Population dip with hunting pressure	Fairly common, recovery with hunting regulation
Least Sandpiper	Population dip with hunting pressure	Fairly common, recovery with hunting regulation
Pectoral Sandpiper	Population dip with hunting pressure	Rare, recovery with hunting regulation
Band-tailed Pigeon	Population dip with hunting pressure	Fairly common, recovery with hunting regulation

have the beneficial effect of keeping down rodent populations. The Bald Eagle, our national symbol, needed special legislation to protect it from extinction due to shooting before DDT kicked in as well. Other hawks and owls needed more legislation to finally safeguard their populations (Matthiessen 1959).

Other types of persecution affected more species. Double-crested Cormorant numbers have been rising in the Puget Sound area, possibly from an end to egg gathering by egg collectors or others looking for food (Vermeer and Rankin 1984). DDT severely hurt Brown Pelican, Osprey, Bald Eagle, and Peregrine Falcon populations (Wahl et al. 2005). Seeing a Bald Eagle or an Osprey in the Puget Sound area in the 1960s and 1970s was a major treat.

Unknown Challenges/Multiple Factors

Washington Department of Fish and Wildlife (WDFW) studies document a significant decline in marine bird species in Puget Sound (Nysewander et al. 2001, 2003). Researchers divided the marine areas of the Puget Sound region into sub-regions and flew aerial transects during December and January 1993 to 2002. In the northern Puget Sound sub-region, ornithologists compared data to a similar study conducted in 1979 to 1980, the Marine Ecosystems Analysis (MESA) program. Over 20 years, the comparison showed a 57 percent decrease for scoters, 72.3 percent decrease for scaup, a 20.1 percent increase for Bufflehead, 188.6 percent increase for Harlequin Duck, 95 percent decrease for Western Grebe, 89 percent decrease for Red-necked Grebe, 82 percent decrease for Horned Grebe, and all loons combined faced a 79 percent decrease. Continued surveys by the re-named Puget Sound Assessment and Monitoring Program (PSAMP), describe further declines through the 2012/13 season for many of these species (Everson in process). Scoter species, considered as a whole, suffered a 50 percent deterioration in numbers from 1993/1994 to 2012/13. Bufflehead

A Cougar shot at the Cross place in 1915. © University of Washington Special Collections, Oliver S. Van Olinda Photograph Collection, UW 14799.

went from an increase in the earlier surveys to holding stable, with perhaps a small decline. Goldeneyes experienced stabilization at the lower level for several years around the turn of the century and then a return to a further slow decline through the 2012/13 season. Mergansers, considered as whole, provided one example of stable population numbers.

The reasons for the major decline across so many marine bird species appear complex and may turn out to be different for each species. For scoters in the north Puget Sound region, it may be as simple as looking at the 94 percent decline in herring in the Cherry Point fishery, a main prey source (Donovan and Bower 2004). For Western Grebes, the herring loss could also be a major problem. Others speculate that there may be concerns with the grebes' breeding habitat. The species hit hardest seem to be those dependent upon fish and spawning events.

The Nysewander data show the central Puget Sound sub-region wherein Vashon lies to be following a more stable trend in marine bird numbers. The Vashon Christmas Bird Count (CBC), begun in 1999, bears that out to some extent. Overall marine bird numbers look steady, but the wintering Western Grebe populations dropped precipitously in the last few years of the count (Trevathan 1999 to 2005). Local birder Dan Willsie routinely counted Western Grebes in Quartermaster Harbor several times a season since the mid-1990s. His counts show that the winter population exceeded 5,000 Western Grebes in the mid-1990s, but by 1999, the first Vashon CBC tallied only 1,619 birds in Quartermaster Harbor. From 1999 to 2013, the Vashon CBC numbers of Western Grebes fell dramatically to 245 birds for Vashon and just 134 for the Quartermaster Harbor part of the circle. The decline from Dan Willsie's mid-1990s Quartermaster censuses to the 2013 CBC exceeds 95 percent. It appears that whatever is causing serious declines noted elsewhere in Puget Sound may be affecting Vashon Island as well.

Other water bird species also experienced declines in the last two decades for unknown reasons. Bonaparte's Gulls and Common Terns both used to move through King County in large numbers (Hunn 2012). Flock sizes for Bonaparte's Gulls dropped in the last two decades, and Common Terns might now be totally missed during their fall migration. Vashon witnessed a definite fall in Common Tern sightings, though the picture for Bonaparte's Gull appears unclear. Vashon's CBC shows a decrease in Bonaparte's Gull, but this gull represents a species that might easily be missed if counters looked at the wrong time of day. Regionally, other CBC locations around Puget Sound experience lower Bonaparte's Gull numbers as well (Wahl et al. 2005). Ornithologists have no explanations for the regional deterioration of these species' populations. Both of these species forage predominantly for fish and may be facing the same challenges as fish-eating birds in the WDFW censuses discussed above.

Other WDFW research indicates that the wintering Brant population totals less than 60 percent of historical levels in Washington State (Davison and Kraege 2002). Vashon residents noticed a significant decline of Brant in the last decade. One theory is that the West Coast population as a whole may not have changed much. The Brant possibly shifted their wintering grounds to south of California. Perhaps this species should be in the above persecution grouping because some think that the move came with disturbance of the birds (Campbell et al. 1990). Unfortunately, the cause remains unknown. Researchers recently began using radio tracking to follow the Brant on their migration route and discover if problems exist along the route or if the decrease represents a shift in wintering grounds (Davison and Kraege 2002).

A long period of cooler and wetter weather stretching from the 1940s to the 1970s may have impacted prey populations for Purple Martins, Tree Swallows, Western Bluebirds, and Common Nighthawks. The decline of Common Nighthawks raises the most questions. Besides the theory that climate change or pollution affected prey populations, some believe that urban sprawl and the related lack of open spaces or new forest clearing in the Puget Sound region may be a factor. Nighthawks briefly adapted to urban areas, often nesting on the roofs of downtown buildings with

Table 10: Species Facing Unknown Challenges/Multiple Factors		
Species	**Historic Status**	**Current Status**
Red-throated Loon	Uncommon to rare winter resident	Uncommon winter resident
Western Grebe	Fairly common winter resident	Declining, still fairly common
Brant	Fairly common migrant	Uncommon migrant
Eurasian Wigeon	Not present	Uncommon winter resident
Common Nighthawk	Fairly common breeder	Rare migrant
Purple Martin	Uncommon breeder, became nearly extirpated	Fairly common breeder
Tree Swallow	Uncommon breeder, became nearly extirpated	Uncommon breeder
Western Bluebird	Not present, became fairly common breeder	Extirpated

Chart 1: Habitat Change Over the Past 225 Years										
Habitat	1800	1825	1850	1875	1900	1925	1950	1975	2000	2025
Old-Growth Forest	■■■■■■■■■■■■■■■■■■■■									
Logging				■■■■■■■■■■■■						
Hardwoods & Mixed Forest					■■■■■■■■■■■■■■■■■■■■					
Agriculture					■■■■■■■■■■■■■■■					
Ponds										
Residential Development							■■■■■■■■■■■■			
Species Introductions Range Expansion										

asphalt or gravelly surfaces (Smith et al. 1997, Wahl et al. 2005). However, roofing methods have changed, and reports of nighthawk nests in urban areas have diminished.

Most of the species affected by climate change actually faced multiple challenges. As mentioned before, the loss of snags that provided nest holes affected Purple Martins, Tree Swallows, and Western Bluebirds. The arrival of the European Starling and House Sparrow then accentuated the problem. However, the introduced species were only a contributing factor (Sharpe 1993). At least with the bluebird, population decline had already begun because of climate issues and habitat change (see the open area and forest management practice sections above). Artificial nest boxes in Western Washington have assisted in population rebounds where habitat is appropriate for bluebirds and martins (Sharpe 1993). Tree Swallows remain rare on the Island, less common than the Purple Martin. The Western Bluebird habitat on Vashon has disappeared to the extent that no new increase may occur. A local nest box program begun in 2001 has been unsuccessful so far in enticing the few remaining migrants to stay and breed. Only one known sighting took place in the last decade.

Ornithologists long recognized Eurasian Wigeons as rare vagrants across the United States (Edgell 1984). West Coast sightings reported to regional editors of *American Birds* increased from fewer than ten each year in the 1950s to over 100 a year by the mid-1980s. That trend continues to the present day, with no theories as to the cause. While two to five Eurasian Wigeons winter each year on Vashon, no known records exist before the last decade.

Conclusion

Old-growth forest was originally the dominant habitat on Vashon. As logging increased, the forest diminished, to be replaced by agriculture and successional mixed woods. The successional mixed woods eventually expanded to replace abandoned agricultural areas. Those farming areas not taken over by forest succumbed to the expansion of residential development. Few natural ponds of any size existed. Usually as part of agriculture's spread, settlers created many artificial ponds. Settlement also brought the introduction of many birds including those arriving as a result of human-caused habitat change across the continent. Chart 1 (opposite page) provides a visual summary of the major habitat changes since European-American settlement. The prevalence of each habitat over time relates to the thickness of the bar.

The sheer volume and variety of change strongly underscores the responsibility Islanders, industry, and other actors in the region bear in maintaining bird populations. As will be discussed in the chapter on habitat, many of the Island habitats face significant challenges, and others could use improvement. Pollution may so degrade the quality of the water surrounding the Island as to cause significant drops in the fish populations, especially herring and salmon. The waterfowl population drawn here in such variety and numbers by these fish face severe impacts if their major prey resource declines. Development and polluted run-off into streams and groundwater can impact the species diversity of invertebrates and fish populations, also impacting bird species.

Fortunately, many capable Islanders are addressing these and other concerns. Over the last two decades, the Vashon-Maury Island Land Trust, joined by other Island groups and County agencies, protected many of the most important wetlands, ponds, and watersheds on the Island. Those efforts hopefully will continue to be successful. The Island still faces the underlying issue of spreading development, which could ultimately lead to the creation of another suburb of the Everett-Seattle-Tacoma metropolis.

Chapter III

Habitats and Conservation

Physiography

Vashon Island is roughly thirteen miles long. With Maury Island thrown in, the Islands together become as wide as 7.5 miles from east to west. Much of the Island ranges three to four miles across. The land area totals about 36 square miles, or 23,000 acres (King County 1975).

Vashon lies in the Puget Trough, a depressed, glaciated area with a considerable portion under the waters of Puget Sound. At least four glacial periods occurred over the last million years, with glaciers advancing and retreating over the Vashon area. The last period, appropriately called the Vashon Glacier, occurred between 13,000 and 15,000 years ago. Around Seattle, ice depths reached as much as 5,000 feet and in the Tacoma area to the southeast of Vashon, 2,000 feet (King County 1975). The general north-south orientation of the Island and the Puget Sound region resulted from glacial movements. The glaciers flattened and scraped the area and then left so much debris that few remnants of earlier geological processes may be found on Vashon. The composition of the Island soils consists almost completely of glacial till left by glaciers at their base or sand and gravel deposited as outwash as the glaciers expanded and declined (King County 1995). As Susie Kalhorn, a consultant on water issues, puts it, "Vashon is a big glacier dump!" She adds that besides sand and gravel, some silt and clay layers formed from settling out in melt ponds and lakes at the front of the glaciers. These silt and clay layers play an important role in the Island's water supply, as discussed later.

The glacial materials continue to shape the Island, as much of the shoreline consists of low to high bluffs that slough off as weather and water bring them down. The disrupted areas created by slope erosion make a disturbed habitat of jumbled trees and brush, somewhat like the disturbances caused by a river. The spit connecting the two islands developed from eroding bluffs made of glacial debris sloughing down, to be rearranged by marine forces.

The Island soils strongly affecting the habitat distribution on Vashon consist almost entirely of the Alderwood soil series, moderately well-drained soils formed in glacial till. Alderwood and Alderwood-Kitsap soils that retain more water cover the north part of Vashon, some parts of the west side, and the wetter north slopes of Maury Island (King County 2009b). The sandy/gravelly Everett-Alderwood soils that drain more extend over central Vashon down to the south end and most of the central and southern portions of Maury Island. Interestingly, the precipitation patterns, to the extent they exist, somewhat follow the soil types such that central and south Vashon and most of Maury tend to be drier than north and west Vashon, which then determines what kind of forest grows over the different sections of the Island.

The climate of the Island generally consists of relatively warm, wet winters and somewhat cool, dry summers. From 1931 to 1954, the mean high temperature in July was 75.2° F, and the mean low was 50.7° F. For the same years, the mean high for rainfall in January was 43.5 inches, and the mean low was 33.3 inches (King County 1995). Rainfall data from rain gauges collected in 1981 to 1982 and 1989 to 1991 show a fairly erratic pattern of rain distribution across Vashon (King County 1995, Vashon-Maury Island Groundwater Advisory Committee 1998). Total amounts of rainfall and their distributions were different each year. J. R. Carr/Associates (1983) noted in the first comprehensive study of Vashon's water supply that rainfall appeared to decrease from west to east across the Island, which roughly corresponds to the placement of forest habitat on the Island. The Vashon-Maury Island Hydrologic Modeling Technical Report in 2009 found that precipitation ranged from 48 inches a year on the western side of the Island to 35 inches on the eastern side (King County 2009b). The forest habitats seem to be somewhat wetter to the west and north, with more Western Hemlock and Western Red Cedar, and drier in the center, south, and to the southeast, with more Douglas-fir and also mixed Douglas-fir/Pacific Madrone habitat along Maury's southeast coast. On the other hand, Point Robinson and the Luana Beach Road area (along the northeast part of Maury Island) showed higher rainfall, matching wet areas on Vashon. Topography contributes significantly to where rain falls (Vashon-Maury Island Groundwater Advisory Committee 1998). The west to east pattern in moisture is therefore only generally descriptive of actual habitat distribution.

Wells and springs provide access to Vashon's water supply. All freshwater on the Island comes from rainfall on the local land surface, making the aquifer a sole source aquifer (J. R. Carr/Associates 1983). No connection exists to off-Island aquifers. Rainwater lies within the sediments left from the advance and retreat of glaciers, filling in the spaces between the grains of sand and gravel and to some extent soaked into the silt and clay. The sand and gravel and the silt and clay form layers that appear to be discontinuous and most likely intermingle with each other (Vashon-Maury

Island Groundwater Advisory Committee 1998), creating a complex series of water pockets. Sand and gravel prove relatively easy for water extraction, but the silt and clay tend to restrict flow.

Vashon's complex aquifer results in the human population obtaining their water in a number of different ways. Water District 19, the largest water purveyor on the Island, uses wells but actually gets most of its water from surface streams, Beall Creek and Ellis Creek. In addition to the several water purveyors, about 1,000 private well systems reach anywhere from about 50 to 600 feet down to find water.

The complicated water situation also indicates two Island environmental vulnerabilities: water quality and water quantity. Because the different layers create areas of easier and more difficult accessibility, a large amount of water may exist in the aquifer, but the amount reachable at a reasonable expense may be much less than the water budget estimates suggest (see more on this in the discussion below). In addition, easier to access water in streams and shallow wells may be affected by development, pollution, and natural causes such as nitrogen from decaying Red Alder, as stands of trees reach the end of their years and die and decompose. Ample sources of pollution exist: pesticide and herbicide use in gardens and on crops, farm animals such as the former Misty Isle herd of cattle, and oil and gas dripping from vehicles onto local roads and driveways. These can reach and be stuck in shallower water layers. So far Vashon has a good report card on water quality (Vashon-Maury Island Groundwater Protection Committee 2011), but water quality needs to be protected in order to maintain the health of the Island's people, the local environment, and water supply.

Studies to understand the total quantity of water available for use on Vashon reach back about 30 years. The J. R. Carr/Associates report in 1983 first established the sole source nature of the Vashon aquifer and came up with the most conservative water budget. That budget predicted the water resource available would support a population maximum of about 11,000 (J. R. Carr/Associates 1983). Since then three additional studies, the Groundwater Advisory Committee in 1998, the King County Water Resource Estimate (WRE) Phase I in 2005, and the Phase II in 2009 arrived at several different estimates. Table 11 shows the various studies' estimates.

The WRE Phase II used increasingly sophisticated modeling showing a significantly higher water budget than the original Carr report (King County 2009b). The Groundwater Protection Committee (VMIGWPC), however, points out that while a greater amount of water appears available, the WRE Phase II model cannot predict water accessibility at any given location (VMIGWPC 2010). Because of the complex geological layers

Table 11: Vashon Water Budget Estimate				
	Water Resources Evaluation Project Phase II: 2009	Water Resources Evaluation Project Phase I: 2005	Groundwater Management Plan: 1998	J. R. Carr/ Associates-Report: 1983
Precipitation Estimate	43.8 inches/year	38.7 inches/year	44.1 inches/year	38.1 inches/year
Water Budget Estimate	13.5 inches/year	12.8 inches/year	16.3 inches/year	4.8 inches/year

Table 11 summarizes four different estimates of what happens with the rain that falls on the Island. It "balances" the amount of water source (i.e., rain/precipitation) with multiple outflows. These outflows include: evapotranspiration, runoff, and groundwater recharge (King County 2009b).

described above, reaching the potential water is a matter of getting what's actually obtainable. District 19, for example, tried to expand its water capacity but was largely unsuccessful when it drilled new wells in the locations chosen by the District. The District eased its water needs in part by emphasizing conservation among its customers. Estimating actual water availability for further development and higher population on the Island or maintaining availability for existing uses remains difficult and will require more study of rainfall patterns and Island geology. The WRE Phase II model built possible impacts from climate change into some scenarios. Climate change effects add another layer of complexity and uncertainty. The implications for wildlife habitat will be discussed under the Conservation heading later in this chapter.

Vashon exists in the Western Hemlock Zone that combines climax Western Hemlock and Western Red Cedar with sub-climax Douglas-fir (Franklin and Dyrness 1988). Forests in this zone grow dominantly coniferous with little hardwood present except in disturbed areas and riparian zones. Human action over the past century converted Vashon's ecosystem from the expected Western Hemlock Zone to a 37-square-mile disturbed area with plenty of streams. Accordingly, a significant hardwood presence developed on the Island. Franklin describes a number of common successional patterns possible for areas clear-cut such as Vashon (Franklin and Dyrness 1988):

1. Vegetation communities including mostly Douglas-fir and Salal, especially in dry areas;
2. Vegetation communities in intermediate dry/wet areas of Douglas-fir, Red and Evergreen Huckleberry, and Salmonberry;

3. Dense, even-aged stands of Douglas-fir that allow for no growth of understory;
4. Vegetation communities dominated by Red Alder;
5. Vegetation communities where Western Hemlock and Western Red Cedar are primary players early in succession.

All of these communities occur on Vashon. The various successional responses by vegetation communities and how they interacted with agricultural and residential development set the stage for the many habitat types on present-day Vashon.

Vashon Habitat Types

The chapter on the history of the Island clearly indicates the link between the size and health of various habitats and the bird populations found in those areas. This chapter describes in detail the various habitats, the species observed within them, and the challenges they face.

Habitat consists of the type of area where birds (and other animals) can meet their basic needs for food, water, and shelter with the correct climate and other environmental conditions that support their ability to address their needs (Morrison et al. 1992). Most popular ornithological literature uses habitat types described by land cover, usually as vegetation categories or physical characteristics of the landscape or depth of water features. More sophisticated methods now exist that define habitat as a set of relationships between groups of species associated with a particular vegetation community as well as the plant community structure (Johnson and O'Neil 2001). The Island covers a small enough area and possesses habitats that conform mostly to the very basic vegetation and physical characteristics used by the Washington State Gap Analysis land cover designations (Smith et al. 1997, Cassidy et al. 1997). This book loosely follows the Gap Analysis land cover descriptions, with more detailed designations for forest areas based on NatureServe habitat descriptions (NatureServe 2009).

Understanding the variety of habitat types on Vashon Island acquaints one with the diversity of wildlife possible for viewing. Over the last 150 years, 251 bird species occurred naturally or were introduced to the Island. This section describes the vegetation and physical characteristics of the habitat types present on the Island: Saltwater; Saltwater Shoreline; Ponds, Wetlands, and Streams; Fields, Farmland, and Pasture; Wet Coniferous Forest; Douglas-fir Forest; Dry Douglas fir/Madrone Forest; Hardwood-Dominated Mixed Forest; Shrubby Thicket; Developed Area; and Aerial Space.

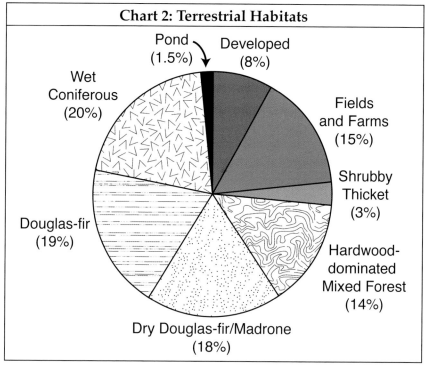

Derek Churchill, a forestry consultant from Vashon, provided much of the information on forest habitat discussed later in this chapter and created Maps 1 to 3 showing the disposition of habitat types on the Island. His maps utilize vegetation designations and data from NatureServe (NatureServe 2009), the Northwest GAP Analysis (Aycrigg et al. 2013), and the United States Forest Service IMAP project (Ohmann and Gregory 2002). The habitat types in the legend of the three maps reflect the types discussed in this chapter with one exception. Open Space, essentially ballfields and other developed parks, shows as a separate category on the map, but is included under the Developed Area heading in the individual habitat type discussions and acreage percentages here.

Chart 2 shows the percentage of total acreage for each terrestrial habitat type based on that mapping data. Improvements in GIS analysis capability and satellite imagery make the data for these current maps and chart more accurate than the information presented in the first edition of the *Birds of Vashon Island*, which based calculations of area upon Alex Moll's 1993 forestry management thesis (Moll 1993). In addition, information for the second edition uses imagery from 2006 to 2008, while Moll employed imagery from the late 1980s to 1990. The earlier mapping software's interpretation of the satellite imagery over-represented developed area at the expense of several habitat types. In this new edition, the Fields and Farms category goes up from 3.5 percent to a much more realistic fifteen percent. Shrubby Thickets moves from one to three percent, and Ponds and Wetlands grows from 0.8 to 1.5 percent. The total forest cover also changes from about 66 to 71 percent. Table 12 shows the habitat preferences of Vashon birds and also locations for habitat types around the Island.

Vashon is dominated by the Saltwater habitat due to its nature as an island. Nearly 50 bird species occur regularly on the surrounding waters, and about 25 species appear exclusively on saltwater. With two-thirds of the landmass covered with forests, the forest habitats come next in significance for the bird species of the Island. All of the forest habitats harbor around 45 species. Early in the 20th century, farmland formed a significant percentage of the habitat, drawing a number of species to Vashon. Later, as open area decreased, those species dwindled or disappeared. Formerly occupying somewhere between a half to two-thirds of the Island's surface, farms and pasture now account for about fifteen percent of the acreage. Shrubby Thicket totals grow fewer as regenerating forest and the spreading Developed Area claim more space. More land surface converts to housing as the population grows. Almost a tenth of the land area of Vashon fits into the Developed Area category, with residential, commercial, and light industrial uses. This category possesses the highest number of species in Table 12 because residential areas often mimic in part the vegetation of the other habitats, attracting more birds. On the other hand, it contributes no specialist species, except perhaps Anna's Hummingbird. Anna's Hummingbirds mostly use feeders and exotic plants, yet also eat enough insects and utilize enough native plants to also use Shrubby Thicket habitat. One often forgets the sky above, even when talking about birds. Aerial Space joins the list of habitat types even though it isn't an actual land or water form or plant community. A number of species on the Island list appear only overhead. Table 12 and the tables showing characteristic species for each habitat arise from the database of Vashon birds, with assistance from Paulson's article, "Northwest Bird Diversity: From Extravagant Past and Changing Present to Precarious Future" (Paulson 1992).

Getting to know the different habitats present on Vashon assists in learning where to find any particular bird species. Some birds, such as the American Robin, appear as generalists found in almost any habitat from the shoreline into the forest. Others, such as Wood Ducks, are very specific about their locations. Wood Ducks utilize only freshwater ponds that possess nest boxes or large trees with large holes for nesting locations. The Hooded Merganser provides an example of a species that uses varying habitats at different times of the year. From fall through early spring,

HABITATS AND CONSERVATION

Hooded Mergansers might be seen on freshwater or saltwater. In mid- to late spring as the breeding season begins, one finds them only on very secluded freshwater ponds with forested cover providing nesting locations.

Knowing the appropriate habitat for a species also helps with identification. For example, a small, green flycatcher seen at eye level in the woods probably represents a Pacific-slope Flycatcher. The very similar Willow Flycatcher utilizes only brushy areas and field edges. Other fly-

Table 12: Habitat Preferences				
Habitat	Description	Examples found on Vashon Island	Number of bird species found in each habitat*	
			Total	Solely
Saltwater	Waters surrounding Vashon	Includes ferry runs and Quartermaster Harbor	48	21
Saltwater Shoreline	Beaches, mud flats, and marsh forming the shoreline	KVI Beach, Fern Cove estuaries, Tramp Harbor, etc.	49	6
Ponds and Wetlands	Ponds, marsh, and associated shoreline	Fisher Pond, Old Mill Road Pond, Singer Pond, etc.	37	4
Wet Coniferous and Dry Coniferous Forest	Evergreen forests on the Island	Wet: mostly NW Vashon; Dry: mostly south Vashon and Maury	45	0
Hardwood-Dominated Mixed Forest	Deciduous and mixed forests on the Island	Ellisport Creek, Paradise Valley, Christensen Creek	62	1
Shrubby Thicket	Brushy areas	Hedgerows around central Vashon, Raab's Lagoon, Paradise Valley	27	0
Fields, Farmland, and Pasture	Fields, farms, and pastures	Wax Orchard, Westside Hwy., south end of Monument Rd.	32	0
Developed Area	Residential, commercial, and light industrial areas	Town area and built-over areas	66	0
Aerial Space	The air above	All over	Most birds	1+

39

catchers utilizing woods, such as pewees and Olive-sided Flycatchers, usually hawk from high perches out on the edge of the forest

Finally, the conservation and preservation of bird species requires knowledge of habitat types. Table 12 gives some indications of possible priority habitat for conservation. For example, with the loss or degradation of freshwater pond and wetland habitat, four species noted as appearing on Vashon only in freshwater habitat would be lost with that habitat.

Chart 2 and Table 12 combined provide a stark example of the importance of habitat when taken in light of the history of the Island. One will note that Farms and Fields habitat, now at only about fifteen percent of the land area, has no remaining specialist species. As discussed in the history chapter, many open-area specialists were present 50 to 80 years ago. The shrinkage of the Fields, Farmland, and Pasture habitat eliminated most of the open-area birds from Vashon.

The rest of this chapter consists of a breakdown by habitat type of the specific vegetation, physical characteristics, and bird life of Vashon Island. The birds discussed include only the regularly occurring species, omitting casual and accidental records. In addition, the accounts follow the various bird species' use of habitat on Vashon. Many of the species utilize additional habitat types in other parts of their breeding or wintering ranges or in migration elsewhere in Washington or North America.

Saltwater

By definition, the island nature of Vashon makes the surrounding open saltwater and the more protected area of Quartermaster Harbor a significant habitat type. Of the 48 species regularly occurring on the waters around the Island, about 21 of those species consist of habitat specialists that only inhabit saltwater when in the Vashon area. Several of these habitat specialists breed or otherwise utilize freshwater bodies or shorelines elsewhere in their range in Washington or North America. The Island's loons, grebes, cormorants, herons, geese, ducks, and gulls form the families of species that one finds in this habitat type.

Referring to saltwater as a single habitat type is a bit deceiving. Within this habitat there exist several distinct sub-categories that have their own specialist species. The sub-categories mainly deal with the depth of the water and the vegetation or fish attracted to the various depths. For example, Pacific Loons generally prefer the deeper waters of Colvos Passage and the west side of the entrance to Quartermaster Harbor. Red-throated Loons like more shallow water and may be found at times in the surf right along the beach.

HABITATS AND CONSERVATION

Dusk falls over Quartermaster Harbor. © Peter Murray

In the near-shore zone, a number of factors attract a great variety of loons, grebes, and waterfowl to the area. The presence of eelgrass and kelp beds furnishes egg-laying habitat for Pacific Herring and also provides juvenile salmonids a foraging area safe from larger fish. Eelgrass beds exist in small and large patches all around Vashon. The eelgrass beds at Ellisport bring Brant close inshore. Salmonids use the shallower waters to escape larger underwater predators. Pacific Sand Lance and Surf Smelt feed in the near-shore zone and spawn in the sandy/gravelly beaches.

Quartermaster Harbor, surrounded by Vashon and Maury Islands with a narrow entrance to the south, shelters about 3,000 acres of water from wind and wave action. The inner harbor features shallow depths of five to six meters, and the outer harbor has depths ranging from eleven to 46 meters (King County 2012a). The designation of Quartermaster Harbor as a National Audubon Society Important Bird Area in 2000 resulted from Islander Dan Willsie's efforts to protect the saltwater harbor habitat. Over the past several years, Christmas Bird Counts verified an average popula-

(Continued on page 48)

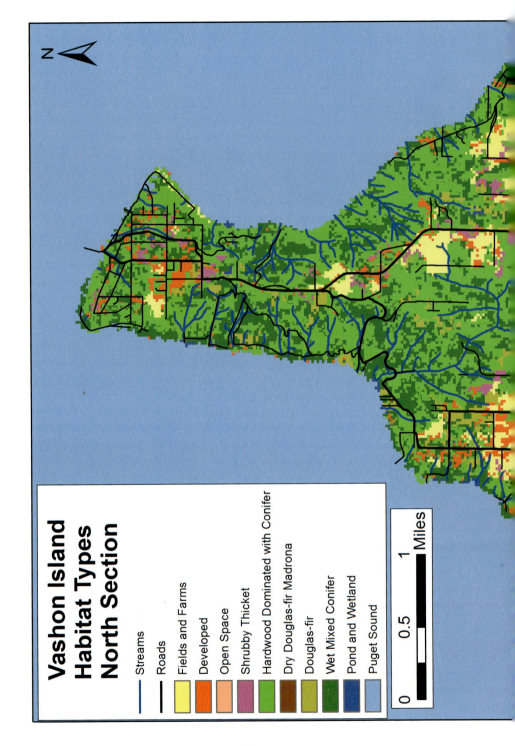

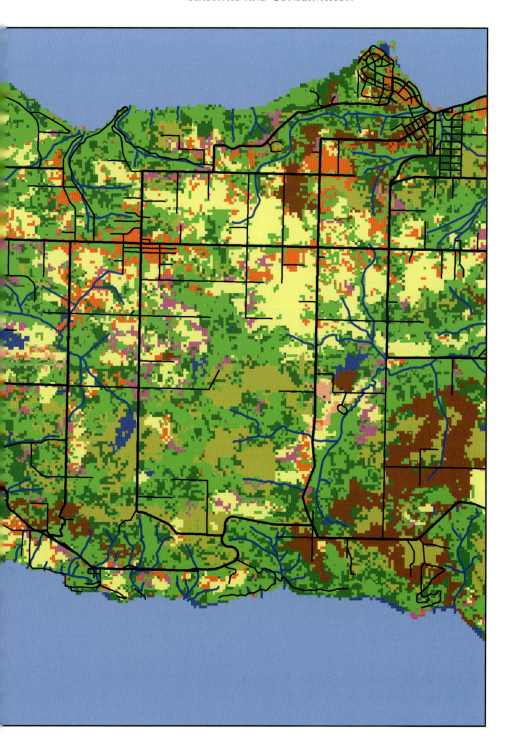

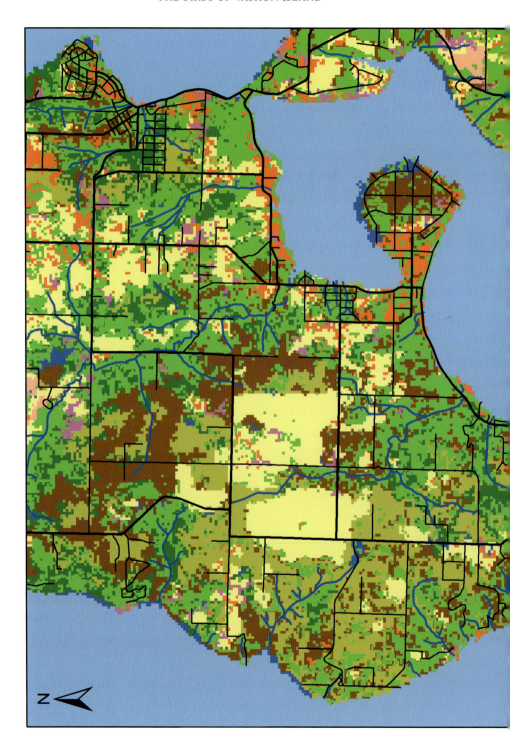

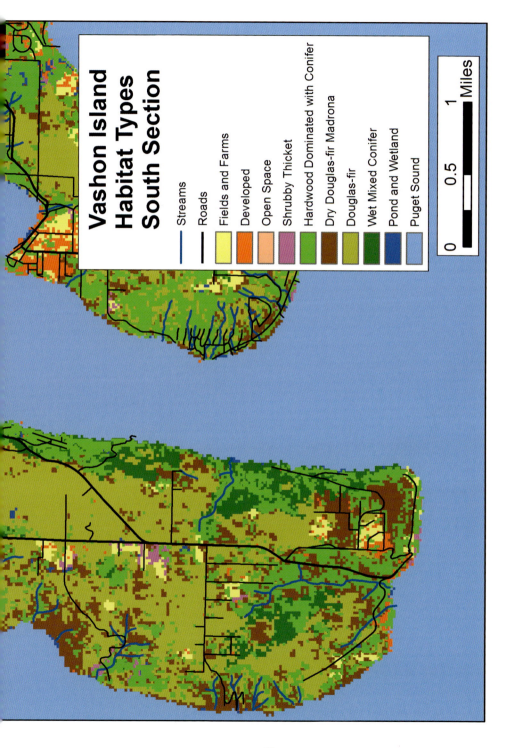

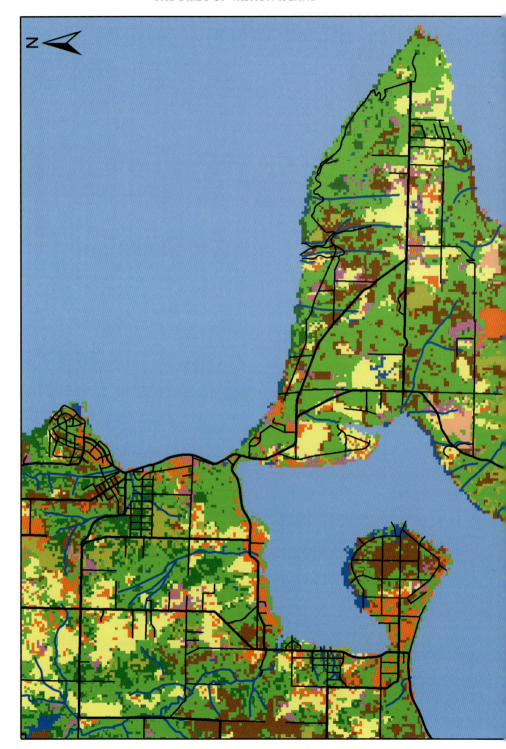

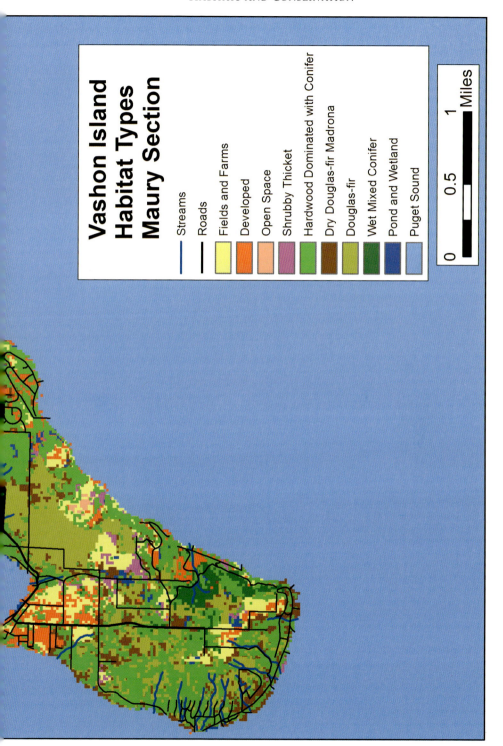

(Continued from page 41)

tion of 3,000 water birds of about 35 species. Before their regional population decline, about eight percent of the wintering population of Western Grebes in Washington State foraged here, arriving each fall and remaining through the spring. Quartermaster Harbor makes a great winter bird area for a number of reasons. It has a spawning stock of Pacific Herring and Surf Smelt, according to Washington Department of Fish and Wildlife spawning surveys (Penttila 1999). These fish populations create a food supply vital for a wide variety of marine fish and bird species. Hundreds of Surf Scoters feed on herring spawn and join other sea ducks to find molluscs in the relatively shallow depths of the harbor. The Black Scoter, only occurring in isolated local populations around Puget Sound, regularly shows up by Shawnee in Quartermaster Harbor and around Manzanita. Because the harbor has very little commercial marine traffic, the area is relatively free of disturbances, allowing birds to feed more easily.

Quartermaster Harbor makes an excellent land location for observing water birds. Manzanita, Dockton, Portage, the marina, the straightaway just south of Burton, and Shawnee provide good viewing points to see most of the loon, grebe, cormorant, and waterfowl species. Point Robin-

Table 13: Characteristic Birds of Saltwater Habitat

Red-throated Loon*	Eurasian Wigeon	American Coot
Pacific Loon*	American Wigeon	Red-necked Phalarope*
Common Loon*	Greater Scaup*	Parasitic Jaeger*
Pied-billed Grebe	Harlequin Duck*	Bonaparte's Gull
Horned Grebe*	Black Scoter*	Mew Gull
Red-necked Grebe*	Surf Scoter*	California Gull
Eared Grebe*	White-winged Scoter*	Herring Gull
Western Grebe*	Common Goldeneye*	Glaucous-winged Gull
Double-crested Cormorant	Barrow's Goldeneye	Western Gull
Brandt's Cormorant	Bufflehead	Heermann's Gull
Pelagic Cormorant	Hooded Merganser	Caspian Tern
Great Blue Heron	Common Merganser*	Common Tern
Brant	Red-breasted Merganser*	Common Murre*
Canada Goose	Ruddy Duck*#	Pigeon Guillemot
Green-winged Teal	Osprey	Marbled Murrelet*
Mallard	Bald Eagle	Rhinoceros Auklet*

* Denotes a specialist for this habitat
# Denotes a species that uses other habitats elsewhere, but for Vashon this consists of its main habitat

son, Tramp Harbor, Ellisport, and KVI offer the best locations on the east side of Vashon. Good spots for examination of Colvos Passage include the end of Bates Road, Reddings Beach Road/Cross Landings Road, Lisabeula Park, 137th Avenue, and Sylvan Beach.

Riding the ferries creates many opportunities for seeing birds in the saltwater habitat. The Tahlequah-Point Defiance run provides the most variety and quantity because of the tide rips that stir Puget Sound across the run. This ferry route gives the best Vashon views of Red-necked Phalarope, Parasitic Jaeger, Caspian Tern, Common Murre, and Rhinoceros Auklet. Brant offer an important highlight in season on the Vashon-Fauntleroy run. The Vashon-Southworth ferry gives one a quick, good glimpse down Colvos Passage for migrating Common Terns and Bonaparte's Gulls. Many ducks, grebes, loons, and cormorants hang out by both ferry docks.

Sandy and Gravelly Shoreline, Mud Flat, and Salt Marsh

Vashon possesses more than 51 miles of saltwater shoreline. Satellite imagery designates about 1,150 acres as nearshore area (Aycrigg et al. 2013, Ohmann and Gregory 2002). These acres are not included in the land surface numbers for Vashon habitat percentages. Over 45 species utilize saltwater shoreline regularly, with six found exclusively in this habitat for the Island. Vashon's shoreline actually represents a collection of several shoreline types, such as rocky shoreline, sandy and gravelly shoreline, mud flat, and salt marsh. Of these, rocky shoreline is practically nonexistent. A pseudo-rocky shoreline exists to some extent in Tramp Harbor at Portage, where riprap is present. Of all the birds preferring rocky shores, only Harlequin Duck, and rarely Black Turnstone, utilize this area. The area remains so small that the many other rocky shoreline specialists very infrequently visit the Island or have never been recorded at all.

In general, Vashon's shoreline is typical of the Puget Sound area, consisting of high bluffs reaching 100 to 300 feet, with narrow beaches formed by the erosion of the bluffs (King County 1975). The beaches vary from some sandy-muddy areas to gravelly areas and cobblestone. This type of shoreline lacks much interest for birds. The sandy, gravelly, and cobblestone shorelines mainly attract crows and resting gulls, mostly Glaucous-winged. Sanderling, a winter resident shorebird, also utilizes this habitat. The value of these types of beaches lies instead in the number of bird species seen in the surrounding waters, both nearshore and deeper. As the Saltwater section outlines, Vashon's beaches create the foundation for extremely important habitat for the fish that the marine bird species eat.

The best shoreline habitat for birds on Vashon exists where streams interact with the shore to create deltas, mud flats, and salt marsh. The most

Exposed mud flat at low tide at Fern Cove. © Linda Barnes

interesting location of this type lies at KVI Beach, where a spring creates a small saltwater estuary. A sand spit built by coastal drift frames the edges of marsh. The salicornia salt marsh here is now an extremely rare habitat in King County (King County 1986). Many waterfowl forage in the salicornia, a low, springy vegetation. At KVI, Green-winged Teal occur from fall through spring in the wet salicornia areas of the estuary, as well as at the muddy pond. The pond-like area hosts a very good shorebird migration every spring and fall. Western and Least Sandpipers make regular visits during migration, as do Greater Yellowlegs and Semipalmated Plovers. Rarities dropping by include Semipalmated, Pectoral, and Baird's Sandpipers. Many ducks and gulls use the estuary, as well as land birds such as Band-tailed Pigeons coming down to drink. The sandy grassy area also attracts a number of rare migrants such as Say's Phoebe, Western Kingbird, Western Meadowlark, and American Pipit.

A small, low salt marsh exists at the mouth of Shinglemill Creek at Fern Cove. It supports saltgrass, pickleweed, and sedges (King County 1986). An extensive mud flat stretches far out to meet Colvos Passage. Fern Cove provides the second-best place to look for shorebirds on Vashon.

Western and Least Sandpipers and Greater Yellowlegs feed on the flats, as does an occasional rarity such as Long-billed Dowitcher or Solitary Sandpiper. Spotted Sandpiper reliably show up here year-round. Many species of migrating gulls and terns using Colvos Passage rest here at low tide.

Other good examples of mud flat deltas at the mouth of a creek include Ellisport and Shawnee. Ellisport often serves as a stopover for shorebirds going to and from KVI Beach. Ellisport hosts a similar diversity of shorebirds in lower numbers for each species. Eelgrass beds attract several waterfowl species as well. A large wintering flock of American Wigeon always forages here, with usually one or two Eurasian Wigeon mixed in. Brant feed in preparation for their northward migration. The old pilings harbor roosting gulls, terns, and herons, as well as nest boxes for Purple Martins placed by Rich Siegrist. These nest boxes house a cloud of young martins every breeding season. At Shawnee, the delta draws wintering Sanderling and a great number of roosting gulls and terns.

The bluffs associated with Vashon beaches provide important nesting habitat for a number of species. Pigeon Guillemots, Belted Kingfishers,

Table 14: Characteristic Birds of Sandy and Gravelly Shoreline, Mud Flats, and Salt Marshes

Double-crested Cormorant	Peregrine Falcon	Herring Gull
Brandt's Cormorant	Virginia Rail	Glaucous-winged Gull
Pelagic Cormorant	American Coot	Heermann's Gull
Great Blue Heron	Killdeer	Caspian Tern
Green Heron	Semipalmated Plover*	Pigeon Guillemot
Gr. White-fronted Goose	Greater Yellowlegs	Belted Kingfisher
Brant	Lesser Yellowlegs	American Crow
Canada Goose	Spotted Sandpiper	Purple Martin
Green-winged Teal	Black Turnstone*	Tree Swallow
Mallard	Sanderling*	N. Rough-winged Swallow
Northern Pintail*#	Dunlin*	Barn Swallow
American Wigeon	Pectoral Sandpiper*	Cliff Swallow
Eurasian Wigeon	Western Sandpiper	American Pipit
Harlequin Duck	Least Sandpiper	European Starling
Bald Eagle	Bonaparte's Gull	Savannah Sparrow
Merlin	Mew Gull	Song Sparrow
	California Gull	

* Denotes a specialist for this habitat
\# Denotes a species that uses other habitats elsewhere, but for Vashon this consists of its main habitat

and Northern Rough-winged Swallows regularly use the bluffs for breeding purposes. Guillemots, kingfishers, and Northern Rough-winged Swallows excavate burrows into soft sides of the cliffs. Examples of all three are easily seen at Point Robinson. Guillemots and kingfishers use several other sites: just north of KVI Beach, the southern bluffs of Tramp Harbor, the bluffs facing Quartermaster Harbor near Raab's Lagoon, the Lisabeula area, and the James Point area, to name a few.

Freshwater: Ponds, Wetlands, and Streams

More than 35 of the species regularly occurring on Vashon use ponds, freshwater wetlands, and marsh to some extent. Three species occur exclusively on ponds or in wetlands on Vashon: Wood Duck, Ring-necked Duck, and Marsh Wren. Northern Shovelers appear almost always at ponds and only rarely on saltwater. The Island boasts no real lakes, though Vashon does possess a few good-sized ponds and many small ponds, marshes, and wet field edges. Freshwater ponds, wetlands, and marsh cover about 1.5 percent of the land area of the Island (Aycrigg et al. 2013, Ohmann and Gregory 2002). (See the three Vashon Island Habitat Types maps on pages 42 to 47.) That percentage may be somewhat higher, as the satellite imagery fails to catch some of the wetlands that have trees. A large wetland south of Cemetery Road, for example, received inclusion into the acreage totals but tends to have so much tree cover that the map misses it and shows it as Hardwood-dominated Mixed Forest. In addition, many of the smaller ponds dry up partially or completely during the summer and early fall months.

Vashon's freshwater ponds provide important habitat for a number of species, several of which would be absent from the Island without the ponds' presence. Both Wood Ducks and Hooded Mergansers breed each year on local ponds, using holes in trees or artificial nest boxes next to wooded ponds. Fisher Pond makes the best spot for Wood Ducks. The ponds of the Island Center Forest create the best opportunities for finding Hooded Merganser broods. They prefer hidden, heavily wooded, and secluded ponds.

Other species that use the ponds include Osprey and Bald Eagle. They frequently check out Fisher Pond for fish. The eagles sometimes catch an unwary duck. Fisher Pond hosts a number of puddle ducks in fall and winter, such as American and Eurasian Wigeon, Green-winged Teal, Northern Shoveler, and an occasional Northern Pintail. Other ducks, especially Ring-necked Ducks, will also appear on Fisher Pond. Ring-necks that utilize Island ponds rarely use saltwater around Vashon. Pied-billed Grebe nest on Fisher Pond. The pond along Singer Road regularly has wi-

The Mukai Pond wetland in the Island Center Forest showing its much reduced size in late summer. © Ed Swan

geon from fall through spring and sometimes a breeding Hooded Merganser. The ponds along the way to Lisabeula Park and those along Westside Highway in the Colvos and Cove area consistently attract wigeon from fall into the spring.

Several good wetland and marsh areas exist. The marsh at Portage attracts Virginia Rail as occasionally do the wet areas around the monument at the end of Monument Road. Marsh Wren, Common Yellowthroat, and Red-winged Blackbirds appear there as well. The small marsh just south of the intersection of Vashon Highway and Wax Orchard Road seems to be one of the first to welcome the blackbirds back in February.

Possibly the best wetland area consists of wetlands on the north and northeast edges of the Island Center Forest. These wetlands include several good-sized ponds, such as Meadowlake and Mukai Pond. Meadowlake, where Marsh Wrens occasionally show up, has a significant band of cattails and open water that attracts many ducks. Several interesting patches of woods exist here as well, a large wood lot of Lodgepole Pine and another of cottonwood. The mixture of wetland and woods has the potential of bringing many more surprises with more observer attention. Mukai Pond attracts many ducks, and the exposed mud in spring and fall

Table 15: Characteristic Birds of Ponds, Wetlands, and Streams

Pied-billed Grebe	Lesser Scaup	Belted Kingfisher
Double-crested Cormorant	Bufflehead	Tree Swallow
Green Heron	Hooded Merganser	Violet-green Swallow
Great Blue Heron	Osprey	Barn Swallow
Gr. White-fronted Goose	Bald Eagle	Marsh Wren*
Canada Goose	Virginia Rail	American Dipper*
Wood Duck*	Killdeer	Yellow Warbler
Green-winged Teal	Greater Yellowlegs	Common Yellowthroat
Mallard	Lesser Yellowlegs	Song Sparrow
American Wigeon	Spotted Sandpiper	Lincoln's Sparrow
Eurasian Wigeon	Western Sandpiper	Red-winged Blackbird
Northern Shoveler*	Least Sandpiper	Brown-headed Cowbird
Ring-necked Duck*	Wilson's Snipe	

* Denotes a specialist for this habitat

entices shorebirds such as the uncommon Solitary Sandpiper. It possesses a large aspen grove with a dogwood understory, attracting many thrushes and warblers, including once a Nashville Warbler. Common Yellowthroat breed in the wet field here. One easily finds 30 species in an hour in spring at either pond, as thrushes, flycatchers, wrens, warblers, and vireos of all kinds abound. Some of the exciting possibilities for this area include Red-eyed Vireo and Hammond's Flycatcher, both rare for the Island.

    The Island Center Forest ponds and wetlands form the headwaters for the Judd Creek watershed, and Fisher Pond forms much of the headwaters for Shinglemill Creek. These create the two large stream systems on the Island. A study by the Wild Fish Conservancy (formerly Washington Trout) in 2002 found 75 streams on Vashon winding for 88 miles altogether. The Wild Fish Conservancy's survey of the Island's streams upgraded the fish-carrying classification of about 40 percent of the streams. Many more streams carried fish than was earlier known. In addition, Wild Fish Conservancy's habitat value for fish and wildlife was much greater than originally thought. Observers found Coho Salmon and sea-run Cutthroat Trout in numerous streams. The Wild Fish Conservancy documented at least 29 streams as fish-bearing, used by fish in a number of ways. The fish utilizing the streams are a key food source for many of the marine bird species around Vashon. The Vashon Nature Center and the King County Department of Natural Resources and Parks Salmon Watcher Program documented salmon and trout over the last decade. They found Coho every year but 2009 and 2010 (2010 had no known observers). Observers saw Chum Salmon and sea-run Cutthroat Trout in some years. The creeks checked included Judd, Shinglemill, Fisher, Christensen, Mileta, and Raab's Creeks (Vashon Nature Center 2013). This data best reflects the presence of fish species and not local population trends. However, if one looks at the numbers of salmon reported each year and then allows for the number of surveys and volunteers, some evidence exists for a decline in salmon in the last decade.

Bianca Perla, director of the Vashon Nature Center, LLC, also analyzed benthic invertebrate information for Vashon streams to better look at local stream health. While water quality chemistry appears good in the streams, the sampling of benthic invertebrates (insects, crustaceans, worms, snails, and clams) came up with low health scores ranging from very poor to at best fair (Vashon-Maury Island Groundwater Protection Committee 2012). These organisms provide an important prey base for fish and birds. Their condition offers an important indicator of habitat quality. Vashon's lower benthic invertebrate numbers in general and in comparison to mainland King County streams may possibly be partially a result of the isolated nature of the Island. Islands tend to be less diverse than mainland habitats and have less ability to replenish species from nearby populations after disturbances occur. In addition, some sample sites in studies may have been more severely impacted than the stream watershed as a whole. A couple of trends did appear to show potential problems for future invertebrate health. Streams with mostly older forest with little or no clearing over the last 30 years were more likely to show stable invertebrate populations. Conversely, even though Vashon is predominantly rural, streams experiencing even very low levels of urbanization/development (less than eight percent of watershed in urban area) seemed particularly sensitive to its effects, including increased sediment and pollution in runoff. Also, many of these species' health correlates to salmon numbers. When salmon populations decrease, some invertebrate species experience declines as well.

Only one bird species relies exclusively on stream habitat, the American Dipper. Salmon watchers alerted birdwatchers to this species in 2000 when Michael Laurie added it to the Vashon bird list. American Dippers eat aquatic invertebrates and their eggs, small fish, fish eggs, and some flying insects (Willson and Kingery 2011). They feed up and down the main stem of Shinglemill Creek in late fall and winter. While only one species is completely dependent on the streams, Pacific-slope Flycatcher, Pacific Wren, Swainson's Thrush, and Wilson's Warbler densely inhabit streamside thickets of Salmonberry in the forested stream areas. Varied

Thrush occasionally nest here as well. Where the streams move along the edges of more open area with deciduous trees and shrubs, Yellow Warbler and Willow Flycatcher show up in late May and June.

Woodlands

Forests as a whole are the largest habitat grouping on Vashon, covering a little over two-thirds of the Island's surface. Forest cover likely peaked in the 1980s or early 1990s. Forest cover from 1992 to 2006 declined from 72 to 70 percent (King County 2012b). The mapping for this second edition, probably using the same satellite data, places the total at 71 percent in 2006 (Aycrigg et al. 2013, Ohmann and Gregory 2002). (See the three Vashon Island Habitat Types maps on pages 42 to 47.) No major clearing occurred from 2006 to 2013, and these numbers likely remain accurate within a percentage point or two for this second edition.

Vashon has four main forest types, each of about the same size: Wet Coniferous Forest at about 20 percent of the land area, Douglas-fir Forest

Wet Coniferous Forest habitat in the Fern Cove Nature Preserve near Shinglemill Creek. © Peter Murray

at nineteen percent, Dry Douglas-fir/Madrone at eighteen percent, and Hardwood-dominated Mixed Forest at fourteen percent (Aycrigg et al. 2013, Ohmann and Gregory 2002). (See the three Vashon Island Habitat Types maps on pages 42-47.) All of the coniferous forest types are dominated by conifer tree species but can contain a significant hardwood component. Hardwood/deciduous trees play a larger role than seems indicated by adding up the acreage percentages of the coniferous-dominated forests. The first edition, with older data and different GIS interpretation capabilities, had separated coniferous forest out at about ten percent, deciduous forest at twelve percent, and 43 percent mixed forest. The new data and interpretation for this edition provided the ability to characterize the mixed forest stands in greater detail.

The Vashon forest mix largely reflects that of the lowland Puget Sound region. The original forest disappeared under waves of logging, agricultural clearing, and industrial, commercial, and residential development. Forests that naturally regenerated after early 20th century logging tend to be quite diverse and structurally complex. Many of these stands are currently developing old characteristics such as large trees (bigger than 24 inches in diameter), snags, downed logs, and multiple canopy layers. However, because of the fragmented nature of Vashon's forests, invasive species, and ongoing human disturbances, many of these stands may not develop into the type of old-growth forest that existed on the Island prior to settlement. The forest along the Shinglemill Creek watershed is a good example of naturally regenerated, older forest.

Forests that originated after agricultural clearing and subsequent abandonment, typically in the 1930s and 1940s, often came back as single layer, hardwood-dominated stands, with mostly Red Alder in patches all of the same age. Some coniferous forests show a history of intensive forestry, starting in the 1950s, resulting in an even-aged monoculture of Douglas-fir plantations with very little understory. These sometimes receive scarce management, growing thickly and close together. This denseness lets a low amount of light in under the canopy, precluding an understory and fostering the presence of many dead lower branches.

Coniferous Forest

Three coniferous forest habitat types exist on Vashon: Wet Coniferous, Douglas-fir, and Dry Douglas-fir/Madrone. While microhabitats of these types spread throughout the Island, generally the Wet Coniferous tends to appear to the north and down the west side of Vashon. Douglas-fir occurs mostly in the middle and south of Vashon. Dry Douglas-fir/Madrone grows mainly to the south and east of Vashon and Maury Island. Soil

Many stands and commercial plantations of same-aged, same-sized Douglas-fir exist in central and south Vashon and on Maury Island. Much of these stands exhibit little diversity in canopy and understory species or in overall structure, as shown by this example of Douglas-fir Forest habitat along Old Mill Road. © Ed Swan

conditions and to a lesser extent precipitation determine their distribution. The north end of Vashon possesses Alderwood loamy/sandy soils that hold somewhat higher moisture content and better support Western Hemlock and Western Red Cedar. The more southern and eastern areas of Vashon and Maury, with the sandy-gravelly, much more drained Alderwood-Everett soils, favor much higher concentrations of Douglas-fir.

Wet Coniferous Forest covers about 20 percent of the Island (Aycrigg et al. 2013, Ohmann and Gregory 2002). (See the three Vashon Island Habitat Types maps on pages 42 to 47.) Tree stands for this forest type range usually from 80 to 100 years old, with very few older trees. These stands tend to be away from development and agriculture and follow a more natural route of succession that in the larger patches might somewhat resemble old-growth characteristics in the decades to come. As described below, both the trees providing the canopy and the understory tend to have a complex, varied structure with a broad mix of species.

Vashon's Wet Coniferous Forest conforms mostly to the North Pacific Maritime Mesic-Wet Douglas-fir-Western Hemlock Forest designation (NatureServe 2009). Douglas-fir, Western Hemlock, and Western Red Cedar dominate the canopy, the latter two the more so where conditions remain moister. Bigleaf Maple and Red Alder occur with a large but not dominant presence as well. Sword Fern, Salmonberry, and Evergreen Huckleberry provide an important part of the understory. A classic example of this habitat exists along the main stem of Shinglemill Creek.

Douglas-fir Forest covers about nineteen percent of Vashon's surface (Aycrigg et al. 2013, Ohmann and Gregory 2002). (See the three Vashon Island Habitat Types maps on pages 42 to 47.) The majority of these stands are 60 to 110 years old. This forest type includes several commercially intended plantations, many of which tend to be quite dense, with trees of a same age that require thinning in order to create a healthier habitat. Other areas grew back from agriculture, and others naturally after logging. The latter example tends to possess the most complex characteristics, with a wider range in tree ages, understory species, and height diversity.

Douglas-fir Forest consists largely of the forest designation North Pacific Maritime Dry-Mesic Douglas-fir-Western Hemlock Forest (NatureServe 2009). Throughout the Puget Sound area it occurs in a mosaic with the Wet Coniferous Forest, as it does on Vashon and occupies the habitat space between the wetter Wet Coniferous Forest and Dry Douglas-fir/Madrone Forest. To some extent, a moisture gradient exists from the wet to the dry coniferous. The difference between the Douglas-fir and Dry Douglas-fir/Madrone Forest types appears to be in a number of conditions which favor Pacific Madrone in the latter habitat. In the straight Douglas-fir For-

At Maury Island Marine Park, Pacific Madrone grows as the dominant tree species in this section of Dry Douglas-fir/Madrone Forest habitat. © Linda Barnes

Table 16: Characteristic Birds of Coniferous Forests		
Sharp-shinned Hawk	Cassin's Vireo	American Robin
Cooper's Hawk	Warbling Vireo	Varied Thrush
Red-tailed Hawk	Hutton's Vireo	Yellow-rumped Warbler
Band-tailed Pigeon	Steller's Jay	Black-throated Gray Warbler
Great Horned Owl	American Crow	Townsend's Warbler
Barred Owl	Common Raven	Wilson's Warbler
Northern Saw-whet Owl	Violet-green Swallow	Western Tanager
Rufous Hummingbird	Chestnut-backed Chickadee	Spotted Towhee
Red-breasted Sapsucker		Song Sparrow
Hairy Woodpecker	Bushtit	Dark-eyed Junco
Northern Flicker	Red-breasted Nuthatch	Brown-headed Cowbird
Pileated Woodpecker	Brown Creeper	Purple Finch
Western Wood-Pewee	Pacific Wren	Red Crossbill
Olive-sided Flycatcher	Golden-crowned Kinglet	Pine Siskin
Pacific-slope Flycatcher	Swainson's Thrush	Evening Grosbeak
	Hermit Thrush	

est, Douglas-fir dominates, with minor amounts of Western Hemlock, Western Red Cedar, and Bigleaf Maple. Salal and Evergreen Huckleberry provide most of the understory, with Oregon Grape joining in where it's drier and Sword Fern in wetter spots. Woods between the high school and elementary school and along much of Old Mill Road and Wax Orchard Road typify this habitat. Typical plantation-type forest patches with no understory include some of the stands in the Dockton/old Glacier Northwest gravel site forest, around Inspiration Point, and along the horse trails between Old Mill Road and Wax Orchard Road south of 220th Street. These areas possess very little of the bird species diversity possible for this type of forest.

The Dry Douglas-fir/Madrone Forest takes over the driest areas of Vashon and especially areas with a history of numerous and extensive fires. Dry Douglas-fir/Madrone forest on Vashon differs from the Douglas-fir forest principally in growing on somewhat sandier soils and having a disturbance history where fires favor the Pacific Madrone life cycle. In addition, some of the Douglas-fir forest might have conditions favorable to Pacific Madrone but regenerate in an area with a lack of a madrone seed source or previous madrone presence providing madrone root crowns for regeneration. Generally in the Dry Douglas-fir/Madrone forest, Douglas-fir provides the primary tree species, but the evergreen broadleaf Pacific Madrone dominates the high-severity fire sites. This forest type covers about eighteen percent of Vashon (Aycrigg et al. 2013, Ohmann and Gregory 2002). (See the three Vashon Island Habitat Types maps on pages 42 to 47.) Locations along the southeast shore of Maury Island provide good examples of this habitat where Pacific Madrone becomes more dominant. Other locations include up Ellis Creek along Ridge Road and some areas in Paradise Valley.

The Douglas-fir/Pacific Madrone-Salal community on the Island, particularly the sections on the south side of Maury, provides one of the best remaining examples of that type in Washington State, according to a site evaluation written by Chris Chappell for the Washington Natural Heritage Program (Chappell 1997). Areas along the southeast shore of Maury Island have Pacific Madrone forest after many fires took place in the first half of the 20th century. At Maury Island Marine Park, a forest exists almost exclusively of Pacific Madrone, with an understory of Salal, hazel, Common Snowberry, and honeysuckle. Madrones regenerate easily from fire by re-sprouting from the root crown. They out-compete Douglas-fir in areas repeatedly burned (Chappell 1997). Douglas-fir require reseeding, taking longer to respond after a fire than the madrone. Multiple fires over the last century eliminated the originally present Douglas-fir, and subsequent fires favored the madrone. The dry slope where this habitat occurs attracts many hummingbirds, including Anna's Hummingbirds. Bushtits often nest here, and Orange-crowned Warblers, Bewick's Wrens, and Spotted Towhees seem to pop from every bush.

The coniferous forest habitats each host about 45 bird species during the course of a year. Coniferous forest possesses no species dependent exclusively on its habitat because those species wouldn't have survived the clearing of the Island's original old-growth forest. A good half of the 45 or so species that utilize this habitat prefer coniferous woods predominantly while still showing up in mixed woods and residential areas. Red Crossbills make a good example of this. Their bills have evolved over time in a cross-wise fashion that enables them to insert their mandibles into a tree's cones and pry them open for their seeds. Crossbills utilize more pure coniferous forest extensively, seek out the cone crop in mixed forest, and occasionally stop at sunflower seed feeders in forested residential areas.

The characteristic birds of the coniferous forests consist of Pacific Wren, Pacific-slope Flycatcher, Varied Thrush, Golden-crowned Kinglet, and Chestnut-backed Chickadee. The sounds in these woods prove very entertaining, with the bubbly, flowing song of the Pacific Wren, the come-here whistle of the Pacific-slope Flycatcher, and the weird whine of the Varied Thrush. Varied Thrush nest in the Wet Coniferous Forest. Overhead the *kip kip kip* of crossbills may be heard.

Hardwood-Dominated Mixed Forest

Hardwood-dominated Mixed (deciduous/coniferous) Forest provides about fourteen percent of the surface area for Vashon (Aycrigg et al. 2013, Ohmann and Gregory 2002). (See the three Vashon Island Habitat Types maps on pages 42 to 47.) While hardwoods dominate in fourteen percent of the Island area, they also present a significant presence in all of the coniferous-dominated forest types. This land cover type has the designation of North Pacific Lowland Mixed Hardwood-Conifer Forest and comprises the main forest type west of the Cascade Range in the lowlands (NatureServe 2009). On Vashon, these forests consist of hardwoods such as Red Alder (primarily), with Bigleaf Maple and a scattering of others such as Cascara and hazel. Mixed in with the hardwoods, large conifers such as Douglas-fir grow in areas with drier soils and less precipitation. Western Hemlock and Western Red Cedar occur with the hardwood mix in the wetter locations. Salal, Salmonberry, Sword Fern, Indian Plum, and Pacific Blackberry fill in the understory, with the invasive Himalayan Blackberry coming in from the edges.

The mixed hardwood-coniferous forests on the Island face increasing change over the next decade because of the life cycle of Red Alder. Red Alder trees make up the majority of the hardwood stands, and many now approach the end of their life. They reach maturity at about 40 to 60 years old

Riparian Hardwood-dominated Mixed Forest growing along the course of Shinglemill Creek. © Michael Elenko

and then begin to decline and die at 60 to 100 years old. Vashon's last large swaths of fires, logging, and agricultural clearing ended in the 1940s and 1950s. The Red Alder that filled in many of the cleared areas now include groups of trees and singles reaching their terminal stage. Conifers should begin to fill in the gaps where they intermingle with the hardwoods. But in areas with especially thick Salmonberry and Himalayan Blackberry, thickets may continue for some time if little or no conifers exist next to the newly opened spaces. Dense layers of thickets and shrubs present a major challenge to tree regeneration. While the hardwood forest type generally has greater bird species diversity than coniferous-dominated stands, this potential diminishes where Red Alder dies and invasive plants such as Himalayan Blackberry, Scotch Broom, or English Ivy move in and choke out other shrubs and early pioneer trees.

Riparian forest, to the small extent that it exists on Vashon, merges with this mixed forest habitat type. Island streams remain too small to have developed flood plains or meandering areas. Their disturbance regime generally follows a very narrow corridor through the woods. The streams change the nature of Island forests to a very small degree. The lowest section of Shinglemill Creek provides a minor exception, with the stream moving back and forth amongst a forest of Red Alder mixed with a few Western Red Cedar and Western Hemlock.

Another forest type worth mention rings Vashon, conforming to the definition of North Pacific Broadleaf Landslide Forest and Shrubland (NatureServe 2009). This forest type develops throughout the northern Pacific mountains and lowlands where steep slopes and bluffs experience periodic mass movements. Vashon has about a hundred acres of this type, where shoreline bluffs collapse, especially after heavy rain events (Aycrigg et al. 2013, Ohmann and Gregory 2002). The disturbance regime usually favors deciduous broadleaf trees such as Red Alder and Bigleaf Maple and shrubs such as Salmonberry and Thimbleberry. This habitat shows patches of different ages associated with differing landslide occurrences. Because of its small amount of acres and tendency to favor hardwood pioneers, this habitat folds into the Hardwood-dominated Mixed Forest category in the acreage totals and on the habitat maps.

The hardwood-dominated forests, with their varied structure and types of plant species, attract a great number of birds. They host over 60 species of birds, with no "specialist" species appearing only in this habitat. Downy Woodpeckers, Black-capped Chickadees, and most of the warblers and vireos prefer the hardwood stands over coniferous forest. Hutton's Vireo and Brown Creeper especially like mixed stands. Red-tailed Hawk and Barred Owl tend to nest in the mixed-wood areas as well. The

Table 17: Characteristic Birds of Hardwood-Dominated Mixed Forests

Sharp-shinned Hawk	Warbling Vireo	Orange-crowned Warbler
Cooper's Hawk	Hutton's Vireo	Yellow Warbler
Bald Eagle	Tree Swallow	Yellow-rumped Warbler
Red-tailed Hawk	Steller's Jay	Black-throated Gray Warbler
California Quail	American Crow	MacGillivray's Warbler
Band-tailed Pigeon	Black-capped Chickadee	Wilson's Warbler
Great Horned Owl	Bushtit	Western Tanager
Barred Owl	Red-breasted Nuthatch	Black-headed Grosbeak
Northern Saw-whet Owl	Brown Creeper	Spotted Towhee
Vaux's Swift	Bewick's Wren	Song Sparrow
Anna's Hummingbird	House Wren	Fox Sparrow
Rufous Hummingbird	Pacific Wren	Dark-eyed Junco
Belted Kingfisher	American Dipper	Brown-headed Cowbird
Red-breasted Sapsucker	Ruby-crowned Kinglet	Bullock's Oriole
Downy Woodpecker	Golden-crowned Kinglet	Purple Finch
Northern Flicker	Swainson's Thrush	House Finch
Pileated Woodpecker	American Robin	American Goldfinch
Western Wood-Pewee	Varied Thrush	Pine Siskin
Olive-sided Flycatcher	Cedar Waxwing	Evening Grosbeak
Pacific-slope Flycatcher	European Starling	

Hardwood-dominated Mixed Forest contains the most bird species diversity for woodland habitats on the Island because it holds a mix of so many forest microhabitats.

Shrubby Thicket

Aerial photos indicate that the Shrubby Thicket habitat category covers as much as three percent of Vashon's land surface, about 800 acres (Aycrigg et al. 2013, Ohmann and Gregory 2002). (See the three Vashon Island Habitat Types maps on pages 42 to 47.) Shrubby thicket occurs mostly in scattered patches rather than in large sections around the Island. This habitat category results mainly from human action, as originally Vashon was wooded down to the shoreline in most areas. It generally occurs around the borders of the various wooded and shore areas and grows up in abandoned fields, vacant lots, next to roadsides, and along power line trails. In shore areas, it often begins as a result of subsidence of bluff edges after wet storm events.

Table 18: Characteristic Birds of Shrubby Thickets		
Sharp-shinned Hawk	House Wren	Fox Sparrow
Ring-necked Pheasant	Ruby-crowned Kinglet	Lincoln's Sparrow
Anna's Hummingbird	Orange-crowned Warbler	Dark-eyed Junco
Rufous Hummingbird	MacGillivray's Warbler	White-crowned Sparrow
Willow Flycatcher	Wilson's Warbler	Golden-crowned Sparrow
Warbling Vireo	Common Yellowthroat	Brown-headed Cowbird
Black-capped Chickadee	Lazuli Bunting	House Finch
Bushtit	Spotted Towhee	American Goldfinch
Bewick's Wren	Song Sparrow	

Thickets in this ecological zone and soil area act as transitional habitat. Thickets give way eventually to forest succession if left to evolve naturally or to suburban and urban development if used by humans. The plant community for this category consists of the various blackberry species, Red Elderberry, Ocean Spray, Oregon Grape, and young Red Alder or Douglas-fir. In moist areas and along streams, Salmonberry grows thickly. The residential sections of the Developed Area habitat category mimic the Shrubby Thicket category to some extent, especially when native plants are used to landscape the grounds.

About 25 different bird species utilize thickets for foraging and nesting. Towhees and a number of sparrow species feed along the ground and sing from exposed perches. Willow Flycatchers dart out from branches to catch insects in midair. Orange-crowned and Wilson's Warblers glean bugs from leaves and branches of shrubs. Sharp-shinned and Cooper's Hawks race through, snatching unwary small birds. Himalayan Blackberries, while detrimental to many native plant species because of their invasive character, still form hedgerows attractive to sparrows, wrens, and towhees. In winter, groups of White- and Golden-crowned Sparrows forage along the blackberry hedgerows, with occasional rare visitors such as White-throated and Harris's Sparrows.

While all of these species use brushy edge zones connected to the other habitat types, some, such as Willow Flycatcher and Common Yellowthroat, require a larger patch for a breeding territory. Common Yellowthroat utilize thickets that border ponds and wetlands. The thickets stretching from the east shore of Mukai Pond host one to four pairs each year. Willow Flycatchers will utilize the same wet thickets or drier fields with young Red Alder and Douglas-fir in their first decade. Once the trees fill in the gaps in the second decade or so, the Willow Flycatchers must

Shrubby Thicket habitat at Raab's Lagoon. © Linda Barnes

find another location. Neither the flycatcher nor yellowthroat can effectively use the faux thickets of residential vegetation like the chickadees, kinglets, juncos, and sparrows do. Retaining the flycatcher or yellowthroat as breeding birds necessitates ponds and wetlands with large borders or cleared lots with a big shrub margin.

A number of very productive thicket areas exist around Vashon. One of the best lies at the base of the hill at Maury Island Marine Park, sheltering Bushtit, White-crowned Sparrow, Bewick's Wren, Lincoln's Sparrow, Anna's Hummingbird, and sometimes rarities such as Lazuli Bunting. The thicket edge of the alder woods at Point Robinson always provides something interesting year-round, especially in migration. Depending on the time of year, four or five kinds of warbler pass through and several sparrow and vireo species. The thickets surrounding the turnaround at the end of Kingsbury Road create a spring hot spot as well. Other locations include the hedgerows along Paradise Valley, Old Mill Road, and around the health center and food bank complex.

Fields, Farmland, and Pasture

Using the Moll study data, the first edition found only 334 acres (about 1.5 percent of Vashon) utilized for agricultural purposes (Moll 1993). Another 510 acres (about two percent) were considered grassland, probably horse pasturage for the most part. In this second edition, improvements in satellite imagery and GIS programming show a more likely accurate fifteen percent of Vashon as farms, fields, pasture, and grassland (Aycrigg et al. 2013, Ohmann and Gregory 2002). (See the three Vashon Island Habitat Types maps on pages 42 to 47.) It appears the earlier imagery interpreted much farm and field area as residential or commercial development.

Most remaining farms form part of the growing organic produce industry. According to a survey for the Vashon Island Growers Association (VIGA), the majority of farms consist of four or five acres, with several acres unused on many farms (Forrester pers. comm. 2005). In many ways, the small size of these new farms tends to make their habitat somewhat similar to residential garden areas. Because most Vashon farmers use organic farming practices, these areas provide safer habitat than many gardens, where people utilize far too many pesticides and fertilizers. Jasper Forrester of Green Man Farm mentions that "many small Island farms also maintain uncultivated areas as wildlife habitat and/or wetlands buffers. This is partly because they appreciate the role birds play in natural pest control but also because they know that such buffer zones are essential to maintaining the health of the whole local ecosystem."

Westside Highway field and barn. © Peter Murray

Table 19: Characteristic Birds of Fields, Farmland, and Pasture

Canada Goose	Rock Pigeon	Common Yellowthroat
Mallard	Eurasian Collared-Dove	Savannah Sparrow
Ring-necked Pheasant	Barn Owl	Lincoln's Sparrow
Great Blue Heron	Merlin	White-crowned Sparrow
Northern Harrier	American Crow	Golden-crowned Sparrow
Bald Eagle	Common Raven	Western Meadowlark
Red-tailed Hawk	Violet-green Swallow	Red-winged Blackbird
American Kestrel	Cliff Swallow	Brown-headed Cowbird
Killdeer	Barn Swallow	House Finch
Wilson's Snipe	American Robin	American Goldfinch
Glaucous-winged Gull	American Pipit	House Sparrow
	European Starling	

The former Misty Isle large cattle operation and smaller farms with livestock such as Singer Farm and the one just west of town provide several hundred acres of pasture. Though the monoculture grass of these fields possesses little avian species diversity, the fields attract rodent prey for raptors and insects for swallows overhead. The Wax Orchard area fields, particularly around the airstrip, serve as the center of raptor species diversity for the Island. Observers noted as many as four Barn Owls at a time swooping over the pasture near the airport along 232nd Street in the summer of 2013. The first Rough-legged Hawk record occurred here in December 2012. Northern Harriers and American Kestrels use the area in winter, and Red-tailed Hawks nest in trees along the edge of the fields. Common Ravens flock in to catch disturbed rodents when the area undergoes mowing in late summer. When left unmowed long enough, pastures such as these provide breeding territories for Savannah Sparrows.

Around 34 species on Vashon use farms and fields as one of several habitats in which to live. No birds specializing just in farmland, fields, or pasture remain. Of the farm and field specialists, which include the American Kestrel and Vesper Sparrow, the Savannah Sparrow remains the only native species present as a breeder. Two raptors that both hunt in a similar manner, the Northern Harrier and Barn Owl, use large fields extensively. Barn Owls can make do to some extent with a patchwork of smaller fields intermixed with other habitats. Northern Harrier need tens or hundreds of acres of continuous open area. The main groups of species utilizing Island open areas include raptors, swallows, and American Pipits. Swallows catch insects overhead and nest on houses, barns, and other outbuildings.

Raptors swoop in and carry off rodents or small birds found in the fields and crops. American Pipits, a nondescript brown, sparrow-like bird, were recently seen migrating through fields along Old Mill Road.

Some particularly good open-field areas lie along Westside Highway in the Colvos and Cove area. Rich Siegrist recently observed several formerly common but now rare species such as Barn Owl and Lazuli Bunting. Wilson's Snipe and Tree Swallows, uncommon for Vashon, also appear regularly. The fields around the monument on Monument Road and on 216th Street between Monument Road and Tramp Harbor also prove very productive. These wet fields produce Common Yellowthroat, MacGillivray's Warbler, Savannah Sparrow, an occasional Virginia Rail, Wilson's Snipe, and a wide variety of other warblers, sparrows, and swallows in spring and summer. In winter, Mallards and American and Eurasian Wigeons forage in the corn stubble field.

With the regeneration of much of Vashon's forests on the one hand and the growth of residential area on the other, it seems as if preservation of what's left of Island farms and fields might need to be moved up to the front burner before they're squeezed out. As forest succession continues, the fields and open areas not only provide habitat in and of themselves, but create the space for the above described Shrubby Thicket habitat. Many field owners possess old fields lightly grazed if at all by animals, growing some small thickets in the midst of the fields. These fields, and those allowing hedgerows and/or interspersed pockets of thickets, attract not only the species listed in Table 19, but many or most of those in Table 18. Such locations boast lists of more than 50 species and thus make a very important contribution to Vashon bird habitat. Finally, from a social/political standpoint, many people choose to live here because of the rural character of the Island. Losing the used and unused farm fields that generate much of the feeling of Vashon's rural character risks weakening the resistance to suburban sprawl that would degrade the current variety of habitat types on the Island.

Aerial

Birds' ability to fly has inspired people all through the ages, though in studying birds, observers often leave out the sky in discussions of habitat. A number of species show up only in the air around Vashon, never or rarely landing on water or alighting on land or vegetation. These birds consist of the ones that migrate high above, catch their food in the air, or use the air to observe their prey down on the ground or in the water. Vaux's Swifts alight only in their nesting cavities in old chimneys or tree trunks, of which there are none known for Vashon. Common Nighthawks

Table 20: Characteristic Birds of Aerial Habitat		
Turkey Vulture	Red-tailed Hawk	Violet-green Swallow
Snow Goose	Common Nighthawk	N. Rough-winged Swallow
Gr. White-fronted Goose	Vaux's Swift	Cliff Swallow
Osprey	Purple Martin	Barn Swallow
Bald Eagle	Tree Swallow	

catch insects in the air from dusk to just before dawn, their unusual *beearnt* call often providing the only evidence of their presence. Former breeders, they now just fly by the Island. Swallows and Purple Martins perch on wires, but sometimes the only way one sees them is overhead as they hunt for airborne bugs. Raptors, such as our common Red-tailed Hawks, Bald Eagles, and Ospreys, gyre overhead looking for their meal down below. Birders note Turkey Vultures as migrants that rarely forage during the summer and less often drop to earth while migrating or foraging. Only a couple of sightings exist of vultures on the ground eating road kill or eating offal from the cattle operation. Several other migrant species such as Snow Goose, Trumpeter Swan, and Tundra Swan almost always make their appearance flying by up high. Nearly all recent Snow Goose records consist of birds winging high overhead. Conservation of this habitat relates mostly to air quality, which may be a factor in the mysterious downward trend of the Common Nighthawk population in the Puget Sound area. One theory hypothesizes that air pollution may have damaged their high-flying insect prey population.

Developed Area

Developed Area, called Town and Garden in the first edition, covers about eight percent of Vashon (Aycrigg et al. 2013, Ohmann and Gregory 2002). (See the three Vashon Island Habitat Types maps on pages 42 to 47.) In this second edition, improvements in satellite imagery and GIS programming show a more likely accurate eight percent figure, as opposed to the 30 percent of the first edition work, which was based on older systems of interpreting the data. It appears the earlier imagery interpreted much farm and field area and some forest as residential or commercial development. Residential areas form by far the largest part of the Developed Area category. Growth, in terms of human presence, occurred comparatively slowly on the Island compared to the rest of the county. That growth appears to eat into the size of all of the other terrestrial habitat types.

Several types of residential development exist on Vashon. The worst, in terms of habitat, consist of those where owners clear the land and re-

An Osprey eyes its nest on the cell phone tower at the corner of Vashon Highway and 204th Street. Ospreys frequently make use of such human-made structures. This nest replaces the original maintained by this pair over several years which burned quickly one evening in spring 2011, killing that year's fledglings. © Ed Swan

place it with a monoculture lawn and a few shrubs or trees. The lack of species diversity in the plants and the lack of structural variety among the plant species create a situation where only Eurasian imports such as House Sparrows, European Starlings, and Rock Pigeons thrive. Robins and Killdeer, very adaptable natives, usually become the few indigenous species to inhabit such deserts. Generally, grass-only yards require intensive use of herbicides and pesticides to maintain, further adversely impacting native wildlife and plants in the area. Eventually, this may possibly degrade Vashon's water supply.

Fortunately, Developed Area with housing need not be a complete loss of usable bird habitat. Much of the residential area retains trees onsite, clearing only for the building site itself. Purple Finches and many of the other forest birds such as Pacific Wren, Varied Thrush, and woodpeckers may be present on such property. Many property owners create areas mimicking the Shrubby Thicket habitat by planting a variety of shrub and small tree types of varying sizes. When residents forego the use of pesticides and carefully dispose of household waste, neighborhoods provide good habitat for a wide variety of warblers, wrens, chickadees, sparrows,

Table 21: Characteristic Birds of Town and Garden Habitat

Canada Goose	Tree Swallow	Black-throated Gray Warbler
Mallard	Violet-green Swallow	MacGillivray's Warbler
Sharp-shinned Hawk	Cliff Swallow	Wilson's Warbler
Cooper's Hawk	Barn Swallow	Common Yellowthroat
Red-tailed Hawk	Chestnut-backed Chickadee	Western Tanager
Merlin		Black-headed Grosbeak
Ring-necked Pheasant	Black-capped Chickadee	Spotted Towhee
California Quail	Red-breasted Nuthatch	Fox Sparrow
Killdeer	Bushtit	Song Sparrow
Glaucous-winged Gull	House Wren	White-crowned Sparrow
Band-tailed Pigeon	Bewick's Wren	Golden-crowned Sparrow
Rock Pigeon	Pacific Wren	Dark-eyed Junco
Anna's Hummingbird	Ruby-crowned Kinglet	Red-winged Blackbird
Rufous Hummingbird	Golden-crowned Kinglet	Brown-headed Cowbird
Downy Woodpecker	American Robin	Bullock's Oriole
Pileated Woodpecker	Varied Thrush	House Finch
Northern Flicker	Cedar Waxwing	Purple Finch
Willow Flycatcher	European Starling	Red Crossbill
Pacific-slope Flycatcher	Orange-crowned Warbler	American Goldfinch
Warbling Vireo	Yellow Warbler	Pine Siskin
Steller's Jay	Yellow-rumped Warbler	Evening Grosbeak
American Crow	Townsend's Warbler	House Sparrow
Purple Martin		

and finches. In just three years, I tallied 84 species of birds on a one-acre property, 25 to 30 being around in any given week.

Adding bird-friendly features to Developed Area habitat can attract even more species. Feeding stations assist a number of species such as Spotted Towhees, Black-capped and Chestnut-backed Chickadees, Pine Siskins, American Goldfinches, House Finches, Dark-eyed Juncos, Song Sparrows, and both hummingbird species. Hummingbird feeders help complete a feeding station, bringing in Anna's Hummingbirds all year-round, Rufous Hummingbirds in spring and summer, and sometimes even finches or warblers trying to drink. Anna's Hummingbirds expanded their range north from California after learning to use hummingbird feeders and to take advantage of exotic flowering plants that bloom at all times of the year. Having a variety of shrubs and trees of different sizes and heights also attracts warblers. Shallow birdbaths draw just about any kind of bird. Other birds characteristic of residential areas include Bewick's Wrens and Downy Woodpeckers.

The town, commercial, and light industrial areas of the Developed Area habitat category form the domain of three species introduced to North America, the House Sparrow, European Starling, and Rock Pigeon. All three adapted long ago to living closely with humans in Europe. House Sparrows and Rock Pigeons on Vashon are generally limited to actual commercial areas, the ferry terminals, and some farm areas. House Sparrows have a particularly strong association with horses, having followed the horses used by settlers as they moved west across the continent.

With relatively dispersed development of residences on Vashon, Developed Area habitat hasn't impacted bird populations in as destructive a manner as in more urban and more thoroughly suburban areas in the Puget Sound lowlands. The habitat supports such a wide variety of species because enough healthy forest and open area still exist, enabling some of the population from these other habitat types to spill over. The future danger exists in that ongoing development may cause Vashon to resemble mainland suburbs. Species diversity would decline extensively and numbers as a whole. Even so, Vashon would still retain quite a few bird species and large numbers of starlings, House Sparrows, robins, crows, and Killdeer that prefer human developed areas.

Conservation on the Island

A good number of organizations pursue conservation of Vashon's ecosystem through three main strategies: political action, education, and land preservation. This section lists many of the groups, but naming them all remains very difficult. So many people take action with various efforts, constantly forming organizations and committees, and then changing the names or combining their work with others. Many groups go dormant for periods of time and reactivate under the same or different name. For instance, Preserve Our Islands, so instrumental in the fight to stop the Glacier Northwest mine and to acquire the land for public use, now remains active on many issues affecting Puget Sound under the name Sound Action. The Vashon-Maury Island Land Trust, the Vashon-Maury Island Audubon Society, the Vashon Hydrophone Project, Vashon-Maury Island Groundwater Protection Committee, Vashon Nature Center, Vashon Beach Naturalists, Vashon Streams Survey Committee, Vashon Forest Stewards, Sustainable Vashon, and the King County Department of Natural Resources and Parks provide a number of ongoing educational classes, forums, and research projects publicizing knowledge of Vashon's ecosystems and the various problems and solutions for the challenges the

Table 22: Important Vashon Wildlife Habitats (King County 1986)

Habitat Location	Values	Protection Status
Shinglemill Creek	Salmon-bearing watershed, least developed in lowland King Co.	Two-thirds of the main stem protected, Needle Creek tributary protected, work continues on more preservation
Fern Cove	Undisturbed salt marsh (rare in King Co.), mud flat	Protected
Whispering Firs Bog	Rare for King. Co. Sphagnum bog, 9 acres	Main body protected; work on surrounding areas continues
Fisher Pond	90 acres of pond, mature forest at headwaters of Shinglemill Creek	Protected and acreage expanded
Island Center Forest	Freshwater pond and wetland, substantial forest	Protected
Meadowlake	Freshwater pond and wetland	Protected as part of Island Center Forest
North Klahanie shore	Undeveloped shoreline, mature forests, smelt spawning	
Ellis Creek ravine	Hardwood riparian forest	Partially protected; work continues
Tramp Harbor Creek	Portage Marsh area	Privately owned, at risk to develop
Judd Creek	Large, salmon-bearing stream, many wetlands	About half protected, more in progress
Shore north of Green Valley	Eelgrass, spawning smelt	
Green Valley Creek	Undeveloped creek	
Christensen Cove	Eelgrass, foraging area for waterfowl	Protected
Christensen Creek	Last remaining old growth, largely undeveloped	Watershed partly protected
Fisher Creek	Salmon-bearing creek	Partially protected
Burton Acres Park	Mature forest with some old-growth trees	Already a park
Luana Beach area	Sometimes breeding location for Great Blue Heron	Land Trust working with private landowners to set protections
Mileta Creek	Great Blue Heron colony	Protected
Shore north of Dockton	Great Blue Heron colony	
Lost Lake area	Pond habitat	About half protected
Tahlequah Creek	Salmon-bearing creek	
Lisabeula Rd. Wetland	Large wetland	
Stanley Natural Area	Mature forest	Already protected
Point Heyer (KVI Beach)	For King Co., rare salicornia salt marsh and largest sand spit	Partially protected; total cover in process

local environment faces. As described below, the Vashon-Maury Island Land Trust works with many groups to acquire and preserve important conservation areas on the Island. The three strategies create a mutually supportive framework that makes a huge difference in protecting the environment and quality of life for Vashon Islanders. Land acquisition and protection holds the most direct link to the above habitat discussion and receives further description below.

In the 1980s, Islanders, nonprofit groups, and public agencies came together to create a list of the critical locations for habitat and wildlife values. They published that list, among other places, in the 1981 and 1986 Community Plan Updates (King County 1986). Of these critical locations, only a few such as Dockton Park, Burton Acres Park, and the Marjorie R. Stanley Natural Area had already received at least some protection. Since 1990, the creation of the Vashon-Maury Island Land Trust resulted in efforts to purchase many of the locations on the list or to obtain conservation easements to protect them. Table 22 shows how many of these priority habitat areas have now been protected in just over two decades' work, primarily by the Land Trust, with assistance from the Vashon Park District, the Vashon-Maury Island Audubon Society, Forterra (formerly the Cascade Land Conservancy), and King County agencies. Many of the properties involved complex alliances of several agencies working together for acquisition, ongoing ownership, and stewardship.

Table 23 totals 2,306 acres in preserves or other forms of public ownership or protection by early 2013 and a further 3,821 acres where tax breaks encourage land be kept from residential or industrial development. The Vashon Island Protected Areas Map (see pages 90 and 91) depicts the locations of the existing preserves, parks, and other open-space resources listed in Table 23. About ten percent of the Island's total land area now receives strong protection as preserves, parks, or conservation easements. About seventeen percent of Vashon's land area currently participates in the King County Current Use Taxation Programs, at a minimum deferring residential or industrial development. Conservation efforts have preserved most of the major ponds and wetlands on the Island, a considerable percentage of several watersheds, and some shoreline so that altogether about a quarter (27 percent) of Vashon receives permanent or tax incentive-encouraged protection.

In Table 23, preserves consist of properties whose primary purpose is to protect wildlife or habitat, permitting little or no human structures such as roads, ballparks, etc. The table lists parks where some development has occurred, such as roads and ballparks, as "Public Parks." The Vashon-Maury Island Land Trust also has some conservation easements with private property owners to protect habitat, especially stream corridors.

Table 23: Protected Property on Vashon*		
Owner/Manager	Type of Property	Acres
Land Trust, Vashon Park District, King County Parks	Preserve	1,620
Land Trust	Conservation easements with private property owners	115
Vashon Park District	Public parks	248
King County Parks	Public parks (Maury Island Marine Park)	323
	Subtotal	2,306
Properties protected in that tax breaks exist for owners as long as they keep the property as open space or agricultural and timber commercial use and not for residential or industrial development.		
King County Current Use Taxation Program	Agricultural Land	643
King County Current Use Taxation Program	Forestland	938
King County Current Use Taxation Program	Public Benefit Rating System (PBRS)	1,450
King County Current Use Taxation Program	Timber Land	790
	Subtotal	3,821
	Total	6,127

*See Vashon-Maury Island Land Trust 2012, Vashon-Maury Island Park & Recreation District 2012, King County Current Use Taxation Programs 2013a and 2013b.

Table 23 also includes private lands that owners maintain especially for conserving habitat values or that may have commercial uses providing quality habitat. The King County Current Use Taxation Programs have four divisions that at least temporarily protect portions of many properties, giving private property owners tax incentives to preserve property or keep it in agricultural or in forest usages. The Public Benefit Rating System (PBRS) offers landowners tax breaks for properties meeting certain standards of improving or protecting habitat and open space on private property. This often results in better protection for local streams, wetlands, and forest. The Timber Land, Forestland, and Agricultural Land Programs involve commercial management and harvest but preclude residential or industrial development while the acreage is in the program. Property can be developed, but then owners must pay seven years of back taxes that were not paid while the property was in the program, often resulting in an unattractive amount to pay. The Timber Land Program covers small parcels between five and 20 acres, while the Forestland Program aims at larger properties greater than 20 acres. While eventual commercial harvest has a large impact, the programs help prevent permanent loss of habitat to housing, retail development, and industry. The amount of acres in the Vashon-Maury Island Land Trust's conservation easements and those in the PBRS, Timber Land, Forestland, and Agricultural Land Programs tend to vary over time as some lands come into a program or leave it for a time.

Some of the important preserved areas owned by the Vashon-Maury Island Land Trust include: Shinglemill Creek Preserve, Whispering Firs Bog, and Paradise Valley Preserve (Judd Creek). King County preserves include the Island Center Forest (435 acres), Maury Island Marine Park, Dockton Forest and Natural Area (which, when including the former Glacier Northwest site, combines to over 350 acres), and Raab's Lagoon. Vashon Park District's preserves and important parks include: Fern Cove, Point Robinson Park, Dockton Park, Lisabeula Park, Paradise Ridge Park, Fisher Pond Preserve, and Agren Park.

The impressive list of protected lands and the overall acreage total show that really most of the important habitat has protection from being directly developed. Forest areas and larger ponds and wetlands are particularly well protected. Areas still vulnerable to direct development consist mostly of stream corridors and the remaining farm and field areas. A success in the proposed project to acquire the former Misty Isle property could in the long run be as important to habitat preservation as the victory stopping expansion of the Glacier Northwest gravel site.

The Future of Vashon Habitats

The chapter on the history of habitat change and this chapter each examine habitat in detail, lending themselves to drawing a number of conclusions about birds and wildlife habitat on Vashon. First, massive habitat change led to sweeping alterations in the bird populations, both in the number of species and in the number of individuals of each species. Second, some of the largest alterations, such as forest clearing, reversed themselves over time, and others brought in as many new bird species as they eliminated existing ones. The rest of this chapter examines the challenges faced by particular habitats and some possible priorities for particular attention.

As discussed above in the protected lands discussion, many of the important areas of Vashon possess direct protection from development. Habitat loss now might come indirectly through problems that originate in one location and spread to neighboring areas or even the whole Island.

The largest concerns for habitat health revolve around water issues, fragmentation of forest, and preservation of farm and field habitat. Saltwater, saltwater shoreline, ponds, and streams face the biggest challenges, mostly from pollution, other water quality problems, and shoreline armoring (bulkheads). Development beyond a certain point could overcome the accessible water supplies, add automotive-related and other pollution into the streams and open water, replace farm habitat, and degrade forest quality through fragmentation.

Saltwater and Shoreline Habitats

From an avian perspective, threats to the shoreline and nearshore areas should be a primary focus of concern on Vashon. Water quality issues could affect a high percentage of Vashon species. The major challenges faced by the saltwater and the shoreline habitat include oil spills, septic tank failure and other sources of nutrients causing algal blooms, non-point pollution (i.e., boats and shipping fuel leakage), and armoring of the shoreline (Dean et al. 1998). Oil spills threatened marine life in Dalco Passage and Quartermaster Harbor twice in 2004. They create immediate consequences by directly damaging birds and other wildlife. Oil spills also hurt the ecosystem by causing long-term problems, where the harm strikes lower down the food chain and gradually affects the predator species over time.

Pollution from surface runoff, septic tanks, oil spills, the industrial use of Puget Sound, and boating form a major concern directly for local waterfowl and shorebird populations. Indirectly, birds face harm through damage to the habitat, such as degradation of eelgrass beds. Working to protect eelgrass beds and other nearshore and shoreline features proves extremely important in maintaining the food source that eelgrass provides in and of itself. An additional consideration consists of the habitat that this vegetation provides for prey species of fish and other aquatic animals that birds require. Damage to these habitats could impact local populations for upwards of 50 species of birds. As discussed in several species accounts in Chapter VII and in the habitat history in Chapter II, a significant decline in the populations of marine birds occurred in much of Puget Sound from 1980 to 2002 (Nysewander et al. 2003) and appears to be continuing to the present (Everson in process). Vashon marine birds overall fared better yet clearly face a serious challenge based on the threat outlined in the research of Nysewander et al.

Quartermaster Harbor faces major challenges from water quality concerns. Streams flowing into the Harbor contribute nitrogen and silica nutrients, and septic systems bring in phosphorus (King County 2010b).

These nutrients support phytoplankton blooms and die-offs, utilizing most of the oxygen in the water (ibid.). The Harbor undergoes low dissolved oxygen concentrations in the late summer and fall at a level below state water quality standards.

Staff for King County's Quartermaster Harbor Nitrogen Management Study continue to conduct monitoring and other research into the sources of nutrients. The problem remains quite complex for a number of reasons:

1. Over the last hundred years, agricultural and industrial groups, with many surrounding farms, shipyards, marinas, and other industrial and commercial activities, dumped materials of all kinds into the underlying sediments;
2. Recent human input from leaking septic systems, runoff from current farms, and automobile-related chemicals washing off roads and driveways have polluted the waters;
3. Nitrogen has been released from decaying Red Alder that covers much of the Island.

The diversity of sources of pollutants and nutrients for algal blooms argues for approaching the problem from a watershed-wide perspective rather than just looking at sediments in the harbor or only at nearshore point sources such as leaking septic tanks or the water quality of in-flowing streams. Low oxygen levels such as Quartermaster Harbor experiences created "dead zones" in nearby Hood Canal in some years and can adversely affect fish and other prey populations for birds.

Armoring involves the practice of using bulkheads, riprap/large rocks, or other artificial hardening of the shore, usually to stop wave erosion. Armoring has a wide number of impacts on species directly and indirectly through habitat change. Some of the effects include: decreased prey production, decreased rearing habitat, reduced vegetation, beach erosion, interruption of littoral drift, reduced spawning habitat, changed substrate size, changed benthic and epibenthic invertebrate species composition, and reduced recruitment of detritus and logs that provide living space for birds' prey species (King County 2012b). Vashon has 25 (48 percent) of its 51 miles of shoreline armored, including a large percentage of Quartermaster Harbor. Because of shoreline armoring, the entire Vashon length of Quartermaster Harbor has entirely lost its sediment source or has less than 50 percent of its sediment source left. Half of the Maury Island side of the Harbor has less than 50 percent of its sediment source left. With climate change raising water levels over the next decades, it will be important to find other solutions to erosion that reduce impact on shoreline hab-

Table 24: Habitat Challenges and Solutions

Habitat	Challenges	Potential Solutions
Saltwater	Pollution in groundwater runoff, septic failure, oil spills	Local and regional efforts to reduce pollution, limit and/or exclude nearshore industrial use
Saltwater Shoreline	Pollution in groundwater runoff, septic failure, beach armoring, oil spills	Limit and reduce beach armoring, replace septic systems, better oil spill protection
Ponds and Freshwater	Disturbance and water quality problems from development	Preservation, regulatory protection, reduce pesticide use
Coniferous Forest	Fragmentation, lack of continued management in "dog hair" stands	Manage forest to develop old-growth characteristics; conservation easements and purchase to protect larger or higher quality stands
Hardwood-Dominated Mixed Forest	Clearing, development, forest succession	Preservation, regulatory protection of stream corridors
Shrubby Thicket	Development, forest succession	Protect agricultural uses and field area, encourage residential development to mimic with native plant landscaping
Farm, Field, and Pasture	Development, forest succession	Assist community-supported agriculture, land use agreements
Developed Area	Pesticide use; monocultural landscaping, loose pets	Reduce availability and use of pesticide products, keep pets indoors/under control, landscaping diversification

itat. An urge to increase armoring to protect land is to be expected, which needs careful consideration because even the current level of armoring is of concern. As sea level rise occurs, beach armoring prevents beach migration inland, which could eliminate spawning habitat for Surf Smelt in the Puget Sound region by 2100 (Krueger et al. 2010). Studies of Pacific Sand Lance spawning indicate that this may be true as well for this species, but adequate data remains too low to absolutely make that claim (ibid.).

Another shoreline concern is the extent of vegetation providing habitat along shorelines. Treed shorelines prove valuable for salmon habitat, as trees drop debris providing shelter for fish and their prey and also directly drop insects and other food into the water. In 2002, dense trees bordered about a third of Vashon's shoreline, and patchy vegetation another fifth. New development or work around existing houses cut a third of a mile of the dense treed shoreline since then (King County 2012b).

Some good population data exist for Quartermaster Harbor fish and bird species that can indicate how the health of the Harbor fares. Pacific Herring spawning biomass peaked in 1995 and then fell through 2012 (Stick and Lindquist 2009, Stick pers. com. 2013), though the stock itself is listed as "stable" 2008 to 2012 by the Washington Department of Fish and Wildlife (WDFW). Since 2010, spawning mass dropped fairly precipitously. The Quartermaster Harbor stock's current status should be classified as depressed since WDFW monitoring began in 1976 (Stick pers. comm. 2013). The Quartermaster Harbor Pacific Herring stock shares the same genetic characteristics as those of most of the other Puget Sound stocks. Experts believe that herring health should be looked at on a Puget Sound-wide scale. However, local herring health may be an indicator of the status of habitat quality in Quartermaster Harbor.

Bird populations in Quartermaster Harbor appear to be largely holding steady over the last fifteen years. Christmas Bird Count data from 1999 to 2013 (Trevathan pers. comm. 1999-2013), specific to Quartermaster Harbor, show that the diving waterfowl looking for fish or for molluscs—birds such as the scoters, goldeneye, scaup, merganser, loons, cormorants, and Horned Grebes—have for the most part stable winter populations. One species, Common Goldeneye, actually appears to have an upward trend in population. Western Grebes, a predator of Pacific Herring, provide a counter example, declining by 95 percent over the last two decades. Like the Pacific Herring discussed above, Western Grebes also peaked about 1995 and then declined, a perhaps related occurrence. It's difficult to say for certain because Western Grebes, for unknown reasons, experienced a decline across the Puget Sound region of 95 percent (Nysewander et al. 2003). While some of the local decline of Western Grebes may be linked to habitat quality in Quartermaster Harbor directly, as well as indirectly through their prey, the decrease in grebe numbers could instead just as easily be mostly part of the overall dip in numbers of the regional Western Grebe population.

Ponds and Wetlands

Freshwater ponds and wetlands increased in the last 200 years through human intervention. Continuing to protect them through wetland regulation, conservation easements, and acquisition for parks or preserves would seem a major priority. A loss or degradation of any of the larger ponds, especially Fisher Pond or the Island Center Forest ponds, would lead to the loss of several bird species on Vashon.

The related riparian corridors need attention because they support such a large variety of birds and most of our neotropical migrants. Vashon streams host salmonids that represent a key food source for the saltwater bird species. The invertebrates in Vashon streams show low numbers, possibly as a result of development causing heavy water events leading to erosion and also more sediments and pollutants to wash into the streams. Birds and fish utilize these creatures as prey. The Vashon-Maury Island Land Trust's work to preserve areas along the Shinglemill Creek and Judd Creek watersheds and to obtain conservation easements that limit disturbances along all Island creeks and streams provides a good example of a continued direction that might improve the health of species dependent on freshwater habitat.

Woodlands

The original massive change, the complete logging of Vashon, has largely been reversed, with forest again covering much of the Island. Some forest stands in patches of larger acreages will likely begin to approach several of the characteristics of old-growth forest habitat in a few decades. Large patches of high quality, complex old-growth habitat are gone, probably forever. It takes about 200 years for old-growth forest to be re-established, and the human-caused changes create different regeneration/succession paths. Some stands may, with natural disturbances or active forest stewardship, attain many old-growth characteristics sooner. Bird species diversity may increase slightly, and many other birds of the coniferous forest will increase or stabilize their local populations.

Climate change is another factor that complicates efforts to restore old-growth forests. Over the next 50 years, projections indicate Vashon will not experience major shifts in vegetation communities. Longer summer droughts will likely lead to reduced abundance and coverage of species such as Western Hemlock. Projected increases in the frequency and intensity of winter storms will lead to more blow-down from high winds, especially of older, tall conifer trees.

A more realistic aim of active forest stewardship involves encouraging the structural and vegetation community species diversity of each of the forest types. In the coniferous forest types, this aims especially at the Douglas-fir plantations which, with their same-age stands, have trees all of the same height, limiting structural variety. The trees grow so thickly together, they shut out the light permitting an understory. These forest patches resemble a desert in terms of bird and other animal species diversity. Thinning and replanting immediately to keep out invasive exotic plants could improve the wildlife habitat potential of many parts of the Island forests.

Invasive exotic plants also present a problem with the hardwood stands where groups of Red Alder reach the end of their cycle simultaneously. When Himalayan Blackberry (the species with the huge canes, not the native Pacific Blackberry vines), Scotch Broom, and English Ivy spread in a recently opened forest setting, they tend to choke out native shrub species and decrease diversity. Weeding out the invasives and planting native shrubs and trees in these areas can help maintain the high quality aspects of hardwood forest.

While forests regenerated to again cover much of the Island, how development interacts with the forest requires watching. Islanders tend to keep their trees when they build a new home, but even when the quantity of trees may not decrease much, the quality of the forest habitat faces a sizable challenge. Many studies show that forest fragmentation from development seriously degrades habitat values for birds. The highest impacts from forest fragmentation for North American birds concentrate on breeding ability. Some work suggests that forest fragmentation in Western landscapes in and of itself may not harm reproductive success (Tewksbury et al. 1998, Marzluff and Restani 1999). Where the wooded landscape remains a patchwork of forest types with only a few non-urban/suburban clearings, reproductive success of birds continues with little detriment. That describes Vashon from the 1940s through about the 1980s; with the decline of agriculture, forest of various kinds took over most of the abandoned fields, though residential development spread into some of it as well. Each forest area usually represents a combination of small woodlots of varying ages and types.

However, forest area for Vashon probably peaked in the last decade or so of the 20th century. Residential area began to cut into and fragment forested area instead of recovering agricultural fields. When forest fragmentation results from increased residential development, it causes significant decreases in breeding productivity in the remaining forest habitats (Marzluff and Restani 1999). Where urban development begins to intersperse itself with forest, the size of the predator community as a whole rises. Introduced predator species such as cats and dogs combine with an increase in native species such as Raccoons, which thrive along the urban/forest interface. Parasitism by Brown-headed Cowbirds also becomes an important factor. Where large forested habitats remain, the amount of total forest cover becomes irrelevant for parasitism rates. The presence of human dwellings provides the key factor in the spread of cowbirds (Tewksbury et al. 1998). Cowbirds use feeders, spilled animal feed, and other human-introduced food sources that give them a stable food supply. On Vashon, even with much new development keeping the trees, the new residential growth inserts more predators and parasites into the forest environment.

The birds most vulnerable to this change appear to be neotropical migrants (Terborgh 1989). They possess a narrow gap of time between migration arrival in mid- to late spring and departure in mid- to late summer. Predators or cowbird parasitism may disrupt the one, brief opportunity these birds have to breed. Neotropical migrants face an increasingly difficult future as habitat loss in their winter range in Central and South America continues as well.

In light of the problems of forest fragmentation, the work putting together the many parcels that now form the Island Center Forest takes on greater importance. The large preserves on Maury Island such as the Dockton Forest and Natural Area, the former Glacier Northwest site, and the Maury Island Marine Park also provide opportunities to build forest patches of good size without splinters of development providing entry to invasive plant and animal species.

Field, Farmland, and Pasture

The Field, Farmland, and Pasture habitat no longer hosts specialist species that will be lost if the habitat disappears. All of the specialist species for this habitat have disappeared with the return of the forests and the increase in Developed Area habitat. Several species would be significantly affected by further loss of this habitat, however, such as Red-tailed Hawk, Northern Harrier, Barn Owl, and Savannah Sparrow. Savannah Sparrow and Red-tailed Hawk would still be present in portions of the Developed Area habitat that were kept open and planted with native species. Northern Harrier would be reduced to an occasional migrant. Barn Owls might still retain a toe-hold but would become much harder to find.

Field, Farmland, and Pasture habitat has a close relationship with the Shrubby Thicket habitat. Field edges and overgrown fields provide the primary locations for thickets outside of Vashon parks or overgrown yards in developed areas. Reductions in the number and size of fields, whether caused by development or forest succession, often result in fewer thickets. Two Shrubby Thicket species, Willow Flycatcher and Common Yellowthroat, require more than just a yard gone wild here and there. Like the Northern Harrier needing large open fields, the flycatcher and yellowthroat each need at least an acre—if not more—to develop successful breeding territories.

From a bird species diversity perspective, two reasons exist for maintaining the current level of farm areas or even expanding this habitat type: protecting raptor habitat and maintaining space for thicket borders and lots. Preserving the Misty Isle site, the most productive Island raptor location, would be one major step toward protecting species diversity on Vashon. Projects to support the Island farming community and to maintain other types of fields should also be a conservation focus. Preserving Vashon farming traditions is one way of strengthening and continuing the Island's rural cultural identity. The rural cultural identity provides one bulwark against attitudes that would let development gradually make Vashon into a true suburb of Seattle, like highly urbanized Mercer Island and quickly developing Bainbridge Island.

Shrubby Thicket

Similar to the Field, Farmland, and Pasture habitat, Shrubby Thicket has lost area to the successional process of the regenerating forests and development. As mentioned above, it continues to survive through farm and field habitat that is no longer actively used. Developed Area habitat, when owners utilize creative landscaping and avoid pesticides, often mimics Shrubby Thicket, which will help many of the species for this category. Keeping some species as breeders or winter residents will require maintaining some fields as shrubby thicket instead of encouraging forest succession. A key problem with these areas will be keeping the thickets free of invasive exotic plants such as Scotch Broom or Himalayan Blackberry. Weeding is costly and time consuming, so solutions for this habitat category will take some careful thinking.

Developed Area

Habitat loss represents the main challenge facing bird populations across the world. The growth of the Developed Area habitat, reflecting increasing residential area on the Island, creates the main source of habitat loss on Vashon. As mentioned in the threats to woodland habitat section above, the rise in predators brought about by mixing residential area with natural habitat makes a very serious problem for birds. The discussion so far has mostly dealt with natural predators and parasites. Predation by domestic cats produces a significant source of mortality for many bird species on Vashon, deserving further mention.

Cats represent a super-predator, producing a major impact. Unlike wild predators, they have a steady source of food requiring no expenditure of effort. Hunting consists of instinctual behaviors that cats act on even if they are well fed. Many people have multiple pets, and a large percentage of households own cats. The density of predators now grows higher than the formerly natural environment, where availability of prey kept predator populations in check. Wild predators also must constantly deal with illness, injuries, or parasites for which most domestic cats immediately receive care. All of these factors make domestic cats a far too effective predator.

A study in Wisconsin by John Coleman and Stanley Temple found that "small mammals like mice and voles make up about 70 percent of their [rural cats'] diets, birds constitute about 20 percent of their kills and a mix of other animals constitute the remaining ten percent" (Coleman and Temple 1996). They contacted rural cat owners and followed 656 cats over an eighteen-month period. One particular cat racked up 1,690 kills during that time. The number of animals killed per cat in the study varied so Coleman and Temple also looked at many other research projects. Their examination of other research showed: "On an annual basis, studies record low estimates of 14 animals per free-ranging urban cat to at least one animal per day for rural cats. Other studies reported 28 kills per year for urban cats and 91 kills per year for rural cats." In the end, their work estimated that rural cats alone killed as many as 219 million birds per year in just the state of Wisconsin.

This problem hits islands extremely hard. Cats and other introduced predators have devastated many seabird colonies in Hawaii and other Pacific islands. In New Zealand, experts consider cats the primary cause in the extinction of eight bird species and the eradication from those islands (but not from the world) of 40 others (Coleman and Temple 1996). On Vashon, cats probably line up right after habitat loss or equal it as the cause of the extermination of the native Sooty Grouse and introduced species such as Gray Partridge (used to be known as "Huns"), Northern Bobwhite, and California Quail.

Controlling cat predation has an easy solution: keep cats indoors. Not only will that protect wildlife, it helps the cat. Not letting cats out keeps them from fighting and being injured by other cats or catching parasites and diseases from prey. Some other things owners can do:

1. Neuter cats so that they don't wander when they do get out and also so they can't propagate more cats.
2. Support groups such as VIPP (Vashon Island Pet Protectors; telephone number (206) 389-1085; website address: www.vipp.org) that promote neutering pets and help control and find homes for feral animals.

3. Don't rely on de-clawing cats or giving them bells—both have been shown to not prevent most cats from killing wildlife (Coleman and Temple 1996).

Developed Area, besides representing habitat loss and importation of exotic plants and predators, also brings resource depletion. One concern with the continued rise in population on Vashon lies in the effect on water quality and quantity. As the water budget discussion at the beginning of the chapter describes, the amount of water available for use by humans and wildlife remains an item for further research. Research of the last few years appears to suggest that much more water exists than the original J. R. Carr/Associates report predicted, meaning that the Island has not as yet reached its carrying capacity related to water. Concerns regarding how increased populations would affect water quality continue, however. Because the accessibility of the water fails in many locations to be workable, as Water District 19 found with some wells, the issue of water quantity will always be one to watch. District 19 continues to work on water sources and successfully educated and encouraged its customers around conservation techniques that are well worth encouraging everybody on the Island to use.

The different types of pollutants associated with development make water quality an important part of the water quantity discussion. Automobile oil and gas leaks and drips, pesticides and other pollutants, leaking septic tanks, and nitrates from manures and fertilizers all go eventually to the Island aquifer or out to the surrounding waters, which as discussed already concerning Quartermaster Harbor, causes problems. The Liquid Assets community report card put out by the Vashon-Maury Island Groundwater Protection Committee shows that so far Vashon groundwater quality appears generally in good condition. Increased development must be conducted in a way to keep the report card looking good or parts of the aquifer will not be usable.

Conclusion

The European-American settlement and development of Vashon transformed the mostly old-growth, coniferous-dominated forest habitat into a more diverse set of habitat types. These habitat types and the bird populations that depend on them now exist in a fairly stable state. Conservation efforts protect from direct development most of the key vulnerable habitat sites. Given the historical trends of the last 150 years, development in the region seems likely to continue, if at a slower pace for Vashon. The key to maintaining Vashon's habitats and birds looks to be:

1. Controlling the water quality and quantity effects development has on both freshwater and saltwater habitats;

2. Looking at ways to limit development's fragmentation of remaining large wood stands; and

3. Exploring avenues for preserving the remaining farm and field habitat. The former Misty Isle fields and stream corridors in general provide good examples of remaining possibilities for acquisition or conservation easements.

Overall, the future of avian diversity looks good for Vashon. Islanders consistently organize to face challenges to Vashon's quality of life. The Vashon-Maury Island Land Trust's work to preserve important habitat in general and vital spots such as the Island Center Forest, Fern Cove, and Fisher Pond, in particular, provides a clear blueprint for continuing to safeguard wildlife on the Island. The creativity exemplified by the energy of groups such as Sound Action (formerly Preserve Our Islands) to address a number of concerns bodes well for dealing with other issues such as the disappearance of open area and the creeping suburbanization of Vashon. If such work continues and focuses on the key goals of preserving wetlands and shorelines, protecting water quality, and limiting the damage from increased residential development, then Vashon should keep its present bird species for the next 50 years.

Killdeer parent protecting its baby on the nest. © Kathrine Lloyd

Chapter IV

Site Guide to Vashon Birding Hot Spots

A day's serious birding on Vashon should find 60 to 70 species in any season. With luck and planning, over 100 species might be possible from mid-November to mid-May. Winter to mid-spring, over 60 species of loons, grebes, cormorants, waterfowl, shorebirds, gulls, terns, and alcids winter and migrate through Vashon. In April and May, neotropical songbirds join the spring water bird and shorebird migration, creating a period of great avian species diversity. The migration from the south builds from early March, with the majority of breeding birds arriving by May before the wintering waterfowl are gone. Fall migration spreads out somewhat, with most breeding birds much harder to find by mid-August and gone by mid-September. Many of the water birds don't return until well into October and November. The period from late June to late July is the slowest. Finding 70 species would be a challenge, as many of the breeding birds present have stopped singing.

For a Big Day or other serious attempt to see as many species as possible, stopping at all or most of the sites at least briefly is strenuous but feasible. In planning any birding on the Island, noting the tides and time of day tends to be as important as knowing how much time and distance lie between the various birding locations. For example, the Virginia Rails at Portage tend to call only at dawn. Shorebirding at KVI Beach is best at high tide, while the same shorebird species are still visible at Fern Cove even at low tide, which fills about half way into high tide. Those thinking about several hours of birding should note that the only locations with public restrooms currently include the public library on the north end of town, the park administration office at Ober Park, facilities at Dockton Park, Jensen Point Park on the Burton Peninsula, a portable toilet at Lisabeula Park on Colvos Passage, the passenger terminal at the north end ferry dock, and portable toilets at Point Robinson.

The ten most productive birding sites of Vashon are: Fern Cove, Fisher Pond, Mukai Pond, KVI Beach, Tramp Harbor, the Burton-Shawnee stretch of Quartermaster Harbor, Point Robinson, Maury Island Marine Park, Raab's Lagoon, and the Tahlequah dock/ferry route. Fern Cove and KVI Beach present the best shorebird hot spots during spring and fall migration and host a good variety of saltwater and passerine species as well.

(Continued on page 92)

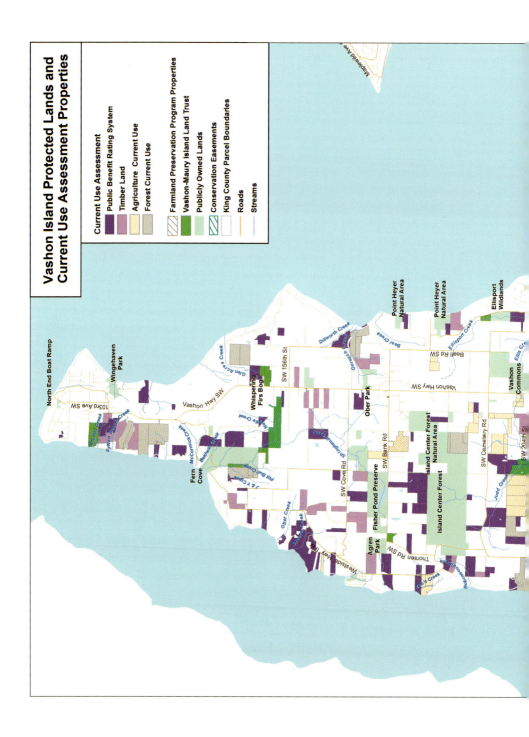

Site Guide to Vashon Birding Hot Spots

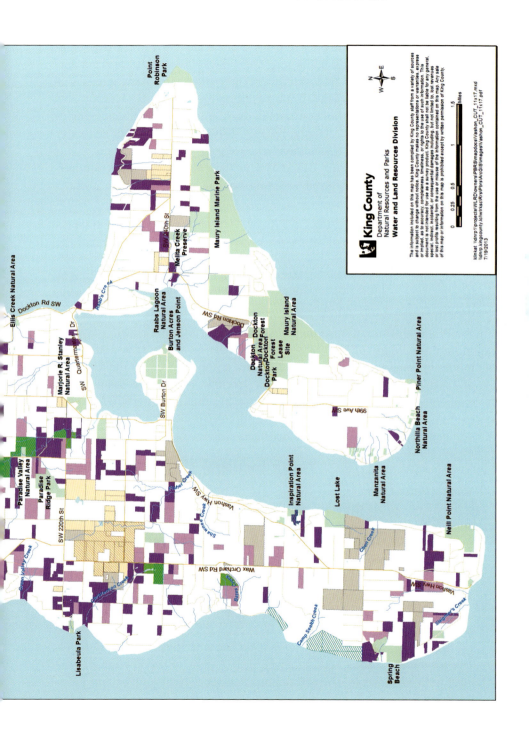

(Continued from page 89)

Fisher Pond provides the only reliable location for many of the duck species on Vashon and hosts many forest and thicket birds. Mukai Pond and Raab's Lagoon possess great thicket habitat that attracts many wrens, vireos, warblers, and sparrows. Tramp Harbor, Quartermaster Harbor, and Tahlequah offer all of the loon, grebe, duck, gull, tern, and alcid species of King County. Point Robinson reliably draws many different saltwater and passerine species. It is known as a migrant trap where many "wild card" birds turn up. Maury Island Marine Park also acts as a migrant trap in spring and provides good breeding habitat for many of the Island's neotropical migrants.

The Vashon Island Protected Areas Map on the previous two pages depicts the locations of all of the parks and preserves on Vashon and the top ten birding hot spots. The street grid on the map shows all of the relevant street names for the top locations, plus most of the other good areas listed in this chapter. Directions accompany each of the locations listed in the Site Guide.

While birding on Vashon, please remember that the Island is a rural community. Many of the roads consist of narrow, twisty lanes. Alternate modes of transportation commonly show up on roads from the roughest of gravel paths to the main highway. Tractors, equestrians, bike riders, walkers, joggers, and young children playing pop up everywhere. Resist the temptation to speed to the ferry and carefully watch for people and domestic animals while driving from one stop to another.

North Vashon

Vashon Ferry Dock: One of the reasons the north end ferry dock produces so many records is the amount of time birders have spent there after just missing the ferry. From fall through mid-spring, Common Loons, Horned and Red-necked Grebes, cormorants, scoters, goldeneyes, and Buffleheads swarm around the docks. Mergansers, other loons and grebes, and Rhinoceros Auklets may join them. Occasionally, a Bald Eagle soars overhead, and rarely, a Peregrine Falcon puts in an appearance. For the last several years, a pair of Harlequin Ducks hung out at high tide in front of the restaurant at the base of the dock. In spring and summer, a Pacific-slope Flycatcher often calls from the woods on the way to the Park & Ride lot. The lot makes a good spot to check year-round for wood-edge passerines, with Swainson's Thrush, wrens, "chicklets" (chickadees and kinglets), and Bushtits usually showing up. The dock in summer usually has a cloud of Barn and Violet-green Swallows. In fall and winter, a large flock of starlings roosts under the pier and swoops in a big ball up, over, and under the dock.

Directions: To find parking for viewing at the ferry dock, go to the nearby Park & Ride lot just uphill from the dock. After exiting the ferry, go uphill to the right immediately at the end of the ferry dock. Coming from Vashon Highway heading toward the dock, turn left at the top of the hill on 103rd Avenue and follow the signs to the Park & Ride.

Vashon-Southworth Ferry: This short ferry run provides a look along the north shore of Vashon and then down Colvos Passage. In August and September, large numbers of Bonaparte's Gulls and now rarely Common Terns float by, with occasional Parasitic Jaegers in pursuit. Red-necked Phalaropes utilize Colvos Passage during their fall migration. A Sabine's Gull was seen on one trip in the fall, and a winter trip found a Merlin crossing the water. Southworth is in Kitsap County, and the King-Kitsap County border lies down the middle of Colvos Passage. Birders enjoy working both county lists on this ferry.

Directions: To take the ferry to Southworth, one embarks at Fauntleroy and goes straight across or leaves Vashon from the same north end ferry dock as the Fauntleroy run. The ride lasts about ten minutes from Vashon.

Vashon-Fauntleroy Ferry: It always pays to be watching along the Vashon-Fauntleroy ferry route. Mid-May through mid-June makes the slowest time, when the highlights consist of Glaucous-winged Gulls and Rock Pigeons. Toward the end of June and continuing into August, the fall migration first brings California Gulls, followed by Bonaparte's, Mew Gulls, and Common Terns. Chasing after the gulls and terns, Parasitic Jaegers cruise by, looking for an opportunity to steal a meal. From October through April, expect three species of loons, three species of grebes, scoters, both goldeneyes, and mergansers. This run and the Tahlequah run (south Vashon) provide the best looks at Red-necked Phalaropes swirling through long strands of debris. From January through March, a few Brant swim in small bands along tidal rips. Small numbers of Rhinoceros Auklets usually show up year-round.

Fern Cove: Largely undeveloped, Fern Cove possesses a salt marsh of mostly saltgrass and a scattering of pickleweed, sedges, and beach grass in the upper part of the marsh. The delta of Shinglemill Creek creates a large mud flat. Mussels and oysters lie strewn across the mud flat. The trail from the parking area heads through mature wet coniferous forest.

The mud flats of Fern Cove regularly produce rarities, especially among the shorebird species. An observer noted the first Long-billed Dowitcher for the Island list here in 2002. This spot offers the most reliable location for Spotted Sandpiper year-round. Small numbers of peeps (sandpipers) and yellowlegs regularly stop by during spring and fall migration. As mentioned previously, shorebirds may usually be found at low tide, and more show up as the tide gets higher. However, the rising tide wipes out all of the mud flat area by about half way in to high tide, so coming too late into the tide cycle limits birding possibilities. Yellowlegs and peeps feed at the water's edge. Dowitchers and Spotted Sandpipers utilize the mud along the stream course across the delta.

The delta here forms a favorite resting place for a wide variety of gull and tern species during low tide. Wigeon, Mallard, and Green-winged Teal forage in the marsh along the streamside. The walk through the woods often brings the sights and sounds of Brown Creeper, Pacific Wren, Pacific-slope Flycatcher, Varied Thrush, Red Crossbill, and Pileated Woodpecker. Band-tailed Pigeons cruise the timber along the shoreline. A wide range of passerines such as Orange-crowned Warblers, chickadees, kinglets, and sparrows show up in the brush along the shoreline as well.

A trail starts from the beach on the south side of Shinglemill Creek and follows the creek, crosses Cedarhurst Road, and goes into the Shinglemill Creek Preserve. The lower part of the trail features much the same birds as mentioned above for the trail down to the beach for Fern Cove.

Directions: The dirt pull-off for parking at Fern Cove may be hard to spot. A few feet down the little dirt driveway is a gate, and a sign identifying Fern Cove Preserve is posted. Please park along the road outside of the gate. The pull-off is on the west side of Cedarhurst Road. Coming south along Vashon Highway, watch for the John L. Scott Real Estate office and turn right at 132nd Place, which becomes Cedarhurst. Proceed 1.2 miles from the highway; Fern Cove will be on your right. Heading north along Westside Highway, go 1.7 miles from the intersection with 121st Avenue. Fern Cove will be on your left. To walk up along the creek to Shinglemill Creek Preserve, park at the pull-off on the east side of the road where Cedarhurst crosses over Shinglemill Creek. It is a hundred yards or so south of the trail down to the cove. The trail starts behind the gate across a dirt road heading east up the creek.

Shinglemill Creek Preserve: The Vashon-Maury Island Land Trust added to the protection of the Shinglemill Creek watershed with purchases covering more of Shinglemill Creek as well as Needle Creek, a tributary. A

Pileated Woodpecker feeding chicks. © Peter Murray

trail leads up from Cedarhurst Road, its entrance about a hundred yards south of the Fern Cove parking area along the road. The trail follows Shinglemill Creek and climbs its canyon several hundred feet in altitude to the edge of some remaining patches of farmland just west of Vashon Highway. Along the lower part of the creek, dipper appear in winter. In summer, kingfishers breed in the banks of the "Grand Canyon," a deep ravine formed by the creek. Wilson's Warbler, Pacific Wren, Western Tanager, and Black-headed Grosbeak may be seen or heard along the whole route. At the top of the canyon, the trail crosses Needle Creek and leads to a parking lot surrounded by shrubby thickets and fields. The brush attracts Hutton's and Warbling Vireos and all of Vashon's possible warbler species. The nearby farm fields host Barn Owl families in some years.

Directions: To reach the upper parking lot, turn west onto 156th Street off of Vashon Highway near the Church of the Holy Spirit. The parking lot is on the north side of the road a little more than half a mile in. To reach the lower parking spots from Cedarhurst Road near Fern Cove, head south about a hundred yards from Fern Cove along Cedarhurst and watch for a small unimproved parking area on the east side of the road.

Fisher Pond: The pond itself consists of about ten acres ringed by spirea, sedges, and rushes on the south side, mature conifer forest around the rest of the shoreline, and a thin perimeter of alder and willow with some Quaking Aspen. Pondweed and lily pads cover the surface in summer. In most years much of the pond dries, leaving expanses of mud.

Pied-billed Grebes, Mallards, and Wood Ducks breed at the pond and stay year-round. In the fall, Green-winged Teal, Northern Shoveler, Ring-necked Duck, Hooded Merganser, and Bufflehead join them. A smattering of other ducks pops up now and then such as wigeon, goldeneye, very rarely a Gadwall, and once, one of the Island's few records of Blue-winged Teal. A Trumpeter Swan visited for a day in the winter of 2002. Bald Eagles swoop down occasionally after the ducks. Ospreys visit for a little fishing.

In October, before the November rains cover up the muddy areas of the pond, this location offers the best spot to find Wilson's Snipe. From July through September, other shorebirds sometimes appear, including Western Sandpipers, Solitary Sandpipers, and rarely a dowitcher. Killdeer show up whenever the water recedes to leave mud exposed.

In early spring, Fisher Pond often has the first sightings of Northern Rough-winged, Violet-green, and Barn Swallows. Tree Swallows, uncommon on the Island, breed sometimes in the nest boxes. The woods along the edge of the pond attract a wide variety of forest birds, such as Townsend's Warblers, Hutton's Vireos, Golden-crowned Kinglets, Brown Creepers, Pacific Wrens, and Pileated Woodpeckers. The brush along the road draws many warbler species, sparrows, and Rufous Hummingbirds.

Directions: From the four-way stop at the intersection of Vashon Highway and Bank Road in town, head west on Bank Road 1.2 miles. From the west, turn off Westside Highway onto Thorsen Road. As you head east, Thorsen turns into Bank Road. It is also 1.2 miles from Westside Highway to Fisher Pond. The best spot to park and bird is a narrow gravel pull-off at the 1.2-mile point from either direction. Fisher Pond lies along the north side of the road behind a wall of brush. A trail leads through concrete blocks about fifteen feet to a view of the east end of the pond. The trail follows along the edge of the pond westward to the end of the pond.

A second location allows access to the west end of the pond and a view along the length of the pond. Turn into the first driveway to the west of the gravel pull-off, about a quarter-mile away at the top of a rise, and follow the driveway to the back of the barn structure. A wide trail runs to the north through the woods to the edge of the pond. This trail links up with the trail from Bank Road and also to another that goes around the north side of the pond to come out on Bank Road on the hill east of the pond. The path provides a very nice walk through the woods but no other views of the pond.

Island Center Forest: These protected woods, wetlands, and ponds have an amazing number of upland microhabitats. There are large stands of conifers, many willows, and several small stands of aspen, cottonwood, and Lodgepole Pine. The preserve has over 400 acres, with trails snaking throughout, reaching many habitat types and attracting many vireos, flycatchers, woodpeckers, wrens, and warblers.

Mukai Pond provides the most variety of species. The first Vashon breeding record for Green-winged Teal occurred here in 2010. Hooded Merganser, Mallard, and Wood Duck regularly hatch broods here. Common Yellowthroat nest in shrubs in the canary grass along the eastside of the pond. The trail around the pond reliably hosts vireos, Black-headed Grosbeaks, Pacific-slope Flycatchers, and sometimes in spring, a Hammond's Flycatcher. Black-throated Gray Warblers call from the firs around the parking lot. Moving into summer, the pond dries, leaving exposed mud that appeals to shorebirds. One can hope for a Solitary Sandpiper in May and August/September. In fall, the brushy areas around Mukai Pond attract sparrows such as Lincoln's and Golden-crowned. The shrubs around the lake host many Swainson's and Hermit Thrushes eating dogwood berries.

Directions: From Vashon Highway, take Bank Road west about three quarters of mile and then turn south onto 115th Avenue. Follow 115th until it turns to gravel and then continue carefully–the road has some big potholes. A trail goes through a gate on the east side of the parking lot to Mukai Pond. Another trail to the south connects into the trail network leading to Meadowlake and to the south entrance of 115th coming up from Cemetery Road.

Three Barred Owl chicks examine their feet. © Peter Murray

Meadowlake has a lot of potential but no easy viewing of the pond for much of the year. Water floods up through the brush and trees down its access trail for much of the year. Sue Trevathan found a Marsh Wren in June 2002, one of the few records since the 1970s, when they were regular at Fisher Pond. Meadowlake possesses a large cattail stand, which is unique on the Island; only small, thin patches are found elsewhere. Hooded Merganser probably nest regularly here. Northern Shoveler and other puddle ducks show up in season. Warbling and Hutton's Vireos and Wilson's Warblers forage and sing around the shelter and parking lot area. Improvements continue to be added to this part of the Island Center Forest complex; perhaps a better trail will be built to allow viewing of the pond and surrounding wetlands. If so, breeding of several duck species will likely be recorded here, and it will create another spot to find wintering freshwater ducks.

Directions: From Vashon Highway, go west on 188th Street to its end, about a mile, and turn right into a gravel parking area. A trail goes north from the shelter to the pond. Another trail connects to the network of trails leading through the forest to Mukai Pond and to Cemetery Road.

Island Center Forest South Entrance: The trail leading from a small parking lot on 115th Avenue as it comes up from Cemetery Road goes into the thick of the forest. Some good-sized patches of dry coniferous forest and mixed hardwood forest as well as small wet coniferous stands attract Townsend's Warblers, many Golden-crowned Kinglets, and Chestnut-backed Chickadees. At night Northern Saw-whet Owls sometimes call, as well as Great Horned and Barred Owls.

Directions: From Vashon Highway turn west onto Cemetery Road, pass the cemetery entrance at Singer Road, and then watch for 115th Avenue, a gravel road on the north side. Follow 115th to its end at a small parking lot. The parking lot at night is the place to listen for owls. During the day, follow the trails through the forest to Mukai Pond or Meadowlake.

Westside Highway fields and ponds: The north section of Westside Highway in the Colvos and Cove area presents a number of small ponds visible from the highway. During the winter months, wigeon, Mallard, and Bufflehead show up regularly. Some of these ponds host domestic geese and swans and other non-native birds, requiring a little checking to understand which birds are truly wild.

The wet field just south of 158th Street has produced breeding Tree Swallows in nest boxes and in winter, Wilson's Snipe. This field and others lining the highway might turn up an occasional Lazuli Bunting. An Islander found the first Vashon record for Yellow-headed Blackbird here.

A good view of Colvos Passage may be found by following 137th Avenue off of Westside Highway down to the water. It turns into a one-lane road, so caution is needed. A turnaround exists at a small power station at the bottom of the road. Expect a good range of loons, grebes, and ducks.

A Common Loon forages for food. The photo, taken in February, shows the bird just beginning to come into breeding plumage. © Michael Elenko

Cedarhurst and Burma Roads: These roads twist through wet coniferous forest and mixed hardwood forest along gullies on the northwest corner of Vashon. Residents regularly report Great Horned, Barred, and Northern Saw-whet Owls calling through the long winter nights. Olive-sided and Pacific-slope Flycatchers, Pacific Wrens, Swainson's Thrushes, Black-headed Grosbeaks, and Western Tanagers abound in summer, and a small population of Varied Thrushes sometimes stays to breed. A small public beach access is available at Sylvan Beach. Sylvan Beach has the usual suspects, Horned and Red-throated Grebes, scoters, and goldeneyes.

Directions: To reach Burma Road, follow Vashon Highway up the hill from the ferry dock, go past the fire station, and turn south. Burma Road is the first street to the right after the highway heads south. It ends at Cedarhurst Road near Fern Cove. Cedarhurst Road is the next turn-off from Vashon Highway after Burma Road. Turn right at the John L. Scott Real Estate office. The actual street turn-off is 132nd Place, which becomes Cedarhurst. Approaching from the south, Westside Highway eventually becomes Cedarhurst Road at the north end of the Colvos area.

South Vashon

Tahlequah ferry dock: Tahlequah always merits a stop in the fall and winter for a number of reasons. The dock area has a great view of Dalco Passage between Vashon and Point Defiance, where many loons, grebes, cormorants, ducks, gulls, terns, and alcids forage. This is sometimes a good spot to watch for Orcas as well. With a scope, the water may be scanned far out for Pacific Loons, Marbled Murrelets, Rhinoceros Auklets, and Common Murres. From fall through mid-spring, many gulls and cormorants roost on a dilapidated dock adjacent to the ferry landing. From time to time, a Brandt's Cormorant might be picked out of the many Double-crested and the handful of Pelagic Cormorants. A Thayer's, Western, or Heermann's Gull or two might be found mixed in with the Glaucous-winged and Glaucous-winged X Western hybrids. The only record of Glaucous Gull came in the 2009 Christmas Bird Count here. The water close to the dock has the usual scoters, goldeneyes, many Buffleheads, a variety of grebes, and often a Eurasian Wigeon.

Bachelor Road, which continues east from the dock, offers more views of the water, providing closer-in looks at a variety of ducks, Rhinoceros Auklets, and Common Murres. Winter passerines utilize the brush and trees along the road in several locations. Yellow-rumped Warblers and Orange-crowned Warblers have been spotted here for the Christmas Bird Count. The Park & Ride lot above the ferry dock often hosts a mixed flock of Golden-crowned, Fox, and Song Sparrows. Thrushes and Hutton's Vireos flit along the forest edge. Common Ravens, Bald Eagles, and Red-tailed Hawks regularly cruise along the shore and above the road. Anna's Hummingbirds utilize several local feeders year-round. At the end of Bachelor Road, Neill Point Natural Area has Band-tailed Pigeon, Barred Owl, and Red-breasted Sapsucker as well as views of water birds at the mouth of Quartermaster Harbor.

Directions: The Tahlequah ferry dock lies at the southern terminus of Vashon Highway. The best place to park is in the Park & Ride lot just above the dock or on the side of the road partway up the hill past the dock.

Tahlequah-Point Defiance ferry: Though nearly all of the water birds are visible from shore with a scope, the advantage of the ferry trip consists of unparalleled close-up views of many harder-to-see species. In fall, Parasitic Jaegers chase the Bonaparte's Gulls and Common Terns, sometimes cruising by at eye-level from the ferry's upper deck. Red-necked Phalaropes show up in their fall migration each year. Rhinoceros Auklets and

Thayer's Gull (right) at Tahlequah ferry dock. Note black wing tips of Thayer's, compared to the gray wing tips of the Glaucous-winged Gull on the left. Also note the more delicate bill of the Thayer's Gull. © Gary Shugart

Male Wilson's Warbler singing on territory. © Gregg Thompson

Common Murres are common in winter and with luck, a Marbled Murrelet may be seen.

Camp Sealth, Paradise Cove/Bates Road, and Reddings Beach: These three locations provide trips through wet coniferous forest or mixed woods down to views of Colvos Passage. Camp Sealth is a Camp Fire facility requiring permission before a visit. Along the wet woods and gullies of both Camp Sealth and Bates Road in winter, watch carefully for Hermit Thrush. The two locations at times offer a wide variety of loons, grebes, and ducks or nothing at all. Reddings Beach has a small marsh attracting a variety of passerines as well as views of marine birds. Spotted Sandpiper visit all three locations throughout the year.

Directions: To reach these roads, take Wax Orchard Road south from its northern point at 220th Street. Reddings Beach Road is .9 miles from 220th, Bates Road is 1.9 miles from 220th, and Camp Sealth is 2.7 miles from 220th. To reach Reddings Beach from Wax Orchard Road, take Reddings Beach Road one mile west and turn right onto Cross Landings Road and follow it about 200 yards. To reach these roads from the Tahlequah ferry, go north 1.8 miles on Vashon Highway from the ferry dock. At that point, the highway curves to the right. To reach Wax Orchard and Old Mill Road, instead go straight ahead onto Wax Orchard Road. Follow Wax Orchard Road another .6 miles to Camp Sealth, 1.4 miles to Bates Road, and 2.4 miles to Reddings Beach Road.

Wax Orchard Road and Old Mill Road: These two parallel roads pass through the largest remaining open area of Vashon. Raptors such as Bald Eagles, Red-tailed Hawks, and accipiters frequently fly overhead. Northern Harriers glide acrobatically over the fields during the day, and in some years Barn Owls at night. The first Rough-legged Hawk for Vashon showed up here in the winter of 2012. An American Kestrel occasionally chooses one of the fields for its winter home. American Pipits migrate through, especially over tilled fields. Savannah Sparrows and Ring-necked Pheasants call from the fields.

Halfway between 220th and 232nd Streets on Old Mill Road, a pond exists hidden behind a dike at the south end of a large field. The pond sits on private property requiring permission for entry. The adjacent trees and brush along the dike may be viewed from the road and provide very productive cover for passerines in spring and fall migration. The brush attracts all of the Island's warbler species but the yellowthroat. It hosts many sparrows as well. Kinglets, wrens, nuthatches, Pine Siskins, and Purple Finches consistently appear.

Mixed forests with many conifers line the southern portions of both roads. Common Ravens often cruise up and down the road at tree-top level, looking for road kill. A trail leads through woods at the Christensen Pond Preserve, coming to a shallow pond that often has Bufflehead and sometimes Hooded Merganser. Pileated and Downy Woodpeckers and Red-breasted Sapsuckers breed in this area. A good range of flycatchers, vireos, and warblers may be heard in spring.

Directions: To reach the Wax Orchard area from central Vashon, go west on 204th Street at the intersection of Vashon Highway and 204th. At the bottom of the hill, 204th curves into 111th Avenue, formerly Paradise Valley Road. One can bird along the valley or head straight at the curve to Singer Pond, as described in the Paradise Valley section. To continue to Wax Orchard Road, follow the curve at 111th south to where it climbs a steep hill, then turns, becoming 220th Street. Go west along 220th. The fields will appear to the left along Old Mill Road at 0.7 miles and Wax Orchard Road in another half mile. Instead of turning left onto Wax Orchard Road, one can continue westbound on 220th to the Lisabeula area. Wax Orchard Road may also be reached from several roads heading west from the Burton neighborhood or from the south as one comes up from the Tahlequah ferry dock. From the Tahlequah dock, Vashon Highway heads straight north. At 1.8 miles, it curves to the right. Instead of following the curve to the right, Wax Orchard Road starts here, continuing the straight path to the north. To walk the trails at Christensen Pond Preserve, follow Wax Orchard Road to the section between 240th Street and Reddings Beach Road. Park along the west side of Wax Orchard Road near 240th and look for the two unmarked trail openings. The more northerly one, 0.2 miles from either 240th or Reddings Beach Road, has the trail leading most directly to the pond. Currently no signs stand at this entrance, but a chain stretches across the trail to prevent vehicle entry. Follow the trail west into the woods a short way and choose the fork that heads north and west to the pond.

Lisabeula area: Heading west past Wax Orchard Road on 220th Street, watch for two small ponds on the left (south) side of the road. These ponds attract puddle ducks such as Mallards and wigeons, including an occasional Eurasian Wigeon, and should be examined for surprises. The wet fields here support Common Yellowthroat in the breeding season. The stretch just before the hard left corner to Lisabeula Park usually has a sparrow flock from fall through early spring, with a number of Golden-crowned Sparrows and sometimes a White-crowned Sparrow, a rarity in winter on Vashon.

Many waxwings, sparrows, and finches feed in the brush and shrubs at the entrance to Lisabeula Park in the fall. Driving down into the park in spring one hears Pacific-slope Flycatchers. The beachfront of the park borders Colvos Passage and provides a good place to watch for Bonaparte's Gulls and Rhinoceros Auklets from fall through spring. Wigeons and bay ducks forage in Christensen Cove next to the park to the south. Spotted Sandpipers bob up and down along the shore.

Directions: Find the Lisabeula area by driving straight west on 220th Street past the intersection with Wax Orchard Road. Reach the park by going left at the curve found at the end of 220th proceeding down a steep and narrow lane.

A winter-plumaged Bonaparte's Gull plucks a fish from Puget Sound. © Tim Kuhn

Burton Acres Park: This park encompasses the interior of the Burton Peninsula and provides a good walk to see forest birds. Bewick's and Pacific Wrens, both kinglets, nuthatches, both chickadees, and woodpeckers abound. Sharp-shinned Hawks prowl the brushy western edge, and Cooper's Hawks venture deeper within the woods. The Jensen Point boat launch offers good views into the inner harbor of Quartermaster Harbor. The park at Jensen Point possesses a primitive but usable public restroom.

Directions: From the intersection of Vashon Highway and Burton Drive at the four-way stop in Burton, head straight east along Burton Drive to the stop sign at a T intersection with 97th Avenue. One entrance to the trail system is found by continuing straight ahead on the small lane and parking at the end of the last driveway. The trail system may also be found by taking 97th to the left or right; 97th turns into Bayview Drive and loops around the Burton Peninsula. Jensen Point Park is on the east side of the loop. The trail head for Burton Acres Park opens directly across the street from Jensen Point Park.

Vashon Clinic/Granny's Attic area (former Nike missile site headquarters): The high ridge here boasts beautiful views of the Cascades, Olympics, and Mount Rainier. Raptors soar over this open area, moving from one part of the Island to the other. The tall poplar trees along the entrance drive often host Townsend's and Yellow-rumped Warblers during spring and fall migration. In fall and winter, the blackberry hedge on the southwestern side serves as a good home to many crowned and Fox Sparrows.

Directions: To access the Vashon Clinic/Granny's Attic area, watch for their signs along the west side of Vashon Highway at 0.3 miles south of the four-way stop at the intersection of the highway with 204th Street.

Paradise Valley: A walk down the hedges of Paradise Valley on 111th Avenue may be very productive during spring and fall migrations. In spring, Common Yellowthroat, Wilson's, Orange-crowned, Yellow-rumped, Black-throated Gray, and Townsend's Warblers sing from the wet fields, brush, or adjacent woods. The wooded area around the intersection of 212th Place and 111th offers one of the most reliable locations for Western Wood Pewee. Barred Owls have nested nearby for at least ten years. Where Judd Creek crosses 216th Street is always good for Steller's Jay and Bushtit, as well as many sparrows and warblers in season. In fall and winter, many sparrows inhabit the hedgerows and visit feeders at nearby houses: Golden-crowned (usually a good flock), White-crowned (one or two), and Lincoln's (one or two). Wilson's Snipe sometimes forage in the wet fields or roadside ditches.

At the north end of the valley, Singer Road leads south from Cemetery Road through several good habitat types. At the north end of Singer Road, the thick coniferous woods by the cemetery and Vashon Sportsman's Club host Pacific-slope Flycatcher and Brown Creeper in spring and Varied Thrush in winter. From the southwest corner of the cemetery, one can look down on a small doughnut-shaped pond visited by ducks and one fall, Greater White-fronted Geese. Going south along Singer Road, look for farm pastures where Red-tailed Hawk perch along the power lines. Many swallows fly overhead in summer. Where Singer Road meets 204th Street, Singer Pond is worth a look for ducks year-round. Late fall through mid-spring, wigeon and Bufflehead visit regularly. In the summer of 2002, Hooded Mergansers nested in the nearby woods and brought young down to the pond. Dark-eyed Junco and Pacific-slope Flycatcher nest in the woods along the road at this intersection. Cassin's and Warbling Vireos, Black-throated Gray Warbler, Yellow-rumped Warbler, Western Tanager, and Black-headed Grosbeak may be noted during the spring migration or the breeding season. A Townsend's Solitaire appeared here in April 1999.

Directions: To visit Paradise Valley, take 204th Street westbound from its intersection with Vashon Highway in central Vashon. At 0.7 miles, 204th curves south, turning into 111th, and follows the length of the valley. Find the north end of the valley by continuing straight west on 204th at this curve. Singer Pond is one mile west of the highway intersection. The area may also be found from the north by heading west from Vashon Highway on Cemetery Road and turning left or south on Singer Road. The north entrance to Singer Road looks like the entry to the cemetery itself but continues south to 204th.

KVI Beach: This location supports a small salicornia salt marsh/estuary surrounding a pond. Consistent migrants include Semipalmated Plovers, Greater Yellowlegs, Western Sandpipers, Least Sandpipers, and Semipalmated Sandpipers, especially in the fall. Black-bellied Plover, Marbled Godwits, and Baird's and Pectoral Sandpipers have each been recorded once or twice at this location. Mallard, wigeon, and Green-winged Teal visit the pond.

More shorebird species may be seen along the sandy beach: Sanderling come every winter, and shoreline rarities noted here include Wandering Tattler and Dunlin. From the beach, loons, grebes, Brant, ducks, and gulls may be spotted out in Tramp Harbor or in Puget Sound. Raptors often fly over this area. Bald Eagles swoop after ducks, Ospreys dive for fish, and more rarely, a Merlin or Peregrine Falcon rockets past and stoops for the shorebirds.

The driftwood and sand grass in this area may reveal Vashon rarities: Say's Phoebe, Western Kingbird, American Pipit, and Western Meadowlark have all been recorded here. Savannah Sparrows are common in migration. Clouds of Purple Martins, Barn Swallows, and Violet-green Swallows fly overhead or roost on the radio tower.

The woods above the salt marsh host Olive-sided Flycatcher, Pacific-slope Flycatcher, nuthatches, and kinglets. Band-tailed Pigeons come down from the woods to drink from the pond.

Directions: To find KVI Beach, head east from the four-way stop at the intersection of Vashon Highway and 204th Street. Pass the high school and continue downhill to the bottom where the road reaches Vashon's eastern shore. Take a left turn to the north onto Chautauqua Beach Road and look immediately to the right to find a dirt parking strip further described in the Ellisport section. Continue north-bound to a four-way stop and turn right, going down a short, steep hill. Park at the bottom and walk out past the gate.

Ellisport: From the parking area along Chautauqua Beach Road, one can often see hundreds of wigeon feeding on eelgrass just a few feet away in the fall and winter. At least one Eurasian Wigeon may usually be found with the flock by December. Brant join them in February or March for several weeks. A few goldeneyes, scoters, and Bufflehead usually come close into shore, and many other loons, grebes, and ducks swim and dive further out. The beach and riprap where the old pilings come to shore hosted a flock of Black Turnstones in December 2002. Purple Martin boxes placed by Rich Siegrist adorn the old pilings. Many Purple Martin adults and young use them during the summer. Double-crested Cormorants, Great Blue Herons, and Glaucous-winged Gulls rest on the pilings in winter. In August, one can compare California, Mew, Bonaparte's, and Glaucous-

A Black Turnstone skims the waters off Ellisport. © Ed Swan

winged Gulls, all washing together in one of the creeks that drain into Tramp Harbor.

Directions: To find the Ellisport pull-off, head east from the four-way stop at the intersection of Vashon Highway and 204th Street. Pass the high school and continue downhill to the bottom where the road reaches Vashon's eastern shore. Take a left turn, or north, onto Chautauqua Beach Road, and look immediately to the right to find a dirt parking strip.

Tramp Harbor: Two pull-offs on the southwestern edge of Tramp Harbor present the best viewing opportunities: the fishing pier and the exercise bikes by the old Portage store where Portage Way intersects Dockton Road. The exercise bikes are a bit of Vashon color—someone started a collection of exercise bikes looking out onto the harbor at the pull-off by the store. One may take a scope out onto the pier to reach farther out into the water or look from the two pullouts at the many species that come close to the shore. A mixed flock of Horned and Red-necked Grebes, Greater Scaup, Barrow's and Common Goldeneyes, Hooded and Red-breasted Mergansers, and Bufflehead may usually be seen here from November through March. White-winged and Surf Scoters spread throughout the harbor in small groups. A large raft of 50 to 100 usually forages farther out from the Portage store. The area near the exercise bikes sometimes hosts Harlequin Ducks very close to shore. Further out, Common, Pacific, and Red-throated Loons and Western Grebes dive for fish. Common Mergansers show up here during the fall migration, and Long-tailed Duck put in rare appearances.

Directions: From Ellisport, head south along the water and watch for the parking area for the fishing pier, about a quarter-mile from the Ellisport pull-off. The pull-off for the Tramp Harbor side of Portage exists a further quarter-mile away, where Portage Way intersects Dockton Road, and currently displays a very visible collection of abandoned exercise bikes across the street from the old Portage store. The store closed in 2004 but hopefully will undergo a reincarnation of some sort someday.

Portage: A brackish marsh best viewed from Quartermaster Drive hides behind the Portage store. The star attraction here consists of Virginia Rails that respond consistently to a tape of their calls.by calling back or sometimes coming out to look for a rival. (Please do not play tapes excessively. Doing so can have adverse effects on birds.) Near-dawn makes the best time to find the rails. Many wrens, woodpeckers, flycatchers, thrushes, vireos, warblers, and sparrows utilize the woods on the western side of the marsh during migration and in winter. A small collection of snags here provides nesting sites for chickadees, wrens, and other birds.

The view of the inner harbor of Quartermaster Harbor at Portage reveals one of the best spots to find Ruddy Ducks around the Island. Many scoters, goldeneyes, and Buffleheads show up here as well. Rarely, Sanderlings or Western Sandpipers join the Killdeers feeding in the mud.

Directions: To view the Quartermaster Harbor side of Portage, one can park along Tramp Harbor or take the short crossroad along the south side of the old store through to the Quartermaster Harbor side. A gravel parking strip exists along the harbor side of Quartermaster Drive. Note the Quartermaster Harbor Important Bird Area interpretive sign.

Quartermaster Harbor (Vashon side): Quartermaster Harbor achieved designation as a National Audubon Society Important Bird Area in 2000, thanks to the efforts of Islander Dan Willsie. He censused the bird populations regularly in the 1990s to provide the documentation showing that as much as eight to ten percent of the wintering Western Grebe population in Washington State showed up here in some years, totaling several

A Western Grebe catches a fish in nearshore waters. © Doug Parrott

thousand birds. With the region-wide decline in Western Grebe numbers, the Christmas Bird Count hopes to find 200 birds now. The south part of Vashon Island holds several good viewing areas for the inner and outer harbors: Portage, mentioned above, and the next three sites below are good locations for viewing the harbor.

Quartermaster Harbor Straightaway and Shawnee: Just south of Burton, along Vashon Highway, a number of pullouts exist with views of the main area of Quartermaster Harbor. These pullouts provide waterfowl-viewing opportunities that rival or better Tramp Harbor. Western, Red-necked, and Horned Grebes are common, as well as loons, cormorants, ducks, shorebirds, and gulls, with at least 35 marine species seen regularly. At the west end before the highway climbs uphill, a stream delta forms at Shawnee, viewed from highway pullouts or from the end of Shawnee Road. From fall through spring, a good number and variety of gulls roost at the delta during low tide. The waters off the delta make a reliable location most years for the uncommon Black Scoter. In winter, Sanderling often rest on the small square docks, as do all three cormorant species. Bald Eagles often fly overhead or watch from high in the tall treetops lining the road.

Quartermaster Harbor Marina: The marina often has many scoters, goldeneyes, and grebes foraging in the open stretches of water and very rarely a Green Heron perched on the boat lines or an American Coot swimming around the pilings.

Directions: The marina may be viewed from pull-offs along Vashon Highway on the north end of the Burton neighborhood.

Mouth of Judd Creek: Dozens of Mallards hang out here in winter. After Portage, this provides just about the only other location for Ruddy Ducks. Sometimes a Northern Pintail visits in winter, mixed in with the Mallards. The usual goldeneyes, Buffleheads, and scoters show up as well.

Directions: To view the mouth of Judd Creek, park in the large pull-off on the southeast corner of the intersection of Vashon Highway and Quartermaster Drive. Walk out along the highway bridge over Judd Creek and look along the stream east to the harbor. The east side of the bridge has a protected pedestrian walkway.

Monument Road: The fields where Monument Road meets Quartermaster Drive prove productive for a wide range of species. The small marsh on both sides of the road sometimes hosts Virginia Rails and Marsh Wrens, as well as more regularly seen birds such as Common Yellowthroat and Red-winged Blackbird. The wet fields occasionally attract Canada Geese, Mallards, and wigeons. Savannah Sparrows buzz from the fields, and Bald Eagles nest to the east. Swallows hawk for insects and light on the telephone lines. The local flock may include Cliff Swallows in some years. The brush attracts many warblers, vireos, and sparrows, depending on the season.

Maury Island

Raab's Lagoon: Formally protected in 2008, this small eighteen-acre preserve proves good for land and water birds year-round. As more observers visited this spot over the years, they discovered that Greater Yellowlegs winter in the protected lagoon, joined at times by Spotted Sandpiper. The only Canvasback sighting for Vashon came from this location when one joined the large scoter and goldeneye flocks that forage offshore in Quartermaster Harbor.

The brush surrounding the cul-de-sac parking area attracts a large variety of passerines throughout the year. In winter Lincoln's, Song, Fox, White-crowned, and Golden-crowned sparrows regularly inhabit the thickets. In spring and fall, Savannah Sparrows join the mix. Spring migration and the breeding season bring many warbler species. An American Kestrel swept through in the winter of 2002, and Red-tailed Hawks and Merlins are present in season. Northern Rough-winged Swallows nest in the bluffs.

Kingsbury Road leading up to Raab's Lagoon is worth a walk in the spring. Remnant migrants from the days of more open areas on Vashon still pass through. Some of the rarities found in the last few years include MacGillivray's Warbler, House Wren, and Lazuli Bunting.

Directions: Raab's Lagoon lies at the end of Kingsbury Road, accessed off Dockton Road. From the stop sign at the intersection of Quartermaster Harbor Drive and Dockton Road denoting the beginning of Maury Island, go 0.3 miles and take Kingsbury Road on the right, or south side, of the road.

Dockton: Dockton Park provides a good place to view waterfowl in Quartermaster Harbor from the Maury Island side. The area around the boat launch sometimes turns up a Northern Pintail with the wigeons and Mallards. Scoters, mergansers, goldeneyes, and Bufflehead are common. The dock often has a collection of Mew and Glaucous-winged Gulls to sort through for gull rarities. Farther out, rafts of Western Grebes swim by in winter. Raptors such as Bald Eagles, Peregrine Falcons, and Merlins should be watched for as well. The park possesses a public restroom.

Dock Street takes one through a residential neighborhood with a few more views of the harbor. A small pond on Stuckey Avenue may produce a few ducks or a Great Blue Heron. Birds attracted to feeding stations may be noted along the street. A Western Scrub-Jay sometimes winters in this set of narrow lanes. Hake Road, a little south of the town, provides a few more water views. As 99th Avenue stretches east of the main neighborhood, watch the wires and telephone poles for a new addition to Vashon's birds, the Eurasian Collared-Dove.

Directions: Dockton Park is 3.6 miles from the stop sign at the entrance to Maury Island where Dockton Road meets Quartermaster Drive. When you climb the hill above the park into the village, the arterial turns east, and Dock Street continues as a small lane straight ahead to the south.

A Greater Yellowlegs rests on one leg. © Doug Parrott

Dockton Forest and Natural Area: The Dockton Forest and Natural Area, over 400 acres of forest and disturbed area, received protection as Vashon organizations organized a public purchase in 2010 of the Glacier Northwest sand and gravel operation. Because the site was so recently acquired, the name of the park/preserve may change, and species aren't completely documented. Much of the forest consists of "dog hair" Douglas-fir forest, closed canopy with little or no understory vegetation. A few Pacific Wrens, kinglets, and chickadees use this, but little diversity exists. Much of the rest of the woods includes mixed patches of dry coniferous and dry deciduous forest similar to other areas of Maury Island, attracting Swainson's Thrush, Wilson's Warbler, and other typical forest birds.

Ironically, the disturbed former sand and gravel site presents the most interesting possibilities for birds as well as incredible Puget Sound and Cascade Range views. Pacific Madrone regenerates here as islands amongst a sea of Scotch Broom. Willow Flycatchers hunt from brushy perches, and many pairs of White-crowned Sparrows defend their territories, while Western Fence Lizards scrabble among the dry leaves. Like Maury Island Marine Park, the warm southeast-facing slopes likely attract good waves of arriving passerine migrants. If/when the Scotch Broom is cleared to be replaced by native vegetation, this location will attract many more warbler, vireo, and flycatcher species in spring and sparrows in fall and winter.

Manzanita: Manzanita offers the most reliable location on the Island for Pacific Loons in late fall and winter. As one looks west across the channel, the loons appear from mid-channel to the opposite shore of Vashon Island. Red-throated Loons may sometimes be found close into shore, as well as the uncommon Black Scoter. The nearby brush often hosts a sparrow flock that should be checked for rarities in winter. The driftwood area, if watched more regularly, has possibilities of birds not yet recorded at the location: pipits and Short-eared or Snowy Owls.

Directions: Manzanita is 6.6 miles from the stop sign at the entrance to Maury Island where Dockton Road meets Quartermaster Drive. Follow Dockton Road to Dockton, where it turns into 99th Avenue, then 99th to where the arterial turns right and becomes 280th Street, shortly after which the arterial turns left and becomes 101st Avenue. Go downhill to the water and then right on through to the end of the pavement. Two small dirt/gravel pull-offs exist on either side of the end of the public road. The road continues on to private property at this point. Park and step across to the beach for viewing the harbor entrance.

Sandy Shores: Sandy Shores furnishes views southeast across Puget Sound toward Federal Way. The usual Red-necked and Horned Grebes, scoters, and goldeneyes swim offshore.

Directions: Find Sandy Shores by driving to Dockton as described above. Continue through the village, heading south on 99th and turn left (east) on 268th Street. At the T intersection with 94th Avenue, turn right (south) until 275th Street. Turn left and follow it down to the bottom of the bluff.

Gold Beach: This residential neighborhood presents more spectacular views across Puget Sound toward Commencement Bay. A number of Anna's Hummingbirds stop at feeders here. Mourning Doves show up regularly in the neighborhood.

Directions: Gold Beach lies on the southeast shore of Maury Island. Follow Dockton Road until the intersection with 75th Avenue just north of the golf course. At this intersection, Dockton Road curves to the right, but visitors to Gold Beach should head straight onto 75th and follow it to the edge of the bluff, then continue down to the bottom toward the beach.

Point Robinson: Just about the whole Vashon list and more might be expected to turn up at Point Robinson at some time or another. At any time of year, some vagrant wanderer might show up. Spring migration seems to be the best bet, but unusual birds appear in all seasons. The reason for all the rarities is two-fold: First, Point Robinson sticks out from the Island into Puget Sound and acts as a migrant trap akin to Discovery Park in Seattle. Second, the park includes a good mix of habitats, attracting a wide variety of resident birds. The area next to the lighthouse on the south side of the point makes the best place to look for interesting marine birds. Migrant warblers, vireos, and thrushes appear especially noticeable in spring and fall along the bluffs to the south, viewed from the beach. The same species, joined by sparrows, utilize the brush at the base of the bluff by the lighthouse. The woods and thickets surrounding the parking lot at the top of the bluff offer additional opportunities to find neotropical migrants.

The park holds twelve acres, with about a half-mile of gravel and sandy shoreline, clay bluffs, some grassy areas, two areas of thickets, and Red Alder forest. Point Robinson attains its greatest species diversity from September through mid-May, especially during spring and fall migrations. Many loon, grebe, waterfowl, shorebird, gull, and tern species stop to forage or stream on by. Rarities include Short-tailed Shearwaters seen during an invasion of the Puget Sound area in 1977 (Hunn 1982), Black Oystercatcher, Whimbrel, Red Phalarope, and Sabine's Gull.

Directions: The entrance to the park at Point Robinson is 3.2 miles from the intersection of Quartermaster Drive and Dockton Road. Follow Dockton Road about half a mile and then go straight at the Y intersection with Point Robinson Road; Dockton Road turns to the right. Follow Point Robinson Road to the end. From the park entrance, one can drive in and park either at the top of the bluff or down at the bottom closer to the lighthouse keeper buildings. Portable toilets are available at both parking lots.

Maury Island Marine Park: The park requires a roundtrip walk of about two miles to reach the areas where more unusual species frequent. The first half-mile proceeds down a ravine of mixed deciduous woods. Towhees and jays actively call on this stretch, and warblers and vireos make appearances, too.

As the trail turns to parallel the beach, the habitat changes to Pacific Madrone, Salal, and huckleberry. This area receives more sun, and lots of birds and Western Fence Lizards use the slope. One observer noted a Rubber Boa along the trail. Rufous and Anna's Hummingbirds abound among the honeysuckle. Anna's Hummingbird, Bushtit, and Hutton's Vireo nest adjacent to this stretch of the trail. Swainson's Thrushes sing in the lower Red Alder patches.

At the bottom of the trail where a flat grassy and brushy area meets the dry hillside, Killdeer nest. Goldfinches, House Finches, Black-headed Grosbeaks, and White-crowned Sparrows sing in the breeding season. Lincoln's Sparrows visit in winter. A Lazuli Bunting stopped by in 2001. A walk along the beach at the bottom provides opportunities to view loons and waterfowl. Spotted Sandpipers appear occasionally along this stretch of beach.

Directions: From the stop sign at the intersection of Quartermaster Drive and Dockton Road denoting the beginning of Maury Island, head toward Point Robinson, going two miles before turning right (south) on 59th Avenue. Watch for 244th Street on the east or left side and turn onto it. The small parking lot for the park sits on the right at 0.3 miles. Park and walk past the gate down the gravel road.

Chapter V

The Vashon Year from a Birding Perspective

Any time of year makes for good birding on Vashon Island. Every season has its specialty and invites one to a different part of the Island. At latest count, 251 species have been recorded for the Island list. Of those, only a fourth, about 60, stay year-round. Over 100 species regularly arrive to breed or over-winter, while others just pass through briefly in migration. Though the characters change from season to season, one can easily find 50 to 60 species in a morning's birding. During migration, with a little luck and planning, one might find 80 to 100.

January: Christmas Bird Count Finds Many Winter Birds

The first Sunday in January hosts the Christmas Bird Count. Participants observe 110 to 120 species annually in the count circle. Brant first arrive early in the month to fatten up for the big trip north. Waterfowl populations have stabilized, with nearly 40 species of loons, grebes, cormorants, geese, ducks, shorebirds, gulls, and alcids in the saltwater habitats. Along the shorelines, Sanderling flocks reinforce the small bands of ubiquitous Killdeer. Tramp and Quartermaster Harbors and Tahlequah make the most rewarding stops during this month.

Bald Eagles dot the dark coniferous coastline, waiting for an opportunity to take an unwary duck. Anna's Hummingbirds hang tight to their feeders and prospect for a few exotic or out-of-season blooms here and there. Mixed sparrow flocks coalesce around seed feeding stations, rarely staying in large groups without human help. Sharp-shinned and Cooper's Hawks swoop through, raiding those gathering around the seeds.

February: Blackbirds Spread Rumors of Spring

Bird populations mostly remain stable, with few new rarities showing up. As the month progresses, the numbers of Red-breasted Merganser begin to decrease, the first of the waterfowl to dwindle, leaving early in the spring. Red-winged Blackbirds return to the wetlands and may be seen at bird feeders in the latter half of the month. Their calls join many species just beginning to sing: Brown Creeper, Hutton's Vireo, juncos, robins, and

Pacific Wren. February and March bring the easiest opportunities for finding the creeper and Hutton's Vireo. A walk along Paradise Valley from Cemetery Road to 216th Street should deliver many of these birds, especially along Judd Creek.

March: Rufous Hummingbirds Return

In the first week, Rufous Hummingbirds begin buzzing around the Island's Salmonberry blossoms and hummer feeders. Once again, one must look carefully to see if a hummer is a Rufous or an Anna's. Any sign of brown or rust on the belly is indicative of a Rufous.

Now the watch begins for returning swallows. Violet-greens arrive in the latter half of the month and the others in April, much later than noted elsewhere in Western Washington. Fisher Pond, Paradise Valley, and the south end of Monument Road make good places to look and listen.

Is that song a junco's or is it the first Orange-crowned Warbler? Usually somewhere on Maury, but then quickly all across the Island, the trill of the Orange-crowned Warbler comes in the third week of the month. Simultaneously, White-crowned Sparrows announce their presence with song as well, and the occasional Say's Phoebe might turn up somewhere.

For those outside and paying attention, the surprise sight and sound of overhead northbound Snow Geese might be heard. Northern Harriers and others seen only during migration unobtrusively make their way over the Island's beaches and fields.

Say's Phoebe at KVI Beach. © Ed Swan

April: Spring Migration Swells, Waterfowl Begin to Leave

The floodgates open and each week brings many more birds. Northern Rough-winged, Tree, and Barn Swallows return in the first week or two. A lucky few observers will spot a Townsend's Solitaire, an uncommon migrant passing through. Savannah Sparrows vibrate the eardrums of listeners as the males sing to establish their territories along wet fields at Monument Road, Wax Orchard, and Paradise Valley.

The middle of the month brings Osprey, Caspian Tern, Common Yellowthroat, and Brown-headed Cowbird. One might find all four at the end of Monument Road near Quartermaster Harbor or at Raab's Lagoon. Scouts for the summer's Purple Martin population drop in at Ellisport and other locations with nest boxes to stake their claim.

The latter half of April brings a flurry of flycatchers, vireos, and warblers. Pacific-slope Flycatchers, Cassin's and Warbling Vireos, Swainson's Thrushes, Black-throated Gray and Wilson's Warblers, Western Tanagers, and Black-headed Grosbeaks fill Point Robinson, Paradise Valley, Maury Island Marine Park, and many other places with song.

The last week brings the shorebird migration to Fern Cove and KVI Beach, rewarding persistent observers with a variety of peeps, yellowlegs, and the occasional Dunlin. A close eye should be kept on the sand grass area at KVI Beach, as American Pipits wander through in late April.

Meanwhile, songs from the Fox Sparrows resonate in many thickets. About mid-April they leave, as do the majority of Ruby-crowned Kinglets and Varied Thrushes. Out on Quartermaster Harbor and Puget Sound, the Red-breasted Merganser disappears and the other waterfowl thin out considerably. By the end of the month, the only gulls are Glaucous-winged. Loon and grebe populations swell and decline as waves of migrants briefly stop and then continue northwards.

May: The Wild Card Month

The first week or two of May makes the best period for a Big Day, since at least a few of each of the wintering waterfowl species remain and all of the uncommon to common regular migrants are back. Finding 100 species should be possible for observers who plan well and have a little luck.

The last regular migrants consist mostly of birds more common in Eastern Washington: House Wrens, MacGillivray's and Yellow Warblers, Lazuli Buntings, and Bullock's Orioles. Except for the Yellow Warbler, all are rare, without consistent returning locations. The last of the flycatchers, the Western Wood Pewee and Olive-sided and Willow Flycatchers, arrive and sing from the woods. Paradise Valley and the woods above KVI Beach make the best places to listen for them.

A trip to Point Robinson, Maury Island Marine Park, KVI Beach, and/or Fern Cove might easily be rewarded with some very interesting birds. Palm Warbler and Black Oystercatcher were added to the Island's list in May. Pectoral Sandpipers and Whimbrels make rare visits. Large migrant fallouts of many species still occur at Point Robinson in the first week. Just about anything might show up, which adds some spice to birding in May.

The flip side of the exciting search for rarities and the return of the breeding species is the departure of the waterfowl. Loons, grebes, and the myriad ducks move to their northern and eastern breeding grounds by the third week of May. The once teeming waters of Tramp and Quartermaster Harbors become empty of all but the Glaucous-winged Gull and nesting Pigeon Guillemot. Saltwater and shoreline habitats remain calm and uneventful until late July. In the upland areas, the Golden-crowned Sparrows depart as well.

Meanwhile, the resident birds busily make babies. Bewick's Wrens, robins, juncos, and others already have one brood and may be preparing for another in June or early July. Small populations of Pacific Wren, Golden-crowned Kinglet, and Varied Thrush remain in the wetter or more mature coniferous woods.

June: The Breeding Season

All of the breeders are active now. The month becomes slower as the singing gradually quiets down except for very early in the morning. The main highlight of this time of the year lies in finding hidden nests and seeing the first fledglings out and being fed. A gaggle of young ducklings follow mother Mallards and Wood Ducks across Fisher Pond. Purple Martins may be heard high above, cruising the skies anywhere around the Island. Spotted Sandpipers parade their young along downed logs or the small dock at Fern Cove.

Interestingly, June also begins the fall migration. The first California Gulls return along the ferry runs or rest at Fern Cove in the last week of the month. A few Western and Least Sandpipers might show up at KVI Beach or Fern Cove. They are adults having already left their young alone in the north to fend for themselves. It will be at least another two months before the juveniles come through on migration. Meanwhile, one or two early-returning, non-breeding Common Loons, White-winged Scoters, and Surf Scoters might provide a surprise in Tramp Harbor.

July: Shorebird Migration Begins

Just as the land birding grows increasingly quiet, with many warblers and vireos already harder to find, the shorebirds return to make birding interesting. Persistent watching at KVI Beach finds the earliest Western Sandpipers by the end of the first week in July. Least Sandpipers join them, followed by Greater Yellowlegs and Semipalmated Plover.

In the last week of the month, the first saltwater species return. Birders who look outward over Puget Sound or Tramp Harbor after looking for shorebirds at the pond at KVI Beach might be rewarded with views of Common Loons, Double-breasted Cormorants, Red-necked Grebes, and Western Grebes. A scattering of Mew and Bonaparte's Gulls also livens things up a bit, usually along Tramp Harbor or at Fern Cove. Overhead, watch for young Osprey learning to fish.

August: Shoreline Areas Become Hot Spots Again

As August progresses, the summer passerines become increasingly harder to find, as most of them begin their migration to the south. Most species hang out in low numbers into September. KVI Beach and Fern Cove become hot spots again as the Western and Least Sandpiper numbers increase and more grebes, cormorants, ducks, gulls, terns, and shorebirds return. Early August brings the return of Horned Grebes and can sometimes produce a rare Semipalmated Sandpiper. Red-necked Phalarope, usually seen from the ferries, should be sought in the lines of weed debris strewn across both ferry routes throughout the month.

Fisher Pond merits watching as it increasingly dries out. The shorebird migration spills over to the pond, with Spotted Sandpipers, Western Sandpipers, and an occasional dowitcher foraging in the mud. Green-winged Teal arrive here in late August.

Other late August birds arriving at a variety of locations include American Wigeons, Pelagic Cormorants, and Common Terns. Large flocks of Bonaparte's Gulls and occasionally Common Terns stream down Colvos Passage and across the Tahlequah ferry route. In the last week of August, Parasitic Jaegers chase through the flocks for a free meal or flap along waiting sinisterly for a chance to steal.

September: Upland Winter Residents Return

Upland winter birds compete for attention with the shorebirds and water birds, as wintering thrushes and sparrows come back to the Island. Early in the month, Lincoln's Sparrows come through at Point Robinson and Raab's Lagoon, and by the third week of the month, Golden-crowned and Fox Sparrows return to Island feeding stations. Ruby-crowned Kinglets, Varied Thrushes, and Hermit Thrushes show up at about the same time. Listeners hear Yellow-rumped Warblers' chips throughout the Island, especially in hardwood stands. Townsend's Warblers should be watched for as well, arriving back from the mountains. The neotropical migrants that bred on the Island over the summer totally disappear by mid-month. With the thrushes, it's just like trading places, as the returning Hermit Thrushes virtually replace the simultaneously departing Swainson's.

Shorebird migration keeps moving on, with Pectoral Sandpipers sometimes gracing the estuary at KVI Beach. Wintering Sanderling take station along the wave line. While looking for shorebirds at KVI Beach, one should watch the beach grass for American Pipits wandering through. In the harbors and coves, the first Red-breasted Mergansers of the fall must be closely observed to ensure separation from the Common Mergansers also visiting the Island.

October: The Remaining Waterfowl Arrive

Each week in October, the number of water birds and species increases. Early to mid-October brings back Red-throated and Pacific Loons and Eared Grebes. Mid- to late October delivers Northern Shoveler, Northern Pintail, both scaups, both goldeneyes, and Bufflehead. Each trip by Tramp or Quartermaster Harbor may show a new bird returning.

On Fisher Pond, the shorebird migration culminates with Wilson's Snipe checking out the mud just as the migration of peeps fades out at KVI Beach and Fern Cove.

November: The Search for Rarities

By early November, thousands of water birds actively dive, dabble, and swim around Tramp Harbor and Quartermaster Harbor, and others scatter all along the shoreline. In the bramble hedges and around feeding stations, flocks of winter sparrows gather. November offers a good time to scan the flocks for something unusual. In past years, Long-tailed Duck have visited Tramp Harbor in November, a Trumpeter Swan checked out Fisher Pond, American Kestrel returned to Wax Orchard, and Black Turnstones dodged the waves at Ellisport.

The flocks of birds at a single, well-stocked feeding station of mixed seed, black-oil sunflower seed, and a hummingbird feeder may approach 150 individuals and fifteen or more species. Chickadees, nuthatches, sparrows, towhees, and finches swarm around the food and scatter as accipiters feed on them. Each winter, a number of White-throated Sparrows join the flocks. Every other year or so, a Harris's Sparrow might be found. Once in a great while, a real rarity such as a Blue Jay or White-breasted Nuthatch shows up.

December: Prepare for the Christmas Bird Count

December appears much the same as November, though the numbers of birds stabilize after the last waves of migrants pass through. The hunt for interesting birds among the big flocks continues as part of the process of scouting for the Christmas Bird Count. The question becomes, where are the wandering foragers such as the Cedar Waxwings, Red Crossbills, and American Goldfinches? They may be common one year or gone the next, depending on berry and seed crop timing. Also, the call goes out for residents to listen for owls calling in preparation for the their early breeding season. Great Horned Owls often end up being rather easy to find at this time, Barred Owls show up perching on utility lines, and Northern Saw-whets call out here and there.

Winter Mallards already beginning to think about the coming spring. © Doug Parrott

Chapter VI

Avian Seasonal Abundance

CHECKLIST FOR THE BIRDS OF VASHON ISLAND, WASHINGTON
2013 EDITION

KEY:		
	▬▬	Common: 25+ seen or heard daily
	▬▬	Fairly common: 1–25 seen or heard daily
	▬	Uncommon: not seen or heard daily
	───	Rare: 1–5 records per year
	- - - -	Very rare: not seen every year
	◄······►	Single bird: duration of stay
	+	Single occurrence of species
	*	Known to nest in checklist area
Italicized species have five or fewer records on Vashon Island.	Intro	Introduced to Vashon
	Ext	Extirpated on Vashon

	J	F	M	A	M	J	J	A	S	O	N	D
___ Greater White-fronted Goose	-	-	-	-	-					▬▬	-	-
___ Snow Goose			▬							▬	▬	
___ Brant			▬	▬▬	▬▬						-	-
___ Cackling Goose	-	-	-	-							-	-
___ Canada Goose*	▬▬	▬▬	▬▬	▬▬	▬▬	▬▬	▬▬	▬▬	▬▬	▬▬	▬▬	▬▬
___ Trumpeter Swan												
___ Tundra Swan												
___ Wood Duck*	▬▬	▬▬	▬▬	▬▬	▬▬	▬▬	▬▬	▬▬	▬▬	▬▬	▬▬	▬▬
___ Gadwall												
___ Eurasian Wigeon			▬	▬	▬							
___ American Wigeon	▬▬	▬▬	▬▬	▬▬	▬▬			▬▬	▬▬	▬▬	▬▬	▬▬
___ Mallard*	▬▬	▬▬	▬▬	▬▬	▬▬	▬▬	▬▬	▬▬	▬▬	▬▬	▬▬	▬▬
___ *Blue-winged Teal*					-	-						
___ *Cinnamon Teal*					-	-						

Avian Seasonal Abundance

	J	F	M	A	M	J	J	A	S	O	N	D
___ Northern Shoveler												
___ Northern Pintail												
___ Green-winged Teal*												
___ Canvasback		+										
___ Ring-necked Duck												
___ Greater Scaup												
___ Lesser Scaup												
___ Harlequin Duck												
___ Surf Scoter												
___ White-winged Scoter												
___ Black Scoter												
___ Long-tailed Duck												
___ Bufflehead												
___ Common Goldeneye												
___ Barrow's Goldeneye												
___ Hooded Merganser*												
___ Common Merganser												
___ Red-breasted Merganser												
___ Ruddy Duck												
___ California Quail, Intro, Ext												
___ Northern Bobwhite, Intro, Ext												
___ Gray Partridge, Intro, Ext												
___ Ring-necked Pheasant*, Intro												
___ Sooty Grouse, Ext												
___ Red-throated Loon												
___ Pacific Loon												
___ Common Loon												
___ Yellow-billed Loon												
___ Pied-billed Grebe*												
___ Horned Grebe												
___ Red-necked Grebe												
___ Eared Grebe												
___ Western Grebe												

The Birds of Vashon Island

	J	F	M	A	M	J	J	A	S	O	N	D
___ *Clark's Grebe*	-	-	-	-	-	-				-	-	-
___ *Northern Fulmar*										+		
___ *Sooty Shearwater*		+										
___ *Short-tailed Shearwater*	-										-	-
___ *Fork-tailed Storm-Petrel*										+		
___ *Leach's Storm-Petrel*												+
___ *Magnificent Frigatebird*									+			
___ *Brown Booby*					+							
___ Brown Pelican						━━━━━━━━━━━━━━━━━━━━━━━━━━━━						
___ Brandt's Cormorant	████████████████████████						██████████████████████					
___ Double-crested Cormorant	████████████████						████████			████████████████		
___ Pelagic Cormorant	████████████						████					
___ Great Blue Heron*	██											
___ *Great Egret*									-	-	-	
___ *Cattle Egret*								+				
___ Green Heron					-	-	-	-	-			
___ Turkey Vulture			-	-	████████				████			
___ Osprey*				████████████████████████								
___ Bald Eagle*	██											
___ Northern Harrier				██████					████████			
___ Sharp-shinned Hawk*	██											
___ Cooper's Hawk*	██											
___ Northern Goshawk								+				
___ Red-tailed Hawk*	██											
___ *Rough-legged Hawk*	-										-	-
___ *Virginia Rail*	██											
___ American Coot	-	-	-	-	-					-	-	-
___ Sandhill Crane					-	-			-	-	-	
___ *Black-bellied Plover*				-	-					+		
___ *Semipalmated Plover*					-			████				
___ Killdeer*	██											
___ *Black Oystercatcher*						+						
___ Spotted Sandpiper	██											

AVIAN SEASONAL ABUNDANCE

	J	F	M	A	M	J	J	A	S	O	N	D
___ Solitary Sandpiper												
___ *Wandering Tattler*								+				
___ Greater Yellowlegs												
___ Lesser Yellowlegs												
___ *Whimbrel*												
___ *Marbled Godwit*					+							
___ Black Turnstone												
___ Surfbird		+										
___ Sanderling												
___ Semipalmated Sandpiper												
___ Western Sandpiper												
___ Least Sandpiper												
___ Baird's Sandpiper												
___ Pectoral Sandpiper												
___ Dunlin												
___ Short-billed Dowitcher												
___ Long-billed Dowitcher						+						
___ Wilson's Snipe												
___ *Wilson's Phalarope*						+						
___ Red-necked Phalarope												
___ Red Phalarope												
___ *Black-legged Kittiwake*												
___ *Sabine's Gull*												
___ Bonaparte's Gull												
___ *Little Gull*		+										
___ Franklin's Gull												
___ Heermann's Gull												
___ Mew Gull												
___ Ring-billed Gull												
___ Western Gull												
___ California Gull												
___ Herring Gull												
___ Thayer's Gull												

	J	F	M	A	M	J	J	A	S	O	N	D
___ Glaucous-winged Gull*	■	■	■	■	■	■	■	■	■	■	■	■
___ *Glaucous Gull*												+
___ Caspian Tern					■	■	■	■	—			
___ Common Tern								─	─			
___ *Arctic Tern*							+					
___ *Pomarine Jaeger*								+				
___ *Parasitic Jaeger*								─	─	─		
___ Common Murre	■	■	■	─						─	■	■
___ Pigeon Guillemot*	■	■	■	■	■	■	■	■	■	■	■	■
___ Marbled Murrelet	■	■	■	■	■	■	■	■	■	■	■	■
___ *Ancient Murrelet*										-	-	-
___ *Cassin's Auklet*								-	-	-	-	-
___ Rhinoceros Auklet	■	■	■	■	■				■	■	■	■
___ *Tufted Puffin*						+						
___ Rock Pigeon*	■	■	■	■	■	■	■	■	■	■	■	■
___ Band-tailed Pigeon*				■	■	■	■	■	■	■	■	■
___ Eurasian Collared-Dove												
___ Mourning Dove*												
___ Barn Owl*												
___ *Western Screech-Owl*	-	-									-	-
___ Great Horned Owl*												
___ *Snowy Owl*	-	-	-	-	-						-	-
___ *Northern Pygmy-Owl*	-	-	-	-	-	-						
___ *Spotted Owl, hypothetical/ext*												
___ Barred Owl*												
___ *Long-eared Owl*											+	
___ *Short-eared Owl*										+		
___ Northern Saw-whet Owl*	■	■	■	■	■	■	■	■	■	■	■	■
___ *Common Nighthawk*						─	─	─	─	─		
___ *Black Swift*					-	-			-	-		
___ *Vaux's Swift*						─	─	─				
___ Anna's Hummingbird*	■	■	■	■	■	■	■	■	■	■	■	■
___ *Costa's Hummingbird*								+				

Avian Seasonal Abundance

	J	F	M	A	M	J	J	A	S	O	N	D
___ Rufous Hummingbird*												
___ Belted Kingfisher*												
___ *Lewis's Woodpecker*										+		
___ *Red-naped Sapsucker*	←···→											←···→
___ Red-breasted Sapsucker*												
___ Downy Woodpecker*												
___ Hairy Woodpecker												
___ Northern Flicker*												
___ Pileated Woodpecker*												
___ American Kestrel												
___ Merlin												
___ Peregrine Falcon												
___ Olive-sided Flycatcher*												
___ Western Wood-Pewee*												
___ Willow Flycatcher												
___ Hammond's Flycatcher												
___ Pacific-slope Flycatcher*												
___ Say's Phoebe												
___ Western Kingbird												
___ *Northern Shrike*		+										
___ *White-eyed Vireo*							+					
___ Cassin's Vireo*												
___ Hutton's Vireo*												
___ Warbling Vireo*												
___ *Red-eyed Vireo*												
___ Steller's Jay*												
___ *Blue Jay*	+											
___ Western Scrub-Jay												
___ American Crow*												
___ Northwestern Crow, Ext												
___ Common Raven*												
___ Purple Martin*												
___ Tree Swallow*												

The Birds of Vashon Island

	J	F	M	A	M	J	J	A	S	O	N	D
___ Violet-green Swallow*												
___ Northern Rough-winged Swallow*												
___ Cliff Swallow*												
___ Barn Swallow*												
___ Black-capped Chickadee*												
___ *Mountain Chickadee*									◄►			
___ Chestnut-backed Chickadee*												
___ Bushtit*												
___ Red-breasted Nuthatch*												
___ *White-breasted Nuthatch*	◄	···	···	►						◄	···	►
___ Brown Creeper*												
___ House Wren*					–	–				–	–	
___ Pacific Wren*												
___ Marsh Wren	–	–	–	–	–	–	–	–	–	–	–	–
___ Bewick's Wren*												
___ American Dipper	–	–								–	–	–
___ Golden-crowned Kinglet*												
___ Ruby-crowned Kinglet												
___ *Western Bluebird*				–	–	–						
___ *Mountain Bluebird*				+								
___ Townsend's Solitaire	–	–	–	–			–	–		–	–	–
___ Swainson's Thrush*												
___ Hermit Thrush												
___ American Robin*												
___ Varied Thrush*												
___ European Starling*												
___ American Pipit					–				–			
___ Cedar Waxwing*												
___ *Snow Bunting*	–	–									–	–
___ Orange-crowned Warbler*			–	–								
___ *Nashville Warbler*						–	–					
___ MacGillivray's Warbler												
___ Common Yellowthroat*												

130

Avian Seasonal Abundance

	J	F	M	A	M	J	J	A	S	O	N	D
___ *American Redstart*						+						
___ Yellow Warbler												
___ *Palm Warbler*					+							
___ Yellow-rumped Warbler												
___ Black-throated Gray Warbler*												
___ Townsend's Warbler												
___ *Hermit Warbler*										+		
___ Wilson's Warbler*												
___ *Yellow-breasted Chat*												
___ Spotted Towhee*												
___ *Chipping Sparrow*												
___ *Vesper Sparrow*												
___ Savannah Sparrow*												
___ Fox Sparrow												
___ Song Sparrow*												
___ Lincoln's Sparrow												
___ White-throated Sparrow												
___ *Harris's Sparrow*												
___ White-crowned Sparrow*												
___ Golden-crowned Sparrow												
___ Dark-eyed Junco*												
___ Western Tanager*												
___ Black-headed Grosbeak*												+
___ Lazuli Bunting												
___ Red-winged Blackbird*												
___ Western Meadowlark												
___ *Yellow-headed Blackbird*												
___ *Rusty Blackbird*												
___ Brewer's Blackbird*												
___ Brown-headed Cowbird*												
___ Bullock's Oriole*												
___ Purple Finch*												
___ *Cassin's Finch*												
___ House Finch*												

The Birds of Vashon Island

	J	F	M	A	M	J	J	A	S	O	N	D
___ Red Crossbill*	━	━	━	━	━	━	━	━	━	━	━	━
___ Pine Siskin*	━	━	━	━	━	━	━	━	━	━	━	━
___ American Goldfinch*	━	━	━	━	━	━	━	━	━	━	━	━
___ Evening Grosbeak				-	━	━	━		-	━	-	-
___ House Sparrow*	━	━	━	━	━	━	━	━	━	━	━	━

Great Blue Heron. © Doug Parrott

CHAPTER VII

Annotated List of Species

The annotated list of species of Vashon Island covers the 251 species of birds documented for the Island. This list includes naturally occurring species, those introduced to the Island, and a few known to have existed on the Island which are now extirpated. Two additional birds that were likely to have existed but for which there are no documented records (i.e., the Spotted Owl and Northwestern Crow) join the list. Each account states the current status of the species and the habitats the species may be found in specifically for the Island. Many of the species might be observed in other habitats in other locations around the state or continent, but unless they use that habitat on the Island, the habitat isn't listed. The body of the account details habitat use and includes information on known population fluctuations and breeding/nesting records for the Island. Following each species's summary are Breeding Bird Survey (BBS) records and Christmas Bird Count (CBC) data. The BBS lists birds seen on a set route by one trained observer following a strict protocol on a chosen day in the breeding season. Christmas Bird Counts involve many volunteers noting birds in a fifteen-mile diameter circle, indicating the presence of a species in winter over the years but not an exact census. Islander Carole Elder collected the BBS data, conducting surveys from 1995 to 1998, from 2000 to 2006, and in 2009. Harsi and Ezra Parker continued the Vashon BBS route in 2013. Sue Trevathan has compiled the Vashon data since the CBC started here in 1999. The Vashon Island count circle has six observer

Seasonal Occurrence	
Occurrence	**Description**
Common	25 or more birds seen or heard daily
Fairly Common	1 to 25 birds seen or heard daily
Uncommon	Not seen every day
Rare	1 to 5 records per year
Very Rare	Not seen every year
Accidental	Out of region species with few records
Hypothetical	Species without sufficient historical or descriptive documentation

Habitat Abbreviations	
Abbreviation	Description
SW	Saltwater
SS	Sandy and Gravelly Shoreline, Mud Flat, and Salt Marsh
FW	Freshwater Ponds, Wetlands, and Streams
FL	Field, Farmland, and Pasture
DC	Dry Coniferous: Douglas-fir and Dry Douglas-fir/Madrone Forests
WC	Wet Coniferous Forest
HW	Hardwood-Dominated Mixed Forest
ST	Shrubby Thicket
DA	Developed Area
AE	Aerial

areas, four covering Vashon and two covering nearby off-Island locations in Pierce and Kitsap Counties. The CBC data is broken down here to show the numbers from only the four sections that cover Vashon.

The American Ornithological Union (AOU) provides the official list of North American birds (AOU 2012). Based on the latest observations and research, updates to the list reflect the latest understandings about the evolutionary relationships and order of avian families. Over the last decade, DNA research, especially, changed the order of the North American species list. Accordingly, this book reflects several changes occurring about the same time as the first edition and a number afterward. Most noticeably, waterfowl and game birds jump to the beginning of the list in front of loons and grebes. Falcons no longer appear closely related to hawks and eagles and now come after woodpeckers in the ordering of species. Many other small changes took place within family groupings, especially among the gulls. This edition also reflects changes in names, such as the recent split creating Pacific Wren from the species formerly known as Winter Wren.

Ducks, Geese, and Swans

Greater White-fronted Goose

(SS, FW, FL, AE) Status: Uncommon fall migrant, very rare winter visitor, and rare spring migrant.

In the spring and fall, listening carefully for the calls of geese overhead might bring the reward of seeing this uncommon goose for King County.

Usually their calling gives the first warning of their approach, hopefully in time for a good look before they pass beyond sight. Most sightings consist of birds migrating overhead. Every once in a while, Greater White-fronted Geese land in some of the small ponds or at farm fields on the Island. Fran O'Reilly enjoyed 20 or so that visited her horse pasture on Maury Island for a week in mid-October 2008. Joy Nelsen saw thirteen on a pond on the Rosford property on Maury Island on 10 November 2001. While leading a Seattle Audubon field trip on 19 October 1996, Rick Sanders and John Friars found them at the small pond in the valley below the cemetery, and Sue Trevathan found a dozen nearby at Singer Pond on 1 October 2011. John Friars observed a single bird with Canada Geese at his house near KVI Beach on 15 April 1992. During Vashon's agricultural past, long-time resident Ed Babcock remembers them landing to feed in local fields.

One individual apparently stayed much of the winter and possibly late into the spring of 2007/2008. Gary Peterson photographed the bird for the Christmas Bird Count at the Vashon Community Care Center pond and fields, and Kathy Kirkland first noted it with Canada Geese at the mouth of Judd Creek. In the Vashon Community Care Center photograph, it associated with a flock of tame Canada Geese, Canada Goose hybrids, and various domestic hybrids. Other observers saw it either with the hybrid flock or with Canada Geese several times that winter. Rick Sanders later in the spring heard a single Greater White-fronted, possibly this bird, flying with Canada Geese along Colvos Passage near Fern Cove.

CBC by area (Trevathan 1999-2013):

Vashon North: 2008

Snow Goose

(FL, AE) Status: Rare to uncommon spring and fall migrant.

In addition to Greater White-fronted Geese, one should watch and listen for overhead Snow Geese. Snow Geese observations increased over the last half decade, likely as a result of additional observer effort and report sharing. Western Washington Snow Goose populations come almost entirely from the Wrangel Island breeding stock, which recovered over the last several decades from major declines in the 1970s (Pacific Flyway Council 2006). With the recovery, numbers wintering at the Skagit delta north of the Island surged, and Vashon probably also experienced more birds overhead. The expansion in reports since the last edition still appears most aptly characterized as the result of more local observers. Only two recent reports of birds actually landing exist: the first in the field behind Vashon Auto Parts in December 2008 and the second at Bella Ormseth's place, a first-year bird on 1 January 2013. All other sightings consist of migrating birds flying over Vashon. Ed Babcock, a resident for 80 years, remembers them as somewhat more common back in the early to mid-20th century. He saw them land in fields on Maury Island. Most flocks over the last ten years ranged from 30 to 50 geese, but a few times flocks of several hundred flew by. Tens of thousands may be seen each winter along the Skagit delta to the north.

CBC by area (Trevathan 1999-2013):
Vashon South: 2013

Brant

(SW, SS) Status: Rare late fall, uncommon winter, fairly common in spring, and one summer record.

> "Black brants are the only geese one is quite sure of seeing from the deck of a steamboat on an average winter day on Puget Sound. While they have their favorite feeding grounds upon the mud flats and in shallow bays, they are widely distributed over the open water also, and their numbers during the spring migrations are such that not all other wild geese put together are to be mentioned in comparison. They sit the water in small companies; and although they are exceedingly wary in regard to rowboats, they often permit an approach on the part of steamers, which is very gratifying to the student." (Dawson and Bowles 1909)

While Brant numbers are drastically lower today, much of what Dawson observed holds true. In December, a few small flocks of half a dozen to a dozen Brant begin appearing along the Vashon-Fauntleroy and Vashon-Colman Dock ferry routes, feeding in the long lines of weedy debris, usually half a mile to a mile out. Larger flocks of 20 to 100 come close inshore to eelgrass beds at KVI Beach, Ellisport, Portage, and Point Robinson in February as migrants returning from the south stage for the return to the high north. Numbers peak in late March and April. Alice Bloch reported the largest flock in recent memory, with over 400 at Point Robinson on 21 April 2008. John Friars found eight off KVI Beach on 6 July 2010 for Vashon's only summer record. Don Kraege writes that small groups showing up in Puget Sound in summer consist most likely of subadults or other non-breeders (Wahl et al. 2005).

Brant numbers in Washington fell dramatically after the 1960s. The Midwinter Waterfowl Survey averages prior to 1970 ranged from 20,000 to 25,000, then dropped to around 10,000 in the 1980s and stabilized at about 12,000 since (Pacific Flyway Council 2004). Puget Sound Ambient Monitoring Program (PSAMP) surveys from 1992 to 1999 indicate a decrease in densities of 66 percent from the same transects in the north Sound from the Marine Ecosystem Analyses of 1978 to 1979 (Nysewander et al. 2001). A limiting factor with these statistics involves their using only data on wintering birds and failing to measure the spring migration staging of birds returning from the south.

No one theory definitively explains the drop in numbers, which appears to be both a decrease in the overall Pacific Flyway population as well as a shifting of the population from Washington, Oregon, and California to Mexico. One Washington State study of eelgrass beds, a critical feeding habitat for Brant, showed a 22 percent decline of beds, associated with a 52 percent drop in the geese at Willapa Bay. A 31 percent decrease in eelgrass had an accompanying 63 percent diminishing of Brant utilization of Dungeness Bay (Wilson and Atkinson 1995). The researchers suggest that the compromised feeding reserves might result in poorer breeding success, causing a lowering of Brant numbers. It might also cause a shift in population to more productive foraging locations. Important factors in this study involve counts over a decade's time and throughout the winter and spring, catching both the wintering and returning spring migration populations. Nest predation by Arctic Fox on the Brants' breeding grounds in the area around the deltas of the Yukon and Kuskokwim Rivers breeding grounds in the late 1970s and early 1980s appears to explain the overall Pacific Flyway population drop since the 1960s, according to some ornithologists (Reed et al. 1998).

CBC by area (Trevathan 1999-2013):
Vashon North: 2006cw, 2010, 2012cw
Maury Island-Tramp Harbor: 2007, 2011

Cackling Goose

(SW, SS, FW, FL, AE) Status: Very rare winter visitor. Six records. Change in Status: The American Ornithological Society gave the Cackling Goose separate species status only in 2004, and local observers rarely paid attention to the subspecies of Canada Goose prior to that change. Observers watching for this smaller goose since its status changed added enough additional sightings to move its status for Vashon from accidental in the first edition to very rare in the second edition. Closer observation of overhead migrants may find this species actually rare to uncommon.

The American Ornithological Union (AOU) split the small forms of the Canada Goose into a separate species, the Cackling Goose, in 2004 (AOU 2004). Only six recent records exist for this species since the split. On 25 January 2006, the author found six small geese with a flock of Great Basin form Canada Geese in the fields at the southeast end of Monument Road. The author checked photos by Peter Murray and Jack Dawdy with expert Steve Mlodinow, showing four of the birds were of the *taverneri* subspecies, Taverner's Cackling Goose, and one, possibly two, were of the *minima* subspecies of Cackling Goose. Rich Siegrist discovered a *minima* subspecies goose hanging out with a Canada Goose flock in the Colvos area and took a photo on 3 March 2009. Bob Hawkins noted another Cackling Goose of indeterminate subspecies with a Greater White-fronted Goose and Canada Geese at Dockton on 13 March 2009. John Friars found a single bird grazing in his lawn on 25 October 2011. Sue Trevathan saw three associating with a flock of Canada Geese at Singer Pond on 3 March 2013. These sightings represent the first ones in over 50 years of birding records. Ed Babcock, long-time resident of the Island, remembers seeing a goose of uncertain subspecies in the 1940s (Babcock pers. com. 2005). Cackling Geese possibly come on a rare basis to Vashon. Prior to the species split, even experienced birders hadn't noticed them in the last couple of decades. Careful watch over goose flocks from fall through spring is required to ascertain their true current status. The last several winters produced few records of Canada Geese other than the Great Basin form. More

Cackling Goose. © Doug Parrott

observers in the Puget Sound region are gaining expertise in separating the two species; their sightings show that Cackling Geese appear to be at least uncommon in the area in migration and winter, just not stopping much on Vashon as of yet. Bainbridge Island observers have noted many flocks overhead; Vashon birders should watch for and listen to goose flocks closely to build up the Island record.

Canada Goose

(SW, SS, FW, FL, DA) Status: Fairly common resident. Breeds.

The large Great Basin form of the Canada Goose makes up 99.9 percent of the Canada Goose sightings on Vashon. All Island nesting Canada Geese consist of birds of this subspecies. Other subspecies visit at least occasionally and probably provided most of the sightings of passing geese in the past. Observer coverage hasn't focused long enough on this possibility for many records as yet. Only two documented occurrences exist. On 9 January 2006, the author noted three unusually small Canada Geese at a pond created by runoff in the corner of fields at Old Mill Road and 220th Street. With help from photos by Peter Murray and Jack Dawdy, the author consulted Steven Mlodinow, one of the editors of *Birds of Washington,* who determined that the birds were of the *parvipes* subspecies, common name Lesser Canada Geese. Gary Shugart found another Lesser at Fisher Pond on 4 December 2010.

In the past, Canada Geese merely migrated through Western Washington along with the smaller Cackling Goose. Breeding occurred only east of the Cascades with small numbers of Great Basin Canada Geese. In the early and mid-20th century, nesting numbers increased along the river systems and around lakes and ponds for a number of reasons: regulated hunting seasons; a lessening of use of rivers as transportation corridors and hunting areas first by Native Americans and subsequently later by settlers; better range management; irrigation and planting of crops (Yocom 1961, Ball et al. 1981).

However, in the 1960s, many officials and bird lovers still worried about Canada Geese numbers because of habitat loss across the country. Wildlife officials and others apparently conducted several introductions in the Puget Sound area with eggs from nests soon to be covered by water backed up from dams (Price et al. 1999). A particularly large such operation took place as the John Day Dam neared completion in 1968 (Williams 2005). Bud Angerman, who worked at the South Tacoma State Game Farm during this time, traces the start of the breeding population of Pierce County Canada Geese to the goslings they raised that came from the John Day operation. At one point, they had over 300 birds to release. The local golf course complained about their poop, but the golfers liked seeing the birds so much that they carried bags of feed in the carts with them (Bud Angerman pers. com. 2009).

Meanwhile, over the last century, humans transformed the Puget Sound area from a region forested to the waterline into a "virtual geese paradise consisting of well-kept lawns, golf courses, parks and recreational fields." (Price et al. 1999) As development spread, hunting and natural predators declined. The mild climate meant birds obtained food easily year-round so that now Great Basin Canada Geese stay all year. Birds counted in the Olympia-Tacoma-Seattle area went from 69 to 5,591 from 1969 to 1997 (Price et al. 1999).

Vashon, fortunately, seems to have manageable numbers, though the geese are uncommon to common throughout the year. Several pairs breed on small residential ponds and protected inlets around the Island. The Vashon Allied Arts Garden Tour can sometimes be a good time to see a nest on some of the private ponds. In the middle of south Vashon, Joe Van Os has a pair in his field every year. Raccoons or Red-tailed Hawks have always taken their young. Goslings appear as early as May, following the adults. By August and September, large groups make the rounds looking for handouts, especially in Paradise Cove and inner Quartermaster Harbor and by Tahlequah.

BBS (USGS 2013): 2000

CBC by area (Trevathan 1999-2013) Trend: Stable.
Vashon North: 1999-2000, 2002-2003, 2005-2010, 2012-2013
Vashon South: 1999-2001, 2004, 2006, 2009cw, 2010, 2012-2013
Quartermaster Harbor: 1999-2003, 2005, 2007-2008, 2011, 2013
Maury Island-Tramp Harbor: 1999, 2001-2013

Trumpeter Swan

(SW, FW, AE) Status: Very rare to rare migrant and winter visitor.

The Trumpeter Swan likely passes by overhead in more winters than it is actually recorded. As with the Tundra Swan, more records depend on having enough birders on the Island observing and having the luck to look up at the right time. Fern Cove and Fisher Pond each have several sightings. Observers report sightings of birds in migration down Colvos Passage, over the center of the Island, and off KVI Beach.

In the 1800s, hunting pressure was so severe that the swan came near extinction. Some thought the U.S. population of the Trumpeter Swan to be down to 73 individuals in the lower 48 states by 1935 (Matthiessen 1959). The Hudson's Bay Company hunted the swans heavily on their northern Canadian breeding grounds from the 1770s through the end of the nineteenth century. Several hundred swans continued to winter in British Columbia as well (Banko 1960). Banko indicates that the Alaskan status of the Trumpeter Swan continued to be unclear for much of the 20th century. It wasn't until 1954 that Monson proved the existence of a breeding population on the Copper River (Monson 1956). The Migratory Bird Treaty and other hunting regulations put in place in the late 1800s and early 1900s halted the decline toward extinction of the Trumpeter Swan.

The recovery of the Trumpeter Swan began seriously in the United States with the creation of the Red Rock Lakes National Wildlife Refuge in Montana in 1935 (Banko 1960). Annual swan censuses started in 1929 show increases from the 1930s into the mid-1950s until the breeding population in the Red Rock Lakes area and Yellowstone National Park maximized the holding capacity of the protected habitat. In Washington State, the recovering population comes from birds breeding in Alaska (Wahl et al. 2005).

One of the current threats to the continued recovery of the Trumpeter Swan consists of lead poisoning from old lead shot present on the birds' feeding grounds. A significant number of swans are found dead in Washington and elsewhere each year after they reach down into the bottom mud of ponds and fields for their favorite vegetation and scoop up old shot (Wahl et al. 2005). Even with the banning of lead shot, so much remains from past years that the problem still haunts the birds. Numbers visiting Vashon in the past may have always been low. Regionally, several hundred swans winter around the Skagit delta area. A few small groups may also be found in various locations in Pierce, Pacific, and Grays Harbor Counties.

CBC by area (Trevathan 1999-2013):
Vashon North: 2008cw, 2009cw
Vashon South: 2013cw

Tundra Swan

(SW, FW, AE) Status: Rare migrant and winter visitor.

The Vashon status of the Tundra Swan remains somewhat uncertain. All sightings involve migrants flying by overhead or birds at some distance in saltwater. It appears they move by in most years, but building up the existing number of records requires the increased number of observers and shared reporting that developed since 2003. Observations mostly come from shoreline areas. Problems with separating identifications of Tundras from Trumpeter Swans compound the status situation.

Wood Duck

(FW) Status: Fairly common resident. Breeds.

"Few if any more exquisitely beautiful creatures have been fashioned in the workshop of Nature than the Wood Ducks of America." (Dawson and Bowles 1909). The population of the colorful Wood Duck contracted and expanded in Washington in response to hunting pressure and habitat change. Rathbun speaks of the Wood Duck as formerly common (in the latter part of the nineteenth century) but rare at the turn of the 20th century in the Seattle area (Rathbun 1902). Dawson describes Wood Ducks as limited to the area around the Columbia River in southwestern Washington (1909). Jewett et al. comment that after game regulation began, the Wood Duck population started to increase again (Jewett et al. 1953). Many hunting groups saw the damage done to Wood Ducks by over-hunting and worked to introduce them again, along with pheasant and quail. On Vashon, Walt Wagner was known for releasing many Wood Ducks, according to Ed Babcock, a member of the local Vashon Sportsmen's Club.

Wood Ducks prefer secluded, wooded ponds and require nest holes in trees and stumps. In some areas, clearing of the trees providing nest sites has likely been a problem. Another aspect of the recent growth in their population is the number of artificial nest boxes placed around ponds that provide alternative nest locations when natural ones are nonexistent. Several boxes stand at Fisher Pond and other locations around Vashon.

On Vashon, Wood Ducks breed at Fisher Pond and can consistently be found there year-round. They also breed, though found less regularly, on several other wooded ponds around the Island. Broods may be seen on Fisher Pond as early as the first week of May. Fledglings dot the pond throughout the summer. In 2002, two groups of very young fledglings showed up in mid-July. At the height of initial nesting attempts in late May, there can be so many Wood Ducks on Fisher Pond that walking to the edge and disturbing them may appear to make the whole surface of the pond go into motion as birds shift to the other end. The ducks use nest boxes but may also use snags at Fisher Pond and some other locations.

CBC by area (Trevathan 1999-2013) Trend: Irregular but highly impacted by years with ponds frozen over.
Vashon North: 1999-2009, 2011-2013
Vashon South: 2000, 2012-2013

Gadwall

(SW, SS, FW) Status: Rare fall through spring visitor. Change in Status: Since the first edition, birders reported many more Gadwall sightings, probably par-

tially as a result of increased observer knowledge and coverage. Another factor may be the higher population of this species in the Puget Sound region now. Gadwall should be considered rare as opposed to the prior status of very rare and may continue to become even more common.

Two records exist by Dan Willsie at Fisher Pond, on 6 and 25 November 1988, probably representing the same bird and the first dated records for Vashon. Ed Babcock, when he still hunted, saw them a few times at the Vashon Sportsmen's Club pond and Fisher Pond. After a gap of many years, in 2005 and 2006, one to two Gadwall began showing up with Mallard and wigeon flocks at Ellisport and KVI Beach. They appeared consistently throughout the winters of 2011/2012 and also 2012/2013.

This dabbling duck species apparently prefers more urbanized wetland and lake areas in Western Washington (Smith et al. 1997). An increase in introduced aquatic plants may also be a factor (Tom Aversa pers. com. 2005). Gadwall expanded their population and became a breeding species possibly as a result of the clearing of coniferous forests in the Puget Sound area. Prior to the 1950s, ornithologists considered Gadwall casual in Western Washington, by the 1960s, an occasional breeder, and by the mid-1970s, a regular breeder in the Seattle area (Canning 1983). Most of the larger Vashon ponds are wooded on their edges, as are many of the smaller ponds, shading out the aquatic shoreline vegetation. This may explain the rarity of sightings of Gadwall on the Island.

CBC by area (Trevathan 1999-2013):
Vashon South: 2013

Eurasian Wigeon

(SW, SS, FW, FL, DA) Status: Uncommon fall migrant and winter resident.

Eurasian Wigeons are Asian strays from the Arctic that migrate south through Alaska rather than Siberia. Generally any large flock of 50 to 100 American Wigeons may hold one or more Eurasian Wigeon. The male, with its reddish head, is easy to pick out from the American Wigeons. A large flock of wigeons congregates at Ellisport each fall. Other good locations include Christensen Cove, the ponds near Vashon Community Care Center, the Lisabeula area ponds along 220th, Tahlequah, the ponds along Westside Highway around the Cove and Colvos area, and the cove by the Cove Apartments at the end of 137th Avenue.

Ornithologists recognized Eurasian Wigeons as regular but rare vagrants across the United States for most of the 20th century (Edgell 1984). West Coast sightings, reported to regional editors of *American Birds*, increased from fewer than ten each year in the 1950s to over 100 per year by the mid 1980s. In his article on the matter, Edgell found that the increase involved more than just the increase in observers over the same time period (Edgell 1984). That trend continues to the present day but with no theories as to the cause. Currently, two to five Eurasian Wigeons show up each winter on Vashon without any known records before the 1980s.

CBC by area (Trevathan 1999-2013) Trend: Stable.
Vashon North: 2003, 2009, 2011-2013
Vashon South: 2000-2001, 2004-2006, 2008, 2009cw, 2010cw,
Quartermaster Harbor: 2010-2011, 2013
Maury Island-Tramp Harbor: 2001-2002, 2004, 2010-2013

American Wigeon

(SW, SS, FW, FL, DA) Status: Common fall and spring migrant and winter resident.

Bowles, a Tacoma ornithologist, reported seeing flocks of 500,000 wigeon at the Nisqually tide flats in the late 1890s, but saw barely a fraction of that in the early 1900s (Dawson and Bowles 1909). Natural fluctuations and heavy hunting caused numbers to vacillate over the last century.

Presently, American Wigeon are common both on saltwater shorelines and small ponds throughout Vashon. A large flock almost always builds up at Ellisport in the mid- to late fall through early winter, with smaller flocks at Cove, Lisabeula, Quartermaster Harbor, and Tahlequah. By midto late winter, the large flocks disperse into smaller groups across the Island's ponds and shore. Fisher Pond, the ponds along Westside Highway and Cedarhurst Road, the ponds along the road down to Lisabeula, and other ponds around the Island generally have wigeon in season. The late fall and early winter flocks in Tramp Harbor since 2007 and 2008 appeared to be impacted by an increased Bald Eagle presence. In some years, eagle predation continually breaks up the Ellisport flock, causing the wigeons to spread out earlier than in the past.

CBC by area (Trevathan 1999-2013) Trend: Somewhat up.
Vashon North: 1999-2000, 2002-2013
Vashon South: 1999-2013
Quartermaster Harbor: 1999-2003, 2005-2013
Maury Island-Tramp Harbor: 1999-2013

Mallard

(SW, SS, FW, FL, DA) Status: Fairly common resident. Breeds.

Truly adaptable breeders, Mallards nest in a large variety of habitats. J. H. Bowles, an early 20th century Tacoma area ornithologist, found a Mallard nest 150 yards from a pond under a pile of brush on a hillside (Dawson and Bowles 1909). He also discovered nests in heavy timber in the crotches of trees. Fledged young appear every breeding season at Fisher Pond. A nest was found at Meadowlake in the summer of 2002. Another at Mukai Pond lay in the middle of the field of canary grass. Mallards nest around many of the small ponds dotting the Island. They breed early and sometimes have more than one brood. Fledged young might be seen anywhere from late April into August.

Mallards on the Island also show up on saltwater, especially around creek mouths. In the fall, the author has noted them several times out at mid-channel along the Tahlequah ferry route. Mallards also drop in on residential yards and gardens and can be found in wet pastures and fields. The increase of their food supply due to the change from timber to agricultural fields, parks, and yards, as well as people's practice of feeding ducks helped expand their population.

BBS (USGS 2013): 1995, 1997, 1998, 2000, 2003-2005, 2009

CBC by area (Trevathan 1999-2013) Trend: Stable.

Vashon North: 1999-2013
Vashon South: 1999-2013
Quartermaster Harbor: 1999-2004, 2007-2013
Maury Island-Tramp Harbor: 1999-2013

Mallard duckling. © Doug Parrott

Blue-winged Teal

(FW) Status: Very rare spring visitor. Four records.

Blue-winged Teal are a fairly common breeder in lowland wetlands in Washington State, with a number of nesting records for King County (Smith et al. 1997). Numbers fluctuate from year to year. In the early 20th century, Dawson considered Blue-winged Teal to be among the rarest of Washington waterfowl (Dawson and Bowles 1909). Their numbers grew tremendously in the last half of the 20th century in Washington, possibly through use of greater habitat opportunities from the building of dams, expansion of agriculture, and irrigation (Wahl et al. 2005).

Only four recent Blue-winged Teal records exist on Vashon. A sighting at Fisher Pond was reported by Rick Sanders on 23 May 1993. Two males were seen by Dan Willsie at the Island Center Forest on 6 May 1993. The third sighting by Jill Andrews at Shawnee a few days after Willsie's was probably the same two males. A somewhat older sighting from 12 May 1982 appears in Phil Mattocks's *Earthcare Northwest* sightings column for that year. In the past, Ed Babcock can remember hunting teal at Fisher Pond and the Island Center Forest (Babcock pers. com. 2005). It would seem Vashon should have at least some more records, but perhaps the wetlands that exist fail to provide enough habitat for a more regular presence. Cinnamon Teal, too, appear in lower numbers on Vashon than one would expect.

Cinnamon Teal

(FW) Status: Very rare spring visitor. Two records. Change in Status: Further research and a recent sighting added Cinnamon Teal to the Island list since the first edition.

Russell Rogers, a biologist for the Washington Department of Natural Resources, spotted a Cinnamon Teal on 27 May 1993 at a marsh in central Vashon. The location was probably Fisher Pond or Mukai Pond (Smith et al. 1997, Rogers pers. com. 2009). Since the first edition, Jeff Adams found and photographed a male and female near the Cove Hotel on 1 May 2011.

Like Blue-winged Teal, Cinnamon Teal have several breeding records in King County and show up regularly at locations such as Montlake Fill in Seattle. In fact they bred each year from 2010 through 2013 at Montlake Fill and appear likely to continue to do so (Connie Sidles pers. com. 2013). Additional Vashon sightings might be expected on a more regular basis. It's unclear why they and Blue-winged Teal fail to appear as at least rare on Vashon. Perhaps wetlands occur in too small an amount and have insufficient age to have attracted these small ducks.

Northern Shoveler

(SS, FW) Status: Uncommon fall through winter.

The Northern Shoveler uses its large, broad, spade bill to prospect for pond vegetation and bugs in freshwater wetlands. Shallow Fisher Pond and Mukai Pond provide the most likely places to find this large dabbling duck. However, shovelers occasionally show up on saltwater at Ellisport and at the unnamed stream delta into Quartermaster Harbor at Portage. When freshwater bodies freeze over, they sometimes spread out to small, protected ponds that resist the cold. The author found a few in the wet fields at farms in Paradise Valley during the 2009 Christmas Bird Count. Occurrence and abundance of Northern Shovelers vary from year to year, with some years having several small groups of five to ten found reliably and other years seeing one or two small groups observed erratically through the season. Some years they stay late into the spring.

CBC by area (Trevathan 1999-2013):
Vashon North: 2005-2007, 2009, 2011
Vashon South: 2004, 2009

Northern Pintail

(SW, SS, FW) Status: Rare to uncommon fall through spring. Change in Status: Since the first edition, birders reported many more pintail sightings, probably partially as a result of increased observer knowledge and coverage. Pintail appear to be more uncommon than rare for Vashon.

A member of the dabbler group, pintails show up only in small numbers on Vashon each year, never more than two or three. An increase in knowledgeable observers resulted in records of at least one to two birds every year, present much or all of the fall through spring waterfowl season. Most records occur in the fall. A few birds visit in the winter and spring. Almost all sightings of pintail find them with Mallards, teal, and/or wigeons.

Pintail usually utilize mud flats created by stream deltas such as those at Ellisport, Dockton, and the mouth of Judd Creek. Records also exist for Fisher Pond. Pintail might show up in the ponds or fields along Westside Highway and Cedarhurst Road in the Colvos and Cedarhurst areas, so these areas should be checked carefully.

CBC by area (Trevathan 1999-2013):
Vashon North: 2011, cw2013
Vashon South: 2002, 2009
Quartermaster Harbor: 2002, 2004
Maury Island-Tramp Harbor: cw2001, cw2002, 2004, 2009

Green-winged Teal

(SW, SS, FW) Status: Breeds. Fairly common to uncommon spring and fall migrant and winter resident, very rare summer. Change in Status: First Vashon record of breeding occurred in 2010.

Green-winged Teal appear so small that the first ones returning in mid-August may easily be overlooked in the mass of young Mallards. By mid- to late September, a solid group of a half dozen to a dozen forage regularly at Fisher Pond or the estuary at KVI Beach. Other regular haunts include Fern Cove, Ellisport, Old Mill Road Pond, and small, wooded ponds around the Island. Numbers never reach more than a dozen or so and sometimes may be as low as a couple of pairs.

Green-winged Teal breed in Eastern Washington. West of the Cascades they nest rarely along sloughs and ponds with shrubby vegetation or trees (Smith et al. 1997). A number of records exist for King County (Hunn 1982). The Vashon-Maury Island Audubon field trip on 12 June 2010 found a male and a female with ducklings at Mukai Pond for the first confirmed breeding instance for Vashon. Generally, Green-winged Teal leave the Island by the first week or so of May.

CBC by area (Trevathan 1999-2013) Trend: Stable to slight upturn.

Vashon North: 2000-2001, 2003, 2005, 2007-2008, 2013
Vashon South: 2003, 2008-2009
Quartermaster Harbor: 2004
Maury Island-Tramp Harbor: 1999-2002, 2004, 2006, 2009-2011

Canvasback

(SW) Status: Very rare visitor. One record. Change in Status: New addition to Island list after the first edition.

Jeff Adams, Ross Adams, and Gary Shugart found the only Island record of Canvasback at Raab's Lagoon on 14 February 2009. Canvasback frequent very localized spots in the Puget Sound area from fall through spring. Why Vashon stays off their list of winter locations probably lies in their winter food preference for tubers and other plant material. Their body design and diving technique aim to help them penetrate deeply into the substrate under the water. They usually prefer larger-sized bodies of water in the form of shallow lakes or mud flat deltas in saltwater or brackish water (Mowbray 2002). Vashon has no lakes, only small ponds, and the eelgrass beds and mud flats tend to be of small size. The Island lacks proper habitat for an extended presence of this species, but it still seems surprising that this sighting provides the only recorded stopover.

Redhead

(SW, FW) Status: Hypothetical. Change in Status: All previous sightings have been determined to be escaped, captive-bred birds.

A few Redheads appear in the Puget Sound area each year in migration, making this a possible future addition to the Island list. Observers noted several birds for Christmas Bird Counts and one spring occurrence. All the sightings occurred near what was later determined to be a location where ducks were artificially hatched. These previous records are now considered escapees, not natural visits. Only saltwater sightings seem probable candidates for truly wild birds.

Ring-necked Duck

(FW) Status: Fairly common fall through spring.

This diving duck usually utilizes only freshwater ponds around the Island. A few show up at Fisher Pond, Mukai Pond, and other small wooded ponds on Vashon. Probably about a dozen or so total stay the waterfowl season. Ring-necked Ducks on Vashon tend to be very wary, staying far to the west end of Fisher Pond and using only secluded ponds. So far, all recent local sightings consist of birds on freshwater ponds. Ring-necks come regularly each year but numbers vary from a hard-to-find few to a bunch easily spotted at the main ponds.

> CBC by area (Trevathan 1999-2013) Trend: Stable to possible decrease but affected by frozen pond conditions.
>
> *Vashon North: 1999, 2001-2003, 2005-2008, 2010, 2013*
> *Vashon South: 2001-2002, 2005-2007, cw2009*

Greater Scaup

(SW) Status: Fairly common mid-fall through mid-spring.

In small numbers, up to four or five dozen, Greater Scaup return each year to Tramp and Quartermaster Harbors. This matches their winter habitat preference for shallow, protected waters, especially silty delta areas (Kessel et al. 2002). They occasionally show up along other saltwater shores of the Island. Greater Scaup eat a variety of foods, such as molluscs, crustaceans, eelgrass, and herring spawn (Angell and Balcomb 1982), all of which occur in Vashon's nearshore environment. Occasionally, a Lesser Scaup or two will be mixed in with a flock of Greater Scaup, serving as a nice comparison.

Greater Scaup around Vashon usually forage in groups of six to eight males and females, with three to five groups spread around various locations. In some years, groups of 30 to 50 might be seen. Washington Department of Fish and Wildlife reports indicate that a 72 percent decrease occurred in the north Puget Sound area based on the Marine Ecosystem Analyses of 1979 to 1980 and the Puget Sound Ambient Monitoring Program surveys of 1992 to 1999 (Nysewander et al. 2001). Vashon, part of the central Puget Sound region, appears to be bucking that trend so far.

CBC by area (Trevathan 1999-2013) Trend: Possible slight decline.
Vashon North: 1999, 2001-2003, 2008-2009
Vashon South: 1999, 2008, 2012-2013
Quartermaster Harbor: 1999-2013
Maury Island-Tramp Harbor: 2000-2002, 2004-2013

Lesser Scaup

(SW, FW) Status: Rare fall through spring.

Lesser Scaup occur on saltwater in areas such as Tramp and Quartermaster Harbors as well as on small freshwater ponds such as Old Mill Road Pond and Fisher Pond. In general, Lesser Scaup utilize saltwater only in migration and usually mix with Greater Scaup. Prior to the early 1900s, the scarcity of open freshwater ponds of any size on Vashon meant that Lesser Scaup were even more uncommon than they are now.

CBC by area (Trevathan 1999-2013):
Vashon North: 2006,
Quartermaster Harbor: 2011
Maury Island-Tramp Harbor: 2003, 2007-2008, 2012

Harlequin Duck

(SW) Status: Fairly common October through March, rare mid-May through September. Change in Status: Increased observer effort and a possible change in foraging locations led to more sightings since the first edition.

Harlequin Ducks breed on fast-moving streams in the state's mountain ranges. In the Puget Sound area, they forage in shallow water, at about one meter deep, often over eelgrass or kelp beds (Hirsch 1980). In migration and winter, Harlequins show up around many shoreline types but prefer rocky areas. Vashon has little to no true rocky shoreline except where stone riprap at locations like Tramp Harbor provides a facsimile. The lack of a true rocky shoreline habitat results in irregular occurrence of Harlequins around the Island. In some years, observers record few if any sightings of these colorful sea ducks, while in other years small groups routinely visit Tramp Harbor, the shore along Luana Beach Road, and Dockton. For the last several years, sightings increased as birds foraged reliably at two more visible locations, the shore just south of the Vashon ferry dock in front of the restaurant and along Luana Beach Road. Harlequins appear year-round, with increased and more regular observations in winter.

Washington Department of Fish and Wildlife reports depict numbers for Puget Sound as somewhat stable, with a possible slight decrease from 1993/94 to 2012/13 (Everson in process). Christmas Bird Count data for the Vashon sections of the count circle indicate an increase from 2007 to 2013, but the higher numbers may partially be an artifact of the ducks foraging in more easily visible locations such as next to the north end dock. The years 2005 and 2006 show "0" as the number seen, but observers noted Harlequin Ducks during the count week so the birds were indeed present during those years as well.

CBC by area (Trevathan 1999-2013) Trend: Irregular but possible slight increase, numbers low.

Vashon North: 2001, 2003, 2007-2013
Quartermaster Harbor: 2002, 2010
Maury Island-Tramp Harbor: cw2002, 2004, cw2005, cw2006, 2007, 2009-2011, 2013

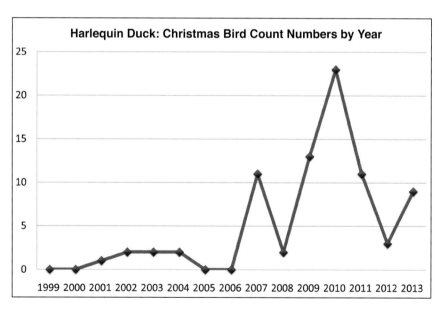

Surf Scoter

(SW) Status: Common fall through spring, rare summer.

Surf Scoters are the common sea duck seen in flocks of ten to 20 around both ferry docks and most saltwater locations around the Island. Large rafts of 50 to 100 or more Surf Scoters, mixed with White-winged Scoters,

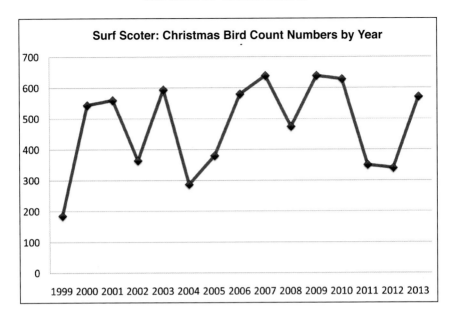

can be found most years at Tramp Harbor, off Portage in inner Quartermaster Harbor, and off Shawnee in outer Quartermaster Harbor. Sometimes the groups reach up to 300+ birds at any one location. Surf Scoters may be seen any month of the year, although usually a gap of occurrence takes place from early June through late July. Sometimes a few non-breeders stay or turn up in the summer.

Scoters busily dive for molluscs, mostly mussels and some clams. Sometimes, standing on the ferry docks, one can see them swim underwater to grab mussels or barnacles attached to the pilings. They also feed on eggs during herring spawning and sometimes move back and forth from different parts of Puget Sound as spawning events occur (Wahl et al. 2005).

Washington Department of Fish and Wildlife reports indicate that a 57 percent decline occurred for all three scoter species, considered as a whole, in the north Puget Sound area based on the Marine Ecosystem Analyses of 1979 to 1980 and the Puget Sound Ambient Monitoring Program surveys of 1992 to 1999 (Nysewander et al. 2001). Numbers in the central Puget Sound, the area including Vashon, showed a more stable pattern (Nysewander 2003). Analysis of data for 1993/94 to 2012/13 by the re-named Puget Sound Assessment and Monitoring Program show a continued, significant, approximately 50 percent decline for the region (Everson in process). The cause remains unknown. However, Surf Scoter data from the Christmas Bird Count for the Vashon sections of the count circle depict a steady population from 1999 to 2013 (Trevathan 1999-2013).

CBC by area (Trevathan 1999-2013) Trend: Variable but apparently stable.

Vashon North: 1999-2013
Vashon South: 1999-2013
Quartermaster Harbor: 1999-2013
Maury Island-Tramp Harbor: 1999-2013

White-winged Scoter

(SW) Status: Common fall through spring, rare summer.

Found around the ferry docks and common along the saltwater shorelines, the White-winged Scoter is another of the sea ducks. Dawson writes:

> "The precise alignment of this great black army is determined in part by the range of the shotgun, and more, perhaps, by the outlines of the reefs, mussel-beds, and barnacle-covered rocks which extend along our shores. The birds follow the fortunes of the tide throughout the day, feeding greedily as the retreat of the water makes otherwise unattainable depths accessible, and following up the return movement no less eagerly yet always a gun-shot offshore." (Dawson and Bowles 1909)

This notation describes fairly well the deployment of both Surf and White-winged Scoters around Vashon. One to several dozen always forage just about anywhere offshore. As with the Surf Scoter, good-sized rafts almost

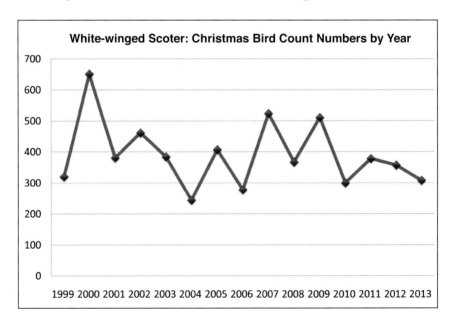

always occur in Tramp and Quartermaster Harbors. Returning White-winged Scoters arrive before the other scoters at the end of the breeding season. More non-breeding White-winged Scoters stick around during the summer months than non-breeding Surf Scoters. Usually, at least one or two and sometimes ten to 20 White-wings utilize Quartermaster or Tramp Harbors in late June or early July. During the rest of the year, they inhabit the same locations as Surf Scoters but in somewhat lower numbers.

Food and foraging habits for White-winged Scoter mimic those of the Surf Scoter, both relying mainly on molluscs and to some extent herring spawn. White-winged Scoters sometimes eat larger prey than other scoters when foraging together (Brown and Fredrickson 1977). Around Vashon, White-wings generally feed in the same areas and depths as Surf Scoters.

Washington Department of Fish and Wildlife reports indicate that a 57 percent decline occurred for all three scoter species, considered as a whole, in the north Puget Sound area based on the Marine Ecosystem Analyses of 1979 to 1980 and the Puget Sound Ambient Monitoring Program surveys of 1992 to 1999 (Nysewander et al. 2001). Numbers in the central Puget Sound, the area including Vashon, showed a more stable pattern (Nysewander 2003). Analysis of data for 1993/94 to 2012/13 by the re-named Puget Sound Assessment and Monitoring Program show a continued, significant, approximately 50 percent decline for the region as a whole (Everson in process). The cause remains unknown. White-winged Scoter data from the Vashon Christmas Bird Count for the Vashon sections of the count circle depict a steady population from 1999 to 2013 (Trevathan 1999-2013).

CBC by area (Trevathan 1999-2013) Trend: Variable but apparently stable.
Vashon North: 2001-2004, 2007-2012
Vashon South: 2000-2006, 2008, 2012-2013
Quartermaster Harbor: 1999-2013
Maury Island-Tramp Harbor: 1999-2013

Black Scoter

(SW) Status: Uncommon fall through spring.

The Black Scoter always arrives as the least common of the three scoter species in Puget Sound. A few dozen Black Scoters winter each year in Quartermaster Harbor and can be seen with the large scoter flock that gathers between Burton and Shawnee, off Raab's Lagoon, and near Manzanita at the harbor mouth. Black Scoters prefer sandy substrates or cobble areas less than ten meters in depth (Wahl et al. 2005). The shoreline between Northilla and Manzanita east of the harbor mouth in Puget Sound fits that description well, and a large flock of ten to 30 often winters there. Black Scoters tend to blend in with their closely related Surf and White-winged relatives, but they are the only ones that regularly vocalize in winter. Listening for the drawn-out, wheezing kazoo whistle of their call provides the best way to determine their presence, especially along the Northilla-Manzanita bluff line where trees block much of the view.

CBC by area (Trevathan 1999-2013) Trend: Up and down with every other year periodicity, possible slight increase over time.

Vashon North: 1999, 2002, 2006
Vashon South: 2004
Quartermaster Harbor: 1999-2003, 2005, 2007-2010, 2012-2013
Maury Island-Tramp Harbor: 1999, 2006-2008, 2010-2013

Long-tailed Duck

(SW) Status: Very rare winter visitor.

A rare sea duck for the central and southern parts of Puget Sound, the Long-tailed Duck appears off Vashon without its long, wispy tail. Sightings occur around Vashon, at most one to two each year. Records come from both ferry routes, Quartermaster Harbor, and Tramp Harbor. The longest occurrence involved two birds seen from the Tramp Harbor fishing pier through December and January of 2007/2008. All other instances consisted of quick, few-minute views.

Washington Department of Fish and Wildlife reports indicate the Long-tailed Duck population as fairly stable with perhaps a slight decline based on surveys by the Puget Sound Assessment and Monitoring Program from 1993/94 to 2012/13 (Everson in process). The duck remains too rare for Vashon to show a significant trend in Christmas Bird Count numbers.

CBC by area (Trevathan 1999-2013):

Maury Island-Tramp Harbor: cw2001, 2006

Bufflehead

(SW, FW) Status: Common fall through spring.

Bufflehead are easily the most common diving duck seen around Vashon. They forage in shallow water, usually three meters or less, diving for insects, crustaceans, and molluscs (Gauthier 1993). Bufflehead appear in ones and twos or even large groups of ten or 20 around the length of the saltwater shore. One or two will show up in about every freshwater pond bigger than a mud puddle. Groups of 50 or more occur in migration.

Washington Department of Fish and Wildlife reports indicate that a 20 percent increase occurred in the Bufflehead population in the north Puget

Sound area, based on the Marine Ecosystem Analyses of 1979 to 1980 and the Puget Sound Ambient Monitoring Program surveys of 1992 to 1999 (Nysewander et al. 2001). Numbers in the central Puget Sound, the area including Vashon, showed a smaller increase (Nysewander 2003). Continued surveys by the re-named Puget Sound Assessment and Monitoring Program depict numbers for Puget Sound as somewhat stable, with a possible slight decrease from 1993/94 to 2012/13 (Everson in process). Vashon Christmas Bird Count data look more complex, with a generally upward trend but experiencing some years of lower numbers (Trevathan 1999-2009).

CBC by area (Trevathan 1999-2013) Trend: Some up and down but generally upward.

Vashon North: 1999-2013
Vashon South: 1999-2002, 2004-2013
Quartermaster Harbor: 1999-2013
Maury Island-Tramp Harbor: 1999-2013

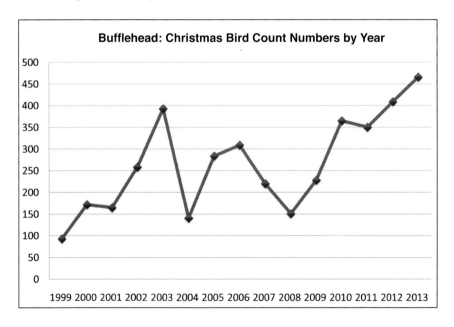

Common Goldeneye

(SW, FW) Status: Fairly common fall through spring.

Common Goldeneyes show up along the saltwater shorelines of Vashon. These medium-sized diving ducks possess omnivorous feeding habits. They eat small fish, slugs, snails, mussels, frogs, and both freshwater and saltwater vegetation (Johnsgard 1978). While saltwater forms the preferred habitat on Vashon, one or two occasionally visit Fisher Pond or Mukai Pond. A female non-breeder stayed the summer around the north end of Vashon in 2004.

Washington Department of Fish and Wildlife reports indicate that a 23 percent decline occurred for both goldeneye species considered together in the north Puget Sound area, based on the Marine Ecosystem Analyses of 1979 to 1980 and the Puget Sound Ambient Monitoring Program surveys of 1992 to 1999 (Nysewander et al. 2001). Numbers in the central Puget Sound, the area including Vashon, showed a gradual decrease through about 2000 (Nysewander 2003). Continued surveys by the re-named Puget Sound Assessment and Monitoring Program depict stabilization at the lower level for several years and then a return to a further slow decline through the 2012/13 season (Everson in process). Vashon numbers in the Christmas Bird Count indicate an increase from 2005 through 2013.

CBC by area (Trevathan 1999-2013) Trend: Significant increase over the decade, with one major dip 2003-2005.

Vashon North: 1999-2013
Vashon South: 1999-2013
Quartermaster Harbor: 1999-2013
Maury Island-Tramp Harbor: 1999-2013

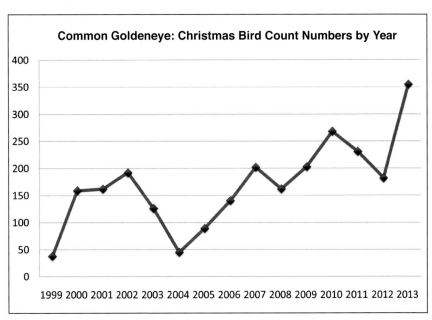

Barrow's Goldeneye

(SW, FW) Status: Fairly common fall and spring, common in winter.

Around Puget Sound, Barrow's Goldeneyes seem to prefer feeding on organisms attached to pilings (Wahl et al. 2005). On Vashon, as with the Common Goldeneye, Barrow's utilize the whole stretch of the Vashon shoreline. Fisher Pond and Mukai Pond make rare destinations. Tramp and Quartermaster Harbors often present great opportunities to compare the two birds together. Barrow's Goldeneye breed in mountainous areas in the north-central and northeastern parts of the state. The author once found a dead Barrow's Goldeneye in his cabin in the Okanogan after it dropped down the chimney in search of a nest site. It failed to get back up because of the damper. Like Wood Ducks and Hooded Mergansers, Barrow's Goldeneyes nest in holes in trees and occasionally use buildings. A study in the Canadian Okanogan found that good feeding opportunities proved more important than the proximity of water in the finding of nesting locations (Cannings 1987). This explains how the author's cabin, more than a mile from the nearest lake, might be chosen.

Washington Department of Fish and Wildlife reports indicate that a 23 percent decline occurred for both goldeneye species considered together in the north Puget Sound area, based on the Marine Ecosystem Analyses of 1979 to 1980 and the Puget Sound Ambient Monitoring Program surveys of 1992 to 1999 (Nysewander et al. 2001). Numbers in the central Puget Sound, the area including Vashon, showed a gradual decrease (Ny-

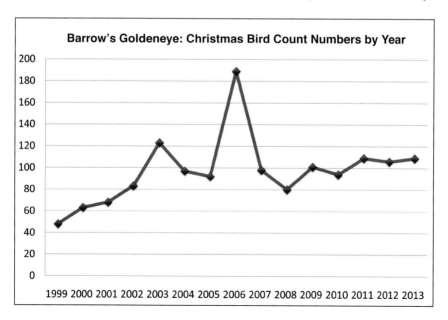

sewander 2003). Continued surveys by the re-named Puget Sound Assessment and Monitoring Program (PSAMP), depict stabilization at the lower level for several years and then a return to a further slow decline through the 2012/13 season (Everson in process). Vashon's CBC numbers differ from the PSAMP data, portraying a fairly stable wintering population with perhaps a slight increase.

CBC by area (Trevathan 1999-2013) Trend: Stable, with a slight increase.
Vashon North: 1999-2013
Vashon South: 1999-2013
Quartermaster Harbor: 1999-2013
Maury Island-Tramp Harbor: 1999-2013

Hooded Merganser

(SW, FW, HW) Status: Uncommon spring through fall, fairly common in winter. Breeds. Change in Status: Increased observer notice found more summer breeding birds since the first edition, moving summer status from rare to uncommon.

This strikingly plumaged diving duck occurs in small numbers on Vashon. From fall through spring, flocks of half a dozen primarily appear on saltwater at locations such as Tramp and Quartermaster Harbors. During this time of year, they show up in ones and twos with less regularity on freshwater. In late spring and summer, female Hooded Mergansers utilize Fisher Pond and other secluded, wooded ponds around the Island. Hooded Mergansers breed regularly on Vashon. They use Wood Duck nest boxes and holes in trees for their nests. Recent nesting locations have included Singer Pond, Old Mill Road Pond, and Mukai Pond. Hooded Mergansers probably did not breed on the Island prior to the creation of many freshwater ponds by farmers in the early to mid-1900s.

CBC by area (Trevathan 1999-2013) Trend: Fairly steady increase.
Vashon North: 1999-2001, 2003-2006, 2008-2009, 2011-2013
Vashon South: 1999-2003, 2006-2007, cw2009, 2010, 2012-2013
Quartermaster Harbor: 1999-2000, 2003-2005, 2007-2008, 2010-2012
Maury Island-Tramp Harbor: 2000, cw2002, 2004-2005, 2007-2011

Common Merganser

(SW) Status: Uncommon to very common fall through spring, rare early and late summer. Change in Status: Since the first edition, flocks of ten to 30 changed in some years to flocks of several hundred. Presence also is much more reliable than in the past.

The most unpredictable of the mergansers on Vashon, the Common Merganser forages along all of the saltwater shorelines of the Island. Sometimes a single bird, though usually in flocks of 30 to 50, these mergansers might be seen working together, heads dipped into the water to search for fish. They swim in a broad line to herd the fish and trap the prey in the shallows. In the winter of 2009/10, a flock hunting Quartermaster Harbor grew to over 400 birds.

Washington Department of Fish and Wildlife reports indicate that wintering numbers for merganser species as a whole remained stable in Puget Sound, based on surveys by the Puget Sound Assessment and Monitoring Program from 1993/94 to 2012/13 (Everson in process). Many other fish-eating waterfowl species experienced declines over the past 30 years for unknown reasons.

Common Mergansers breed on rivers and streams in King County and can be expected on larger ponds and lakes (Smith et al. 1997). No freshwater records exist for Vashon, because of the small size of the Island's streams and ponds. Christensen Cove near Lisabeula Park provides the most reliable location to find these ducks. They often rest on the shore there. The Tahlequah ferry run and locations around Quartermaster Harbor such as Dockton and the marina in the inner harbor offer other potential spots for finding them. Female Common Mergansers are easily confused with the ubiquitous females of the Red-breasted Merganser species, probably causing some undercount of their presence around the Island.

CBC by area (Trevathan 1999-2013) Trend: Stable with spikes for years with large flocks.

Vashon North: 1999-2001, 2008-2012
Vashon South: 1999, 2002-2013
Quartermaster Harbor: 2000, 2002-2005, 2007-2013
Maury Island-Tramp Harbor: 2004, 2006-2007, 2009-2013

Red-breasted Merganser

(SW) Status: Common fall through spring.

Red-breasted Mergansers make up the majority of mergansers seen in winter on Vashon. They leave before the other waterfowl species in the spring and return after the scoters in fall. Usually they spread in small groups fairly evenly around the Island. Large numbers sometimes fly into the mouth of Quartermaster Harbor just before dark for shelter during the night. Frequently four or five hang out around the ferry docks, Tramp Harbor, and the straightaway south of Burton in Quartermaster Harbor.

Washington Department of Fish and Wildlife reports indicate that wintering numbers for merganser species, as a whole, remained stable in Puget Sound, based on surveys by the Puget Sound Assessment and

Monitoring Program from 1993/94 to 2012/13 (Everson in process). Many other fish-eating waterfowl species experienced declines over the past 30 years for unknown reasons.

CBC by area (Trevathan 1999-2013) Trend: Irregular but appears stable.
Vashon North: 1999-2010, 2013
Vashon South: 1999-2013
Quartermaster Harbor: 1999-2013
Maury Island-Tramp Harbor: 1999-2002, 2004-2013

Ruddy Duck

(SW, FW) Status: Rare in winter.

Fairly common in many areas around the Sound, Ruddy Ducks on Vashon can be hard to find. Quartermaster Harbor between Portage and the mouth of Judd Creek provides the most reliable location for them. Ruddies breed mainly in Eastern Washington. A few nest in areas such as the Kent Ponds in King County (Smith et al. 1997). Almost all Island records occur on saltwater, though single birds showed up in March at Fisher Pond on at least two occasions. Ruddies breed in large wetlands and winter in highest densities in major natural and human-made estuarine habitats. Vashon's small scale seems to preclude a bigger presence of these ducks.

CBC by area (Trevathan 1999-2013) Trend: Too irregular to characterize.
Vashon South: 2001
Quartermaster Harbor: 2000-2003, 2005, 2007, 2010-2013

Quail

California Quail

(FL, ST, DA) Status: Introduced, extirpated. Former breeder. Change in Status: Only possibly extirpated at last printing; no sightings of birds not hatched by humans occurred since 2003.

The list of Vashon's introduced game birds includes the California Quail. Old-time Islanders remember them as abundant as far back as the mid-1920s (Carey 1976). The gradual change of habitat away from clear-cuts and agricultural fields reduced quail habitat. They utilize garden areas to some extent, creating a slight offset for loss of agriculture and open fields. That adaptability may account for their longer survival when the other small game bird introductions disappeared. Their lack of success compared to the pheasant on the Island may be in part because of fewer introduction attempts and their smaller size, making them more vulnerable to feral cats and dogs. The last consistent locations for quail on Vashon include Old Mill Road, Burton Hill, and parts of Maury Island. Since 2003, even these areas no longer possess quail, adding them to the Island extirpation list. Isolated sightings after 2003 appear to be released birds.

BBS (USGS 2013): 1996, 1997

CBC by area (Trevathan 1999-2013):
  CBC: *Vashon South: 1999, 2000, 2001, 2002, 2003*

Northern Bobwhite

(FL) Status: Introduced, extirpated.

The Northern Bobwhite, like the California Quail, was once common on the Island. Sportsmen first introduced them around Washington during the beginning of the 20th century (Smith et al. 1997). Kitchin noted them around Quartermaster Harbor in 1925 (Kitchin 1925). John Friars, an Island native and birder, remembers bobwhites as common into the 1940s (Friars pers. com. 2005). About the mid-1940s, they began a Puget Sound-wide decline reaching Vashon a little later. Ed Babcock remembers that the Vashon Sportsmen's Club re-introduced them again in 1955, but the bobwhite failed to survive (Babcock pers. com. 2005). The decline of open areas contributed to the final extirpation of the bobwhite population on the Island (John Friars pers. com. 2005, Larrison 1952). In addition, feral cats and unmanaged pets likely contributed heavily to their decline. Every once in a while, escapees and some deliberate introductions show up. An observer noted one bird on Blake Island in 2001. In 2007, one enthusiast released several birds, and reports came in over several months, then tapered off and ended. An unidentified person hatched and released an unknown, large number of bobwhite in early 2009. Over a score of sightings from all of Vashon (but none from the Maury Island area) came in over several months but finally faded to none.

Partridges and Grouse

Gray Partridge

(FL) Status: Introduced, extirpated.

Formerly called Hungarian Partridge or "Huns," Gray Partridges were introduced in many locations around the state (Smith et al. 1997). They still live in good numbers in the dryland wheat farms of Eastern Washington but died out west of the Cascades, including on Vashon. Possible reasons for their failure include lack of enough grassland habitat and an increase in predation by feral cats and dogs. Open fields steadily disappeared as the forests reclaimed more area of the Island. From the memories of Islander Ed Babcock, it appears that Gray Partridge developed a long enough presence, probably at least a decade, meriting them a spot on the Vashon list (Babcock pers. com. 2005).

Chinese Bamboo-Partridge

(FL) Status: Introduced, extirpated. Change in Status: Placed on the Vashon list for the first edition, further discussion indicates that listing as an error. Apparently these partridge only lasted a few seasons after introduction.

Ed Babcock, with the Vashon Sportsmen's Club, recalls that "Bamboo Quail" were introduced to the Island in 1955 (Babcock pers. com. 2005). A member of the club, who was a pilot, worked with local game officials and the Japanese government for an exchange of California Quail from the U.S. for Bamboo Quail from Japan. The birds died out sometime later.

Ring-necked Pheasant

(FL, ST, DA) Status: Introduced. Fairly common resident. Breeds.

Ring-necked Pheasant are the only introduced game bird on Vashon to develop something close to a sustainable breeding population. The birds were probably first released around the beginning of the 20th century. Since then, the Vashon Sportsmen's Club and others release new birds on the Island at least once a decade. The latest release the author knows about occurred in August 2002. A number of already established birds generate successful broods, maintaining the base population. Ring-necked Pheasants' ability to use a greater range of open habitat types may be one reason for their success compared to other game birds on the Island. Their larger size may protect them to some extent from feral cats and unmanaged pets.

Vashon Christmas Bird Count data over the last decade indicate a fairly consistent period of decline. This also matches anecdotal evidence consisting of a general sense that fewer birds remain. The Vashon population may be headed for extirpation. The large Raccoon population, major numbers of cats and dogs, and an expanding Barred Owl and Bald Eagle presence may be combining with a declining habitat base to eliminate the Island's Ring-necked Pheasants.

BBS (USGS 2013): 1995-1998, 2000-2006, 2009

CBC by area (Trevathan 1999-2013) Trend: Indicates decline then stable at very low numbers.

Vashon North: 1999, 2001-2006, 2008-2009, 2011-2012
Vashon South: 1999-2008, cw2009, 2010-2013
Maury Island-Tramp Harbor: 2001-2005, 2008-2011

Sooty Grouse

(DC, WC) Status: Former breeder, extirpated. Formerly known as Blue Grouse.

Sooty Grouse bred down to the waterline in the Puget Sound area before European settlers arrived. Early ornithologists found Sooties nesting in what is now Seward Park in Seattle (Rathbun in Bent 1963). David Hutchinson, owner of Flora & Fauna Books, knows of these grouse still being on Harstine Island in the 1990s. Observers historically found Sooty Grouse more in disturbed, second-growth Douglas-fir or burnt-over forests in the Puget Sound area and on Vashon (Ed Babcock pers. com. 2005; Campbell et al. 1990; Jewett et al. 1953; Rathbun 1902).

Until the 1940s, habitat was apparently good for them on Vashon. Ed Babcock, with the Vashon Sportsmen's Club, remembers hunting Sooty Grouse for years until they declined in the late 1940s and disappeared in the mid-1950s (Babcock pers. com. 2005). Roland Carey, the late Island author, also mentions them as common in *Isle of the Sea Breezers* (Carey 1976). Larrison writes of them on Vashon in his *Field Guide to the Birds of King County* (Larrison 1947). While forests covered pre-European settlement Vashon, local Native Americans kept open a number of areas by controlled burns. In the mid-1850s, the first surveyors for the state noted several large, possibly naturally burned-off areas. Many waves of logging and forest fires occurred between the 1870s and 1950s. The amount of logging on Vashon diminished extensively by World War II, creating fewer disturbed areas. Fire prevention disrupted the natural fire regime that provided snags and semi-open areas in the woods. After the last major wave of fires and logging on the Island immediately following World War II, the Sooty Grouse fell into decline and disappeared on Vashon.

Babcock feels that the decline of the Sooty Grouse was caused by the end of major burns and cutting on the Island (Ed Babcock pers. com. 2005). Degradation of habitat creates vulnerabilities, allowing other factors to overcome a species' population. Hunting pressure was probably partly responsible yet unlikely the sole reason for their demise; feral cats and dogs possibly contributed more than hunting did. As the habitat declined and more people moved to the Island, their pet castoffs and uncontrolled pets would have had a devastating effect on a once fairly predator-free area.

Loons

Red-throated Loon

(SW) Status: Uncommon fall and spring migrant, fairly common winter. Change in Status: Better observeration coverage indicates these loons are fairly common in winter rather than uncommon.

The best location for a close look at the Red-throated Loon is in Quartermaster Harbor between Dockton and Shawnee, out in the middle of the outer harbor, or the inner harbor near Portage. These loons may be found along any saltwater shoreline area around the Island; other reliable locations, if from afar, include the north end ferry dock and the Tramp Harbor fishing pier. Red-throated Loons may come quite close inshore, sometimes into the surf. They hunt for bottom fish, molluscs, and crustaceans, which leads them to fish the close inshore waters (Angell and Balcomb 1982). In his Western Grebe censuses, Dan Willsie found these loons by watching for them fishing close by but separately from the rafts of Western Grebes in Quartermaster Harbor (Willsie pers. com. 2005).

Red-throated Loons appear to be the least common of the regularly occurring loons on the Island and may sometimes be missed when mistaken for a Pacific Loon. Usually the loons forage in small numbers, with from one to five or six birds present. Larger groups sometimes move through. In the winter of 2008/09, a large flock stayed around for several weeks, making them easy to view in Tramp and Quartermaster Harbors.

Red-throated Loons show a serious decline in their Puget Sound population, according to Washington Department of Fish and Wildlife studies (Nysewander et al. 2003). Vashon CBC numbers for this loon appear erratic, with numbers showing more declines than up years in the first decade of the 21st century. The last four CBCs, 2010 through 2013, depict steady, steep increases, back up to the earliest high marks recorded for the Vashon count. These dramatic up and down swings in numbers make it difficult to determine a definitive trend for this species around the Island.

CBC by area (Trevathan 1999-2013) Trend: Erratic.
Vashon North: 1999-2000, 2002, 2006-2009, 2012-2013
Vashon South: 2001, 2003
Quartermaster Harbor: 1999-2005, 2007-2013
Maury Island-Tramp Harbor: 1999-2000, 2002-2004, 2008, 2010-2012

Pacific Loon

(SW) Status: Uncommon fall and spring migrant, fairly common winter. Change in Status: Better observer coverage indicates these loons are fairly common in winter rather than uncommon.

Pacific Loons tend to stay farther out and use deeper waters than Red-throated Loons, but views of them are possible along any saltwater shoreline area. Tramp Harbor and the west side of Quartermaster Harbor across from Manzanita provide the most reliable locations for Pacific Loons. In the last few years, the Tramp Harbor fishing pier allowed some good views, with birds at times swimming under the dock. They also show up along the various viewing areas of Colvos Passage. Vashon waters have a herring population, one of the prey populations for the Pacific Loon (Angell and Balcomb 1982).

CBC by area (Trevathan 1999-2013) Trend: Appears stable but variable.
Vashon North: 2000-2003, 2006-2007-2011, 2013
Vashon South: 1999-2000, 2002-2004, 2006-2007, 2009
Quartermaster Harbor: 1999-2002, 2004, 2007, 2010-2011, 2013
Maury Island-Tramp Harbor: 2000, 2007-2013

Common Loon

(SW) Status: Fairly common fall through spring, rare and local in summer.

Common Loons bred in many areas across Washington but now nest on a very few mountain lakes in King County and the northern tier of counties (Smith et al. 1997). On the Island they may be found along any shoreline area, especially KVI, Tramp Harbor, Quartermaster Harbor, and Point Robinson. Vashon's ponds appear too small to attract loons. Occasionally these water birds might be heard or spotted flying overhead across the Island. Sue Trevathan noted three over Paradise Valley in the spring of 2001. In many years, one or two non-breeders spend some of the summer in Tramp Harbor. Otherwise Common Loons absent themselves during the breeding season. The first birds arriving in the fall still possess their breeding plumage.

CBC by area (Trevathan 1999-2013) Trend: Stable but variable.
Vashon North: 1999-2004, 2006-2013
Vashon South: 2002-2003, 2006-2010, 2013
Quartermaster Harbor: 1999, 2001-2013
Maury Island-Tramp Harbor: 1999-2013

Yellow-billed Loon

(SW) Status: Very rare winter visitor. Six records.

The Yellow-billed Loon ranks as very rare to rare in King County. Only six records exist for Vashon, three likely representing the same bird. One was observed in late winter off Vashon Island in the late 1970s (Hunn 1982), another showed up off the Tahlequah ferry on 17 November 1984 (Bock 2008), and Gene Hunn discovered an immature from the Tramp Harbor fishing pier on 25 January 2008 (Hunn 2012). Walter Wehtje took excellent photos of one in Tramp Harbor on 28 December 2012, and observers saw it for an additional two days. Subsequently, Kathryn True and Karen Fevold possibly saw the same bird off the north end ferry dock on 9 February 2013, as did Isadora Wong on 9 March 2013 at Fern Cove. An albino

individual spent several winters on nearby Commencement Bay around the turn of the millennium.
CBC by area (Trevathan 1999-2013):
Maury Island-Tramp Harbor: cw2013

Grebes

Pied-billed Grebe

(SW, FW) Status: Fairly common resident, breeds.

The weird call of the Pied-billed Grebe, sounding like some jungle creature or twisted squirrel, can be heard regularly at Fisher Pond. It remains on the pond year-round and possibly breeds there regularly. The first nests weren't observed until the spring of 2003. A pair built nests at both the east and west end of the pond (Dan Willsie pers. com. 2003). The author noted adults feeding two striped-headed young on 3 September 2012 for the first record of young birds seen.

Pied-billed Grebes are common breeders in the Puget Sound area, using emergent vegetation to attach a floating nest (Smith et al. 1997). Other freshwater locations Pied-billed Grebes visit in spring include Ernst Pond along Old Mill Road and Mukai Pond. The fishing pier and Portage in Tramp Harbor provide the best saltwater spots for this small grebe from fall through spring. Saltwater observations prove considerably less common than fresh.

CBC by area (Trevathan 1999-2013) Trend: Indeterminate, not counted too many years. Numbers undoubtedly affected by years where ponds freeze over.

Vashon North: 2000-2002, 2006, 2013
Quartermaster Harbor: 2007-2009
Maury Island-Tramp Harbor: 1999-2000, cw2002

Horned Grebe

(SW) Status: Common fall through spring, very rare to rare summer. Change in Status: Since the first edition, a Horned Grebe stayed through summer in two, possibly three, years.

Undoubtedly the most common and easy to find of all the grebes around Vashon, Horned Grebes show up in small groups all around the Island. Sometimes a larger group of fifteen to 20 will come together and dive for fish as a unit, making quite a swirl in the water as they dive in a coordinated manner and then reappear simultaneously. They forage for fish and some crustaceans primarily in shallow waters. All Vashon records occur on saltwater because while possible on freshwater, Horned Grebes prefer medium- to large-sized lakes. Most birds leave by the end of May, but for at least two years, possibly three, an adult stayed the summer in the Portage area of Quartermaster Harbor.

CBC by area (Trevathan 1999-2013) Trend: Periodic ups and downs edging upward.

Vashon North: 1999-2013
Vashon South: 1999-2013
Quartermaster Harbor: 1999-2013
Maury Island-Tramp Harbor: 1999-2013

Red-necked Grebe

(SW) Status: Fairly common fall through spring.

Usually the first to arrive of all the grebes, the Red-necked Grebe sometimes appears in the fall in its namesake breeding plumage. From late August through September, a noticeable migration, with flocks of 20 to 30 or more, moves through Tramp Harbor. While much more localized in occurrence than Horned Grebes, Red-necked Grebes can be regularly found around the north end ferry dock, Tramp Harbor, KVI Beach and Quartermaster Harbor, and Tahlequah. These grebes often utilize areas with eelgrass beds (Wahl et al. 2005).

CBC by area (Trevathan 1999-2013) Trend: Variable but edging up.

Vashon North: 1999, 2001-2013
Vashon South: 2000-2007, 2009-2011, 2013
Quartermaster Harbor: 1999-2007, 2009-2013
Maury Island-Tramp Harbor: 1999-2013

Eared Grebe

(SW) Status: Uncommon to fairly common fall through spring. Change in Status: Increased numbers of observers with the knowledge to differentiate this species from Horned Grebe resulted in many more sightings each year.

Around Vashon, the Eared Grebe utilizes shallow saltwater habitat like the similar Horned Grebe. Groups of Horned Grebes should be scanned for one or two Eareds for comparison. In migration, sometimes many small groups move through. Tramp Harbor from the fishing pier to Portage and Quartermaster Harbor off Shawnee provide the most reliable locations for finding this grebe, though it might appear along any of the Island shores.

CBC by area (Trevathan 1999-2013) Trend: Increase over second half of period.

Vashon North: 2000, 2008
Vashon South: 1999, cw2005, 2008-2009
Quartermaster Harbor: 1999-2001, 2003, 2005, 2007, 2009-2013
Maury Island-Tramp Harbor: 2005, 2007, 2011-2012

Western Grebe

(SW) Status: Common fall through spring.

Western Grebes form large rafts of birds in Quartermaster Harbor every winter. They usually hang out in the middle of Quartermaster Harbor, the outer edge of Tramp Harbor, or out in the middle of Colvos Passage. Close-in looks happen much less frequently. Smaller groups might be seen along the ferry routes or along any of the shoreline areas from time to time. In the fog, their presence can only be told by the sound of their scratchy call reverberating in the mist.

In the early to mid-1990s, as much as eight to ten percent of the state's wintering population stayed in Quartermaster Harbor. The National Audubon Society designated the harbor as an Important Bird Area because of the over 5,000 Western Grebes censused regularly. Unfortunately, a decline in numbers started about the time of the designation. Vashon Christmas Bird Count data show a decline from over 1,600 grebes counted in the 1998/99 count to seventeen for 2008/09 in the Quartermaster Harbor section of the Vashon count circle (Trevathan 1999-2013). For the last several years, winter flocks in Quartermaster Harbor range only from 100

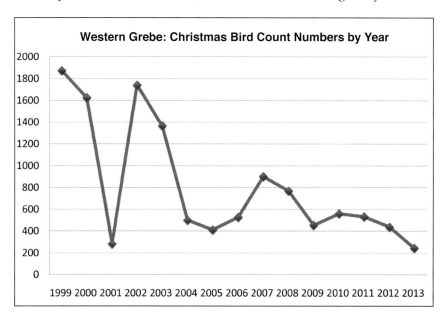

to 200 birds. For all the Vashon-only sections of the count circle, the numbers went from 1,873 for the 1998/99 count to 245 in the 2012/2013 count.

Washington Department of Fish and Wildlife (WDFW) studies show a significant decrease in marine birds of many species in Puget Sound over the last 20 years (Nysewander et al. 2001, 2003). Western Grebes in the northern sub-region of Puget Sound show a 95 percent decline. The cause for the decline remains unexplained. Speculation as to the reasons ranges from disturbances to the birds and their habitat on the breeding grounds to declines in key prey populations such as herring (Donovan and Bower 2004). Numbers for the Western Grebes in WDFW research originally held stable for the central Puget Sound area around Bainbridge and Vashon Islands. But the decline evidenced by Vashon CBC figures for the last several years indicates that these areas begin to match the similar reduction in population seen in the northern region of Puget Sound. Studies by WDFW involving the Quartermaster Harbor Pacific Herring stock describe a peak in numbers in 1995 followed by a decrease through 2012 (Stick and Lindquist 2009, Kurt Stick pers. com. 2013). As the fall in Western Grebe counts parallels that of herring, there may be a correlation between the two. While WDFW considers the Vashon herring stock depressed since monitoring began, the overall Puget Sound herring population health appears stable. Western Grebe numbers diminished across the region, so issues with herring numbers can be but a part of the problem for the grebe.

CBC by area (Trevathan 1999-2013) Trend: Dramatically down throughout the period.

Vashon North: 1999-2003, 2006-2010, 2012-2013
Vashon South: 2000-2013
Quartermaster Harbor: 1999-2013
Maury Island-Tramp Harbor: 1999-2004, 2007-2008, 2010-2013

Clark's Grebe

(SW) Status: Very rare winter. Three records.

This Western Grebe look-alike is extremely rare around the Island. The Clark's Grebe was identified as a separate species in the 1800s, then lumped together with the Western Grebe until being split into a distinct species again in the 1980s. Clark's Grebes are rare but regular winter visitors in Puget Sound. Listed as very rare in winter, Clark's Grebe will likely be recorded increasingly as more experienced observers become available to check out the flocks of Western Grebes that winter near Vashon. Bill color is the best way to tell the Clark's from the Western. The Clark's has a bright yellow to orange bill, while the Western's is a duller yellow. In breeding plumage, the black cap extends over the eye in the Western

Grebe but not in the Clark's. Only three records exist: a sighting on 23 October 1994 by Rick Sanders at his house near Fern Cove (National Audubon Society 1971-1994, *AB*49:92), two seen at the mouth of Quartermaster Harbor by Bent Blichfeldt on 19 April 2005, and one for the 2012 Christmas Bird Count in the inner harbor by the author on 31 December 2011.

CBC by area (Trevathan 1999-2013):
Quartermaster Harbor: 2012

Shearwaters and Petrels

Northern Fulmar

(SW) Status: Very rare fall visitor. One record.

A pelagic species common off the Washington coast, the Northern Fulmar rarely visits the lower Puget Sound area. In some years, storms may blow normally pelagic birds such as fulmars into the central and southern Puget Sound. In mid-October 2003, a number of fulmars strayed as far south as Nisqually after a large storm (*WOSNews* 92, August/September 2004, page 9). Kevin Li spotted one Northern Fulmar probably just outside the area covered in this book. He observed the bird from a boat just past mid-channel toward the West Seattle side, parallel with Lincoln Park, on 14 October 2003. Rick Sanders found another at mid-channel off the Vashon ferry on 13 November 2003.

Sooty Shearwater

(SW) Status: Very rare fall and winter visitor. One record.

The Sooty Shearwater closely resembles the Short-tailed Shearwater and is often seen off the coast in the tens of thousands. Sibley describes the Short-tailed as "distinctly smaller-billed and rounder-headed than the Sooty. Averages smaller with narrower and more angled wings..." (Sibley 2000). Shearwaters rarely enter deep into Puget Sound, and only a few records exist for King County. Either ferry or the waters off Tahlequah and Point Robinson make for the best possibilities for viewing this species. Steve Caldwell has the only record with a 30 January 1996 sighting off the north end ferry dock.

Short-tailed Shearwater

(SW) Status: Very rare fall and winter visitor. Two records.

Normally a pelagic species, the Short-tailed Shearwater occasionally wanders or is blown in by a storm to the lower Puget Sound. Either ferry or the waters off Tahlequah and Point Robinson make the best possibilities for viewing this species. The first record for King County was off the south end of Vashon Island on 18 January 1942 by J. Slipp. Intense winter storms brought pelagics of several species as far south as Nisqually (Hunn 1982, Slipp 1942b). Alan Richards saw four off Point Robinson on 18 November 1977 during the largest inshore incursion by Short-tailed Shearwaters recorded up to that time in Washington's inner waters (Hunn 1982).

Fork-tailed Storm-Petrel

(SW) Status: Very rare visitor. One record.

Fork-tailed Storm-Petrels breed on rocky islands along the northwest tip of Washington State and generally live as a pelagic species. A major storm brought several into Puget Sound in mid-October 1997. Many were seen up and down the Sound. Dave Beaudette saw ten off the Vashon-Fauntleroy ferry on 14 October 1997 and single birds on 16 and 17 October 1997.

Leach's Storm-Petrel

(SW) Status: Very rare visitor. Two records.

Leach's Storm-Petrels breed on the outer coast, like the Fork-tailed Storm-Petrel. One wandered far into the inner waters of Puget Sound. Observers noted it from 14 to 25 December 1995 off the Vashon-Southworth ferry (Wahl et al. 2005). Another bird may have been in Vashon waters when Erik Steffens saw it off Alki Point while on the passenger-only ferry. It or a different one was also seen near the Fauntleroy dock by Rick Sanders on 8 September 2010.

Frigatebirds

Magnificent Frigatebird

(SW) Status: Accidental. One record. Change in Status: Added to the Vashon list since first edition because of new research into records of past sightings.

Magnificent Frigatebirds breed in tropical waters off both coasts of Central America and in the Caribbean. Jeff Zimmerman and Marcye Miller noted one that flew from Point Defiance up Colvos Passage to Point No Point on 8 October 1988. It stayed around Point No Point for several days (Mattocks 1988, Hunn 2012).

Boobies

Brown Booby

(SW) Status: Accidental. One record. Change in Status: Added since the first edition because of new research into records of past sightings.

Brown Boobies breed in the Hawaiian Islands, the Gulf of California, and other areas in tropical waters worldwide. They often range hundreds to thousands of miles from colonies. One rode a boat's mast from Blake Island to Tacoma, passing through Vashon waters on 18 May 2002 (John McMillan *WOSNews* 82, December 2002/January 2003, page 11; Hunn 2012).

Pelicans

Brown Pelican

(SW) Status: Rare spring through fall visitor. Change in Status: Since the first edition, Brown Pelicans have appeared more often; they are now seen every year.

Brown Pelicans spread up the coast from California and have become common along the Pacific shores in summer and fall (Wahl et al. 2005). Occasionally, they wander into Puget Sound and should be watched for off any Island waterfront. Brown Pelicans, along with many raptors such as the Bald Eagle and Peregrine Falcon, faced severe population reductions from egg thinning caused by the use of DDT. The spread up the coast from California came as their numbers rebounded with the banning of DDT. The change in status for Vashon reflects their continued increase in numbers in Washington.

Brown Pelican. © Gregg Thompson

Dave Beaudette observed ten Brown Pelicans on 17 October 1997, as part of the same storm drift that brought the Fork-tailed Storm-Petrels mentioned above, providing the first Vashon record (Dave Beaudette pers. com. 2005). Observers then noted birds every couple of years in the fall. Beginning in 2006, several sightings occurred each year from late April through mid-November, ranging from off the north end ferry dock to Tahlequah. Most records consisted of pelicans flying by. Once at Point Robinson, several stopped and rested for some time. All but two of the observations took place off the east and south passages of Vashon. Alan Huggins watched one off Jensen Point in Quartermaster Harbor on 30 August 2008. Bob Hawkins saw one by Dockton in Quartermaster Harbor on 28 May 2006.

Cormorants

Brandt's Cormorant

(SW) Status: Fairly common fall through spring. Rare to uncommon summer. Change in Status: Since the first edition, numbers and locations have increased and a summer presence is now noted, moving the species to fairly common from uncommon.

Brandt's Cormorants formerly showed up in late fall and in recent years moved their return from breeding to early or mid-summer. They should be looked for along any saltwater shoreline area. Like the Pelagic Cormo-

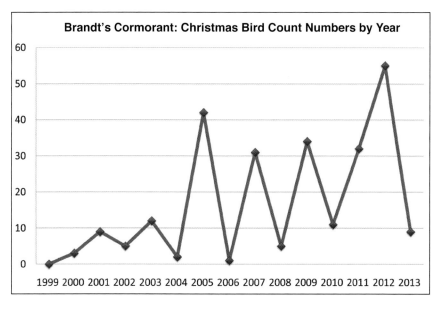

rants, they appear quite localized in their occurrence around Vashon. In the 1990s, while some observers noted them elsewhere, the Brandt's largely used buoys and small unattached docks from the mouth of Quartermaster Harbor to Shawnee and also the pilings at the end of the Tahlequah dock. Finding them was hit or miss, and generally only small numbers were counted. In the last half decade, they began utilizing the pilings at the north end ferry dock, staying in full breeding plumage until at least the end of May. Half a dozen to a dozen are nearly always present fall through spring, sometimes showing up in early summer. They prefer to forage in deeper waters, depths greater than 20 meters (Wahl et al. 2005), which likely explains their smaller numbers compared to other cormorants around Vashon.

> CBC by area (Trevathan 1999-2013) Trend: Shows periodic every other year up and then down, with an overall upward movement. Seen in only one to two count sections for the first twelve years of counts but seen in all four for the last three.
> *Vashon North: 2011-2013*
> *Maury Island-Tramp Harbor: 2011-2013*
> *Vashon South: 2003, cw2004, 2005-2006, 2008-2013*
> *Quartermaster Harbor: 2000-2005, 2007-2013*

Double-crested Cormorant

(SW, FW) Status: Common fall through spring, irregular in summer. Change in Status: Over the last few years, this cormorant extended its presence to include small numbers during the summer months.

The Double-crested Cormorant's very common status around Vashon relates to its preference for feeding in shallow waters. One or two might be found swimming or perched on a piling along any saltwater shoreline area. They are nearly always present at the ferry docks, often with 50 or more at Tahlequah in the late fall and winter. Double-crested Cormorants are the only local cormorant species that appears on freshwater. They show up frequently on Fisher Pond, Mukai Pond, and other ponds. While generally absent during the summer, one or two non-breeders visit from time to time. Double-crested Cormorant numbers appear to be increasing in Washington (Wahl et al. 2005). Apparently egg-gathering for food and oologist collections reduced numbers early in the 20th century (Vermeer and Rankin 1984). Their numbers increased dramatically over the last three decades across the country. Twenty-four states currently allow shooting to reduce numbers, rightly or wrongly considering them a threat to fish populations (Gary Shugart pers. com. 2005).

CBC by area (Trevathan 1999-2013) Trend: Appears stable.
Vashon North: 1999-2013
Vashon South: 1999-2013
Quartermaster Harbor: 1999-2013
Maury Island-Tramp Harbor: 1999-2013

Pelagic Cormorant

(SW) Status: Fairly common to uncommon fall through spring, irregular summer. Change in Status: Over the last few years, this cormorant extended its presence to include the summer months in small numbers.

Much less common than Double-crested Cormorants, Pelagic Cormorants can generally be seen around the ferry docks in ones or twos. While possible around other Island saltwater shoreline areas, observers noted them in Tramp Harbor only a few times and not consistently in Quartermaster Harbor. They look much smaller than the other cormorants and have a thin, snaky neck. As breeding season approaches, they develop two white patches low on their flanks that easily differentiate them from the other two cormorants. Pelagics breed mostly on the outer coast and the north

Pelagic Cormorant. © Ed Swan

end of Puget Sound. A colony formed in 2003, using a Bremerton bridge as its breeding site, which possibly provides the cause for their new summer presence since 2011 at the north end ferry dock. They prefer rocky cliffs rather than the Island's clay bluffs (Jewett et al. 1953), making nesting here unlikely.

> CBC by area (Trevathan 1999-2013) Trend: Shows periodic ups and downs, with slightly upward movement.
>
> *Vashon North: 1999-2004, 2006-2009, 2013*
> *Maury Island-Tramp Harbor: 2000, 2006, 2008, 2012-2013*
> *Quartermaster Harbor: 2001, 2006, 2009-2013*
> *Vashon South: 1999-2009, 2011*

Herons and Egrets

Great Blue Heron

(SW, SS, FW, FL, HW) Status: Fairly common resident. Breeds.

Great Blue Herons are one of the emblematic birds of Vashon. They show up just about everywhere: on the shore, at docks, out in fields, and up high in trees. Often, especially just before dawn, one sits on the dolphin (a structure aiding docking) by the ferry dock watching the boats leave and come in from Fauntleroy.

These big herons feed opportunistically, eating all sorts of prey from frogs to fish to mice, which is why they show up in many different locations and habitats. The characteristic view of these birds consists of them posing motionless, silently staring into the water, poised to spear fish from a dock or shoreline. In freshwater ponds, they stalk fish and introduced Bullfrogs, which do so much damage to indigenous amphibians. Out in the farm fields, they might find a mouse, vole, or a snake.

Great Blue Herons create an odd sight when making an ungainly landing high in the forest. Though it may seem strange, these wading birds nest high up in trees, breeding in loose colonies called rookeries or heronries, located in riparian areas. Mileta Creek on Maury Island hosted the largest such local rookery. Several others existed around Vashon. In the last decade, Bald Eagles severely impacted the breeding productivity of Great Blue Herons on Vashon. Eagles disrupted and/or destroyed every major heronry. The herons seem to be trying to adapt by spreading out into smaller groups.

Rayna Holtz monitored the herons at Mileta Creek and around Vashon in general for several years. She reported in 2005:

"Herons have not completed a nesting season at the Mileta Creek site in years (since 1994). Of the 130 nests that were there in 1990, I believe there are now less than ten. The first big abandonment was in 1994, when eagles and crows evidently began serious harassment. Meanwhile, a heronry started near Spring Beach in 1994 or 1995, which grew to about 20 nests before eagles chased the herons off around 1997. Another started at Raab's Lagoon in about 1996, and there were fourteen nests in alder east of the lagoon until eagles chased them off the second year (a local resident observed several conflicts). A few nests along the west shore of the lagoon were disturbed both by land clearing and eagles, and were abandoned. A single tree in Don Raleigh's yard on the Burton Peninsula hosted nests for a few years. In one year during the mid-1990s, two nests successfully raised young. A nest in a tall tree on the neck of Burton Peninsula produced young in 2001, but eagles may have taken them before they fledged. At this site, herons skipped two years, then began nesting again in 2004 but were driven away in May 2005, again by eagles. A single nest above a pond at the north end had three young in 2002, but the owner observed an eagle harassing them, and subsequently the parents abandoned their effort. The tree itself has been snapped by a winter storm. In 2005 there were several nests on Burton Hill, but an observer saw a mob of over 50 crows driving off the parents and eating eggs. It is not clear yet whether any more eggs will be laid or hatched, though nesting activity has taken place since the crow attack." (Holtz pers. com. 2005).

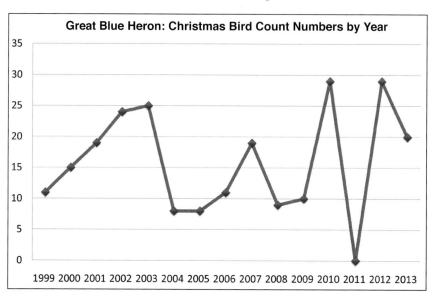

Rayna's account from 2005 pretty much describes the experience since that date. The only confirmed nesting attempts since 2005 occurred on the Burton Peninsula or on Burton Hill. A few herons achieved success for one year, but in every case by the second year, Bald Eagle attacks killed all the chicks.

Great Blue Heron Christmas Bird Count statistics hold stable for Vashon. The herons' population may not be affected by the nest predation as yet. Bald Eagle numbers continue to rise around Vashon and Puget Sound in general. The relationship between the two species shows the complexities of the changing ecological balance in the region. Curbing the use of pesticides like DDT and stopping persecution brought the Bald Eagle back from endangered status. At the same time, the population of one of their main food stocks, salmon, declined precipitously over the past decades. Now a new equilibrium and ecological web will eventually be established since the old, pre-settlement web received such a comprehensive shake-up. Observers can only watch and learn at this point to see what sort of new balance will be created.

BBS (USGS 2013): 1995-1997, 2001, 2002, 2004, 2006

CBC by area (Trevathan 1999-2013) Trend: Variable but apparently stable.

Vashon North: 1999-2003, 2005-2010, 2012-2013
Maury Island-Tramp Harbor: 1999-2010, 2012-2013
Quartermaster Harbor: 1999-2010, 2012
Vashon South: 1999-2002, 2004-2006, 2008-2010, 2012-2013

Great Egret

(SS) Status: Very rare visitor. Three records.

Great Egrets breed east of the Cascades in Washington. Their post-breeding exodus often brings wanderers west of the mountains or up from farther south in the late summer or fall. Three records exist for Vashon: one on 7 September 1991 observed by Dan Willsie and Rich Siegrist at Ellisport, one seen by Russell Rogers on 6 August 1996 (*WOSNews* 47, February 1997, page 8), and one found in late August 2004 by Joe Henke at Fern Cove.

Cattle Egret

(FL) Status: Accidental. One record.

Joy Nelsen found a Cattle Egret in a pasture in Dockton on 24 November 1992 for the sole record (P. Mattocks, archival notecards, Seattle Audubon Society). This rarity may be seen on Vashon again because post-breeding birds wander regularly into Washington State.

Green Heron

(SS, FW, HW) Status: Very rare spring through fall visitor. Change in Status: Since the first edition, there has been only one sighting of this species, resulting in a change in status from rare to very rare.

Green Herons are an elusive, quiet marsh bird. They began expanding north into Washington in 1939 as part of a range expansion up the coast of the Pacific states (Smith et al. 1997). Many juvenile egrets and herons display a post-breeding northward dispersal. The wandering of young, first-year birds appears to have led to the range extension of the Green Heron (Campbell 1972).

Related to the Great Blue Heron, Green Herons appear much smaller and generally prefer marshy, reedy ponds or shorelines. Their quiet, secretive nature makes it difficult to determine how many visit Vashon. One dependable fall location is the marina in Quartermaster Harbor, where they perch on mooring lines, boats, and docks. The adjacent mud flats at low tide, from the marina to the mouth of Judd Creek, seem to produce some sightings. Records exist for most of the Island's ponds and the Tahlequah dock on sev-

Bald Eagles are opportunistic hunters, sometimes catching their own food—herons, reptiles, or fish (as shown here)—and sometimes stealing from others, especially Ospreys. © Tim Kuhn

eral occasions. Peter Murray photographed a juvenile at the Vashon Golf & Swim Club, possibly bred on Vashon. This species may nest on Vashon. Murray's bird may alternatively have flown in from off-Island.

New World Vultures

Turkey Vulture

(FL, AE) Status: Rare late winter and early summer, uncommon spring and fall migrant. Change in Status: Better observer coverage increased sightings of this species, moving the Turkey Vulture's status from rare to uncommon.

Turkey Vultures migrate over Vashon in late March through April and again from late September through early October. The return for spring begins as early as February for the Puget Sound region. One bird flew over Point Robinson on 5 February 2006. Sightings come from the whole length of the Island. Records range from a single bird to groups of 30 to 50 or 100 birds. Most observations consist of birds flying by. Rich Siegrist noted one landing in a recently cut field on 28 June 2009, presumably to scavenge dead mice. Crows and a raven chased it off. It appears a few vultures wander over Vashon from late May into July, probably birds breeding on the slopes of the Olympics to the west.

Hawks and Allies

Osprey

(SW, FW, AE). Status: Fairly common spring through fall. Breeds.

Many birds of prey, including Osprey, became more common again after the discontinued usage of the pesticide DDT (Ehrlich et al. 1988). Legal protection against shooting by fishermen who feared competition from the Osprey provided further assistance in population regeneration. Dawson and Bowles (1909) and Jewett et al. (1953) comment on the persecution faced by this raptor. In the last decade or so, the construction of nesting platforms on all sorts of structures boosted Ospreys' breeding success.

Ospreys nest in several locations on Vashon, the number in 2012 reaching up to at least six or seven. The top of a cell phone tower in the middle of the Island served as the sole nesting location from around 1999 to 2004, and that site has continued to the time of printing of this edition. Listeners hear peeping birds from that nest in summer near the Vashon Center area. In 2004, Ospreys built an additional nest on another cell tower by the golf course on Maury Island, and in 2006 a third pair nested on the cell tower along the highway by the Episcopal church. Since then, at least one additional pair joined the rest about every other year, occasionally utilizing cell tower sites. One pair near the entrance at Camp Sealth used a tree. Cell towers sometimes present hazards. The nest on the CenturyLink building cell tower on Vashon Highway burst into flames on the evening of 19 June 2012, killing that year's young. Officials listed the cause as "spontaneous combustion," but more likely adults or young moved nesting material against a live wire.

Ospreys prove to be very successful fishers. In over 30 years of birding, the author has rarely seen an Osprey miss its meal. They soar over ponds, lakes, and slow rivers seeking fish. They also hunt over saltwater and sometimes in the surf. They occasionally catch a fish so large that they float with their talons down in the water, getting a better grip, before they work their way airborne again. On Vashon, they check out every little pond as well as the shorelines and Dalco Passage.

BBS (USGS 2013): 2003

Bald Eagle

(SW, SS, FW, DC, WC, HW, AE) Status: Fairly common resident. Breeds.

The Bald Eagle approached extinction in the United States because of shooting and the egg-thinning effects of the pesticide DDT (Ehrlich et al. 1988). Dawson and Bowles comment that they were common in the Puget Sound region in the late 1800s. Their population dropped precipitously in the last two decades of the nineteenth century through persecution (Dawson and Bowles 1909). The author remembers Bald Eagles being rare in Puget Sound when he was a teenager in the 1970s, whereas presently, not

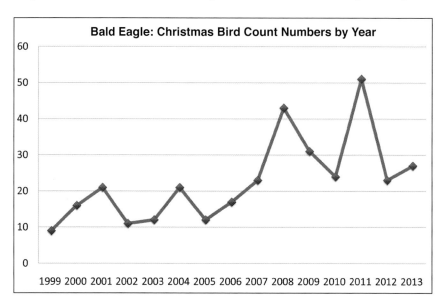

seeing a Bald Eagle on any given day causes comment. They show up year-round, though they spend the late summer and early fall in most years off-Island, presumably checking out rivers and streams with larger numbers of salmon than Vashon has. Their numbers continue to increase under protection. They now nest in many of the major parks in Seattle and in several locations around Vashon. Each year, a number of pairs utilize nest sites in large coniferous trees and snags. Periodically, storms blow the big nests down, and a pair will need to start building all over again.

Bald Eagles show up most commonly hunting, scavenging, or stealing food from other birds and animals along the shorelines of the Island. Their diet is correspondingly widely varied, consisting of fish, mammals, and birds, dead or alive. Tramp Harbor makes a good place to watch them diving on the large waterfowl populations in winter. The author speculates that the wigeon gathering in fall at Ellisport may actually be dispersing earlier, at least in some years, because of pressure from the increasing number of Bald Eagles. This book also discusses the eagles' impact on the nesting success of Great Blue Herons in the heron account. Island chicken farmers know to watch out for eagle predation. The eagles catch fish near the surface of the water and may sometimes actually be in the water for a few moments like an Osprey. The author received some frantic calls about an eagle "hurt" or "stuck" in the water near Burton in March 2004. Peter Murray determined later that the eagle had caught a Surf Scoter that it was attempting to bring to shore. Six to seven other eagles waited nearby to see if they could get a piece of the duck. The author once watched an eagle hounding an otter with a large perch at Reddings Beach. The otter, noticing the author, quickly changed course up the beach to pass nearby, successfully using the author to get the eagle to back off long enough for the otter to escape with the fish.

BBS (USGS 2013): 1997, 2003, 2006

CBC by area (Trevathan 1999-2013) Trend: Shows increase that appears to be getting even larger over the last five years.

Vashon North: 1999-2013
Maury Island-Tramp Harbor: 1999-2013
Quartermaster Harbor: 1999-2013
Vashon South: 1999-2013

Northern Harrier

(FL, AE) Status: Uncommon spring and fall migrant, rare winter. Change in Status: Northern Harrier was originally noted only in migration, but since the first edition, observers saw birds once in the winter of 2007, several times in the winter of 2011/12, and throughout the winter of 2012/13. Its status may eventually

change to uncommon in winter. The status change may be a single bird choosing to return each year post-breeding but may also be due to better observer coverage.

When more farm fields and unused pasture provided suitable habitat, observers often saw harriers flying back and forth across the Island's open areas, stalking rodents. They have a characteristic low, rapid glide over the grass, expertly maneuvering in any sort of breeze or wind. With the decrease in open areas, Northern Harriers now show up primarily in migration. About half of the migration sightings occur along shorelines and the other half wherever the appropriate habitat still exists, such as Wax Orchard, Paradise Valley, and the farm area around Colvos. Usually the observer gets a quick glance, only long enough for identification as the harrier moves along. During the last two winters, watchers noted a male and sometimes a female in the large open fields of Wax Orchard. This may be a permanent change in status for the species on Vashon. The large set of fields at Wax Orchard appears to provide enough open country to sustain one to two harriers. The only other possible locations for wintering might be along Westside Highway in the Colvos area, to the west of Vashon Highway around 140th Avenue, and the area west of the old K2 site.

CBC by area (Trevathan 1999-2013):

Vashon South: 2013

Juvenile Sharp-shinned Hawk trying to get at the author's chickens. © Ed Swan

Sharp-shinned Hawk

(FW, FL, DC, WC, HW, ST, DA, AE) Status: Uncommon resident. Breeds.

This little accipiter often hunts small birds around bird feeders. Avian prey makes up 90 percent of a Sharpie's diet (Johnsgard 1990). This raptor's preference for birds made young chickens a favorite item, although adult hens would be too large. Three fledgling Sharp-shinned Hawks born in the woods next to the author's home in 2013 tried to go after the author's hens. They gave up each time at the last moment as they realized the hen was twice their size. Farmers and "sportsmen" gunned many hawks down by the thousands until they were protected. On the east coast, their quite pronounced migrations provide a great spectacle. Hundreds of hawks fly by a single location in one day. Bent notes in one instance at Cape May, the great fall migration trap in New Jersey, gunners shot over 1,400 sharp-shins in a single day. In nearby Pennsylvania, a hunting party "in a remarkably short-time" killed 90 sharp-shins, sixteen goshawks, eleven Cooper's Hawks, 32 Red-tailed Hawks and two Peregrine Falcons (Bent 1961a).

Sharp-shinned Hawks utilize open areas along the woods all around the Island. Their numbers likely fluctuated greatly with the clearing of the forests, the coming of agriculture, the advance of residential areas, and subsequent reforestation. Their population probably grew with the increase in edge areas bordering coniferous woods.

Sharp-shinned Hawks nest in coniferous forest and present an extremely difficult challenge to find in the breeding season (Smith et al. 1997). Brenda Sestrap on Maury Island and Erin Kenny on Paradise Ridge found Sharp-shinned nests in coniferous forests in 2003. Sue Trevathan watched young begging for food from adults and being mobbed by jays at the Island Center Forest in August 2004. Five young were very actively learning to fly and hunt behind the author's house on Paradise Ridge in mixed forest in August 2005.

BBS (USGS 2013): Unidentified accipiters noted 1997, 1998, 2002

CBC by area (Trevathan 1999-2013) Trend: Stable, numbers always low.
Vashon North: 1999-2003, 2006, 2011, cw2013
Maury Island-Tramp Harbor: 1999, 2001, 2003-2004, 2006-2009, 2011-2012
Vashon South: 2000-2001, 2003-2009, 2011-2013

Cooper's Hawk

(FW, FL, DC, WC, HW, ST, DA, AE) Status: Uncommon resident. Breeds.

A larger version of the Sharp-shinned Hawk, the Cooper's Hawk utilizes forested areas and open edge areas along forests, such as yards and gardens (Smith et al. 1997). The clearing of the Island's original woods likely created a significant dip in their populations (Raphael et al. 1988). The subsequent succession of mixed forest indicates that their numbers expanded to be higher now than before European-American settlement.

Cooper's Hawks breed more openly in deciduous forest or mixed woods than Sharp-shinned Hawks do (Smith et al. 1997). They still often act secretively around the nest, and only the loud peeping, begging calls of young birds give their presence away. Many more Vashon nesting records exist for Cooper's than for Sharp-shinned. Joy Nelsen found a nest in the late 1990s behind the Country Store and Gardens in Vashon Center. In 2001, nests were active above Tramp Harbor and in the woods north of Old Mill Road. In August 2005, a young bird, apparently still learning the ropes, landed on Rebecca Davies's back as she worked in her garden on Maury Island. Both human and bird were a little startled, then the hawk flew a short distance into the trees. For several years, a pair nested across the street from Fisher Pond and raided the pond for young Killdeer, Mallard, and Wood Duck. Cooper's Hawks soar from time to time, but like the Sharp-shinned, they are probably most often found swooping through flocks of birds at bird feeders.

Birds make up about 50 percent of a Cooper's Hawk's diet (Johnsgard 1990). In the past when there were more farms on Vashon, Cooper's Hawks occasionally hunted chickens and domestic pigeons, sometimes coming right into the chicken coop to take their meal (Bent 1961a). As with the Sharp-shinned Hawk, this led to even greater persecution than hawks usually face.

BBS (USGS 2013): 2004, Unidentified accipiters noted 1997, 1998, 2002

CBC by area (Trevathan 1999-2013) Trend: Stable, numbers always low.

Vashon North: 2003, cw2004, 2007, 2009-2011
Maury Island-Tramp Harbor: 2000-2003, 2005-2010, 2012-2013
Vashon South: 1999-2000, 2002, 2004-2005, 2007, 2009, cw2010, 2011-2013

Northern Goshawk

(WC) Status: Very rare. One record.

Probably resident before clear-cuts ended the reign of old-growth forests on the Island, the largest accipiter rarely visits Vashon. Goshawk formerly nested down to the waterline in mature forests throughout the Puget Sound area (Wahl et al. 2005). The proper habitat remains too small on Vashon for them now. Ray Mielbrecht gave a good, detailed description of one in the Lisabeula area in August 2001.

Red-tailed Hawk

(FL, DC, WC, HW, ST, DA, AE) Status: Uncommon resident. Breeds.

The most common large hawk on the Island is the Red-tailed Hawk. Bald Eagle and Osprey are the only other birds of similar size. Both grow significantly larger than the Red-tail, and the adults develop white heads. When one sees a big hawk flying in the sky on the Island, so big it seems like an eagle, it's almost always a Red-tailed Hawk unless the white head of an eagle shows. Sub-adult Bald Eagles have a dark head, yet appear about a third larger than a Red-tail.

While there aren't any other big hawks on the Island, Red-tailed Hawks can be a little difficult to identify because they can display quite a bit of variety. Their plumage ranges from a light brown back and very light front to all black with a red tail. The most common form of the Red-tail in Washington has a brown head and a bright red tail. The breast shows white with a streaked reddish-brown bellyband ("a varsity shirt," as the author's wife calls it) and white underparts. Most of the Island's Red-tails seem to be on the lighter side. For several years, a very dark bird lived in the Tahlequah area. It was colored a deep, chocolate brown with reddish breast and tail. Observers in the Puget Sound area occasionally see Harlan's Hawk, another subspecies of the Red-tail. These birds look blackish like the dark western Red-tail but have vertical white streaks on the breast and a smudgy gray tail with a black tip.

Red-tails show up everywhere on the Island except in thick woods. Even there they might be seen overhead passing through. They use many habitats, including fields, forest edges, and especially the edges of the bluffs following the shorelines. Rodents are their main source of food. Given the rat population on the Island, Red-tails find plenty to eat. They forage opportunistically, catching an unwary bird or snake now and then. Joe Van Os observed adults feeding garter snakes to young in nests in the Old Mill Road area. The increase in open areas on Vashon since the 1800s undoubtedly led to an increase in the numbers of Red-tails. Some of the more likely places to see them are Lisabeula, Wax Orchard, Old Mill Road near the pond, Point Robinson, and Maury Island Marine Park. Coming south from the Vashon ferry, one can nearly always see a Red-tail gyring overhead in the late afternoon in the big fields along the highway.

On 6 September 2006, Bent and Marie Blichfeldt noted an oddity about a Red-tail at their place in Dockton. The bird had an elongated upper mandible that curved extensively down. According to the Falcon Research Group, x-rays indicate "Long-billed Hawk Syndrome" comes from accelerated growth of the keratin sheath, not the underlying bone (Falcon Research Group, 2009). Alaska has the largest concentration of this phenomenon, especially in Black-capped Chickadees, followed by the Pacific Northwest. Examples pop up around the country. The cause is unknown.

BBS (USGS 2013): 1996, 1998, 2000, 2002, 2005, 2013

CBC by area (Trevathan 1999-2013) Trend: Stable.

Vashon North: 1999-2006, 2008-2009, 2011, 2013
Maury Island-Tramp Harbor: 1999-2013
Quartermaster Harbor: 2010
Vashon South: 1999-2013

Rough-legged Hawk

(FL, AE) Status: Very rare winter visitor. One record. Change in Status: First record since first edition.

Rough-legged Hawks live in open country, breeding north on the tundra and wintering in mostly treeless areas such as fields, prairies, marshlands, and shrub steppes. In Washington, they are fairly common east of the Cascades in winter and in farm country such as the Skagit delta west of the mountains. They are rare in King County. Ezra Parker found the first Rough-leg for Vashon along the grass airport runway at Wax Orchard on 7 December 2012. The bird stuck around for about a month.

CBC by area (Trevathan 1999-2013):

Vashon South: 2013

Rail and Coot

Virginia Rail

(SS, FW) Status: Uncommon resident. Breeds.

This elusive marsh bird shows up regularly at the wetlands at Portage. Its secretive nature lessens the chances for observation. Using a tape of its call in the early morning is probably the best means to hear and/or see the Virginia Rail. (Please do not overdo tape playing, especially during breeding season.) Virginia Rails use a number of freshwater wetlands and may be widespread in spring and summer. Alan Huggins found a road-kill immature along the highway around 140th on 27 August 2002, confirming breeding. At Lisabeula on 30 December 2000, Dan Willsie found one captured by a pet, looked it over, and set it free. Observers record them annually for the Christmas Bird Counts at Portage Marsh. Steve Caldwell heard them at the Monument Road marsh in the spring of 2001, and Sue Trevathan had a summer record at Old Mill Road Pond on 28 June 2002.

CBC by area (Trevathan 1999-2013) Trend: Stable.

Vashon South: 2001-2008, 2011, 2013

American Coot

(SW, SS, FW) Status: Very rare visitor fall through spring. Change in Status: Coot sightings dwindled in number since the first edition, with no records in half of the years, changing their status to very rare from rare.

Coots prefer larger freshwater ponds and lakes and require large quantities of emergent vegetation for nesting (Smith et al. 1997). With only one large freshwater pond and one small pond possessing significant patches of cattails, Vashon lacks preferred habitat. Coots do little more than visit the Island. The pilings at the Quartermaster Harbor marina, at Ellisport, and the Tramp Harbor pier attract the occasional coot, and a number of winter records exist for Mukai and Fisher Ponds.

Crane

Sandhill Crane

(SS, FL, AE) Status: Very rare spring and fall migrant. Seven records. Change in Status: Sightings of cranes dropped, with only two records in the years between the first and second edition, moving their status to very rare from the original rare standing.

Sandhill Cranes formerly bred on both sides of the Cascades (Jewett et al. 1953). The loss of wetlands to development reduced Sandhill Cranes to migrants in Western Washington. All but one of the Vashon records occurred in fall migration. Carole Elder noted the latest occurrence, at least one heard overhead at Camp Sealth on 31 March 2013. Peter Murray observed three Sandhill Cranes flying over the golf course on 13 October 2003. Bob Seibold saw one in the fields behind the K2 plant in the fall of 2002. John Friars saw one flying over his house in September 2000, and Joe Van Os reported seeing them from his place on Maury Island in the past.

Plovers

Black-bellied Plover

(SS) Status: Very rare spring and fall migrant. Four records.

Dan Willsie found one Black-bellied Plover at KVI Beach on 20 September 2002. The bird looked like it was in juvenile plumage. Two spring records exist for KVI as well, one seen by the author on 3 May 2006 and another by Margie Morgan on 23 April 2013. The author found the fourth observation for Vashon at Fern Cove on 24 April 2013. This shorebird is regularly found elsewhere around the Puget Sound region in the larger estuaries in winter on sandy and muddy flats or roosting in nearby agricultural land. Vashon lacks the habitat in the size required to attract more than the occasional plover.

Semipalmated Plover

(SS) Status: Uncommon fall and rare spring migrant, very rare winter visitor.

Semipalmated Plovers visit Vashon's sandy beach areas, estuaries, and mud flats in low numbers. They look somewhat like a smaller, single breast-striped version of the more common Killdeer. KVI Beach and Fern Cove provide the most consistent locations for finding these plovers. They also show up at the stream delta of Ellisport and the sandy point of Point Robinson. One late winter record exists, a bird seen at KVI Beach by John and Ellie Friars on 1 February 2007.

Killdeer

(SS, FW, FL, DA) Status: Fairly common resident. Breeds.

The "robin" of the shoreline, Killdeer have a pattern of scooting across the beach similar to that of a robin crossing a lawn. They shoot across the sand or grass for a few feet, then pause and go again. Killdeer are easily found and heard on most sandy and pebble beaches around the Island. They utilize other open areas such as wet fields, pasture, and ball fields. Killdeer are quite noisy and can be heard sounding the alarm at any time of day or night. Anywhere from four or five to 20 hang out year-round at KVI Beach, and in August at Fern Cove numbers often top 50 birds. From mid-summer to mid-fall when Fisher Pond dries up, many Killdeer move from shoreline areas to the pond, foraging in the large developing mud patches.

Ample breeding evidence exists for Killdeer on Vashon. Their nests sit right out in the open as just a simple dip, perhaps lined with little stones. Killdeer use loud calls as they run from the nest or drag a wing to fake injury in order to distract predators from their eggs and young. A family has bred several years in a row in a horse pasture near Vashon Center. Locations with nests found include Agren Park by Sue Trevathan, Point Robinson and Mukai Pond by Dan Willsie, and the cemetery by Rich Siegrist.

BBS (USGS 2013): 1995-1998, 2000-2003, 2005, 2006, 2009, 2013

CBC by area (Trevathan 1999-2013) Trend: Appears highly variable but likely stable.

Vashon North: 1999-2001, 2003-2005, 2007-20102
Maury Island-Tramp Harbor: 1999-2001, 2003-2005, 2008-2013
Quartermaster Harbor: 1999-2000. cw2001, 2002, 2004, 2009-2010, 2012
Vashon South: 1999-2006, 2008-2013

Oystercatchers

Black Oystercatcher

(SS) Status: Very rare visitor. One record.

As denizens of the coast's rocky shores, Black Oystercatchers rarely reach into the King County portion of Puget Sound, where there are only three records, including Vashon's only sighting (Hunn 2012). The nearest breeding sites for Black Oystercatchers exist around Port Angeles and Deception Pass, Whidbey Island (Smith et al. 1997) in the northern part of the Sound. The author saw one fly by Point Robinson on 18 May 2002 for Vashon's sole record. The middle and southern Puget Sound areas' sandy/cobble shorelines have little of the rocky habitat typical of much of the outer coast favored by oystercatchers.

Sandpipers, Phalaropes, and Allies

Spotted Sandpiper

(SS, FW) Status: Uncommon resident. Possible breeder.

Dipping and bobbing its tail up and down, the Spotted Sandpiper often shows up walking along a fallen log in Fisher Pond, at Ellisport, or along a Colvos Passage beach. Adults with young show up yearly at Fern Cove and sometimes Christensen Cove. The young fly, indicating families may have fledged on the Island or flown over from the other side of Colvos Passage. They appear absent in June; breeding on the Island occurs rarely, if at all, and probably only at remote locations such as Green Valley.

Spotted Sandpiper. © Kathrine Lloyd

A couple of unusual records exist. Don Norman and Sherry Hudson found thirteen at Camp Sealth on 6 August 2006. Spotted Sandpipers remain generally solitary except in late summer. Usually only one family makes up the flock, so this sighting likely included more than two broods or a number of migrants. On 26 July 2007, the author observed a leucistic bird, all white except for yellow legs and beak and a few dark breast spots.

CBC by area (Trevathan 1999-2013) Trend: Appears highly variable but likely stable.

Vashon North: 1999-2009, 2011-2013
Maury Island-Tramp Harbor: 2000, 2006, 2009, 2012
Quartermaster Harbor: 2010
Vashon South: 2003-2005, 2011-2013

Solitary Sandpiper

(SS, FW) Status: Rare spring and fall migrant.

Solitary Sandpipers breed in British Columbia and migrate in small numbers on both sides of the Cascades (Wahl et al. 2005). They almost always utilize freshwater ponds or muddy wetlands, especially enjoying ponds that partially dry up with the advance of summer (Paulson 1993). They joined the Vashon list as late as 2003, probably because of their preference for freshwater ponds. Mukai Pond, the first sighting location, became more publicly accessible at that time. Solitary Sandpipers superficially resemble Spotted Sandpipers, possibly causing confusion in identification. Nearly all sightings occurred at Mukai Pond, with a few taking place at Fern Cove and Fisher Pond. Fern Cove records consisted of a bird at the mouth of Shinglemill Creek and two following the creek out into the mud flat. While usually solitary, as their name suggests, multiple birds may forage at a location. Gary Shugart and Steve Caldwell discovered three feeding at Mukai Pond on 4 September 2005.

Wandering Tattler

(SS) Status: Very rare visitor. One record.

The author observed Vashon's sole record for Wandering Tattler at KVI Beach on 30 August 2002. Like turnstones and Surfbirds, tattlers prefer rocky shoreline almost entirely absent as a habitat on Vashon. Tattlers rarely visit Puget Sound shorelines (Wahl et al. 2005).

Greater Yellowlegs

(SS, FW) Status: Uncommon fall through spring. Change in Status: Increased observer coverage revealed that one or more Greater Yellowlegs winters on Quartermaster Harbor.

A few Greater Yellowlegs show up once or twice in spring and fall on Vashon. The exposed mud at KVI Beach and Mukai Pond and mud flats opened up by the fall of the tide provide its preferred Island habitat. Better coverage of KVI Beach and Quartermaster Harbor shores by observers would probably increase the number of sightings per year. Other reliable locations include the mud flats at Ellisport and the Island Center Forest. In winter, at least one bird appears to forage each year along Quartermaster Harbor. Most sightings come from Raab's Lagoon, Portage, and the mouth of Judd Creek.

CBC by area (Trevathan 1999-2013):
Maury Island-Tramp Harbor: 2008, 2011

Lesser Yellowlegs

(SS, FW) Status: Very rare spring and fall migrant, winter visitor. Change in Status: Sightings of Lesser Yellowlegs did not occur in most years since the first edition, so a very rare rating reflects its status better.

The Lesser Yellowlegs is the somewhat smaller twin of the larger Greater Yellowlegs. One tells the difference between these otherwise look-alike birds by comparing their size to a nearby Killdeer (Paulson 1993). Lessers appear smaller, while Greaters look larger than Killdeer. The bill length provides another clue. The bill of the Lesser measures about the same length as the length of its head. The Greater's bill length shows quite distinctly longer than the length of its head.

Observers find Lesser Yellowlegs on Vashon at much the same places as Greater Yellowlegs: KVI Beach, Mukai Pond, and Raab's Lagoon. Peter Murray photographed one bird at the Quartermaster Harbor marina on 26 December 2003 for one of two winter records on Vashon. The increase of knowledgeable observers did not translate into a larger number of sightings. This species appears to be an inconsistent visitor to Vashon.

Whimbrel

(SS) Status: Very rare spring and fall migrant. Eight records.

Whimbrels visit Vashon rarely, with anything from a short fly-by to a stay of several days. Their large size and long bill make an exciting sight that quickly distinguishes them from any other shorebird on the Island. Recent observations include one at Point Robinson on 8 May 2005 seen by Gilbert and Jean Findlay, and four noted flying past there on 18 May 2002 by the author. Dan Willsie found one at the beach in front of his house on the northwest corner of the Island on 4 June 2001 and another at KVI Beach in the 1990s. John Friars observed one at KVI Beach from 14 to 19 September

1995. Whimbrels utilize many different habitats: rocky shore, mud flat, sandy beaches, salt marsh, and wet fields (Paulson 1993). The likeliest locations continue to be along the shorelines on Vashon.

Marbled Godwit

(SS) Status: Very rare. One record.

Interior sightings for this large shorebird are rare anywhere in Washington (Wahl et al. 2005). Only one record exists for Vashon, a single bird making a brief stop at KVI Beach in front of John Friars's house on 24 April 1995.

Black Turnstone

(SS) Status: Uncommon fall through spring. Change in Status: Increased observer coverage found this species more consistently fall through spring.

Black Turnstones breed far to the north and visit the outer coast of Washington in migration and winter. Their preferred habitat usually consists of rocky beaches. To some extent they also utilize cobblestone and sandy/muddy stretches. They utilize scattered Pierce and King County beach locations such as Alki and the log booms on Commencement Bay regularly in winter. A group often hangs out at the southern tip of Bainbridge Island. Fern Cove provides the only consistent location on Vashon, especially the spur of cobblestone on the north edge of the cove. Single birds or small flocks stop in at Ellisport in some years. They sometimes rest on docks and ferry pilings. Don Norman found ten at the Tahlequah ferry dock on 25 December 2006. Several times in the winter of 2010, Rich Siegrist, Sharon Helmick, and the author found a handful using the pilings and the passenger-only ferry dock during very high tides.

   CBC by area (Trevathan 1999-2013):
   Vashon North: 2004, 2008
   Maury Island-Tramp Harbor: 2003, 2008

Surfbird

(SS) Status: Very rare winter visitor. Two records.

Birders find Surfbirds uncommon on the south end of Bainbridge Island or along the rocky shore at Blakely Rock and Restoration Point (Ian Paulsen pers. com. 2005). They undoubtedly stray a few more miles south to Vashon occasionally. Dan Willsie noticed them on 6 February 2005 along the beach on northwest Vashon. The author found others on 14 November 2005 at Fern Cove for the only two Island records as yet. Little rocky shore exists on Vashon to entice them.

Sanderling

(SS) Status: Uncommon fall through spring.

The winter months usually find a flock of 20 to 40 Sanderling working sandy beaches on the Island where the waves meet the sand. One will see a number of robin-sized white puffs scurrying along the shore. The most consistent locations seem to be KVI Beach, Fern Cove, and Quartermaster Harbor between Burton and Shawnee. Sometimes they roost on the little square floating docks at Shawnee or on logs in Dockton after the tide covers up the mud flat. Spring migration appeared particularly noticeable in 2004. Several flocks ranging from 20 to 150 were noted regularly at KVI Beach and Fern Cove during the last two weeks of April 2004.

> CBC by area (Trevathan 1999-2013) Trend: Appears variable but apparently stable.
>> Vashon North: 2000-2001, 2004-2005, 2008-2009
>> Maury Island-Tramp Harbor: 2004-2006, 2008
>> Quartermaster Harbor: 1999, cw2001, 2002-2003, 2007, 2010-2013

Semipalmated Sandpiper

(SS, FW) Status: Rare fall migrant.

Flocks of Western and Least Sandpipers should be checked for this small sandpiper that usually migrates through the center and eastern portions of North America. Dan Willsie made the first record with one at KVI Beach on 8 to 24 August 1991. Since 2000, increased observer effort led to many more sightings, most at KVI Beach and predominantly in late August.

Western Sandpiper

(SS, FW) Status: Uncommon spring and fairly common fall migrant.

Hundreds of thousands of Western Sandpipers rush to parts of western Alaska and northeastern Siberia each spring to breed (Paulson 1993). After only a few short weeks, they begin their journey south again. In the space of a week or so in mid- to late April, a major proportion of the world population of Western Sandpipers funnels through Bowerman Basin in Grays Harbor County. The author has seen Peregrine Falcons whipping in, stirring up a couple hundred thousand Western Sandpipers as well as thousands of birds of other shorebird species there. It's quite something to see the synchronized flash of dark and white as the birds turn this way and that to dodge the falcon. Fall migration spreads out much more over time than spring migration, taking many months rather than weeks.

Adult Western Sandpipers begin flooding back through the state as early as the last week of June, still in their full breeding plumage (Paulson 1993). In this plumage, they appear as small, sparrow-sized shorebirds with a rufous cap and rufous and brown scalloped back. They also possess black legs and a fairly long bill for probing the mud and sand. As fall progresses, their plumage changes to a light brown above and white below. Juvenile birds start making their way from their birth place to Washington in early August and by the end of the month outnumber the adults. Some birds show up into winter in places along the coast and Puget Sound, though generally not on Vashon.

Spring migration on Vashon usually comes through lighter than in the fall. Groups of one to 20 and, less commonly, up to 50 appear in mid- to late April. In the fall, over 100 birds might show up in a day in August.

Checking the estuary at KVI Beach or Fern Cove regularly beginning in the last week of June and first week of July provides the best way to find Westerns on Vashon. Flock size fluctuates widely during the season and from year to year. Often a number of Least Sandpipers mix in, and rarely a Semipalmated Sandpiper shows up. Fern Cove offers a good location, though not quite as reliable as KVI. Westerns also show up at Ellisport, Fisher Pond, Mukai Pond, Lisabeula, and occasionally along other shorelines around the Island. Only one winter record exists.

Hunting pressure severely impacted the population of the Western Sandpiper in the late 1800s. Passage of the Migratory Bird Treaty helped bring about a recovery in its numbers. At the turn of the 20th century, Rathbun, a Seattle area birder, made these comments:

> "But large as the numbers of the western sandpiper still appear to be, they are not comparable to those of fifteen or twenty years ago, and the cause of this decrease in their numbers is the same old story. It seems hardly possible that a bird so small could have been regarded as game and its hunting come under the name of sport, but such was the case and it brought about the logical results." (Bent 1927)

The Migratory Bird Treaty, signed with Mexico and Great Britain (acting for Canada), protected game birds, insectivorous birds, and other non-game birds (Matthiessen 1959). The treaty set seasons for game birds, not to exceed three and a half months. It also prohibited egg collecting except for scientific purposes. The enforcement of this treaty resulted in the recovery of many shorebird populations made noticeably low by hunting.

CBC by area (Trevathan 1999-2013):
Vashon North: 2004

Least Sandpiper

(SS, FW) Status: Uncommon spring and fairly common fall migrant, very rare winter.

The world's smallest "peep," the Least Sandpiper commonly mixes in with flocks of Western Sandpipers. It also appears in its own single species flocks and in some years outnumbers the Westerns. These sandpipers look noticeably darker on their backs, are smaller, and possess yellowish legs in contrast to the very black legs of the Western Sandpiper. In breeding plumage, Leasts have more of a black and brown patterning on their back instead of the rufous noted on a Western. Paulson observes that Leasts will always stand out as the darker birds when foraging or in flight with Westerns (Paulson 1993). The best locations for Least Sandpipers consist of KVI Beach, Fern Cove, Fisher Pond, and Mukai Pond. Their period of occurrence on Vashon matches fairly closely that of the Western Sandpiper. Partly because of their smaller size and partly because of some of their food preference differences, the Leasts sometimes forage higher up out of the water than Westerns. They often mix with the Westerns right at the waterline or even a little into shallow water. Two winter records exist.

CBC by area (Trevathan 1999-2013):

Vashon North: 1999

Baird's Sandpiper

(SS) Status: Very rare fall visitor. Twelve records.

Baird's Sandpipers breed on the arctic tundra and largely migrate through the Great Plains migratory corridor (Paulson 1993). Only a few make it to Washington State, and fewer yet migrate down the west side of the Cascades. Dan Willsie saw a member of this shorebird species for Vashon's first record at KVI Beach on 22 September 1990. Most subsequent records came from KVI Beach, with additional single sightings at Ellisport and Point Robinson. Baird's Sandpipers prefer sandy beaches and mud flat areas. At a location such as KVI Beach, they might be found on the actual beach area or in the muddy pond area.

Pectoral Sandpiper

(SS) Status: Very rare spring and fall migrant. Fifteen records. Change in Status: Only three sightings since the first edition take this species down from rare to very rare.

Pectoral Sandpipers feed by hunting insects and crustaceans in salt marsh (Angell and Balcomb 1982). Accordingly, a few of these medium-sized sandpipers show up each year at KVI Beach, which possesses the most appropriate habitat on Vashon. Almost all records consist of fall visitors, although Sue Trevathan found one spring migrant on 10 May 2002, and Ezra Parker spotted another at Fern Cove on 26 May 2013. Pectoral Sandpipers belong to the list of shorebirds that faced heavy losses due to unrestricted hunting in the nineteenth century (Bent 1927). It's unknown how Vashon populations fared during that time.

Dunlin

(SS) Status: Very rare fall through winter, at times uncommon in spring.

Dunlin winter in large flocks of many thousands in several locations along the coast and at the Skagit delta. Small groups stay in several spots around Puget Sound (Paulson 1993). Vashon hosts only a few, possibly because most of the mud flats here are not large enough to sustain a group over winter. Most sightings in fall and winter on the Island feature a single Dunlin mixed in with a Sanderling flock. During fall migration, Dunlin show up along the eastern and west shores, and wintering birds might be at Fern Cove, KVI Beach, Shawnee, or the small floating docks of Quartermaster Harbor. Larger groups visit during the spring migration. Better observer coverage changed the status of Dunlin from very rare to rare to uncommon for Vashon in spring over the last few years. More observer effort to spy out the Dunlin in a larger Sanderling flock would likely change the very rare status in fall and winter to rare and possibly uncommon.

CBC by area (Trevathan 1999-2013):
Vashon North: 1999, 2012
Maury Island-Tramp Harbor: 2004, 2009

Short-billed Dowitcher

(SS) Status: Very rare fall visitor. Seven records.

Paulson notes that Short-billed Dowitchers move through the Northwest in good numbers mostly on the outer coast. Relatively few pass through the Puget Sound area. He states generally, but not definitively, that Short-bills prefer saltwater shore habitat over freshwater locations (Paulson 1993). They usually come in large numbers and more likely utilize mud flats rather than shore vegetation at the beach edge.

Both dowitchers forage in the company of the other. With the two birds extremely difficult to tell apart, vocalizations make the best method for identification. The Short-billed issues a *tututu* somewhat like a Lesser Yellowlegs, and the Long-billed calls *keek* or *peep*, either singly or a number of times together. When a Long-billed Dowitcher showed up at Fern Cove, the author spent an hour with Sue Trevathan and Ron Simons closely observing the bird. All were still somewhat undecided about identification until vocalization settled the issue.

As he has with many Vashon shorebirds, Dan Willsie saw the first of this species, with one on 20 July 1991 at KVI Beach. KVI Beach provides three other records, and Ellisport, Fern Cove, and Fisher Pond each one, for a total of seven Vashon records. It's likely that Short-billeds will upgrade in status to rare as the work of more observers continues to come into play. Unless their actual population status in the region changes, it's unlikely that they will ever show up as more than rare on the Island.

Long-billed Dowitcher

(SS, FW) Status: Very rare spring and fall visitor. Twelve records. Change in Status: Even with increased observer coverage, sightings occurred about every other year since the first edition, changing the status from rare to very rare.

Long-billed Dowitchers appear commonly in small groups across the state around both saltwater and freshwater habitats such as mud flats, drying ponds, and salt marsh (Paulson 1993). Rick Sanders probably saw the first Long-billed Dowitcher for Vashon. Sue Trevathan later found the same bird when leading a field trip to Fern Cove on 28 July 2002. One spring record exists of two birds found together at KVI Beach by Bob Hawkins on 6 May 2013. All other sightings came as single birds in the fall migration from mid-July through late September. The best locations for Long-billed Dowitchers include Fern Cove, Fisher Pond, and KVI Beach, with one record occurring at Lisabeula.

Wilson's Snipe

(SS, FW, FL) Status: Uncommon fall through spring. Change in Status: Increased observer coverage finds them at a large number of locations across the Island several times each year, moving their status from rare to uncommon.

Checking the expanses of mud at Fisher Pond may yield this long-billed shorebird in the fall. Sometimes appearing as early as September, Wilson's Snipe usually present themselves by the end of the first week in October and may be seen throughout that month. Because they sit out in the open in the mud, this provides the most likely place and time of year to find snipe. Rich Siegrist finds them in the fields near his house on Cedarhurst Road in winter and spring. In winter, they show up at other marshy locations and wet fields, such as those at the south end of Monument Road, Paradise Valley, Portage, and Mukai Pond. Snipes' ability to blend in and hold still makes them difficult to see, causing observers to under-report their actual occurrence. They nest in marshy areas without tall vegetation in other parts of the Puget Sound lowlands. Vashon has no breeding records. The wet fields where they spend the winter on the Island possibly do not remain wet enough for long enough into the nesting season. The author found one very actively feeding and running from place to place in eelgrass washed ashore at Ellisport on 10 October 2012, atypical behavior and location for Vashon.

CBC by area (Trevathan 1999-2013):
Vashon North: 2000, cw2005, 2008, 2011
Vashon South: 2009-2010, 2012

Wilson's Phalarope

(SW, FW) Status: Very rare visitor. One record. Change in Status: New addition to the Island list since the first edition.

Carole Elder discovered Vashon's first and only Wilson's Phalarope on 11 May 2008 at Tahlequah. It was surface-feeding with some gulls close inshore. Wilson's Phalarope rarely appear on saltwater or out toward the coast. Birders shared a number of sightings in wetlands in the Puget Sound area in the spring of 2008; Elder's record provided the only saltwater observation. Though rare west of the Cascades, Wilson's Phalarope breed in good numbers in Eastern Washington. They favor freshwater habitats such as wetlands and ponds. Nesting populations tend to move opportunistically as pond conditions change over time (Smith et al. 1997). E. A. Kitchin found a disjunct breeding pair or two in the formerly extremely productive Tacoma tide flats in the 1930s (Kitchin 1934). Observers noted others nesting at Nisqually National Wildlife Refuge up to 1975. No recent westside breeding records exist since the Nisqually population disappeared (Smith et al. 1997).

Red-necked Phalarope

(SW, SS, FW) Status: Uncommon fall and very rare spring migrant.

John Friars, an Islander since the 1930s, remembers Red-necked Phalarope as much more common during migration than they now occur. Small numbers still pass through during fall migration along the Fauntleroy and Point Defiance ferry runs. From the ferry runs, watch for them feeding in drifting seaweed. Look for the long strands of floating green weed or driftwood and then for the bobbing and spinning forms of phalarope in the midst of it. Offshore at KVI Beach and Tramp Harbor also provides possibilities where the weed strands wash in. On 26 August 2010, the author found one Red-necked Phalarope in the small pond at KVI Beach for the only Vashon freshwater sighting.

Red Phalarope

(SW) Status: Very rare fall migrant and winter visitor. Eight records.

Red Phalarope migrate predominantly off the outer coast of Washington. A few birds move through Puget Sound, generally after or during a storm. Dave Beaudette found ten off the ferry after a storm in October 1997 that produced other pelagic rarities (Dave Beaudette pers. com. 2005). On other occasions, storms off the coast brought birds inland that later strayed into Quartermaster Harbor.

Gulls, Terns, and Allies

Black-legged Kittiwake

(SW, SS) Status: Very rare fall visitor. Two records. Change in Status: New addition to the Island list since the first edition, due to new research and a single new sighting.

Black-legged Kittiwakes generally forage in pelagic waters off Washington's coast, with a few showing up on the actual coastline. An early 20th century inspector for the Biological Survey, George Cantwell, reported seeing kittiwakes at Burton on 16 December 1918 (Jewett et al. 1953). This sighting appears in Jewett et al. with comments before and after indicating the possibilities of mistaken identification. At that time very few mid- to lower Puget Sound records existed for the kittiwake. Knowledge of the Black-legged Kittiwake's distribution grew considerably with increased observers and offshore surveys since Jewett's time, according to Wahl et al. (2005). Wahl et al. consider kittiwakes to be rare in migration in inland waters. Kittiwakes are common off the coast as migrants and winter residents. Over the past three decades, at least ten records exist for Pierce County, mostly from around Point Defiance, just a couple of miles south of Cantwell's report. Dan Willsie discovered the only recent Vashon Black-legged Kittiwake on the beach at his place near the northwest corner of the Island on 3 December 2007. It perched long enough to give him a good look before flying off.

Sabine's Gull

(SW, SS) Status: Very rare fall visitor. Two records.

Two Vashon records exist for the Sabine's Gull, a pelagic species usually seen far offshore along Washington's coast. Dave Beaudette saw one while on the Southworth ferry on 14 October 1997 during the same storm event that yielded storm-petrels, pelicans, and other birds that generally stay on the outer coast. Rich Siegrist and Dan Willsie found a Sabine's off Point Robinson on 7 September 1991.

Bonaparte's Gull

(SW, SS) Status: Fairly common spring and fall migrant, uncommon winter resident, uncommon in summer as part of the early fall migration.

The small Bonaparte's Gull appears in all seasons around Vashon. During migration, flocks of hundreds and sometimes thousands of birds stream through Dalco Passage and Colvos Passage. In mid-April 2004, a flock of over 3,000 birds lined the shore of Quartermaster Harbor at Burton. Locations along Colvos Passage and around Tahlequah seem to be the best for winter sightings. Summer sightings actually consist of mid-July precursors to the full fall migration. These observations tend to be of gulls flying along Colvos Passage or of gulls resting at Fern Cove. With Common Terns, Bonaparte's Gulls make the main local targets for trouble from Parasitic Jaegers. Jaegers time their visits to Vashon with the height of the Bonaparte's Gull and Common Tern fall migration through the area. The large flocks of Bonaparte's Gulls should also be scanned for Little Gull.

Bonaparte's Gull numbers dropped in King County since the 1980s for unknown reasons (Hunn 2012). Christmas Bird Count (CBC) data from around the Puget Sound region show declines (Wahl et al. 2005) as does Vashon's (Trevathan 1999-2013). At least on the Vashon CBC, counting

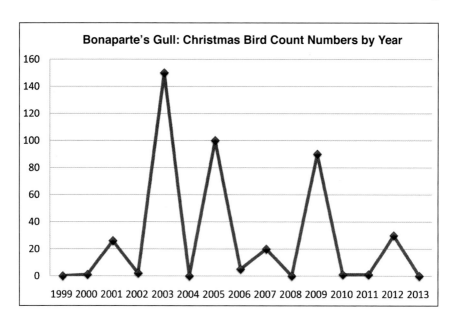

Bonaparte's Gulls presents a challenge. Unless observers specifically pick the time of day correctly with Bonaparte's Gull as the main target, they may miss this species if tide and other conditions aren't right. As noted above, large flocks still move through Vashon's waters in season. Judging any change in status remains difficult for this gull on Vashon.

CBC by area (Trevathan 1999-2013) Trend: Appears variable with possible decrease.

Vashon North: 2006, 2010-2011
Quartermaster Harbor: 2006-2007
Vashon South: 2000-2003, 2005, 2007, 2009, 2012

Little Gull

(SW, SS) Status: Very rare fall through spring. One record.

Russell Rogers has the only Little Gull record for Vashon, off the ferry to Southworth on 5 February 1993. "I saw it from the ferry between Vashon and Southworth....The bird was flying around and then sat on the water about 30 to 40 feet away from the ferry as it went past.One of the best looks at a Little Gull that I have ever had, actually." (Rogers pers. com. 2009).

With careful scans of gull flocks along Colvos Passage and around Tahlequah, observers should add more Little Gull records. In most years at least one shows up in the Puget Sound area each fall, generally in association with flocks of Bonaparte's Gulls. Through the 1990s, one often appeared at nearby American Lake in Pierce County, and it likely passed by Vashon with other gulls regularly.

Like the Franklin's Gull, the Little Gull only recently joined the Washington list in 1972 (Wahl et al. 2005). Not known to nest in North America until 1962, the small population of Little Gulls appears to be slowly expanding in both North America and Western Europe for unknown reasons (Ewins and Weseloh 1999).

Franklin's Gull

(SW, SS) Status: Very rare fall through early winter. Ten records. Change in Status: Increased observer effort altered this species's status from accidental to very rare.

The Vashon status for Franklin's Gull changed from accidental in the first edition to very rare at present because of the larger number of knowledgeable observers. Vashon now has ten records, eight from 2006 to 2010. Wahl et al. (2005) consider Franklin's to be uncommon in fall in the Puget Sound area; intensive looking for this gull on the Island each year might bring its status up to uncommon or at least rare, with a sighting or two every year.

J. W. Slipp scored the first record for Washington in Pierce County at Waughop Lake (Slipp 1942a). Washington numbers of Franklin's Gull sightings gradually increased in the intervening years since Slipp's first observation, possibly through a general westward expansion of this species. These gulls bred originally in the continent's interior prairies, with a small and growing breeding population in eastern Oregon (Wahl et al. 2005).

Franklin's Gulls show up mostly at low tide, feeding out on exposed mud flats at Fern Cove and Tramp Harbor, often in association with the somewhat similar Bonaparte's Gull. Others turn up in the flocks of Bonaparte's streaming down Colvos Passage or by the Tahlequah ferry.

Heermann's Gull

(SW, SS) Status: Rare fall visitor.

Heermann's Gulls breed to the south in California and then expand their range northward during the fall. Mostly seen on the outer coast, a good number turn into the Straits of Juan de Fuca. Some Heermann's reach King County and Vashon. Heermann's Gull sightings on Vashon appear to rise with the numbers of observers. These gulls turn up mostly at the Tahlequah dock and with less regularity off the ferries, at Point Robinson, or on pilings at Ellisport. The windstorms of October 2003 brought many Heermann's Gulls into the south Puget Sound area, where observers saw them from a number of spots around the Island. Gary Shugart had the highest count, with nine at Tahlequah on 30 October 2003. Observers noted these gulls there regularly in fall 2004. For the last three years, one or two birds roosted almost daily at the Tahlequah dock from October through December.

CBC by area (Trevathan 1999-2013):

Vashon North: 1999

Mew Gull

(SW, SS) Status: Fairly common spring and fall migrant, common winter resident and very rare in summer. Change in Status: In the summer of 2011 and 2012, a few birds were present into May and arrived earlier than usual in July, perhaps also in June.

The Mew Gull is the common small winter gull seen around Puget Sound. Adults have a dainty look that, along with size, differentiates them from the other possible gull species in the area. A few Mew Gulls show up at mid-summer, as foreshadowers of the larger fall migration. In two recent years, some of these gulls possibly stayed the whole summer, or at least late into May and present in early July. This may be a new trend or just a fluke. At mid-winter, Mews and Glaucous-winged Gulls comprise 95 percent or more of the Vashon gull population.

CBC by area (Trevathan 1999-2013) Trend: Appears variable but stable.
Vashon North: 1999, 2003-2005, 2007-2009, 2011, 2013
Maury Island-Tramp Harbor: 1999-2001, 2003-2005, 2007-2013
Quartermaster Harbor: 1999-2005, 2007-2013
Vashon South: 1999-2013

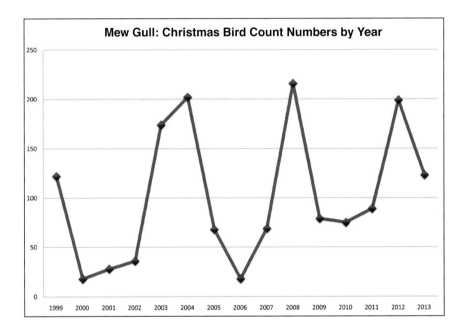

Ring-billed Gull

(SW, SS) Status: Rare visitor year-round.

While common across the water in Seattle and Tacoma, only a few Ring-billed Gulls wander over to Vashon. Sightings are most likely in migration periods. Observers who are used to seeing them frequently in the urban areas and lake settings of Seattle need to be careful in identifying them in the saltwater habitat of Vashon. Ring-bills might be confused with Mew and California Gulls, which, like the Ring-bill, have black wing tips and often a dark mark on the bill in some plumages. Mew and California Gulls show up more consistently and in greater numbers than Ring-billed Gulls.

It's not completely clear why Ring-billed Gulls only rarely visit Vashon. They use harbor fronts, freshwater lakes, and garbage dumps in the Seattle and Tacoma areas, which may explain their rarity. They possibly showed up frequently in the past when Vashon had an open landfill that attracted many gulls.

> CBC by area (Trevathan 1999-2013):
> *Vashon North: 1999*
> *Maury Island-Tramp Harbor: cw2005, 2011*
> *Quartermaster Harbor: 2012*
> *Vashon South: 1999*

Western Gull

(SW, SS) Status: Rare fall through spring.

The Western Gull is a rare visitor to Vashon from Washington's outer coast. In King County, a few Westerns show up each year mixed in with the more common Glaucous-winged Gull. Some of these Western Gulls visit Vashon. The two birds extensively hybridize in Western Washington, creating a hybrid called by some "Olympic Gull." Observers must take care confirming identification of Western Gulls in this area. Westerns possess backs that look dark gray and have dark gray wing tips. The back of the head remains clear in winter with adult Westerns, differentiating them from Glaucous-winged and Herring Gulls in winter. Glaucous-winged have light gray backs, with wing tips only a little bit darker. The hybrids mix and match these characteristics. As many as one-third of the birds on much of Washington's coast consist of hybrids (Smith et al. 1997). In the Puget Sound area, Olympic Gulls comprise a large percentage of the birds in the Glaucous-winged/Western Gull species complex. Gull roosts at Fern Cove, Ellisport, and Tahlequah supply the most likely locations for observation of Western Gull on Vashon.

> CBC by area (Trevathan 1999-2013):
> *Vashon North: 1999, 2008, 2013*
> *Maury Island-Tramp Harbor: 2007-2009*
> *Vashon South: 2006*

California Gull

(SW, SS) Status: Fairly common fall migrant, uncommon to rare winter resident and spring migrant, rare late spring and summer. Change in Status: In 2011 and 2012, California Gull occurrence changed from birds being present for part of the summer to being around all summer. The summer stay didn't occur in 2013 and needs watching in future years.

Small numbers of California Gulls show up around Vashon on the ferry runs and along KVI Beach, Tramp Harbor, and Fern Cove. A few gulls start the fall migration in mid-summer, usually seen off the ferry runs, resting at Fern Cove, or flying along Colvos Passage. The population swells in August and September and then falls to only a few birds seen on the Christmas Bird Count. Numbers rise during spring migration and then fall to nearly zero until mid-summer. Finding the winter birds usually takes the effort of checking all the gull roosts of Quartermaster and Tramp Harbors.

In 2011 and 2012, California Gulls extended their presence from part to all of the late spring and summer. At some point in June, Tahlequah had the highest counts for this species for all of Puget Sound, not a common experience with gulls on Vashon. As noted above, this phenomenon didn't repeat in 2013. It's difficult to know yet whether the year-round presence will continue regularly or only occasionally.

CBC by area (Trevathan 1999-2013) Trend: Appears stable at always low numbers.

Vashon North: 1999
Maury Island-Tramp Harbor: 2000-2002, 2004-2005, 2008-2012

Herring Gull

(SW, SS) Status: Very rare winter visitor. Change in Status: Only a few sightings over the last five to six years indicate this species is very rare rather than rare for Vashon. Several earlier records may be misidentifications.

A careful look at the Glaucous-winged Gull flocks around the ferry docks and on pilings at Tahlequah rarely reveals one or two Herring Gulls in winter. Over the last five years, observers noted Herring Gulls only four times. Records in earlier years may reflect misidentifications. Look for a light gray mantle contrasting with black wing tips above and below. A close look is often needed to find the yellow eye because the "Olympic Gull," the common hybrid offspring of the Glaucous-winged and Westerns Gull, lives year-round in the area. Olympic Gulls often have dark wing tips and light gray mantles like the Herring Gull, creating the possibility for misidentification. In addition, Glaucous-winged Gulls and Herring Gulls hybridize, producing Herring-like gulls with brown eyes. Gary Shugart, Islander and Collections Manager for the Slater Museum of Natural History at the University of Puget Sound, collected and identified a dead Glaucous-winged X Herring Gull for the Vashon Audubon chapter bird skin collection in the winter of 2004. The Thayer's Gull, split from the Herring Gull as a full species in the early 1970s, provides more chances for confusion. The identification problems may mask slightly the status and almost certainly the extent of the Herring Gull presence during the year, as shown in the bar graphs for the seasonal occurrence chart in Chapter VI.

Herring Gulls likely show up earlier in the fall and later in the winter. All current records fall in December and January except one in early spring.

CBC by area (Trevathan 1999-2013):
Vashon North: 1999
Quartermaster Harbor: cw2001, cw2002, 2005
Maury Island-Tramp Harbor: 2013
Vashon South: 2001-2003

Thayer's Gull

(SW, SS) Status: Rare fall through spring. Change in Status: Gary Shugart found one to two Thayer's Gulls regularly October through mid-May over the last several years, bringing the status of this species up from very rare to rare.

It takes persistent checking of the winter gull flocks to find a Thayer's Gull on Vashon. On a localized basis, these gulls remain in the Puget Sound area in large numbers during winter. A big flock roosts at the Port of Tacoma each year, just a few miles from Vashon. On the Island, these birds happen to be rare, with usually only one to two birds around. Thayer's Gulls show up with other gulls around the Island, but Gary Shugart finds them most regularly at the Tahlequah dock as he commutes back and forth to Tacoma. Identification problems occur as with the similar Herring Gull, from which it was split as a separate species in the early 1970s. Despite identification issues, enough records exist from knowledgeable observers to make the seasonal occurrence bar graphs in Chapter VI accurate. As the number of experienced watchers expands, the rare status might possibly move to uncommon.

CBC by area (Trevathan 1999-2013):
Vashon North: 2002
Maury Island-Tramp Harbor: 2007, 2013

Glaucous-winged Gull

(SW, SS, FW, FL, DA, AE) Status: Common resident. Breeds.

The large Glaucous-winged Gull takes the prize as the most common gull year-round for Vashon. The ferry docks and shorelines always produce at least a few of these birds. They occasionally fly overland, especially in winter. They sometimes rest overnight in open areas such as the playing fields of the high school. These gulls nest on sandy shores, gravelly roof tops in the city, and on pilings (Smith et al. 1997). Many Glaucous-winged Gulls breed each year in King County. Vashon nesting records remain few. A nest on a deck near Glen Acres in the mid-1990s produced young that were taken by a Bald Eagle (Joy Nelsen pers. com. 2005).

In Western Washington, Glaucous-winged Gulls interbreed extensively with the Western Gull of the outer coast (Smith et al. 1997). Some call the hybrid offspring the "Olympic Gull." These gulls make identification somewhat difficult in figuring out the few true Westerns that come by. Sometimes this problem arises with Herring or other large gulls as well. See the Herring Gull and Western Gull accounts for further discussion of the hybrid identification problem.

BBS (USGS 2013): 1995-1998, 2001-2005, 2009, 2013

CBC by area (Trevathan 1999-2013) Trend: Stable.
Vashon North: 1999-2013
Vashon South: 1999-2013
Quartermaster Harbor: 1999-2013
Maury Island-Tramp Harbor: 1999-2013

Glaucous Gull

(SW, SS) Status: Very rare fall through spring visitor. One record. Change in Status: New addition to the Island list since the first edition. It was just a matter of time until observers noted a Glaucous Gull and made it part of the official record.

Glaucous Gulls show up as rare to uncommon migrants and winter residents in Western Washington. The first and only record for Vashon was a bird that paid a short visit to the Tahlequah dock during the Christmas Bird Count on 28 December 2008. The author, Peter Murray, and Nancy Miracle viewed the bird for a few minutes, and Michael Perrone and Kathy Kirkland independently discovered the bird at about the same time. This species is likely to be seen again on Vashon every few years. It will probably never reach a status higher than very rare.

CBC by area (Trevathan 1999-2013):
Vashon South: 2009

Caspian Tern

(SW, SS, AE) Status: Fairly common spring and summer; status may change.

Caspian Terns were not listed by Dawson and Bowles in the early 20th century for Washington State (Dawson and Bowles 1909). Jewett et al. considered them as rare or casual along the coast and a rare breeder east of the Cascades (Jewett et al. 1953). Caspian Terns expanded their breeding range north into Washington State over the last 30 years, responding largely to human-created opportunities (Smith et al. 1997, Wahl et al. 2005). Caspian Terns developed nesting colonies in a number of locations in the Puget Sound area and along the coast, usually around dredging or construction sites. Humans then destroyed these new nesting opportunities for various reasons (Smith et al. 1997). The Grays Harbor County colony was wiped out during dredging. Builders covered the site at Everett with plastic to discourage nesting while they constructed the new Navy base. Colonies built on islands in the Columbia River suffered deliberate disruption as well. Most recently and relevant to Vashon, agencies eliminated the colony near Point Defiance in 2002 for fear of these birds preying on salmon. Some groups characterize Caspian Terns as a threat to endangered native salmon stocks. Gary Shugart, an ornithologist with the Slater Museum of Natural History, asserts that proponents of this theory fail to take into account that the vast majority of young salmon in Washington waters are hatchery fish, not native offspring (Shugart pers. com. 2013). It seems unlikely that the terns actually take significant numbers of native salmon.

Even after the destruction of the colony at the former ASARCO plant near Point Defiance, a few Caspian Terns forage in Dalco Passage at Tahlequah. Others work their way along the north/south shorelines of the Island or into Quartermaster Harbor. Apparently, a few pairs found alternative nesting sites in the Pierce County area in 2002 and 2004. What the future will bring remains uncertain, as these birds are still unjustly blamed for the size of their salmon take.

BBS (USGS 2013): 1997, 2000, 2002

Common Tern

(SW, SS) Status: Rare fall migrant. Change in Status: Formerly uncommon to fairly common. Since the first edition, only one sighting per year and in a couple of years, none.

Flocks of Common Tern appear during the fall migration, first showing up in August. The best locations to look for Common Terns consist of Tahlequah, through Colvos Passage, in Ellisport, and along both ferry runs. Common Terns often associate with Bonaparte's Gulls, and both suffer harassment from the Parasitic Jaeger. For about two months in late summer to fall, flocks of these graceful terns migrate by, only to be gone until the next year. Flock size tends to vary considerably, from small groups of a handful or so to assemblages of 50 to 100.

Numbers in Puget Sound dropped over the last decade for unknown reasons (Hunn 2012). The status of Vashon's terns changed as well since the first edition, moving from fairly common fall migrant to rare. Both occurrence and flock size fell around Vashon over the last eight to ten years. Many fish-eating seabird species tracked by the Washington Department of Fish and Wildlife faced significant declines over the same time period. Because Common Terns forage along Puget Sound looking mainly for fish and sometimes crustaceans, they may be facing challenges like those of other seabirds in the region.

Arctic Tern

(SW, SS) Status: Very rare fall migrant. One record. Change in Status: New addition to the Island list since the first edition.

Arctic Terns predominantly migrate along and off the outer coast of Washington. Some migrate through Puget Sound, and a small, disjunct colony existed formerly in Everett for many years. Gene Hunn found Vashon's only record at KVI Beach on 27 August 2008. "I noticed a small tern struggling against the wind headed south 100 yards or so offshore," he says. "It fought the wind for nearly five minutes, eventually coming in to within less than 50 yards. I was able to follow it in my scope at 25x. At first I thought it might be another Forster's Tern like I saw last week on Lake Washington, as it showed a clear pale gray mantle to the tips of the primaries above. It showed a subtle but noticeable dusky carpal bar (thus it was not a full adult) and a very narrow black margin at the tips of the primaries beneath. The cap was reduced to the cowl of a winter adult or immature Common or Arctic, complete across the nape, ruling out Forster's. The clincher was that the bill was notably short, black, and the round head and bill projected noticeably less ahead of the wing than the tail projected behind. A translucent triangle showed on the underside of the trailing edge of the wing. A graceful and elegant bird. I would judge it to have been a first summer Arctic Tern. Last seen about 2:45 p.m. heading south towards Point Robinson. A first for King County for me and one of very few documented records." (Tweeters 2008)

Pomarine Jaeger

(SW) Status: Very rare. One record.

Like the Parasitic Jaeger, the Pomarine Jaeger mostly steals its meals from terns and gulls when away from its tundra breeding grounds. In Washington, it moves through predominantly as a pelagic species, seen several miles offshore. During migration, one or two appear in Puget Sound or east of the Cascades (Wahl et al. 2005). Dave Beaudette observed one on 10 September 1998 off the Vashon-Fauntleroy ferry (*WOSNews* 59, March 1999, page 12).

Parasitic Jaeger

(SW) Status: Rare to uncommon fall migrant.

While one might see Parasitic Jaegers by using a spotting scope at the Tahlequah dock and Point Robinson, the best and most likely way to see these predators involves watching from either on the Tahlequah or Vashon-Fauntleroy ferries. The jaegers allow close looks as they cruise by looking for fish-laden Common Terns or Bonaparte's Gulls to chase. Once they sight their target, they become relentless acrobats, harrying the tern or gull until it at last gives up its dinner for the jaeger to seize midair. There is something indescribably sinister to the flight of the jaeger that immediately tips one off that this is not just another gull. Dawson writes: "Hard upon the migrating hosts of Terns come these cruel tyrants of the sea, Jaegers." (Dawson and Bowles 1909) He comments that "at the height of the season, one may see a dozen birds in the course of a steamboat ride from Tacoma to Seattle, or a hundred between Seattle and Victoria." Those numbers are much higher than today's data, when only two to three may be seen between Tacoma and Seattle in any given year. Sometimes a dozen work the gull flocks just to the north in Kitsap County at Point No Point. Records for both dark and light morphs exist off Tahlequah.

Alcids

Common Murre

(SW) Status: Fairly common fall through spring, rare summer.

The ferry runs present the best opportunities to view Common Murres because they generally swim or fly fairly far out in the water. The easiest land views come from Point Robinson, Tahlequah, and the various Colvos Passage locations, especially Reddings Beach or Lisabeula or on Bachelor Road at the south end. No records exist for Quartermaster Harbor.

Common Murres around the Island usually forage in small groups of two to five, though larger groups of ten to 20 show up. They dive for fish and crustaceans. In British Columbia, observers found them feeding around herring spawn events (Campbell et al. 1990). The Washington population appears stable, though breeding success appears often negatively affected by El Niño events (Wahl et al. 2005). Common Murres breed along Washington's outer coast.

    CBC by area (Trevathan 1999-2013) Trend: Stable.
        Vashon North: 2000, 2002-2003, 2009, 2012-2013
        Maury Island-Tramp Harbor: 2008, 2010-2012
        Quartermaster Harbor: 1999-2004, 2009, 2012-2013

Pigeon Guillemot

(SW, SS) Status: Fairly common resident. Breeds.

Other than the ever-present Glaucous-winged Gull, the open saltwater of Puget Sound offers only Pigeon Guillemot to birdwatchers in much of

June and July. About half the size of a Mallard, these black birds with white wing patches hang around the ferry docks and shorelines with bluffs. Pigeon Guillemots act somewhat less pelagic than other alcids, for they sometimes perch on rocks along the shore. In *Life Histories of North American Diving Birds* (Bent 1963a), Dawson comments that these birds hover at the face of a bluff and dig a hole with their beak and claws. They then build a tunnel with a turn at right angles to provide a nesting den. Artificial sites such as docks and pilings in addition to burrows in bluffs provide nest sites in the Puget Sound area. The nest itself consists only of a bare surface, sometimes with rock chips. Out on the outer coast, guillemots nest on cliffs and haystack rocks alongside the breeding colonies of other birds. Pigeon Guillemots nest by themselves or in small colonies.

As the most widely distributed seabird in the state, Pigeon Guillemots nest in almost every small marine inlet in Washington (Smith et al. 1997). On Vashon, they show up just about everywhere along saltwater shores. The bluffs at Point Robinson provide an easy location to see them flying back and forth from the water to their burrows. On 19 May 2002, the author saw at least 30 sitting on the rocks along the shore or diving in the water at Point Robinson. Another 25 or so occupied Tramp Harbor near Portage, where Dan Willsie has noted their nests in the past. Their burrows create good-sized holes in the bluff. Kingfishers sometimes use past year's guillemots' burrows. Sue Trevathan noted guillemots utilizing the pilings at Maury Island Marine Park. Gary Shugart saw them employing

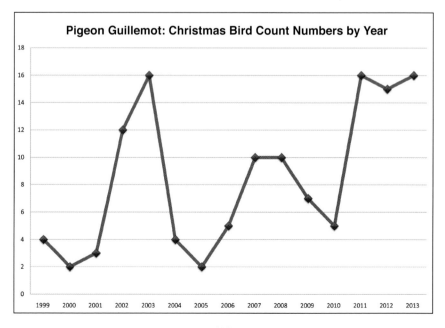

the ferry dock at Tahlequah for nesting sites. The author observed adults coming to nests under the north ferry dock and the Tramp Harbor fishing pier. They make a *pee-pee-peee-peeeee-peeeeeeeeee* call as they fly in and out from under the docks in the breeding season.

BBS (USGS 2013): 2000, 2002, 2005, 2006

CBC by area (Trevathan 1999-2013) Trend: Appears variable but stable.

Vashon North: 2002, 2003, 2006-2013
Maury Island-Tramp Harbor: 1999-2002, 2003, 2006-2013
Quartermaster Harbor: 1999, 2001, 2003, 2007, 2009-2013
Vashon South: 2001-2009

Marbled Murrelet
(SW) Status: Rare in all seasons. Possible former breeder.

Instead of nesting high on a rocky island cliff like the other alcids, the Marbled Murrelet builds high in a tree. For decades, no one knew how they nested in the Northwest. Some Native Americans claimed to find them high in the mountains in hollow trees (Bent 1963a). Others put them in all sorts of interesting locations. As Dawson states it:

> "The nesting of the Marbled Murrelet hereabouts is an engaging mystery....The Quileute Indians say that they do not nest like the other seafowl upon the rocky islets, but that they colonize upon some of the higher slopes of the Olympic Mountains where they lay their eggs in burrows and one of the Indians claims to have come upon such a colony several years ago while hunting in company with a white man.
>
> "It sounds fishy, I know; but I have one slight confirmation for such an hypothesis. At Glacier, on the North Fork of the Nooksack River, and near the foot of Mount Baker, having risen before daybreak for an early bird-walk, on the morning of May 11, 1905, I heard voices from an invisible party of Marbled Murrelets high in air as they proceeded down the valley, as tho to repair to the sea for the day's fishing." (Dawson and Bowles 1909)

It wasn't until 1963 that observers discovered the first nest in a tree in Siberia and 1975 for one to be found in North America in California (Smith et al. 1997). It turns out that Marbled Murrelets need the huge boughs of old-growth trees that have beds of dwarf mistletoe or moss on which to build their nests. Many nests have now been found in the Olympics and Cascades. The addition of the murrelet to the endangered species list led to a major amount of research that resulted in nest discoveries. Most sites are high in the mountains because those areas provide the only remaining old-growth forest.

As logging of old-growth forests wiped out most of the mature coniferous forest in Western Washington, the Marbled Murrelet grew increasingly rare. Washington Department of Fish and Wildlife reports indicate that a 96 percent decrease occurred in the north Puget Sound area, based on the Marine Ecosystem Analyses of 1979 to 1980, and the Puget Sound Ambient Monitoring Program surveys of 1992 to 1999 (Nysewander et al. 2001). Vashon might once have been a breeding location, but now we'll never know. Kitchin noted several pairs in Quartermaster Harbor in the summer of 1925 (Kitchin 1925).

Breeding success presents an additional problem (Ralph 1994). The fragmentation of forests possibly increased the vulnerability of nest sites to predators such as Steller's Jays and squirrels. Even the existing, reduced population may not be sustainable because of the lower reproductive rate.

Marbled Murrelets still show up in breeding season on Vashon either as non-breeders or possibly as foragers from the mountain breeding locations. Records exist for all seasons of the year, but most come from the spring and fall. The most reliable areas for murrelet sightings include Point Robinson and the ferry runs.

CBC by area (Trevathan 1999-2013) Trend: Appears erratic with always low numbers.

Vashon North: 2002
Maury Island-Tramp Harbor: 1999, 2002-2004, 2008, 2011, 2013
Quartermaster Harbor: 2003, 2005

Ancient Murrelet

(SW) Status: Very rare winter visitor. Five records.

Ancient Murrelets prove uncommon in King County from October through December (Hunn 2012). Vashon has just five records. Three sightings exist for Vashon off the ferry to Fauntleroy. Dave Beaudette reported fifteen seen on 16 November 1998, two chased by a Peregrine Falcon on 22 November 1998, and four on 8 December 1998. Gary Shugart found six off the Tahlequah ferry on 9 November 2004 and a flock far off Point Robinson on 23 November 2007. Brad Waggoner noted a very rare summer sighting of a lone adult Ancient Murrelet in the Puget Sound area 16 July 2005 (Tweeters 2005).

Cassin's Auklet

(SW) Status: Very rare fall visitor. Three records.

Cassin's Auklets live as a pelagic species off the outer coast and breed on offshore islands along the northwest tip of Washington (Smith et al.

1997). Three sightings of vagrants to Vashon exist. Rick Sanders described a single auklet off KVI Beach in August 1990. Dave Beaudette discovered one on 19 September 1998 off the Vashon-Fauntleroy ferry (*WOSNews* 59, March 1999, page 12). Joe Van Os saw one near Point Robinson off Luana Beach Road on 6 December 2011.

Rhinoceros Auklet:

(SW) Status: Fairly common fall through spring, rare in summer.

Seen all year from the ferry runs, the Rhinoceros Auklet also comes close enough to shore for observation in winter near the ferry docks, locations along Colvos Passage, and Point Robinson. Rhinoceros Auklets forage mostly for fish, preferring depths of greater than fifteen meters (Gaston and Dechesne 1996). No records exist for Quartermaster Harbor, probably because of its relatively shallow water. A colony of 34,000 adults bred at Protection Island near Port Townsend in 1980. A large population still exists there (Smith et al. 1997). This represents the auklets' southernmost nesting outpost in Puget Sound. A few straggle down to Vashon during the summer. Numbers rise highest in winter, when many groups of ten or more work the tidal rips in Dalco Passage. Flocks of 25 to 50 showed up in the winters of 2010, 2011, and 2012.

CBC by area (Trevathan 1999-2013) Trend: Indeterminate.
Vashon North: 2000-2002, 2008, 2010-2013
Maury Island-Tramp Harbor: 1999-2000, 2003, 2005, 2009-2012
Quartermaster Harbor: 2000, 2003, 2009-2012
Vashon South: 2000-2004, 2009-2010, 2012

Tufted Puffin

(SW) Status: Very rare. One old record.

These colorful alcids breed on the rocky outer coast around Neah Bay and the Strait of Juan de Fuca. A very few wander south into Puget Sound. Kitchin noted one in Quartermaster Harbor on 25 July 1925 (Kitchin 1925).

Pigeons and Doves

Rock Pigeon

(SS, FL, DA) Status: Introduced. Common resident. Breeds. Formerly known as Rock Dove.

European settlers introduced Rock Pigeons to North America with the very first colonies in the early 1600s (Smith et al. 1997). The birds spread westward along with the immigrants. Fortunately, unlike the starling and House Sparrow, no large adverse effects to indigenous wildlife occurred with the pigeons' range expansion. Rock Pigeons specialize in living in urban areas and farmlands. Some nest on cliffs along the Columbia River far away from human structures in Eastern Washington (Smith et al. 1997). On Vashon, they live around the ferry docks, farmhouses, fields, and the business district. They nest under the ferry docks, in other old dock structures such as those at Maury Island Marine Park, and around farm buildings. Dan Willsie found them nesting under the docks at the marina over many years.

Vashon Rock Pigeons display an interesting behavior in flying back and forth between passing ferries. They commute to and from Fauntleroy to Vashon and vice versa regularly, riding on the boats. Some Rock Pigeons fly across the water from one ferry to the other and go back from whence they came. It's somewhat amusing to be out in the middle of Puget Sound and to see and hear a flutter of wings, all ready for the sight of some interesting bird, only to find it to be a Rock Pigeon trading ferries.

BBS (USGS 2013): 1996, 1997, 2001, 2003

CBC by area (Trevathan 1999-2013) Trend: Stable.
Vashon North: 1999-2006, 2008-2013
Maury Island-Tramp Harbor: 1999-2013
Quartermaster Harbor: 1999-2002, 2004-2005, 2007, 2010-2013
Vashon South: 1999-2011, 2013

Band-tailed Pigeon

(DC, WC, HW, DA) Status: *Fairly common spring through fall, variably rare to fairly common winter. Breeds.*

Band-tailed Pigeons inhabit coniferous forests or mixed forests with large coniferous trees. Jewett et al. (1953) write of them as filling in Northwest forests the ecological niche held by the Passenger Pigeon in the East. Hunting pressure in the late 1800s almost added the Band-tail to the extinction list along with the Passenger Pigeon (Bent and Kitchin in Bent 1963b). Federal and state laws and a wide range throughout Northwest forests saved it from the same fate.

On Vashon, observers mostly see them flying quickly from one patch of forest to another. If one fails to watch closely for them, Band-tails might be thought to be less common than they are in actuality. Some fairly regular spots to look for them include Fern Cove and KVI Beach. At the latter they may be seen coming down to the little pond for a drink. Bird-feeding stations at the edge of forested areas often receive Band-tails as visitors. A

Band-tailed Pigeons. © Gregg Thompson

Band-tailed Pigeon can clear out a mixed-seed feeder in a minute's time. In fall and winter, as Pacific Madrone berries ripen, flocks of pigeons search out the fruit and form large multi-species flocks with other birds to eat the trees out. Dan Willsie discovered the only nest located on Vashon so far in the Burton area, although they likely breed regularly on the Island.

> BBS (USGS 2013): 1995-1998, 2000-2003, 2005, 2006, 2009, 2013
>
> CBC by area (Trevathan 1999-2013) Trend: Appears stable with jumps in good Pacific Madrone crop years.
>
> *Vashon North: 1999, 2001, 2003-2004, 2006-2008, 2011, 2013*
> *Maury Island-Tramp Harbor: 2002-2003, 2007-2010*
> *Vashon South: 2000-2006, cw2008, 2009-2010, cw2012*

Eurasian Collared-Dove

(FL, DA) Status: Uncommon visitor year-round. Change in Status: New addition to the Island list since the first edition, due to range expansion by this species.

Eurasian Collared-Doves arrived in North America in 1974 in the Bahamas (Smith 1987), possibly as stock for a pet shop. They escaped captivity, bred prolifically, and then spread to Florida. They expanded primarily through Florida and then the Southeast before exploding westward across the continent. Some intentional and unintentional introductions occurred in several locations across the country as well. Washington's first record came on 2 January 2000 (Wahl et al. 2005). Over the last five years, they spread thoroughly around the state.

Katrina Lande called the author with Vashon's first record for Eurasian Collared-Dove at the Lande farm north of Vashon town on 22 April 2010. By that fall, Marie Blichfeldt began the first of regular reports from Dockton of one or more birds, where they now likely breed.

Eurasian Collared-Doves utilize mostly agricultural and suburban habitat, coming to feeders and getting spilled grain. They like to perch on power poles and wires in village and farm areas.

BBS (USGS 2013): 2013

CBC by area (Trevathan 1999-2013):

Maury Island-Tramp Harbor: 2013

Mourning Dove

(FL, DA) Status: Uncommon visitor year-round. Breeds. Change in Status: Considered rare in the first edition, increased observer effort finds Mourning Doves several times each year over all parts of Vashon. A pair mated and apparently brought young to a feeder on south Vashon.

The center of the Washington Mourning Dove population occurs in open areas east of the Cascades. West of the Cascades, doves are much less common and local. Formerly common in south King County (Larrison 1952, Hunn 1982), a few now breed around Auburn. Prairies and farmland form their primary habitat, but recently cleared forest provides for some range expansion in Western Washington (Smith et al. 1997). When Islanders utilized more land as farm fields, Mourning Doves appeared more common than at present. Island birders John Friars and Dan Willsie remember their presence in the 1940s. These doves also show up during the same time period in the journals of Roland Carey, the late Island author (Carey, undated notebook). Then the forests regenerated, replacing most farmlands. Residential area overtook the fields and pastures, causing the Mourning Dove population to decline for Vashon.

Mourning Doves tend to show up in residential and open spaces all over the Island, favoring no particular month or season. Over the last five years, they showed up regularly at feeders in Dockton and the Camp Sealth area. In 2011, a pair consistently visited a feeder at Ron Simons's place, where Ron saw them mate. Later in the summer, four showed up, most likely the two adults with two young. Other probable locales for sightings include Point Robinson, Gold Beach, the Old Mill Road/Wax Orchard open areas, and the northern stretches of Westside Highway.

CBC by area (Trevathan 1999-2013):
Vashon North: 1999, cw2013
Maury Island-Tramp Harbor: 2012
Vashon South: 2013

Barn Owl

Barn Owl

(FL, DA) Status: Uncommon resident, breeds. Change in Status: Increased observer effort and the sharing of sightings resulted in more records.

The return of the forests reduced suitable habitat for Barn Owls on the Island. Barn Owls hunt small rodents by gliding and flapping silently back and forth across open fields. They appear to require a good-sized patch of fields but not quite so much as the Northern Harrier, which hunts in a similar fashion.

In the mid-20th century, Larrison listed them as uncommon in the Puget Sound area, appearing mostly in dairying areas along the larger river valleys (Larrison 1952). They were probably uncommon to fairly common breeders on Vashon when more agricultural habitat existed. They once nested at the old Nike missile site in the area of central Vashon. One recent nesting site used by Barn Owls seemed an unusual place, fifteen feet off the Chautauqua Elementary School playground. An old snag with a hole in the top about 25 feet up provided a successful nesting location in 2005, 2006, and 2008. Birds stared out apparently undisturbed as the loud playground noise rolled in. Several residents in farm areas on north Vashon report these owls regularly in barns, with possible nesting.

Recent locations where multiple sightings have been reported include Rich Siegrist's driveway in the Colvos area, the Lisabeula fields, the old Beall greenhouses, and the farm fields just north of the Vashon Community Care Center. In the summer of 2013, up to four Barn Owls at a time could be seen hunting the Wax Orchard fields around the grass runway and across the street to the south. The considerably increased sightings of the last several years may be the result of increased observer effort and more sharing of information.

CBC by area (Trevathan 1999-2013):
Vashon North: 2003, 2011
Vashon South: cw2005, 2013
Maury Island-Tramp Harbor: 2007

Typical Owls

Western Screech-Owl

(HW, DA) Status: Very rare visitor. Two records.

Known for its "bouncing ball" call, the Western Screech-Owl makes a whistle-like hoot that starts slowly and then accelerates. That call remains rare on the Island despite appropriate habitat. These owls like riparian areas and deciduous woods with a thick understory (Smith et al. 1997). Both exist in the mixed woods along many of Vashon's streams. One of the few recent records includes the owl Sue Trevathan found for the 1999 Christmas Bird Count along Judd Creek in Paradise Valley. The only other recent Island sighting was by Rick Sanders at his house by Fern Cove in the 1990s. J. H. Bowles mentions in Bent's work that Western Screech-Owls were common along both freshwater and saltwater in deciduous growth bordering open areas in the south Puget Sound region (Bent 1961b).

On the Island, the screech-owl may be another bird on the decrease because of the decline of open fields and thicket areas. Two additional factors may account for the rareness in sightings of this species. First, few observers spend any effort attempting to find them, due to their nocturnal activity. Second, large numbers of Barred and Great Horned Owls reside on the Island. Both species include smaller owls as potential prey.

CBC by area (Trevathan 1999-2013):

Vashon South: cw2000

Great Horned Owl

(FL, DC, WC, HW, DA) Status: Fairly common resident. Breeds.

The Great Horned Owl is one of the easiest of all of the owls to find on Vashon because it hoots all year-round. Its call, a hoarse *hoo! hu hu hu hoo! hoo!* echoes from a little after dark until just before dawn. When hunting, Great Horned Owls sometimes make a rather blood-curdling scream that sounds like a cat being mauled. Camping out near Walla Walla, the author heard that call in the hour before dawn and was brought straight up in his sleeping bag. Luckily, he just happened to see the large, dark shape of the owl flying fast over the grass, or he would have wondered what might be coming for him. The young, when hungry, create a bewildering variety of whistles and shrieks as they follow their parents and beg for food. William Dawson, one of Washington's turn of the 20th century ornithologists, writes about the sounds outside his window in Tacoma:

Great Horned Owl with chick. © Peter Murray

"Murder most foul was being committed on the roof just outside the open window, and the shrieks of the victims were drowned by the imprecations of the attacking party. Peering out into the moonlight, I beheld one of these Owls perched upon the chimney of the church hard by, gibbering and shrieking like one possessed. Catcalls, groans and demoniacal laughter were varied by wails and screeches, as of souls in torment...." (Dawson and Bowles 1909)

Mostly nocturnal, Great Horned Owls also hunt in the early morning or late afternoon. They inhabit forested areas all over the Island. Burton Hill and Old Mill Road formerly provided consistent locations on the Christmas Bird Count. They use nests already built by Red-tailed Hawks, other owl species, or crows (Smith et al. 1997). Rich Siegrist found a pair with two fledged young using an old Red-tail nest near his place in the Colvos area. Few animals give more entertainment than a nestful of several-week-old owls, craning their whole bodies around every which way, with their heads doing a 360 to look around. One of the ways to find an owl during the day involves watching when a large flock of crows appears to be harassing a large bird. The Great Horned Owls return the favor at night, as they sometimes pick off the crows in their roost one by one. Some decline in general sightings seems to be occurring in the last half-decade.

The 2002 Christmas Bird Count (CBC) totaled eight Great Horned Owls for the highest number for all the CBCs so far; recent counts find at most one. Observers usually still discover at least one nest each year.

CBC by area (Trevathan 1999-2013) Trend: Always low numbers.
> Vashon North: 2000-2001, 2005, cw2006, 2008, 2012-2013
> Maury Island-Tramp Harbor: 2003, 2007
> Vashon South: 1999-2003, 2005-2006

Snowy Owl

(SS, FL, DA) Status: Irregular winter visitor, no recent records.

About once a decade, an irruption of this arctic owl brings a large flight to the Puget Sound area. Rich Siegrist remembers seeing a few Snowy Owls on Vashon in the 1940s and at his place near Colvos in the 1970s. Jim Pappin may have seen one during the irruption to this area in the late 1980s in the fields of the Lisabeula area. Though all seen on the Island occurred in upland fields, the likeliest locations in the Puget Sound region involve sites with driftwood, generally in the fields near big estuaries such as the Skagit. Good Vashon locations to watch include KVI Beach, Point Robinson, Maury Island Marine Park, and possibly Manzanita. Unfortunately, no confirmed sightings occurred with the big invasions into the Puget Sound area in 2011/12 and 2012/13.

Northern Pygmy-Owl

(DC, WC) Status: Very rare visitor. Three records.

Jamie Acker of Bainbridge Island discovered pygmy-owls breeding nearby his home (Acker pers. com. 2005). Northern Pygmy-Owls favor coniferous forests in Washington (Smith et al. 1997). They prove somewhat less common in the Puget Trough, as much of the second growth consists of hardwood species (Smith et al. 1997). Acker found an active calling pair in three different years on Bainbridge and witnessed copulation. This should indicate nesting activity. He heard and saw them in large open forest tracts with tall trees and little understory, bordering meadows. On Vashon, Rick and Kathleen Sanders recorded pygmy-owls twice near their home in the Fern Cove area on 11 January 1995 and 14 March 1996. Alan Huggins found another at the Heights water tower on 17 December 2011. Northern Pygmy-Owls might increase on Vashon as the Island forests mature.

Spotted Owl

(WC) Status: Hypothetical past resident, now extirpated.

Spotted Owls probably lived on Vashon prior to European-American settlers' clearing of old-growth forests on the Island. The logging of the woods would have eliminated their presence by 1900. Breeding pairs require 2,000 to 5,000 acres of coniferous forest, primarily Douglas-fir (Smith et al. 1997). Bent collected three birds in Kirkland in 1911 (Bent 1961b), and other lowland records exist. It isn't unreasonable to expect that a few pairs resided on Vashon before the clearing of the late 1800s. As loggers and settlers cut the woods and fragmented them into smaller sections, the owls would have left. No record exists of their presence.

Barred Owl

(DC, WC, HW, DA) Status: Fairly common resident. Breeds.

Barred Owls first spread to Washington through British Columbia from the other side of the Rockies in the 1970s (Smith et al. 1997). They utilize many types of forests. Barred Owls expanded their range as logging created a patchwork of forests of many different types and ages across the whole West. Ron Simons observed the first recorded presence of a Barred Owl on Vashon on 9 September 1995. Several nesting sites were identified in the late 1990s. The Barred Owl population increased over the last decade while that of the Great Horned Owl has seemed to fluctuate. Some speculation occurred, wondering if the rise of the Barred Owl had some relation to the decrease of Great Horned Owl breeding reports and sightings in general. The substantial size and aggressiveness of the Great Horned Owl, however, makes it unlikely that Barreds could displace the larger owl.

Barred Owls inhabit most of the forested areas of Vashon. They prefer mixed woods along stream courses. Judd Creek has at least three pairs successfully raising young in some years. Probably every drainage with a year-round stream has at least one pair. One nesting site in Paradise Valley hosted an owl family for at least the last decade. Young are heard being fed as early as late April. They make a variety of weird sounds, including a strange, mechanical sound, an ascending whine that assists in finding them by day. Especially when feeding young, Barred Owls remain active all day long. It's not unusual to see an adult perched on a wire along the road in July and August. Besides Paradise Valley, other regular locations include near Dockton, Fern Cove, the Colvos area, and around the north fire station.

BBS (USGS 2013): 2003

CBC by area (Trevathan 1999-2013) Trend: Always low numbers.
Vashon North: 1999, 2001, cw2002, 2005, cw2006, 2007, 2010-2013
Maury Island-Tramp Harbor: 2007, cw2008, cw2010, 2011
Vashon South: 1999, cw2001, 2003-2007, cw2008, 2009-2011, 2013

Long-eared Owl

(FL) Status: Very rare. One record.

This owl dwells commonly in Eastern Washington, with only a few records west of the Cascades. Joe Van Os heard one near Burton in December 1980 for the only record for Vashon (Hunn 1982).

Short-eared Owl

(SS, FL) Status: Former resident, now very rare fall migrant. Two records.

Formerly seen in grassy fields on Vashon, Short-eared Owls join the open field species that benefited for a time from the conversion of Vashon forests to farms and fields. As forests reclaimed areas and residential coverage grew, their habitat shrank. Any possible breeding population disappeared. Short-eared Owls now show up as only very rare visitors to the Island. Dave Beaudette saw two on 11 November 1998 from the Fauntleroy ferry, about two-thirds of the way to Vashon, separated from each other by 150 to 200 feet. Ron Simons noted one at Point Robinson on 31 October 2005.

Northern Saw-whet Owl

(WC, HW) Status: Uncommon winter resident, rare breeder.

Formerly at least as common on Vashon as the Great Horned Owl, the Northern Saw-whet Owl is much harder to spot because of its small size and nocturnal nature. These owls might be found in any significant stand of trees. The wet coniferous woods of the northwest part of Vashon and the Island Center Forest seem especially productive for these owls. Saw-whets possess both a whistling call and a screech like a saw being sharpened, a cry that gives the species its name. It makes quite an eerie sound to hear. Most campers in the wet woods of the Northwest have probably heard this owl beeping/tooting away, especially in late winter and early spring. Joe Van Os reports up to eight calling at once in his yard one year. Confirmed breeding occurred in a nest box built for a flicker at one location on Maury Island. Some long-term Island observers have felt numbers may now be falling, possibly in reaction to the increase in Barred Owls on the Island, a potent predator. On the other hand, with the increase of birders sharing information over the last half decade, sightings appear to come in on a regular basis.

CBC by area (Trevathan 1999-2013):
Maury Island-Tramp Harbor: 2003
Vashon South: 1999-2000, 2007, 2010

Nighthawk

Common Nighthawk

(FL, DC, WC, AE) Status: Rare summer visitor. Rare breeder.

The Common Nighthawk declined over the past few decades in Western Washington for unknown reasons. It adapted somewhat to urban environments. Observers documented nests on the tops of buildings in downtown Seattle (Hunn 1982). Several theories have been proposed for its decline without any conclusions yet. Some suggest a cold, wet weather interlude around the 1970s and pollution decreased the availability of their insect prey. In the Vancouver area, one suggestion concludes that the decline in burns and clear-cuts where they formerly nested affected their numbers (Campbell et al. 1990). In the cities, fewer buildings possess the gravelly composition roofs that they formerly used. Gulls appear to be using many of the remaining available sites (Wahl et al. 2005). For whatever reason, the Common Nighthawk declined seriously since the early 1970s and appears rarely in the Puget Sound area. Joy Nelsen reported a nest in fields near Point Robinson for the summer of 1998, making a rare contemporary breeding record. Almost all recent sightings come from birds passing through in June, with two September records.

Anna's Hummingbird. © Peter Murray

Swifts

Black Swift

(AE) Status: Very rare spring and fall migrant and summer visitor. Four records.

Every once in a while, Black Swifts wander from their nest locations in the Cascades down into the Puget Sound lowlands. They show up when stormy weather forces them out of the mountains to feed. Vashon's sightings could come from breeders in the mountains or from spring or fall migrants. Dan Willsie saw some on 10 June 1990 in Paradise Valley. John Friars observed swifts over his place near KVI on 9 May 1996. Joe Van Os noted them in migration coming down Puget Sound from his place on Maury Island. The author contributed the latest sighting on 2 September 2003, seeing one along the cow pasture on Old Mill Road.

Vaux's Swift

(AE) Status: Rare spring and fall migrant, very rare summer visitor.

Vaux's Swifts generally reside in forested areas throughout the state, especially old-growth forest (Smith et al. 1997). Their abundance remains unknown for the period before settlement on Vashon. The habitat existed for a breeding population prior to the clearing of the Island's woods. The elimination of old-growth forest would have discouraged nesting on the Island. Throughout the West, Vaux's Swifts adapted over time to neighborhood chimneys and urban situations, except in areas like business cores (Smith et al. 1997). They now breed in the region in remnant old-growth or chimneys on old houses and other old buildings. Vaux's Swifts feed very actively over many of Seattle's neighborhoods, especially along Lake Washington. Despite proximity to these foraging areas, Vashon receives few visits. Spring and fall migrants provide the few sightings recorded.

Hummingbirds

Anna's Hummingbird

(HW, ST, DA) Status: Fairly common resident. Breeds.

Anna's Hummingbirds join the line of Californians that have come north. As more people put out hummingbird feeders and planted exotic plants that bloom at all times of the year, these hummingbirds expanded their range (Smith et al. 1997). The earliest Washington record appeared in Seattle in 1964, with the first breeding record coming from Tacoma in 1976. As Islanders learn more about their presence, more residents keep hummingbird feeders up during winter. Christmas Bird Count numbers have increased each year. One of the reasons Anna's Hummingbirds winter here may be that they eat more insects, giving them an additional food resource, as compared to other North American hummingbirds that rely primarily on nectar (Terres 1991).

Anna's Hummingbirds sometimes nest as early as January or February. Shaylon Stolk saw them gathering nesting materials on 20 February 2006. Gilbert and Jean Findlay observed them taking lint from a ball of cotton put out for nest builders on 4 March 2007. Rich Siegrist saw fledged young on 4 May 2010.

BBS (USGS 2013): 2013
CBC by area (Trevathan 1999-2013) Trend: Shows dramatic, consistent increase from less than ten to more than 60.
Vashon North: 2001-2013
Maury Island-Tramp Harbor: 1999-2013
Vashon South: 1999-2000, 2002-2013

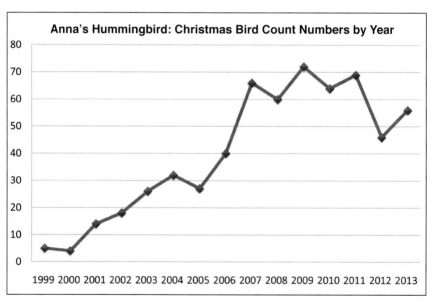

Costa's Hummingbird

(DA) Status: Accidental. One record.

Kathleen and Rick Sanders saw a male Costa's Hummingbird on 20 September 2004 at their place near Fern Cove on the northwest corner of Vashon. Both got good views of the bird sitting on a bush next to a male Anna's Hummingbird and going to their several hummingbird feeders. The Sanderses are familiar with Costa's Hummingbirds from observing them in their usual Southern California range. *A Birder's Guide to Washing-*

ton notes three records since 1998 in the Puget Sound lowlands (Opperman et al. 2003).

Rufous Hummingbird

(HW, ST, DA) Status: Fairly common spring and summer. Breeds.

The Rufous Hummingbird utilizes a wide range of habitats. These birds live off a variety of flowers from the shoreline up into the mountains, in open shrubby areas, and in both deciduous and coniferous forests. Besides adding insects to its diet, the Rufous Hummingbird drinks sap from the wells created by Red-breasted Sapsuckers in tree trunks (Terres 1991). These wells provide sap and attract insects for the Rufous to glean.

The Rufous usually times its arrival in spring to coincide with the flowering of pink Salmonberry or currant flowers. In several years, early scouts arrived as early as the first week of February. By late July and August, only a few remain, with many August and any September birds mostly passing through as migrants. Joe Van Os found active nests on both islands. Ralph Moore photographed a nest placed three stories high in a Douglas-fir near Tahlequah. Sharon Helmick noted one picking up dryer lint for its nest on 20 April 2011.

BBS (USGS 2013): 1995-1997, 2000, 2001, 2003, 2005, 2006, 2013

Kingfisher

Belted Kingfisher

(SW, SS, FW) Status: Fairly common resident. Breeds.

Kingfishers fly along saltwater shores and small ponds on Vashon. They like riverbanks and clay cliffs for nesting and use holes in the bluffs at Point Robinson, where they use burrows next to the Pigeon Guillemots in early May. Ann Spiers found them utilizing holes in the high banks of the "Grand Canyon" of Shinglemill Creek on 23 June 2002, deep in the Shinglemill Creek watershed. Sue Trevathan observed them using the banks near Raab's Lagoon. One or two often hang out at either ferry dock or perch on the wires in the Portage area.

BBS (USGS 2013): 1998, 2000, 2004, 2013

CBC by area (Trevathan 1999-2013) Trend: Shows a decline followed by a return to original levels.

Vashon North: 1999-2007, 2009-2011, 2013
Maury Island-Tramp Harbor: 1999-2006, 2008-2013
Quartermaster Harbor: 1999-2005, 2008-2013
Vashon South: 2000-2007, cw2008, 2009-2013

Woodpeckers and Allies

Lewis's Woodpecker
(DC) Status: Very rare visitor. One modern record.

Once erratic breeders and regular migrants through the lowlands of Puget Sound, Lewis's Woodpeckers now rarely visit Western Washington. Mating was seen in the Kirkland and Redmond areas in 1911 (Jewett et al. 1953). Jewett et al. note: "In our experience it is seen more frequently in burned areas in the forest than in any other habitat; the blackened standing dead stubs afford it nesting sites, and as a rule a considerable variety of plant and insect life is available for food." Rathbun writes of the Lewis's Woodpecker west of the Cascades: "In western Washington this woodpecker nests in June. Almost invariably the excavation for its nesting place is in a dead tree, the trunk of which is more or less blackened by fire, and this may be one reason why the bird is partial to old burns." (Bent 1964d)

The European Starling usually gets the blame for the disappearance of this bird from the area. Given the forest practices of the last 75 years, habitat change seems a more likely primary culprit. As with the Western Bluebird and Sooty Grouse that like disturbed and burnt-over areas, the Lewis's Woodpecker declined as burns decreased significantly and cutting vastly lowered the number of snags for nesting. In many areas of the Puget Sound lowlands, especially Vashon, urban and suburban areas expanded while forests matured and reclaimed semi-open and burned areas. The starling makes a possible, important secondary factor, hogging the few nest sites available in what's left of the appropriate habitat.

Campbell et al. (1990) came to the same conclusion for the decline of Lewis's Woodpecker in southwestern British Columbia. Previously these birds were considered an abundant breeding species around Vancouver and the southeastern tip of Vancouver Island, with observers noting them amid the habitat created by burns and logging that left snags from at least 1920 to 1940 (Campbell et al. 1990). After 1940, with fires tightly controlled and the removal of snags required, a population decline ensued. They note that Lewis's Woodpeckers continue to breed in the Okanogan area of British Columbia. Observers witnessed the woodpeckers successfully fending off starlings from nest sites.

Larrison mentions Lewis's Woodpeckers, in particular, as one of many "interesting" species for Vashon (Larrison 1952). No other records exist for the species on the Island. It probably wasn't around for much longer on Vashon, as the last wave of significant forest fires and clearing took place in the 1940s, about the time Larrison gathered material for his book.

The first Lewis's Woodpecker on Vashon in five decades eats a bug. © Peter Murray

John and Ellie Friars found the only Lewis's Woodpecker record for Vashon in 50 years, with a bird in their yard along the bluff above KVI Beach on 10 October 2005.

Red-naped Sapsucker

(DC, WC, HW, DA) Status: Very rare. One record.

Richard and Susan Rogers found and photographed a Red-naped Sapsucker at their home in a small, old apple orchard frequented by Red-breasted Sapsuckers. Local observers saw it several times from late November of 2003 through January 2004. Very few records exist for this species west of the Cascade foothills. See the Red-breasted account below for occurrence of hybrids.

CBC by area (Trevathan 1999-2013):

Vashon South: cw2004

Red-breasted Sapsucker

(DC, WC, HW, DA) Status: Uncommon resident. Fairly common in spring when tapping to claim territory. Breeds.

The Red-breasted Sapsucker lives up to its name, drilling rows of holes in trees to drink the sap. Other birds, especially hummingbirds, use the holes afterward to drink sap and to catch bugs attracted to it (Terres 1991).

One of the endearing habits of sapsuckers—like flickers—includes using a house's drainpipe as a territorial drumming instrument at 4:30 in the morning during breeding season. They also like to use street signs, and one can often drive right up to them without disturbing the bird. In spring, setting out the breeding territories makes them so visible they reach fairly common status. A pair nested in a tall alder snag at the Wolczkos' off Cove Road in north central Vashon for several years. This is one of several Vashon breeding records. In fall and winter, many Red-breasted Sapsuckers move through or down from the cold weather in the nearby Olympics and foothills, but their status lowers to uncommon as they become less visible and vocal and can't dependably be found at any particular location.

As bole nesters, Red-breasted Sapsuckers likely faced a major decline after so much of the Island converted to fields of stumps and agriculture (Raphael et al. 1988). They inhabit both mixed and coniferous forests in Western Washington (Smith et al. 1997). As the forests regrew on Vashon, their numbers again increased.

Where Red-breasted and Red-naped Sapsucker ranges overlap in the Cascades, hybridization occurs (Smith et al. 1997). Hybrid birds may then spread to other areas. A Vashon-Maury Island Audubon field trip found one such bird on 9 June 2007. Originally thought to be a Red-naped, the sapsucker turned out upon examination of photographs to be a hybrid (Steve Mlodinow pers. com. 2007).

BBS (USGS 2013): 2013

CBC by area (Trevathan 1999-2013) Trend: Shows a slight to moderate increase.

Vashon North: 2000, 2004, 2006, 2009, 2011-2013
Maury Island-Tramp Harbor: 2000, cw2002, 2006-2007, 2009-2012
Vashon South: 2002-2006, cw2007, 2008-2013

Downy Woodpecker

(DC, WC, HW, DA) Status: Fairly common resident. Breeds.

Downy Woodpeckers prefer deciduous and mixed woods on the Island. They were probably uncommon before the Island was cleared of the coniferous forest. As alders, maples, and other hardwoods spread in many areas, especially riparian zones, Downy Woodpecker numbers would have increased considerably. Nests have been found in several locations around Vashon.

BBS (USGS 2013): 1995, 1996, 1998, 2000, 2005, 2009, 2013

CBC by area (Trevathan 1999-2013) Trend: Stable.

Vashon North: 2000-2013
Maury Island-Tramp Harbor: 1999-2013
Vashon South: 1999-2000, 2002-2007, cw2008, 2009-2013

Hairy Woodpecker

(DC, WC, HW, DA) Status: Very rare visitor. Change in Status: No sightings since 2005 brings this species from its rare status in the first edition to very rare.

Ornithologists consider Hairy Woodpeckers fairly common in Western Washington in the appropriate habitat (Wahl et al. 2005). These woodpeckers prefer conifers, utilizing mixed forests to a lesser extent (Smith et al. 1997, Wahl et al. 2005). They would presumably have occurred in healthy numbers on the Island prior to European-American settlement, given the forest makeup back then. When loggers cut the original conifer forest, their numbers would have declined. Because of a lack of observers keeping records, no known sightings are available for Vashon prior to observations by birders over the last two decades. Hairies now persist only as rare residents or visitors. Records include one seen by John Friars at Point Robinson on 11 October 1992, another seen by Pam and Jack Dawdy in Paradise Valley on 20 September 2005, and birds seen on the Christmas Bird Count. Hairy Woodpeckers may breed on the Island in small numbers as they do elsewhere in the Puget Sound area. No breeding evidence exists for Vashon, possibly because too small a population exists or because of a lack of observer coverage. Recent sightings might be from residual population or from re-colonization efforts.

CBC by area (Trevathan 1999-2013):
Vashon North: 1999, 2002
Maury Island-Tramp Harbor: 2005
Vashon South: 2003, cw2005

Northern Flicker

(SS, FL, DC, WC, HW, ST, DA) Status: Fairly common resident. Breeds.

The robin of the woodpecker family, flickers breed in all sorts of habitats throughout the state. Any habitat holding some open area and a standing pole creates nesting area for them (Smith et al. 1997). Dan Willsie discovered a nest in an old stump by his former house in Burton. Flickers forage along the edges of woods, in open or agricultural areas, and in the gardens and yards around Vashon. A significant population probably already existed prior to European-American settlement, using the forests and forest clearings. The mix of habitat now available would have resulted in an increase in flicker numbers.

The local birds used to be known as "Red-shafted" Flickers until lumped in with the "Yellow-shafted" Flicker. The Yellow-shafted occurs east of the Rockies and up to Alaska. A few drift to Western Washington, and hybrids of the Red- and Yellow-shafted also occur. A true Yellow-shafted has yellow under the wings and a red crescent on the back of the head/neck. Males possess a black mark on the cheek instead of red, as with the Red-shafted. Rich Siegrist found a Yellow-shafted Flicker at his place on 2 October 2001. The author had several visits from one in December 2002. Gary Shugart of the Slater Museum at the University of Puget Sound received a specimen of a true Yellow-shafted killed by a car 21 March 2009. Red-shafted X Yellow-shafted Flicker hybrid birds show up regularly.

BBS (USGS 2013): 1995-1998, 2000, 2001, 2003-2006, 2013

CBC by area (Trevathan 1999-2013) Trend: Moderate increase.

Vashon North: 1999-2013
Maury Island-Tramp Harbor: 1999-2013
Vashon South: 1999-2013

Northern Flicker in the snow. © Michael Elenko

Pileated Woodpecker

(DC, WC, HW) Status: Fairly common resident. Breeds.

A big, crow-sized bird, Pileated Woodpeckers make themselves very visible and audible around Vashon. They forage widely and may be seen and heard flapping from one forest stand to another. While they do not exist in large numbers, they are hard to miss in a day's birding across the Island.

The Pileated Woodpecker population probably fluctuated greatly with the clearing of the forests and the resurgence of the woods through forest succession. Their numbers very likely decreased 40 to 50 percent with the complete clear-cut Vashon received (Raphael et al. 1988). Pileateds require large trees for nesting (Smith et al. 1997). Their ability to use a wide variety of species and types of trees enabled them to survive the cutting of the coniferous forests. In the Puget Sound area, they adapted to the new hardwood and mixed coniferous/deciduous forest stands.

Many recent nesting records exist for Vashon. In May 2001, KB Jones discovered a pair excavating a nest hole in an old, broken-off Red Alder. The hole was about 35 to 40 feet from the ground. Erin Kenny has found them nesting in the coniferous woods along the unpaved section of Old Mill Road. In mid-July 2002, Wally Woods saw a family of Pileated Woodpeckers, with the two fledged young looking like they had bright red Mohawk haircuts.

BBS (USGS 2013): 1996-1998, 2000, 2001, 2003-2005, 2013

CBC by area (Trevathan 1999-2013) Trend: Stable with possible increase.
Vashon North: 1999-2000, cw2001, 2002-2007, 2009-2013
Maury Island-Tramp Harbor: 1999-2000, cw2001, 2002-2004, 2007, 2009-2011, cw2012, 2013
Vashon South: 1999-2013

Falcons

American Kestrel

(FL) Status: Rare spring and fall migrant, uncommon winter resident, former breeder. Change in Status: Since the first edition, kestrels stayed the winter regularly at Wax Orchard, changing their status from very rare in winter to uncommon in winter. Recent ornithological research also moved the falcons from being grouped with hawks and eagles into a separate grouping, landing after woodpeckers in the evolutionary tree.

American Kestrels used to be fairly common on the Island, according to long-time residents. The shift away from farm fields, pasture, clear-cuts, and burns toward heavier wood cover decreased their habitat. Kestrels bred in earlier times, possibly up into the early 1990s, at Wax Orchard. Wax Orchard appears to have been the central habitat for this species, with other locations visited primarily by birds in migration. At least one kestrel still winters along Wax Orchard Road and Old Mill Road fields, often perching on wires along 232nd Street.

CBC by area (Trevathan 1999-2013):
Vashon South: 2004-2008, cw2010

Merlin

(SS, FW, FL, DC, WC, HW, ST, DA, AE) Status: Uncommon fall through spring, very rare summer.

The roughly pigeon-sized Merlin is Vashon's most common falcon. In migration and winter, Merlins utilize the open fields and gardens of the Island and shoreline areas. Around farms and fields, they hunt for sparrows and birds up to starling and robin in size. On one of the Christmas Bird Counts, the author saw a Merlin rocket across the sky over the fields of central Vashon, making all of the other birds in the area drop like rocks into the bushes. Along the beaches, Merlins dive down on Sanderlings and Killdeers or any other small birds moving along the waterline.

Historically, only a few Puget Sound Merlin breeding records exist. According to Bud Anderson of the Falcon Research Group, Merlins staged a breeding range expansion in Western Washington over the past few years, with several pairs now nesting in Seattle (Anderson pers. com. 2005). That expansion may reach Vashon in the next few years. In a very rare Island summer sighting, Dan Willsie saw a Merlin chasing a Violet-green Swallow on 3 July 2005.

CBC by area (Trevathan 1999-2013) Trend: Stable:
Vashon North: 1999, 2008-2009, 2012-2013
Maury Island-Tramp Harbor: 2003, 2007, 2009, 2011-2013
Vashon South: 2001, 2005, 2008-2009, 2013

Peregrine Falcon

(SS, AE) Status: Rare visitor year-round.

Peregrine Falcons visit the Island year-round. The migration and winter seasons record the most observations. Vashon's lack of rocky cliffs provides few if any suitable nesting locations for Peregrine Falcons. Several peregrines breed in the Puget Sound area, some using special nest boxes on tall buildings and bridges in downtown Seattle, Tacoma, and Olympia.

Peregrine Falcon populations plummeted, as did those of many other birds, from the heavy use of the pesticide DDT (Ehrlich et al. 1988). After DDT was banned, the release of captive-hatched young birds and assistance with artificial nest boxes helped bring peregrines back from the edge of extinction. According to Bud Anderson of the Falcon Research Group, the population of peregrines in the San Juan Islands rebounded from no breeding pairs in the mid 1970s to eighteen by the turn of the millennium (Anderson pers. com. 2005). Many consider starlings to be a nuisance, but they provide an abundant source of prey to the rebounding falcon population. Researchers usually find starling bones and feathers in large quantities at most peregrine nesting sites, according to Anderson.

Around Vashon, peregrines generally hunt only along the shorelines. They seek out and eat ducks and shorebirds feeding along the beaches and in the small estuaries. Most sightings of peregrines come from near the ferry docks or Point Robinson. In the last couple of years, one hunted in winter from the Dockton area to the pond at Monument Road and Quartermaster Drive. Green-winged Teal make a favorite meal of peregrines, so KVI Beach and Fisher Pond offer two other places to watch for them. On 23 November 2003, the author visited KVI Beach and observed a Mallard and a teal in the pond, watched by a Peregrine. The author walked toward the ducks, trying to scare them up, but they knew of the falcon and wouldn't fly until the author got close and threw a large stick at them. The falcon came down a little slow off the mark, probably worried about the author. The ducks escaped going flat out, skimming close to the ground, and then flew to Tramp Harbor as fast as they could.

Dave Beaudette tells a great story about a peregrine he saw hunting out over the open water:

"On November 22, 1998, at about 11:00 a.m., one was flying a few feet over the surface of the water in very windy conditions. It just came over a wave as two Ancient Murrelets surfaced. The peregrine darted to the side after them, and the ancients dove and got away. This happened in mid-Sound on the Fauntleroy to Vashon ferry. Was the peregrine hunting murrelets, or did it accidentally come across the murrelets? My guess is that it was hunting, since it was using the waves as an element of surprise and was flying just a few feet over the surface of the water in very windy conditions, which costs a lot of energy." (Beaudette pers. com. 2005)

CBC by area (Trevathan 1999-2013):
Vashon South: 2008
Maury Island-Tramp Harbor: 2004

Tyrant Flycatchers

Olive-sided Flycatcher

(DC, WC, HW) Status: Fairly common summer resident. Breeds.

Some birds' calls evoke a whole landscape. For the author, the calls of Olive-sided Flycatchers take him back to near timberline in the Olympics. Their emphatic *whut, whee year* makes him think of hiking up a switchback, looking for them calling from the top of a snag or tall tree. For fun, many write the call as *quick, three beers*.

Olive-sided Flycatchers hunt for flying insects from high at the top of conifers, making it hard to get a close look at them. They specialize in utilizing the edges of clearings, burns, parks, gardens, and occasionally mixed forest (Sharpe 1993). In his *Life Histories* series, Bent notes that they inhabit woods all the way from sea level to the timberline of the high Cascades and Sierras (Bent 1963d). Rathbun, an early Seattle area bird observer, remembers a Lake Washington with an unbroken shoreline of conifers down to the water. Olive-sided Flycatchers staked out separate territories about every mile along the lake (Bent 1963d). They act quite territorially and fiercely settle boundary disputes with each other.

On Vashon, they appear widespread in coniferous forest of the northwest of the Island and seem more localized in conifer patches elsewhere. Early returning birds often call from the woods above KVI Beach. Breeding evidence includes Dan Willsie's observation of a crow's raid on a nest on the north end of Vashon and Rich Siegrist's views of adults feeding juveniles in the Colvos area.

BBS (USGS 2013): 1995-1998, 2000-2006, 2009, 2013

Western Wood-Pewee

(DC, WC, HW) Status: Fairly common summer resident. Breeds.

Pewees seem very local on Vashon. Paradise Valley and the Colvos area provide two of the few easy locations to find them. They breed in riparian woodlands (Smith et al. 1997). Raphael projected a 79 percent increase in their population in his study area in Northern California after major clearing of the coniferous forest (Raphael et al. 1988). It would seem that they should be more common on the Island, with all of the various stream corridors available. A big burst of activity begins in May as migrants arrive.This decreases as most of the birds continue on to breeding territories across western Canada. Large numbers of pewees sometimes appear after a major front has passed through. Point Robinson would be a good place to look after a big downpour in early to mid-May. Rich Siegrist found a nest in a Bigleaf Maple near his place. Two eggs survived to hatching, but only one bird made it to fledgling status.

BBS (USGS 2013): 1995-1998, 2000-2006, 2009, 2013

Willow Flycatcher

(FL, ST, DA) Status: Fairly common spring and summer resident, probable breeder.

The Willow Flycatcher possesses a two-syllable *fitz-bew* call sounding quite emphatic, similar to a sneeze. This helps differentiate it from the Pacific-slope Flycatcher. Willow Flycatchers prefer brushy, new-growth areas, especially those with alders. They arrive almost a month later than the Pacific-slope, showing up in mid- to late May. Because increasingly fewer brushy fields survive on Vashon, Willow Flycatchers take more effort to find than the other flycatchers. They probably breed, but no evidence has been found. Increased observer effort should find nesting activity.

BBS (USGS 2013): 1995-1998, 2000-2006, 2009, 2013

Hammond's Flycatcher

(DC, WC, HW, ST, DA) Status: Rare spring and fall migrant.

Hammond's Flycatchers move through in small numbers in the lowland Puget Trough at altitudes below 150 meters, and at best breed rarely (Wahl et al. 2005, Smith et al. 1997). Thick, mid-elevation coniferous forest provides its main nesting areas throughout the state, though hardwood and mixed forest in low to mid-elevations west of the Cascades host these birds uncommonly (Smith et al. 1997). Old-growth coniferous forest presents the optimum habitat for this species (Manuwal 1991). Because these birds are largely absent from developed parts of the lowlands, some observers believe Hammond's were common in the Puget Sound area and then decreased with the cutting of the Douglas-fir forests.

Few observers with the skills to differentiate the various *Empidonax* flycatchers have looked for Hammond's on Vashon. The first records for the Island date back to the 1980s, when Joe Van Os banded two. No further records occurred until 2004. At most, two records come in each year from that date to the present.

Pacific-slope Flycatcher

(DC, WC, HW, DA) Status: Fairly common spring and summer resident. Breeds.

Mid-April sees the return of the most common of the Western Washington flycatchers, the Pacific-slope Flycatcher. These flycatchers utilize every type of forest on Vashon and show up in any significant wood lot.

Their Latin name is *Empidonax difficilis*. That gives an idea as to the difficulty in telling them apart from the other species of the *Empidonax* genus that occur in Washington. Disciplined study of *Empidonax* field marks permits one to separate the species. Pacific-slope, Hammond's, Dusky, Willow, and Least Flycatchers all belong to this group. On Vashon, the main species consist of the Pacific-slope and Willow Flycatchers. Hammond's, as noted above, comes as a rare migrant. Least Flycatchers theoretically might visit during migration, but no records exist for Vashon. They all look like little green to yellow-green birds with white wing bars. The slight differences in size and plumage remain similar enough to the eye that the variations within a species might be as great as or greater than those between the various species. A few expert birders attain the capability to identify them without actually holding them in the hand.

Knowing their vocalization provides the best method of differentiation. The songs for each bird are diagnostic for almost all of them. The Pacific-slope gives a *sooweet!* reminiscent of a whistle blown to get someone's attention. The extent of forested area on Vashon makes the Pacific-slope Flycatchers easy to find. They almost always remain within the woods and not out in the open. The other *Empidonax* that shows up on the Island, the Willow Flycatcher, almost always perches out in brushy areas. It makes a different call, and its eye-ring is much less visible.

Good places to look for Pacific-slope Flycatcher include Lisabeula, Point Robinson, the forest above KVI Beach, the parking lot by the north end ferry dock, and Fern Cove. Several nesting records exist. A 20 May 2001 field trip visited a nest location at Singer Road and 204th Street. The cup-shaped nest was about five feet up on a branch next to the trunk of an alder in mixed woods. That same spring, another bird nested in the rafters of Ellen Kritzman's entryway on north Vashon. A pair nested on top of an outdoor light fixture on the wall of the author's home in July 2005. Other nests show up sometimes in open porches and carports.

BBS (USGS 2013): 1995-1998, 2000-2006, 2009, 2013

Say's Phoebe

(SS, FL) Status: Very rare late winter, early spring visitor. Two records. Change in Status: With only one record in the first edition, this species was considered

accidental; a second sighting brings its status to very rare. It's unlikely to be seen more than once every few years.

Common in the dry, open scrub and steppe of Eastern Washington, the Say's Phoebe sometimes makes a wrong turn and ends up on the west side of the Cascades. This occurs particularly in spring migration (Wahl et al. 2005). Brian Bell found one perching on beach logs at KVI Beach on 5 April 2002. The author saw another in the same location almost exactly a decade later on 10 April 2012.

Western Kingbird

(SS, FL) Status: Very rare spring migrant. Seven records. Change in Status: Increased observer effort resulted in very rare but regular sightings of this migrant over the last decade.

The Western Kingbird breeds commonly in open areas in Eastern Washington. Small numbers migrate west of the Cascades each year. Pierce, Skagit, and Whatcom Counties produced a few recent breeding records (Smith et al. 1997). The loss of open areas and prairies on this side of the mountains led to a decline in Western Kingbird numbers in the Puget Sound area. Rich Siegrist observed one on Vashon along his driveway in the Colvos area in June 1991 for the first record. Since 2004, increased observer effort and reporting resulted in at least one sighting every other year. The birds all showed up as migrants along shoreline open areas such KVI Beach, Point Robinson, and Maury Island Marine Park. The only exception consisted of a bird seen by Harsi and Ezra Parker on 12 June 2012 at Wax Orchard.

Shrike

Northern Shrike

(FL, ST, DA) Status: Very rare winter visitor.

On 15 February 1987, Doug Dolstad found a Northern Shrike at the old Nike missile/Vashon Health Center site (P. Mattocks, archival notecards, Seattle Audubon Society). This 20-year-old record remains the only sighting, for unknown reasons. Northern Shrikes regularly show up as uncommon to fairly common from October through March in King County and the Puget Sound region as a whole. This holds true for the San Juan Islands, so the island nature of Vashon fails to explain their absence. While the open habitat preferred by shrikes declined over the last half century, enough survives and should attract at least one or two birds each year.

Vireos

White-eyed Vireo

(FW, FL, HW, ST, DA) Status: Accidental. One record.

The only record for White-eyed Vireo in Washington State consists of one bird found on Vashon. Ornithologist Phil Mattocks saw this stray from the eastern United States at his home on 12 July 1981 (Hunn 1982).

Cassin's Vireo

(DC, WC, HW, DA) Status: Uncommon spring migrant and summer resident. Breeds.

Around the state, Cassin's Vireos inhabit mainly dry coniferous forests. Early observers in Washington noted them using the vanishing oak prairies that were once more common in the southern Puget Sound region (Jewett et al. 1953, Dawson and Bowles 1909). On Vashon, this species generally dwells along riparian areas in mixed woods where conifers form the dominant part of the mix. When the early settlers cleared the coniferous forests, the Cassin's population would have taken a significant hit, declining by as much as 25 to 30 percent (Raphael et al. 1988). The Cassin's ability to survive in stands other than pure conifers, and the regrowth of some stands even as others were cut, offer possible reasons for its presence on the Island.

Over the last decade, in some years, observers found only one or two briefly in spring migration. In other years, birds showed up throughout the summer into the fall. Places to check for Cassin's Vireos include the Island Center Forest with its stand of cottonwoods and Lodgepole Pine, as well as the forests of southern Vashon and Maury Islands. Rayna and Jay Holtz hosted them for many years in their forested property off Cove Road. Dan Willsie found a nest in Paradise Valley for the sole breeding record, but Cassin's Vireos possibly breed each year.

BBS (USGS 2013): 1996, 1997, 2000, 2006

Hutton's Vireo

(DC, WC, HW, ST) Status: Fairly common resident. Breeds.

Hutton's Vireos prove almost as common as Warbling Vireos on the Island, especially when their calling in spring makes them easy to find. In other times of the year, they tend to be quiet and inconspicuous. They remain resident throughout the year with probably no change in numbers, though their unobtrusive habits make them appear uncommon.

Hutton's Vireos reside in mixed deciduous and coniferous forests (Wahl et al. 2005), a common habitat on Vashon. These birds would have lived here in some numbers before European-American settlement. Those numbers would have increased significantly as the Island went from predominantly coniferous woods to successional hardwood and mixed deciduous and coniferous woods.

From mid-February through April, this vireo's *wheo wheo wheo* call, a two-note strong whistle, resounds throughout Vashon. Singing continues to a lesser extent into the summer and occasionally in the midst of winter. Hutton's Vireos breed earlier than most of the migrants. Rich Siegrist found a nest being built on 6 April 2002 in Maury Island Marine Park, placed on an alder branch. He later saw the female sitting on the nest.

During the winter, Hutton's Vireos forage singly or in mixed flocks in the company of kinglets, chickadees, and nuthatches. Hutton's look much like Ruby-crowned Kinglets but have a thicker, vireo bill, blue legs, and generally much slower movements. Paradise Valley, Point Robinson, Westside Highway in the Colvos and Cove area, and the Island Center Forest are some of the best places to search.

BBS (USGS 2013): 1997, 1998, 2000-2006, 2009, 2013

CBC by area (Trevathan 1999-2013) Trend: Stable and then down for last five years but always such low numbers that the trend is not very useful.

Vashon North: 1999, 2003-2004, 2006, cw2013
Maury Island-Tramp Harbor: 2001, 2004-2010
Vashon South: 1999-2003, 2006-2007, 2009

Warbling Vireo

(HW, ST, DA) Status: Fairly common spring to early fall. Breeds.

At the end of April, Warbling Vireos burst upon the scene singing their insistent song from deciduous growth in gardens and riparian settings. Just about any wet patch of hardwood forest will have at least migrant birds if not pairs staying to nest. Warbling Vireos would have become more common in the 1900s as the clearing of the timber in the late nineteenth century created brushy regrowth and more deciduous woods than previously existed. As the Island's forested stands mature, become larger as a whole and more coniferous, the Warbling Vireo population will likely drop to some extent. Enough open area exists, especially in the expanding residential areas of the Island, for Warbling Vireos to continue their fairly common status. The Island Center Forest, Point Robinson, and Paradise Valley make excellent locations to look for this vireo. The vireo breeds prolifically on the Island. Dan Willsie observed an adult feeding four young in a nest out on a limb at the yacht club at the marina in Quartermaster Harbor on 14 May 2001. Rich Siegrist found a female incubating eggs in a nest in a Red Alder along Westside Highway. The adults later abandoned the nest after a period of extremely cool, wet weather. Joe Van Os had an active nest at his office on south Vashon. Ornithologist J. W. Slipp found an adult feeding downy young on 7 July 1940 (Slipp 1939-1956).

BBS (USGS 2013): 1996-1998, 2000-2006, 2009, 2013

Red-eyed Vireo

(HW) Very rare spring visitor. Three records. Change in Status: Through a typographical error, listed as rare in first edition when actually very rare.

Red-eyed Vireos breed in cottonwood groves, usually in riparian areas in Washington (Smith et al. 1997). Vashon has very few cottonwood patches, making these vireos a rare migrant. One place to watch would be the patch of cottonwoods at the Island Center Forest in May and early June. Gary Shugart found several birds, likely migrants, in June at Point Robinson. The only other confirmed recent records occurred at Carole Elder's home on 20 June 2006, and one seen by Adam Sedgley at Dockton on 15 May 2012.

Crows and Jays

Steller's Jay

(DC, WC, HW, DA) Status: Fairly common resident. Breeds.

Steller's Jays demand attention in pretty much every habitat on Vashon. If the bright blue of their plumage doesn't grab the eye, the loud *jay! jay! jay!* of their scolding assaults the ears. These jays act extremely curious and eat just about anything, hence their propensity to find food wherever they turn up.

In urban and suburban settings, Steller's Jays empty a feeder of its food just to pick out the particular type of seed that suits their fancy. They audaciously raid dog and cat food left out on the porch or even inside a house next to an open window or door. Under the forest canopy or along any bunch of trees, jays can be seen starting at the bottom of a tree, flapping diagonally across to a higher opposite branch over and over again until they reach the upper levels. Then the process will repeat after a long glide down to the bottom of the next tree. The procedure gives them the ability to spot any nests with eggs or young to eat, any fruit to pluck, and any beetles, wasps, or spiders to glean. Along the forest perimeter, field edges, and hedgerows, they plunder the hazelnuts or opportunistically spear a frog or other small creature with their beak.

The jays lead the other birds in noticing and mobbing any intruder to their areas. Cats walk along stubbornly pretending that three or four jays are not just out of reach, screaming penetratingly, *shack, shack, shack*. Hawks and owls receive similar yet somewhat more cautious treatment, as these larger predators hunt the jays. Steller's Jays have a remarkable ability to mimic the scream of a Red-tailed Hawk and sometimes use the ability to flush prey or parents from nests to be plundered.

While resident in Washington State, some latitudinal and altitudinal migration occurs. Several studies show some northern birds moving south in the late fall and bolstering the size of more southern populations (Campbell et al. 1990). Sharpe in *Olympic Peninsula Birds* reflects that jays hesitantly cross bodies of water. In the San Juans, many of the smaller Islands appear empty of jays because of the need to fly across water (Sharpe 1993). Large groups have been seen flying out from the tip of Vancouver Island. It is thought that the birds return to land again on the island. Banding studies found the birds remain on the island later in the season after banding. After their initial flock creation, they spread out in small groups in that region (Campbell et al. 1990). The author noted this phenomenon on Maury Island when, on 6 May 2000, more than 30 Steller's Jays gathered on the radar towers at Point Robinson. Repeatedly they flew out over the water a good distance, only to return. Observers noted this behavior in other years as well.

For being so obvious and loud, Steller's Jays act quite elusive during the breeding season. It takes careful observation to find their nests. Sue Trevathan has discovered nests in her yard in the Paradise Valley area. Dan Willsie spotted one at his former residence in Burton. Joe Van Os had an active nest at his office on south Vashon.

BBS (USGS 2013): 1995-1998, 2000-2006, 2009, 2013

CBC by area (Trevathan 1999-2013) Trend: Stable.

Vashon North: 1999-2013
Maury Island-Tramp Harbor: 1999-2013
Vashon South: 1999-2013

Blue Jay

(DA) Status: Accidental. One record.

A single Blue Jay visited Mary Fitch's house during the winter of 1991 to 1992 (National Audubon Society 1971-1994, *AB*46:309).

Western Scrub-Jay

(HW, ST, DA) Status: Rare visitor and winter resident. Change in Status: Range expansion into the Puget Sound area by this species has resulted in an increased number of sightings such that visits now occur yearly, and sometimes a bird stays the winter.

The list of California invaders includes the Western Scrub-Jay, a large, blue and white jay. This bird historically resided in open areas and open forests. It adapted extremely well to residential development. With increased development on the West Coast, it grew in numbers in its original areas and expanded its territory northwards. A very rare breeder along the Columbia River at the turn of the millennium, it now extends its breeding range to British Columbia (Smith et al. 1997).

First seen by Joy Nelsen on Maury Island on 18 November 1992, scrub-jays in the beginning visited Vashon only every few years. Most records consisted of brief visits to yards or hazelnut tree patches. Since the first

American Crow bathing. © Doug Parrott

edition of this book, they now come every year, and one spent the winter and early spring at Bob Hawkins's place in Dockton in 2008/09.

CBC by area (Trevathan 1999-2013):
Maury Island-Tramp Harbor: cw2006, 2009, 2001

American Crow

(SS, FL, DA, AE) Status: Common resident. Breeds.

American Crows in Western Washington increased their population greatly as urbanization grew (Marzluff et al. 2001b). University of Washington researcher John Marzluff finds that crow populations in urban areas expanded rapidly despite many challenges to breeding and individual survival. Crows face problems such as cars, toxins, and predators of adults such as Red-tailed Hawk and Great Horned Owl. The many large, relatively protected populations of nest predators, i.e., Raccoons and Eastern Gray Squirrels, pick off many of the young crows. A concentration process developed in urban areas, where crows flock in from suburban and rural environments, attracted by the large amount of food in garbage and refuse containers (Marzluff et al. 2001b). Many consider the increased crow population a threat to urban breeding success for other bird species. Using nests mimicking canopy, ground, and shrub nesters, studies conducted by Marzluff found that crows represented a relatively insignificant part of the overall nest predator picture that includes mice and rats, squirrels, Raccoons, and jays.

American Crows are very visible on Vashon, cruising shorelines, ruling the commercial areas, harassing any raptor in the farms and fields, and swooping in on garbage and tidbits in yards and gardens. They largely avoid the forested areas that form the raven's redoubt. Crows breed on the Island, visibly building nests, as they fly by with big sticks in their beaks.

BBS (USGS 2013): 1995-1998, 2000-2006, 2009, 2013

CBC by area (Trevathan 1999-2013) Trend: Stable.
Vashon North: 1999-2013
Maury Island-Tramp Harbor: 1999-2013
Quartermaster Harbor: 1999-2013
Vashon South: 1999-2013

Northwestern Crow

(SS) Status: Extirpated, probable formerly common resident.

"After lengthy discussion it is pretty well settled that the Crow of the northwestern sea-coasts is merely a dwarfed race of the *Corvus brachyrhynchos* group; and that it shades perfectly into the prevailing western type, *C. b. hesperis,* wherever that species occupies adjacent regions. This area of intergradation lies chiefly south and west of Puget Sound, in Washington; for the Crow is ever fond of the half-open country, and does not take kindly to the unmitigated forest depths, save where, as in the case of the Fish Crow, he may find relief upon the broad expanses of shore and tide-flats....

"It is impossible, therefore, to pronounce with certainty upon the sub-specific identity of Crows seen near shore in Mason, Thurston, Pierce, or even King County; but in Clallam, Jefferson, San Juan, and the other counties of the Northwest, one has no difficulty in recognizing the dwarf race." (Dawson and Bowles 1909)

The American Ornithological Union recognizes two crow species for Western Washington, the American Crow and the Northwestern Crow. For Washington ornithologists, Dawson's words above ring as true today as they did a hundred years ago. Argument continues back and forth, but local ornithologists have not recognized the Northwestern Crow as a separate species for decades. In 1961, David Johnston's *Biosystematics of American Crows* forcefully argued that they were one species, convincing most local authorities.

A highly specialized shoreline crow, the Northwestern Crow once existed on shorelines from the Puget Sound and Olympic Peninsula to southeastern Alaska. The American Crow inhabited the territory east of the Cascades and spread west along major river valleys only as the woods west of the Cascades were cut and farmland and urban area were developed (Wahl et al. 2005). In general, this mirrors the westward movement of the American Crow in other regions, as European settlement changed the habitat in areas across the continent (Marzluff et al. 2001b). In the Puget Sound area, the two forms either quickly interbred to the point where it is impossible to distinguish between the two, or the larger American Crow pushed the other out. Marzluff believes the Northwestern Crow probably existed as a subspecies headed toward full speciation but found its population re-mixed and swamped by the American Crow in the last century and a half.

Mitochondrial DNA studies by Renee Robinette-Ha at the University of Washington show that two genetically distinct populations exist in Washington (Robinette-Ha pers. com. 2005). The crow population on the state's outer coast appears similar to that of crows along the coasts up through Alaska, but different from the American Crows in the rest of Washington. Across the country, Robinette-Ha says, American Crow DNA remains consistent, without genetically different populations. Combined with the different behavior of the Northwestern Crow, it would seem that the DNA evidence confirms a separate species. However, the project needs much more DNA analysis to be conclusive.

Finding out if Puget Sound Northwestern Crow populations merged with American Crows or were pushed out will require nuclear DNA research. While a population of Northwestern Crows probably existed around Vashon prior to the 1800s, birds in this area now match the behavior and DNA of American Crow (Renee Robinette-Ha pers. com. 2005).

Common Raven

(SS, FL, DC, WC, AE) Status: Fairly common resident. Breeds. Change in Status: The Island population continues to expand, such that the Common Raven is now hard to miss.

Ravens are rare in the urbanized lowlands of the Puget Sound. Vashon has hosted a breeding pair since at least the early 1990s. Each Christmas Bird Count records five or six at least, and the trend seems to be heading higher over the last decade (Trevathan 1999-2013). Because ravens range the whole length of the Island, it's difficult to say without netting and banding the birds how many actually reside on Vashon. Ravens appear to visit from Kitsap County across the narrow Colvos Passage, adding to the local population.

John Marzluff, expert on ravens worldwide, mentions that the Common Raven population expanded across the North American West over the last decades (Marzluff per. com. 2013). Vashon's own population is

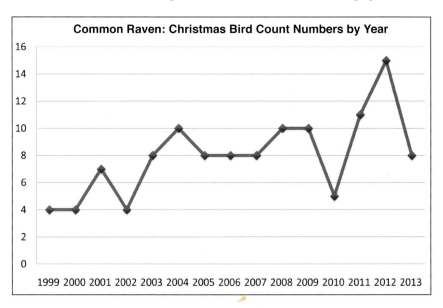

likely growing at the same time as more birds spread out from other territories in rural Kitsap and western Pierce Counties. As persecution decreases and food sources such as road-killed deer increase, survival becomes much easier for this corvid.

In the mid-1990s it appeared as though a pair nested in the Shinglemill Creek watershed north of Fisher Pond, another in the Old Mill Road woods, and one to two others around Point Robinson. These successfully raised broods over the years, indicating that perhaps two or more nesting pairs now exist on Vashon. Everywhere west of Vashon Highway, most of south Vashon, and Maury Island have ravens flying along the shorelines or up and down the roads looking for roadkill. When workers mow the fields at Wax Orchard in August, ten to 25 ravens might be found looking for rodents. Alan Huggins and Kathryn True noted groups of ten or more playing in the winds over the north end of Vashon in 2010 and 2011.

It is appropriate that among the Celts, ravens were said to foretell outbreaks of plague. The first known death of an indigenous animal in Washington State due to West Nile virus was a Common Raven in Pend Oreille County in the state's northeastern corner (Ostrom 2002). By January 2005, West Nile virus was known to have infected 284 species in North America, according to the Centers for Disease Control (CDC). The corvids, the family of birds including ravens, crows, and jays, appear to be hit exceptionally hard, with high mortality rates (Marra et al. 2004). Data collection skews these statistics in that crows and ravens, as large birds, prove much easier to find and keep track of when they die compared to small songbirds. So far, Christmas Bird Count and Breeding Bird Survey data in highly affected areas show only small dips in species populations overall (ibid.) Individual regions, such as around Chicago, showed an 81 percent decrease in crows after a severe outbreak in 2002 (Chu 2003). Research into the long-term effects on wildlife remain in the very early stages at this point. Marra et al. (2004) hypothesize that, currently, only endangered populations like the Hawaiian Crow are at risk. Experts anticipated West Nile virus to impact Washington on as large a scale as it affected other states. This has not occurred as yet. Perhaps Washington will escape die-offs, and the introduction of West Nile to the region will be slow enough for species to become accustomed to it.

BBS (USGS 2013): 1997, 2002, 2003, 2009, 2013

CBC by area (Trevathan 1999-2013) Trend: Moderate increase.

Vashon North: 1999-2001, 2004-2010, 2012
Maury Island-Tramp Harbor: 2001-2002, 2003-2007, 2009, 2012-2013
Vashon South: 2000-2013

Swallows and Martins

Purple Martin

(SS, AE) Status: Fairly common summer resident. Breeds.

In the 1990s, the warbling call of the Purple Martin seldom reached the shores of Vashon. Like Tree Swallows, these birds historically nested in dead snags along shorelines. According to Jewett et al. (1953), they also used oak meadows, such as the remnant around Joint Base Lewis-McChord. These meadows found favor with early farmers in the mid- to late 1800s. Soon the farmers converted them to agriculture, wiping them out. Wholesale clear-cutting, removal of snags and trees along shorelines, and farming of the oak prairies eventually limited the number of potential nest sites for martins. Purple Martins fortunately adapted to using holes, cracks, and ledges on human structures. Their population might have even risen as they used all of the new potential locations provided by the rapidly growing number of settlers around farms, towns, and cities. By the turn of the nineteenth century, Jewett et al. note that martins occurred only around the growing urban centers of the Puget Sound region: Bellingham, Port Townsend, Everett, Seattle, Tacoma, Olympia, and a few other sites.

Another of the state's birding pioneers, William Dawson, noted in 1909: "It will prove a sad day for the martins when the English Sparrows [House Sparrows] take full possession of our cities." (Dawson and Bowles 1909, Sharpe 1993) The prediction proved accurate because the martin's decline began with the coming of the urban-dwelling and scrappy House Sparrow, veteran of millennia of co-existing with human habitation. House Sparrows claimed most of the nest holes and would literally steal the food from the martin young's mouths. Starlings soon piled on to worsen the situation. The coming of the aggressive, hole-nesting European Starling to Washington in the 1950s just about finished the martins off.

Washington's cool, wet, late spring/early summer weather may have affected martins as well. According to the American Ornithological Union's *Birds of North America* series, "Adverse weather kills more Purple Martins than all other sources of mortality combined." (Brown 1997) As recently as 1972, an East Coast hurricane killed 90 to 100 percent of the nestlings and thousands of adults in a number of states. It took more than ten years before martins returned to some parts. Cool, wet weather also impinges on or keeps down the high-flying insect populations that martins depend upon, causing starvation of adults or nestlings. It's not hard to imagine a couple of wet Junes here in Washington impacting local martin populations just as nesting begins. The combination of one or two serious weather events as well as competition from starlings and House Sparrows may have been the cause of the disappearance of Purple Martins from the state for so many years.

By the early 1980s, the Purple Martin essentially disappeared from Washington State (Sharpe 1993). A few pairs still nested out of the Bon Marché building in downtown Seattle, and a nest box project in the Olympia area had a few takers. Around Vashon, local birders such as Rich Siegrist hadn't seen martins for quite a while. Then one day in 1993, on the west side, just north of where the old Colvos Hotel used to be, Siegrist observed two pairs using some pilings out over the water. Siegrist had heard of the nest box project down in Olympia and others that were trying to assist martins in gaining a toehold again in Western Washington. The next year, he put out three boxes, all of which hosted pairs. The rest, as they say, is history.

Siegrist's martin box program now comprises over 70 "holes" or nesting cavities around Vashon on pilings. Boxes contain one, two, or three nesting cavities. By 2004, about 72 pairs bred around Vashon in boxes at Sylvan Beach, Fern Cove, Colvos Passage, Dockton, Ellisport, and Tramp Harbor, and two pairs made their own nests in pilings (Rich Siegrist pers. com. 2013.) In 2005, there were 72 pairs in boxes plus four pairs in pilings; 2006 had 67 pairs plus three pairs in pilings; and 2007 had 69 pairs plus two pairs in pilings. In 2008, an early spring got the martins to start nesting early, but then the weather turned very cold for weeks. Siegrist found some martins dead in the boxes, and many others left. Only sixteen pairs stuck around that year, and in 2009, only nineteen. Numbers began to rise

Two Tree Swallows. © Doug Parrott

starting in 2010, reaching 39 pairs using boxes in 2012. No pairs utilized pilings from 2008 to 2012.

Putting a number of houses close together works well because Purple Martins nest colonially. For some reason, West Coast martins prefer single-hole houses, though Siegrist has shown that they will use a three-hole bird box. All of Siegrist's boxes sit on pilings over water, which remains the case for almost all known martin nests in Washington (Smith et al. 1997). Siegrist carves a rectangular hole with the long side horizontal, making it harder for starlings to enter. Sometimes the starlings still need to be evicted. Siegrist recently started to look for some locations along shorelines in order not to depend upon pilings. Most of the pilings exceed 80 or 90 years of age and will require eventual replacement.

Other caring birders have successfully put up boxes in British Columbia, around the Columbia River estuary, in Commencement Bay in Tacoma, around the Olympia area, and at several other locations. On the East Coast, martins readily take to multiple-hole houses. One birder in New Jersey, in 1947, counted pairs in 270 holes of a 379-room birdhouse (Terres 1991). Native American peoples in the South started the practice of helping the martins by putting up gourds. European settlers found Native Americans attracting the martins, possibly to help control insects.

Siegrist says that male martins arrive around mid-April and stake out a box. The females follow them in a few weeks. More and more arrive through May until they begin nesting in June. Nest box locations along the shorelines provide almost certain sightings of martins in summer. Their larger numbers mean that they show up overhead hunting for insects just about anywhere around the Island. The author often hears them up high over the very center of the Island. In late August and early September, many adults and the year's young concentrate in big flocks around the radio tower at KVI Beach.

These largest of North American swallows grow a full inch and a quarter larger than the ubiquitous Barn Swallow. The males look all dark, a glossy purplish-blue-black. Females and juveniles appear dark gray-purple on the back and gray to light gray below. After they finish the summer here, martins migrate all the way to South America to avoid winter.

BBS (USGS 2013): 2006, 2009

Tree Swallow

(SS, FW, FL, DA, AE) Status: Uncommon spring and summer resident. Breeds.

Tree Swallows appear quite localized on Vashon. Where Violet-green Swallows show up just about anywhere on the Island, Tree Swallows almost solely inhabit areas near water. As hole-nesters, they face the same challenges as Purple Martins meet with House Sparrows and starlings. Logging of snags and trees, especially along the shorelines, would have negatively affected the Tree Swallow population. Tree Swallows utilize nest boxes built to special dimensions, just as do martins. Rich Siegrist sometimes finds them using his martin boxes, as well as boxes he placed in a wet field near his house. They also use a nest box at Fisher Pond. Checking these artificial nesting sites seems to be the only certain method of finding a Tree Swallow on the Island. Tree Swallows often arrive in mid-February in Western Washington but not until late April or May on Vashon. It is hard to find them once young have fledged.

Violet-green Swallow

(SS, FW, FL, DC, WC, HW, DA, AE) Status: Common spring through fall. Breeds.

This very common and noisy swallow actively hunts airborne insects all over the Island. Violet-green Swallows inhabit most upland habitats as well as freshwater and saltwater shorelines. They demonstrate more adaptability in nest site choice than their near-relative, the Tree Swallow. Violet-green Swallows make use of nest holes in a variety of sites from cavities in snags, to nest boxes, to crannies in buildings or cliffs. Their exploitation of artificial structures as nest sites helped them keep ahead of the destruction of natural hollows in snags and trees. Dan Willsie organized a nest box project that placed many boxes around Vashon. A number of Violet-green Swallows use these boxes and several of the birdhouses put up in hope of attracting migrating Western Bluebirds back to Vashon. They nest in both upland and near-water sites around the Island. Locations near a pond and or other shore receive preferential attention for nest sites. Large groups hawk for insects over the fields along Wax Orchard Road, Paradise Valley, and the waters over Tramp and Quartermaster Harbors. Violet-green Swallows arrive as early as February and usually by early March in Western Washington. On Vashon, migrants often show up only in the third week of March. Migrants might be seen passing through in the fall into late October. Most local birds leave by the second or third week in September.

BBS (USGS 2013): 1995-1998, 2000-2006, 2009, 2013

Northern Rough-winged Swallow

(SS, FW, HW, AE) Status: Fairly common spring and summer. Breeds.

A few of these chocolate-brown and white swallows nest in the cliffs and banks at Point Robinson, KVI Beach, and Raab's Lagoon. They prefer saltwater shorelines, river shores or streamsides, and ponds with banks for nesting. Rough-wings show up in early April sometimes even before the Violet-green and Tree Swallows that for some reason come to the Island later than elsewhere in the Puget Sound region. Early arrivals in spring often occur first at Fisher Pond or the Island Center Forest. Later in April, their breeding locations around the shorelines of Vashon make the best places to look for Rough-wings.

BBS (USGS 2013): 1996, 2001, 2002

Cliff Swallow

(SS, FL, DA, AE) Status: Rare breeder and summer resident.

Cliff Swallows in Western Washington benefited from the clearing of woods and the building of structures, especially bridges (Jewett et al. 1953, Smith et al. 1997). Originally, Cliff Swallows inhabited the rocky cliffs of the Columbia Gorge, with only a few localized breeding areas west of the Cascades (Dawson and Bowles 1909). They expanded their range by using many human-built structures for nesting sites. On Vashon, Steve Caldwell noted them as nesting from time to time on buildings at the high school. Joy Nelsen found their nests on a house in north central Vashon. Cliff Swallows formerly nested on the hangers of the airport along Cove Road. Despite these known breeding locations, Cliff Swallows remain quite rare for the Island; any sighting represents a lucky find. Gary Shugart documented the most recent breeding with a photo of an adult feeding two fledglings on a wire along 232nd Street in the Wax Orchard area on 11 July 2009. Other records in the past few years involve small numbers of Cliff Swallows mixed in with other swallow species at Mukai Pond in the late summer, KVI Beach in fall migration, and other locations during migration.

Barn Swallow

(SS, FW, FL, DA, AE) Status: Common spring and summer resident. Breeds.

This large, fork-tailed swallow utilizes any open area around the Island. Like Cliff Swallows, only more so, they gained in population since European-American settlement, taking advantage of artificial structures for nest sites (Dawson and Bowles 1909, Smith et al. 1997). In the past, they nested on rocky cliffs, few of which exist in this area. Now Barn Swallows rarely use a "natural" location, as opposed to some human structure. All over Vashon, they nest on houses, garages, barns, and the ferry docks. As they hunt for their insect prey, they are as likely to be found skimming out over the water as they are to be seen over farm fields in the center of the Island. Most local Barn Swallows leave by the second or third week of September. Passing migrants show up often high overhead late into October.

BBS (USGS 2013): 1995-1998, 2000-2006, 2009, 2013

Chickadees

Black-capped Chickadee

(HW, ST, DA) Status: Fairly common resident. Breeds.

Following forest succession, Black-capped Chickadees extended their range in Western Washington over the last century (Smith et al. 1997). They expanded around the Puget Sound region as logging decreased coniferous forest and provided suitable deciduous thickets and woods. The expansion through the islands of Puget Sound and the San Juans took place slowly, as Black-capped Chickadees are mostly non-migratory and dislike moving over large stretches of open water (Sharpe 1993). Observ-

Black-capped Chickadee feeding young. © Doug Parrott

ers confirmed breeding in the San Juan Islands only in the 1990s (Smith et al. 1997). No confirmed sightings exist for Vancouver Island (Campbell et al. 1990).

If Black-capped Chickadees existed on Vashon prior to European-American settlement, they utilized the limited thickets in disturbed or riparian areas. The vast majority of pre-1870 Vashon consisted of old-growth Western Hemlock and Douglas-fir, habitat preferred by the Chestnut-backed Chickadee. Even the short trip across Colvos Passage doubtless required sufficient appropriate habitat both on Vashon and the surrounding lowlands. That hardwood habitat probably didn't grow sufficiently until the 1870s or 1880s even after clearing of coniferous forest. As early as 1925, a visiting ornithologist, A. E. Kitchin, found Black-capped Chickadees fairly common along Quartermaster Harbor (Kitchin, 1925), but Hunn still wrote of them as rare on Vashon in the late 1970s and early 1980s (Hunn, 1982). Dan Willsie, a master birder and Island native, remembers them as being rare to uncommon before the 1990s.

Those reports indicate that Black-capped Chickadees appear to be colonizing and re-colonizing parts of the Island as the habitat shifts from shrubby areas into woods and from woods and farms to residential. Joe Van Os, a local ornithologist and wildlife guide, saw no Black-capped Chickadees on his older second-growth parcel on Maury Island for years until logging and development approached right up to its border. As ornamental plantings and regrowth of young alder came nearer to his property, Black-caps appeared. At present, Black-caps are common in the residential sections of Vashon, many of the open brushy areas, and the areas with alders and maples. The author noted nests in hardwood snags at Portage. Rich Siegrist found a nest in a dead Red Alder at Maury Island Marine Park in 2002.

BBS (USGS 2013): 1995-1998, 2001-2006, 2009, 2013

CBC by area (Trevathan 1999-2013) Trend: Stable.

Vashon North: 1999-2013
Maury Island-Tramp Harbor: 1999-2013
Vashon South: 1999-2013

Mountain Chickadee

(DC, WC, DA) Status: Very rare. One record.

A Mountain Chickadee put in a brief appearance during the lowland invasion by montane species in the winter of 2004/05. Gilbert and Jean Findlay first observed the bird at their feeder and alerted others. Given the reluctance of the similar species Black-capped Chickadee to cross bodies of water, this Mountain Chickadee gave many a pleasant surprise. However, during the 2004/05 invasion, Puget Sound birders discovered Mountain Chickadees had crossed water in many shoreline areas (Tweeters). Participants in Vashon's Christmas Bird Count once found Mountain Chickadees in the off-Island, Kitsap County portion of the count circle (Trevathan 1999-2013).

Chestnut-backed Chickadee

(DC, WC, HW, DA) Status: Fairly common resident. Breeds.

Chestnut-backed Chickadees are Vashon's native chickadee. They inhabit any area with a significant chunk of coniferous trees. They venture out of such territory, but they require a coniferous base. A small flock resided at the author's former house in Vashon Center, though the nearest patch of Douglas-fir and hemlock was a quarter-mile away. The Island's two main chickadee species show different habitat preferences and also exhibit dissimilar foraging patterns. Sharpe notes that Chestnut-backs feed higher in the canopy and out further to the narrow tips of branches, whereas Black-caps stay lower in the canopy on larger branches (Sharpe 1993). Chestnut-backs look for insects in a largely upright manner along the upper surface of a branch. Black-caps hang upside down as they pry and examine cones and the underside of branches. Both chickadees enjoy sunflower seed feeders. Rich Siegrist hosted Chestnut-backed Chickadees in nest boxes at his place in the Colvos area several times over the last decade.

BBS (USGS 2013): 1995-1998, 2000-2006, 2009, 2013

CBC by area (Trevathan 1999-2013) Trend: Stable.

Vashon North: 1999-2013
Maury Island-Tramp Harbor: 1999-2013
Vashon South: 1999-2013

Long-tailed Tit

Bushtit

(HW, ST, DA) Status: Fairly common resident. Breeds.

For a fairly common species on Vashon, Bushtits can be very local in some years and unaccountably difficult to find. Bushtits wander in flocks of ten to 50 through brushy thickets and gardens. In winter, they might join in with roving mixed-species bands of kinglets, chickadees, and nuthatches.

Bushtits make highly visible breeders. Many nests have been found each year at Point Robinson, Maury Island Marine Park, and several other locations around Vashon. Their nests look like hanging woolen socks, often way out at the end of a branch. Crows easily find many of these nests and raid the eggs and young. Ocean Spray provides a favorite brush for Bushtits to glean through. It often serves as a nesting site, since the droopy foliage conceals nests better than other shrub species. Bushtits strongly defend their territories. One used to attack the side mirrors on the author's truck and the shiny woodstove chimney on the side of the house every morning. In the early spring, the usual flocks of 20 or so birds split up into breeding pairs. The first groups appear again as small family units in mid-May, when young learn to forage with the adults. Nest building begins as early as the first week of April. More than one brood may be attempted, as pairs have been observed copulating as late as the last week in May.

Bushtits are wary sentinels. One observer in Bent relates a practice which the author has also observed when Bushtits face a threat:

> "A flock of bush-tits will be foraging as usual, with the ordinary uncertain medley of location-notes, when suddenly one or two birds utter several of the sharp alarm notes and then begin a shrill quavering piping. This is taken up by the whole flock, until there is a continuous monotonous chorus. At the same time every member of the scattered company strikes a stationary attitude in just the position it was when the alarm was first sounded, and this attitude is maintained until the danger is past....The remarkable thing about this united cry, is that it is absolutely impossible to locate any single one of the birds by it. The chorus forms an indefinably confusing, all-pervading sound, which I know from personal experience to be most elusive." (Bent 1964b)

BBS (USGS 2013): 1996, 1997, 2001, 2002, 2003, 2005

CBC by area (Trevathan 1999-2013) Trend: Appears stable, with possible slight decline.

Vashon North: 1999-2000, 2002-2003, cw2004, 2005-2008, 2011
Maury Island-Tramp Harbor: 2002-2006, 2009-2011, cw2012, 2013
Vashon South: 1999, 2001-2003, cw2005, 2006-2010

Nuthatches

Red-breasted Nuthatch

(DC, WC, HW, DA) Status: Fairly common resident. Breeds.

The nasal *nyank, nyank, nyank* call of the nuthatch is the first signal that it is around. It quietly moves up tree trunks looking for bugs and has feet designed to let it hop or crawl downwards headfirst. Nuthatches breed in coniferous forest and also utilize mixed woods and yards with bird feeders. Nuthatches enjoy flitting in to grab a sunflower seed from amidst the squawking finches at the feeder. Sometimes, in late fall and winter, nuthatches join mixed-species flocks of chickadees, kinglets, Bushtits, warblers, and juncos. Dan Willsie found a pair using a nest box at his former residence in Burton. Marcy Summers found adults feeding young at her feeders on 1 June 2010.

> BBS (USGS 2013): 1995-1998, 2000-2006, 2009, 2013
> CBC by area (Trevathan 1999-2013) Trend: Stable.
> *Vashon North: 1999-2013*
> *Maury Island-Tramp Harbor: 1999-2013*
> *Vashon South: 1999-2013*

White-breasted Nuthatch

(DC, WC) Status: Very rare. One record.

Carole Elder heard a White-breasted Nuthatch at the Huggins place on north Vashon on 7 November 2004. Amy and Alan Huggins later saw it and shared views of it with many others. Eventually, the Hugginses noted at least two birds at the same time. White-breasted Nuthatches are rare west of the Cascades. The Slender-billed subspecies breeds in oak prairie, a quickly disappearing habitat in southwestern Washington (Smith et al. 1997). The winter of 2004 witnessed a lowland invasion by montane birds, especially Mountain Chickadees (Tweeters). The Vashon nuthatches might as easily be visitors from Washington's east of the Cascades population as from the rare Slender-billed group to the south. Peter Murray took several clear photographs, but a subspecies determination wasn't possible.

> CBC by area (Trevathan 1999-2013):
> *Vashon North: 2005*

Creeper

Brown Creeper

(DC, WC, HW, DA) Status: Fairly common resident. Breeds.

Denizens of mixed woods, Brown Creepers are very hard to spot as they quietly creep up and down tree trunks. Their brown plumage provides good camouflage against the bark. For nest sites, they prefer hardwood trees with loose bark in mixed coniferous/deciduous woods (Smith et al. 1997). This preference often leads them to use riparian areas that provide such a mix. Given the large number of stream areas and lots of mixed woods on the Island, they appear well distributed on Vashon. Creepers also like mature Douglas-fir for nesting locations because of the deep ridges in the bark, which provide locations for nest building. Artificial nests can be made for them, as the late ornithologist J. H. Bowles states:

> "I selected trees with very smooth bark, or else cut the bark down smooth, and nailed against them bark shelters fifteen inches or more in length, and three or four inches in width, leaving a space inside of about three inches between the bark and the tree. This inside space will, of course, be tapering towards the bottom, but creepers require a considerable depth for their nests, which are started by a large foundation of twigs, on top of which is built the nest cup of soft bark, feathers, etc." (Bent 1964)

Carole Elder found a natural nest in the woods by the Vashon Sportsmen's Club, where creepers can often be heard calling. Rich Siegrist found another nest in a rotten alder tree, producing surviving fledglings. From mid-February to mid-April, when creepers sing the most, a walk through just about any forested area of the Island produces them fairly easily. Some of the best locations for finding creepers consist of Paradise Valley, along Shinglemill and Judd Creeks, and Point Robinson.

BBS (USGS 2013): 1997, 2000, 2001, 2002, 2003, 2005, 2009, 2013

CBC by area (Trevathan 1999-2013) Trend: Stable.
Vashon North: 1999-2000, 2002-2004, 2006-2007, 2009-2013
Maury Island-Tramp Harbor: 2000-2007, 2009-2013
Vashon South: 2000, cw2002, 2003, 2005-2009, cw2010, 2011-2013

Wrens

House Wren

(HW, ST, DA) Status: Rare spring migrant and summer resident. Breeds.

Vashon would have hosted few to no House Wrens before the clearing of old-growth forest on the Island. House Wrens then colonized the open areas provided by agricultural fields, clear-cuts, and yards. The Island's forests gradually grew back, leaving less open area. As the orchards, farms, and berry fields of the Island fill in with houses or woods, less open habitat remains. House Wrens breed very rarely on the Island now. One pair utilized a nest box along Old Mill Road at Joe Van Os's office for much of the 1990s and on to 2012. In 2007 and 2008, males prepared sites at nest boxes in the Center (9 June 2007) and Lisabeula (17 May 2008) areas of Vashon but failed to attract a mate. The author found one singing on the edge of a clearing in the Old Mill Road woods on 17 June 2009 but it, too, apparently found no female to join it.

BBS (USGS 2013): 2003, 2005

Pacific Wren

(DC, WC, HW, ST, DA) Status: Fairly common resident. Breeds. Change in Status: Formerly known as Winter Wren.

In Western Washington, Pacific Wrens utilize just about any type of forest habitat, from various types of conifers to deciduous woodlands to mixed forest. They usually situate nests close to the ground, often in the tangled roots of an upturned tree. Dan Willsie found a nest with young in Burton. On Vashon, they usually hang out in the more thickly wooded areas, especially larger parcels of forest and wet woods from June through mid-September. They then show up more widely the rest of the year. Pacific Wrens act quite curious, scolding one from cover and then popping up at one's face or scurrying around one's feet. The author remembers deer-hunting as a teen, sitting on a stump at the edge of clear-cut at first light. Pacific Wrens silently hopped all along the stump checking him out, not quite landing on him.

Pacific Wrens make incredible songsters. Generally, they sing for six to eight seconds but can go longer. In that time, they can trill over a hundred separate notes (Terres 1991). Their song is very beautiful and at the same time hard to describe. They sing all year, most extensively from March through June and sometimes July. They produce a *tick tick* call heard year-round. A walk down the path to Fern Cove in spring is sure to treat the visitor to their song.

When the Pacific Wren was known as the Winter Wren and considered the same species all across the northern hemisphere, we shared it with Ireland and Britain, where it is known simply as the Wren. On St. Stephen's Day (December 26) in Ireland, boys "hunt the wren." They bring their capture to neighbors in their community, who then give them a treat or some money. This practice, in turn, probably derived from ancient Ireland, where the Druids held the wren sacred throughout the year. They hunted the wren for a ritual sacrifice around the time of the winter solstice. The ritual relates to the periodic sacrifice of the divine king to protect and rejuvenate the land. Believers sacrificed the wren in place of the divine king. This and other such hunting rituals appear associated to the belief in the turning of the wheel, the old year ceding its place to the new.

In many parts of Britain, the wren, like the robin and swallow, was considered sacred. It is believed that anyone who harmed these birds would pay a high price. In Ireland it was called the *Drui-en,* or Druid bird. In Welsh, the word *Dryw* signifies both a Druid and a wren. In Brittany, the Celts held that the wren brought fire from heaven. It began burning in flight and handed the fire off to the robin. (The British robin is a small thrush, somewhat smaller than a bluebird but similar in shape, with a wash of rusty red across its breast.) The robin also burst into flames, and it was the Sky Lark that finally brought fire down into the world.

Wrens got their title of king of all birds from a legend in which the birds held a contest to see who could fly the highest. All of the birds strove to fly as high as they could, but a great eagle soared high in the sky above all others. It thought to claim the title of king of birds, when a wren sprang from its hiding place on the eagle's back and won the tourney. The author listened to the wren song on the Chieftains' *The Bells of Dublin* album for several years, wondering what the song was talking about.

> "The wren, the wren, the king of all birds,
> On St. Stephen's Day was caught in the furze,
> Although he is little, his family is great,
> I pray you, good people, give us a treat."

BBS (USGS 2013): 1995-1998, 2000-2006, 2009, 2013

CBC by area (Trevathan 1999-2013) Trend: Stable.

Vashon North: 1999-2013
Vashon South: 1999-2013
Maury Island-Tramp Harbor: 1999-2013

Marsh Wren

(FW) Status: Very rare, possible year-round. Change in Status: Although this species was seen every year but 2005 from 2002 to 2008, there have been no sightings since 2008.

The Marsh Wren's specific habitat requirements account for its very rare status on Vashon. Marsh Wrens prefer wet areas with emergent vegetation, preferably cattails or bulrushes (Smith et at. 1997). Within that specificity, Marsh Wrens utilize a variety of wetland types: saltwater, freshwater, ditches, ponds, and wet fields. Vashon possesses little freshwater or saltwater habitat with the wide swath of cattails that Marsh Wrens like best.

Since 1998, birders have found Marsh Wrens at only a few locations. Before that date, the gap in sightings stretches back to the late 1970s and early 1980s, when Hunn mentions them at Fisher Pond (Hunn 1982). Observers find these wrens usually at Mukai Pond or the cattails along Monument Road bordering the farm fields at the road's south end. One record exists for Meadowlake, near the 188th Street entrance to the Island Center Forest. Meadowlake hosts open water and a thick cattail border on one side, perfect for a few Marsh Wrens to set up shop. The pond has no good viewing locations, creating little opportunity for better observer coverage, making it difficult to establish the wren's actual status for this location.

The Marsh Wren acts as a wetland counterpart to the Pacific Wren of the region's wet forests. It's somewhat larger, with a more prominent eyestripe, but it's basically a little brown bird. Like the Pacific Wren, it can be quite elusive when it chooses. Marsh Wrens are seldom found at the same spot where they disappeared into the cattails. They move very quickly and pop up or scold far into the midst of their domain. Even when singing their distinctive song, they often perch deep in a marsh, only a few inches up the stem of a cattail.

Bewick's Wren

(HW, ST, DA) Status: Fairly common resident. Breeds.

Bewick's Wrens like gardens, brushy areas, and brambles around the Island. They have a beautiful song, and each bird sings a number of variations. They actively scold intruders of all kinds and sizes that enter their territory. These wrens belong to the list of birds that benefited greatly from the clearing of the woods that created many new habitats in the regenerating clear-cuts and residential areas.

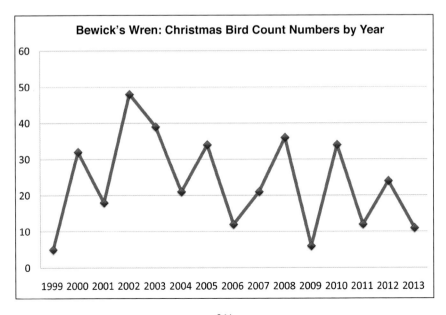

J. H. Bowles aptly describes their adaptability in finding nest sites:

"The building sites chosen by this wren for its nests are so variable that hardly anything can be considered typical. It may be in the wildest swampy wood far removed from civilization, but it is quite as likely to be found in a house in the heart of a city. A few of the nesting sites I have recorded are in upturned roots of fallen trees, deserted woodpecker holes, in bird boxes in the city, in a fishing creel hanging on a porch, under a slab of bark that has scaled away a few inches from the body of a tree, or an open nest built on a beam under bridge." (Dawson and Bowles 1909)

Rich Siegrist noted adults feeding fledged young as early as mid-May. He found a nest in an old piece of machinery in his tool shed. The nesting attempt failed, evidently from egg robbing.

BBS (USGS 2013): 1995-1998, 2000-2006, 2009, 2013

CBC by area (Trevathan 1999-2013) Trend: Stable but with possible slight downward tilt.

Vashon North: 1999-2013
Maury Island-Tramp Harbor: 1999-2012
Vashon South: 2000-2013

Dippers

American Dipper

(SS, FW) Status: Very rare winter resident. Nine records. Change in Status: Dippers should have been listed as very rare in the first edition; they show up only once every few years on Vashon.

American Dippers, formerly known as Water Ouzels, breed on mountain streams in Washington State. Their characteristic activity is a constant bobbing up and down as they perch or walk along streams. They go beyond dabbling along the streamside to actually swimming like a duck out into the water of fast-moving streams. They also dip down into the water to walk on the stream bottom. On Vashon, all records come from along streams, but at times these birds might also be seen on the saltwater shoreline where streams meet the saltwater's edge in other locations around Puget Sound.

Dippers likely winter in some years on faster-flowing and steeper streams on Vashon. Salmon monitor Michael Laurie first added them to the Vashon species list in October 2000. Many subsequent sightings occurred along several sections of the Shinglemill Creek watershed. Changes in the salmon monitoring program brought fewer people up Shinglemill Creek for several years. A subsequent tapering off of sightings occurred, generating no new records for years. Jim Bazemore saw one on 1 March 2007 at the 216th Street culvert on Judd Creek. Michael Laurie caps the list sightings with his latest sighting, again on Shinglemill Creek, on 27 October 2012. Sharpe lists a number of lowland breeding locations in the Puget Sound region (Sharpe 1993). No breeding season observations have yet occurred on Vashon.

CBC by area (Trevathan 1999-2013):
Vashon North: 2001, 2002

Kinglets

Golden-crowned Kinglet

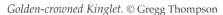

(DC, WC, HW, ST, DA) Status: Fairly common fall through early spring, uncommon spring and summer. Breeds.

The Golden-crowned Kinglet flitters and spins as it gleans for bugs. Birders usually hear it without seeing the bird as its high pitched string of *see see* calls floats down from high in a conifer or maple. The kinglets' practice of foraging far up in the trees makes it rewarding to learn their distinctive call. They retreat in summer to breed in the wetter and thicker coniferous forests of the Island. The rest of the year, they inhabit mixed woods. Several breeding records exist. Joe Van Os discovered an active nest in the

Golden-crowned Kinglet. © Gregg Thompson

Ruby-crowned Kinglet. © Gregg Thompson

woods of his property on Maury Island. Rich Siegrist found one carrying food to young in a large fir in the Colvos area but was unable to actually view the nest. The author found adults feeding a juvenile cowbird several times their size at Chautauqua Elementary School.

Golden-crowned Kinglets often associate with Chestnut-backed Chickadees that have a similar habitat preference. While generally high up in a conifer, they occasionally come down low into the brushy understory of a wood lot. In winter, a bigger flock of 30 or 40 birds might form, including both kinglet species, both chickadees, nuthatches, wrens, Hutton's Vireos, and Townsend's Warblers.

BBS (USGS 2013): 1995-1998, 2001-2006, 2013

CBC by area (Trevathan 1999-2013) Trend: Stable but with possible downward tilt.

Vashon North: 1999-2013
Vashon South: 1999-2013
Maury Island-Tramp Harbor: 1999-2013

Ruby-crowned Kinglet

(DC, WC, HW, ST, DA) Status: Fairly common fall through spring.

The Ruby-crowned Kinglet's audacious behavior makes it easily seen as it is one of the common "scolding" birds of the forest edge and brushy areas. In a jazzy rhythm, its call goes *tch tch tch tch tch* as it moves through a thicket. A little "spishing" with one's lips almost always gets a little kinglet to pop out of a brush patch around here. In migration, waves of Ruby-crowns pass through. During most of the fall, winter, and early spring, they appear more in twos and threes when part of a mixed flock of chickadees, kinglets, wrens, and vireos. Ruby-crowns show up from their mountain and northern breeding areas in mid-September and leave by late April or early May.

CBC by area (Trevathan 1999-2013) Trend: Stable.
Vashon North: 1999-2013
Vashon South: 1999-2013
Quartermaster Harbor: 2009
Maury Island-Tramp Harbor: 1999-2013

Thrushes

Western Bluebird

(FL) Status:Very rare late winter, early spring migrant. Former breeder, two modern records.

Western Bluebirds like open areas such as farm fields, orchards, cutover woods, and burns. As hole nesters, they utilize cavities in snags, live trees, fence posts, and nest boxes (Rogers 2000). Their population took a big nose dive throughout the western United States for a variety of reasons in the late 1940s.

Back in the 1940s, Western Bluebirds, while not common, regularly occurred in spring and summer on Vashon (John Friars pers. com. 2005, Dan Willsie pers. com. 2005). Through the early part of the 20th century, observers considered them commonly in appropriate habitat in Western Washington and rarely to uncommonly east of the Cascades (Jewett et al. 1953, Herlugson 1978, Sharpe 1993). Sharpe (1993) provides a good review of the published bluebird records for Western Washington, showing their widespread distribution and fairly good numbers. In Sharpe's account, the author noted that a distant relative of his, James G. Swan, found bluebirds using the open areas created by marshes in the wooded Neah Bay area in the 1850s. In Jewett et al.'s *Birds of Washington State* (1953), Cantwell, a Washington birder active in the late 1800s and early 1900s, noted a flock of 25 bluebirds feeding with juncos on a ranch on Harstine Island, just a few miles to the south of Vashon.

On Vashon, Dan Willsie and John Friars, both Island natives and expert birders, remember seeing them regularly in the open areas, especially around Vashon Center and the Dockton area of Maury Island. Friars remembers one incident in the 1940s when he saw them along the driftwood line, eating bugs and sand fleas. Several Washington ornithologists and early Audubon members noted bluebirds in about the same period. Kitchin found a nest with young near Quartermaster Harbor in 1925 (Kitchin 1925). Slipp found one at Manzanita on 7 July 1940 (Slipp 1939-1956). Violet Cannon recorded one on 13 February 1952 (*AFN*6(3):211).

A number of factors led to the bluebirds' decline nationally and locally in the Puget Sound area. Change in habitat constitutes one commonly cited factor. Old forests across the country possessed plenty of snags and dead trees that provided nest holes needed by the cavity-nesting bluebird. Timber practices such as clear-cuts that completely removed all trees, including snags that often contain nest holes, certainly posed a part of the problem. Further, the tendency to totally suppress fires, leaving little burnt-over habitat certainly affected bluebirds further. On Vashon, the last large wave of logging took place in the 1940s as well as the last fires producing cutover or burnt-over areas. Over the last 50 years, the woods grew, retaking much open area. No fires spread to create open areas or park-like woods that bluebirds like. Similar to Purple Martins, bluebirds adapted to some extent to using human-created sites such as wooden fence posts. Orchards provided some potential nesting cavities. But even the human-created nesting sites became limited as forests regenerated or suburbs and cities replaced the orchards and open agricultural areas. In addition, metal increasingly took the place of wood in fence post usage on farms, eliminating another source of holes for nests.

Two exotic introductions to the continent created another threat. Introduced to North America in the 1850s, the House Sparrow soon entered Washington and grew common by the turn of the nineteenth century (Smith et al. 1997). The European Starling became common in Washington by the 1970s, creating another threat (ibid.). These exotic species really represent more of a hindrance to a bluebird comeback than an original causative agent in the bluebird decline. Starlings, often cited as the cause for the decrease in bluebird populations, arrived long after the fall in bluebird numbers began. Breeding Bird Survey data for Eastern Washington survey routes between 1968 and 1976 showed no statistically significant relationship between bluebird and starling numbers (Herlugson 1978).

Sharpe outlines another factor often not considered when such easy culprits as House Sparrows and starlings remain at hand. Western Washington from the 1940s through the 1970s experienced a period of cooler, wetter weather that may have affected the bluebirds' ability to find their insect prey. On the west side of the mountains, the Puget Sound area forms the northern extent of their breeding range; therefore weather events could be a major factor in their reproductive success.

Russell Rogers, a biologist for Washington Department of Fish and Wildlife, mentions a possible pesticide connection that would have combined with the weather to hold down prey populations for the bluebirds (Rogers 2000). DDT use grew excessively in the 1930s and 1940s and extended into the period of bluebird decline. Rogers found only one study showing a slight impact from DDT on bluebirds. He believes the earlier mentioned fall in nest hole numbers to be the most prominent factor (Rogers 2000). DDT use in Washington decreased at about the same time that the weather improved, the late 1970s. Species usually rebound over time from weather events and trends. If the starling and House Sparrow affected bluebirds, the effect consisted of suppressing bluebird recovery by intense competition for nesting opportunities.

By 1981, one pair of bluebirds nested at the only known remaining breeding location in Western Washington, the prairies of Joint Base Lewis-McChord (Sharpe 1993). Two birders, George Walters and Carol Sheridan (later continued by Sam Agnew), helped turn the population dive around by building bluebird boxes and placing them throughout Pierce and Thurston County prairie areas. Within ten years, they counted 215 nesting pairs (Rogers 2000). That number declined but then held steady around 170 during the 1990s. Now, a few locations along Hood Canal and the Sequim area host a few pairs as well. On Vashon, no bluebirds have been seen except as migrants since at least the mid-1970s. Interestingly enough, one of the few recent sightings took place at a newly clear-cut area on Maury Island in the mid-1990s. Joy Nelsen found the bird in a disturbed area that still had some trees, typical bluebird habitat. Only one other modern record exists, a bird seen visiting an orchard on the south end of Vashon in January 2008.

Mountain Bluebird

(FL) Status: Very rare. One record.

Mountain Bluebird appear as a rare spring migrant in lowland Western Washington (Wahl et al. 2005). Carole Elder saw a small flock on 7 April 1988 along Cemetery Road for Vashon's sole record (National Audubon Society 1971-1994, *AB*42:1334).

Townsend's Solitaire

(DC, HW, ST, DA) Status: Rare spring migrant, very rare winter and very rare fall migrant.

Townsend's Solitaires breed in dry coniferous montane forests in Washington. They pass through Vashon in April, usually seen flycatching along the edges of woods. Sightings of solitaires range widely across Vashon in the last few years, though Point Robinson provides the most consistent single location. Three winter records exist and two in fall migration. Joe Van Os had one stay through the winter one year at his office in south Vashon Island.

CBC by area (Trevathan 1999-2013):
Maury Island-Tramp Harbor: 2009

Swainson's Thrush

(DC, WC, HW) Status: Common spring migrant and summer resident. Breeds.

Every year, Vashon performs a dance with two thrushes where we trade one off for the other. Spring brings the Swainson's Thrush, to be replaced in fall and winter by the Hermit Thrush. The Hermit Thrush leaves again in early May just before the return of the Swainson's. Telling the two apart visually is quite a task. They're both medium-sized songbirds about two-thirds the size of a robin. Swainson's Thrush appears bigger overall, about half an inch over the Hermit Thrush (Sibley 2000). They both possess russet brown/olive backs with pale, dotted breasts. The Hermit Thrush's dots are somewhat larger and more emphatic, but in most lighting conditions that might not be easily noticed. The Hermit Thrush also has a contrasting orange/reddish brown tail that is brighter and more reddish than that of the Swainson's Thrush. Again, lighting conditions might not make that very obvious.

Sally Marrone found this rare Townsend's Solitaire in spring 2008. © Kevin Lickfelt

Both birds act quite shy and retiring, making them hard to see. Tracking them by voice provides the best way to find and identify them. The Hermit Thrush has a reedy, flute-like song that seems to hang in the air. Bent describes the Swainson's Thrush's upward spiraling song as: *whip-poor-will-a-will-e-zee-zee-zee* (Bent 1964a). Swainson's Thrushes create a whistle-like call, similar to a drip into water. Each fall, the author checks for their continued presence in the pre-dawn darkness by whistling their call note and listening for their answer. Swainson's hunt down the sound of a call note in their territory until they're quite close, giving several opportunities to track them as their movement gives away the location of their camouflaged bodies.

Swainson's Thrushes prefer woods with some sort of deciduous thicket. Sharpe found them in both coniferous and deciduous forests of all ages, as long as there was an understory of shrubs taller than ferns (Sharpe 1993). They like regenerating forests and the edges of natural and human-created meadows. Swainson's Thrushes appear abundantly spread throughout the woods of Vashon. While these birds were undoubtedly present before European-American settlement changed the Island habitats, the increase in brushy edges to the forested areas and deciduous woods means that their numbers rose in modern times (Smith et al. 1997).

Swainson's Thrushes start appearing around the end of April and reach good numbers on the Island by the second or third week of May. Breeding begins immediately. Rich Siegrist noted young being fed by mid-June in the Colvos area.They leave in September, with a few possible stragglers up to October. An early Washington ornithologist, R. H. Lawrence, observed that they "arrive about the time the salmon berries blossomed and left when the fruit was gone." (Sharpe 1993) In winter they migrate as far south as northern Argentina.

BBS (USGS 2013): 1995-1998, 2000-2006, 2009, 2013

Hermit Thrush

(DC, WC, ST, DA) Status: Uncommon fall through spring.

The ethereal, angelic fluting song of the Hermit Thrush inspired two of its many old-fashioned names: "American Nightingale" and "Swamp Angel" (Terres 1991). Unfortunately, Hermit Thrushes breed up in the Olympics and Cascades, creating few local opportunities to hear their song, as they are seasonally mute during their tour of Vashon.

Hermit Thrushes come down out of the mountains in September, generally after the Swainson's Thrush has just left. Most birds fly through the area to winter in the southern U.S. or Mexico. A few winter in the Puget

Sound lowlands each year. The berries in the shrubs around the pond at the Island Center Forest provide a great attraction to the Hermit Thrushes as they arrive in the fall. In winter, look along roadsides and wood edges for them checking out leaf detritus.

Hermit Thrushes make a single-note *chuck* scold, somewhat like the Varied Thrush call note. It also sounds slightly like a Fox Sparrow's scold call. Look closely at the bird making the *chuck* call because the Fox Sparrow's plumage appears a little similar. Both species look closely matched in size. However, the body shape is different, providing a way to quickly tell them apart. The head of a Hermit Thrush also comes down to a pointier face and beak. The author saw his first Hermit Thrush for Vashon Island in April 2001 as it hawked and chased down both flying and crawling bugs in a hazelnut tree in his yard. The returning northern migration begins in late March and peaks in April. The April migration period greatly swells the Island thrush population for a brief time. The Hermit Thrush mostly completes its migration before the Swainson's Thrush shows up at the end of April or early May.

CBC by area (Trevathan 1999-2013)Trend: Stable at generally low numbers with occasional high peaks.

Vashon North: 1999, 2004-2005, 2008, 2011, 2013
Maury Island-Tramp Harbor: 2002, 2004, 2007-2009, cw2010, 2011, 2013
Quartermaster Harbor: 2004
Vashon South: 1999, 2003-2006, 2008-2009, cw2010, 2011-2012

American Robin

(SS, FW, FL, DC, WC, HW, ST, DA) Status: Common resident and breeder.

Robins utilize all habitats on the Island except open water. They benefited from the changes in the landscape since development occurred, openly enjoying the monoculture grass lawns of the suburbs that provide so little for most other species except starlings. They seem equally at home chasing bugs on the beach or in the deep woods. During the summer of 2003, at the height of the tent caterpillar infestation, they busily shook down every alder for the hatching moths, picking them off the branches or hawking them out of the air.

The cries of begging young robins pervade the air in May and June. July and August see birds with speckled breasts dotting the lawns and filling the birdbaths with splashes. Robins use a variety of trees in woods, thickets, and yards to place their nests. The author found one nest on 30 April 2002 that was about 20 feet up in an alder along Judd Creek, full of young making a racket. Others robins nest in exotic shrubs along heavily frequented walkways. In 2012, the author found a robin building a nest on a joist under a second-story deck on the 22nd of April. It eventually built one between each joint—thirteen—before laying eggs in one by the 4th of May. At least three hatchlings called for food on the 13th of May and fledged, flying from the nest on the 25th of May.

In September, small flocks begin building up into larger groups, as the birds seek out ripe fall berries in laurels, hollies, and hawthorns. Most of the local breeders leave for the south, to be replaced later by birds from farther north.

BBS (USGS 2013): 1995-1998, 2000-2006, 2009, 2013

CBC by area (Trevathan 1999-2013) Trend: Stable with some large peaks.
Vashon North: 1999-2013
Maury Island-Tramp Harbor: 1999-2013
Vashon South: 1999-2013

Varied Thrush

(DC, WC, HW, DA) Status: Fairly common fall through spring, rare summer. Breeds.

The eerie calls of the Varied Thrush filter through the mixed and coniferous woods of Vashon during the winter months. Similar in size and shape to a robin, these birds have a dark band across their orange breast that distinguishes them from their relative. Walking along any of the roads through dark, wet woods and listening for their song provides the best way to find them. They seem easiest to discover in late September and April, when good numbers migrate through. The Shinglemill Creek watershed, Christensen Pond, and the wet, wooded roads down to the Colvos Passage off of Wax Orchard Road offer some of the best locations to search for this elusive thrush. Dan Willsie found an active nest in Burton. Harsi and Ezra Parker noted a female gathering nesting material on 29 March 2013. They saw two adults collecting food for several days starting on 26 April 2013, suggesting breeding still occurs in some years. The Parkers live near a forested wetland suitable for Varied Thrush nesting habitat. Observers heard Varied Thrush singing during the 26 May 2013 bioblitz project along Shinglemill Creek near Fern Cove, also good potential nesting habitat.

CBC by area (Trevathan 1999-2013) Trend: Stable.
Vashon North: 1999-2013
Maury Island-Tramp Harbor: 1999-2013
Vashon South: 1999-2013

American Robin. © Gregg Thompson

Starling

European Starling

(SS, FL, HW, DA) Status: Introduced, common resident. Breeds.

Someone, trying to make sure New York had every bird species mentioned in Shakespeare, introduced the starling in 1890. The starling spread across the country to Washington by 1943 and to the Puget Sound area by 1949 (Smith et al. 1997). Starlings prefer urban, residential, and agricultural habitats. They easily spread to any habitat that borders on favored areas. Starlings penetrate every habitat on the Island except for heavily wooded areas and open waters. Large flocks roost under the ferry docks and move along beaches and fields looking for food. They nest semi-colonially or spread out to individual nesting sites.

Their huge success as exotic invaders makes them suspect in the decline of several species across the continent, as mentioned in several of the other species accounts. They aggressively take over already occupied nests and kill young. This behavior forced many species over the last few decades to learn to beat off such attempts. In addition, as resident birds, starlings get first dibs at available nesting holes and very successfully expand into every potential nesting site before migrants return. Habitat and weather changes better explain the first causes of most species' decline on Vashon and in Western Washington. On the other hand, the population rebound of the birds in decline appears severely impacted by the starlings taking up so many nest holes. Clearing of snags and other factors decreased the number of nest holes available at the same time as starlings invaded the area. When nest box programs increase the number of nesting sites again in appropriate habitat, species like the Purple Martin rise in population. Locally, Rich Siegrist checks his Vashon martin boxes for starling and House Sparrow infestations and tosses these birds out to further improve martin breeding success.

Starlings mimic sounds well and replicate just about any bird call imaginable. California Quail, Olive-sided Flycatcher, and Red-winged Blackbird, in particular, seem to be starling favorites on Vashon. One has to check into the source of these birds' calls because starlings so effectively mimic their sounds.

BBS (USGS 2013): 1995-1998, 2000-2006, 2009

CBC by area (Trevathan 1999-2013) Trend: Stable, with some large peaks.

Vashon North: 1999-2013
Maury Island-Tramp Harbor: 1999-2013
Vashon South: 1999-2013

Pipit

American Pipit

(SS, FL) Status: Uncommon spring and fall migrant.

Pipits sweep through in good numbers in the Puget Sound lowlands (Hunn 1982) and the lowlands of the Olympic Peninsula (Sharpe 1993).

Around Vashon, pipits utilize two typical habitats: beach grass and farm fields. KVI Beach and Point Robinson provide consistent shoreline grassy locations. The stubble fields and pasture along Wax Orchard Road and Old Mill Road offer upland grass habitat. The pipit migration probably took place in a more pronounced manner when a greater number of agricultural fields existed on the Island. Most sightings in the last decade occurred in spring and fall among the logs, grass, and salicornia at KVI Beach. In 2002, Ron Simons found a large flock along Old Mill Road in the sheep dog trial field just south of 220th. Follow-up investigation revealed that flocks of various sizes use this field for at least a month in the fall migration. These and like fields usually lack interest for Island birders, and access to many fields is limited. In the past, that led to underestimating pipit numbers for Vashon. Increased searches of other big fields around Vashon might yield more pipit sightings and possibly add Horned Lark to the Island list.

Waxwing

Cedar Waxwing

(FW, DC, HW, ST, DA) Status: Irregularly common spring through fall, rare winter. Breeds.

One of the more pleasant sounds of summer is the *ceeee, ceeee* of Cedar Waxwings flying overhead or settling onto the end of a high branch. Cedar Waxwings live on the Island year-round. They wander widely and may be absent for long periods of time during the year. They seem to be most visible in mid- to late May when summer breeders migrate through. Many remain to be seen and heard through summer into fall. Cedar Waxwings breed comparatively late (Wahl et al. 2005), often waiting until August to nest. They possibly time their nesting for the most berries to be ripe. In 1998, a pair successfully nested and fledged several young in an apple tree at Rich Siegrist's place in the Colvos area. Joe Van Os has also had an active nest at his office on south Vashon. Judith Hinderer took a cute photo of several young birds huddled together apparently dumped out of their nest at the golf course on 12 July 2012.

Their liking for berries propels Cedar Waxwings to move constantly to find a new crop to harvest. They forage high in madrones, low in elderberries, and everywhere in-between looking for a juicy bite. Part of their courtship rituals involve passing berries back and forth to each other (Ehrlich et al. 1988). Waxwings sometimes gorge on so many berries that they become flying-impaired, drunk on fermented berries. Their diet changes more to insects when feeding young and when fruit is scarce. In summer, at the Island Center Forest, they actively catch flying bugs of various kinds on the wing. An interesting local story comes from Islander Phil Gleb. As a boy in the 1940s around Tahlequah, he remembers Cedar Waxwings in the neighborhood. Once, as he sat out on the edge of his window, he stuck his hand into the breeze while holding a piece of string. A waxwing flew by, taking the yarn for its nest.

BBS (USGS 2013): 1995-1998, 2000-2006, 2009, 2013

CBC by area (Trevathan 1999-2013) Trend: Erratic and irruptive.
Vashon North: 2004, 2006
Maury Island-Tramp Harbor: 2003, 2006, 2008-2009, 2012-2013
Vashon South: 2003, 2006, 2008-2009

Snow Bunting

Snow Bunting

(SS) Status: Very rare winter visitor. One record. Change in Status: New addition to the Island list since the first edition.

On 6 December 2005, Sue Trevathan added the Snow Bunting to the Island checklist. She found a single bird, probably a first-year male, at the interface between beach logs and beach grass on the north shore of Point Robinson. Many birders observed the bunting several times over the next couple of weeks. None were seen on the Christmas Bird Count, though Joy Nelsen discovered one again on 14 January 2006. Nelsen noticed the

Cedar Waxwings. © Michael Elenko

Snow Bunting taking a bath. © Gregg Thompson

bird hopping up and down the beach after sand fleas, starting and stopping like a plover or other shorebird. Other birders noticed two buntings in the following days, and Joe Van Os capped the sightings off, counting six at once on 28 January 2006. Snow Buntings were last seen in the second week of February 2006.

Snow Buntings visit stubble fields in Eastern Washington in winter, with flocks sometimes numbering into the several hundreds. Numbers vary from year to year. In Western Washington, sightings generally occur only along shorelines on the outer coast and Puget Trough (Wahl et al. 2005). Most records consist of only one or two or a handful of birds. Snow Buntings eat grass and weed seeds and along the coast, "take tiny crustaceans and other small forms of marine life, sometimes following the retreating waves or gleaning in pools like sandpipers...." (Edward Forbush in Bent 1968). Observers note buntings in some years along the beach at Discovery Park in Seattle, a point similar to Point Robinson. Snow Buntings likely stop by at Point Robinson or KVI Beach every few years and just haven't been noticed.

Wood Warblers

Orange-crowned Warbler

(HW, ST, DA) Status: Fairly common spring through fall and very rare winter. Breeds.

The Orange-crowned Warbler utilizes shrubby thickets amidst other habitat types, especially in hardwood or mixed forest (Smith et al. 1997).

These warblers often visit and nest in residential areas where yards with a mix of shrubs and trees resemble, in essence, the shrubby thicket habitat. Orange-crowned Warblers undoubtedly benefited from clearing over the last 150 years, as clear-cuts created new brush area.

From early April through early July, their song spreads throughout the Island. The song forms a long trill, like a junco. It differs from the junco by wavering up and down the scale a bit, unlike the junco's steady two-note trill. Migrant fallouts often seem to hit the south shore of Maury Island. In early April at Maury Island Marine Park, one hears an Orange-crown singing about every hundred feet down the road. From early July to early August, adult Orange-crowns feed young in the bushes of local thickets and gardens. The Breeding Bird Survey shows an every other year rise and fall in numbers, overall status holding fairly stable (USGS 2013). Joe Van Os has had active nests on his property on Maury Island. In fall and winter, one or two birds occasionally stay as the others migrate south. Observers find an Orange-crown in some years on the Christmas Bird Count.

BBS (USGS 2013): 1995-1998, 2000-2006, 2009, 2013

CBC by area (Trevathan 1999-2013):

Vashon North: 2003
Maury Island-Tramp Harbor: 2002, 2003
Vashon South: 2005

Nashville Warbler

(DC, WC, HW, ST, DA) Status: Very rare spring and fall migrant. Five records.

The Vashon status of the Nashville Warbler should change with the increase of observers on the Island. Currently, only one older and four recent sightings exist. Ornithologists consider Nashvilles uncommon in spring migration and rare in fall migration in the Puget Sound lowlands (Wahl et al. 2005). Vashon records increased with the awareness of the possibility of this species occurring on the Island. Brenda Sestrap saw the first recent observation at her place on 5 May 2003. That was followed by a sighting by Dan Willsie at the Island Center Forest on 6 May 2003; the author found another at Point Robinson on 2 May 2008; and most recently Steve Caldwell photographed one in his yard on 22 April 2012. One old fall record exists for 28 November to 6 December 1974 (Wahl et al. 2005).

MacGillivray's Warbler

(HW, ST, DA) Status: Rare spring and fall migrant, rare in summer.

A few MacGillivray's Warblers appear in brushy areas, gardens, and shrubby yards around Vashon each year. It's likely that their preference for disturbed habitat, clear-cuts, and brushy areas led to colonization and an increase in numbers on Vashon as woodlands were cleared. If numbers actually were higher in the past, forest succession covering the brushy areas provides the probable cause for today's low population. MacGillivray's Warblers might have nested when Vashon still possessed the correct habitat. Over the last decade, a number of sightings in June raise the possibility that breeding might be taking place. However, no historical or recent breeding records exist for MacGillivray's on the Island. The likelihood of breeding continues to fall as forest succession continues.

BBS (USGS 2013): 1996, 2003

Common Yellowthroat

(FW, FL, HW, ST) Status: Fairly common spring migrant and summer resident. Breeds.

Common Yellowthroats prefer marshes and brambles on the edges of wet fields. Sometimes they inhabit large, open Scotch Broom patches, especially if a wetland is nearby. They respond readily to "spishing" though they often stay in deep cover. Wet fields created by the clearing of woods and the rise in agriculture increased the population of yellowthroats on Vashon. Some of the regular locations in which they appear are Mukai Pond, Point Robinson, Fern Cove, the marsh by the monument on Monument Road, and the wet fields and brambles of Paradise Valley. In 2003, Dan Willsie discovered three pairs nesting on the edge of the Canary Grass at Mukai Pond.

BBS (USGS 2013): 1995, 1997, 2000, 2005, 2006, 2013

American Redstart

(HW, ST, DA) Status: Very rare. One record.

A male American Redstart put in an appearance at the Vashon airport on 30 June 2004. It sang as if on territory in a swampy area suitable for redstart habitat. A few more records exist for King County, but this warbler rarely migrates west of the Cascades. A small breeding group returns each year to ponds along the Skagit/Whatcom County border for the only known westside nesting location (Smith et al. 1997).

Yellow Warbler

(FW, HW, ST) Status: Fairly common spring migrant and uncommon to rare summer resident. Possible breeder.

The Yellow Warbler arrives nearly last of the Island warblers each year. In mid-May when these birds first reach Vashon, they come in a large wave.

During that initial surge, almost any deciduous shrub area might sport a Yellow Warbler or two. As the month progresses, the Judd Creek watershed probably becomes the center of their population on the Island. The retention pond on the west side of 188th Street provided most of the first sightings over the last few years.

Listening for its sweet song offers the easiest way to find a Yellow Warbler. Peterson's field guide describes the song as *tsee tsee tsee tsee titi wee* (Peterson 1990). Yellow Warblers prefer riparian habitat, foraging and breeding around streams, rivers, and lakes with hardwood cover. Conifers and closed canopies line many of Vashon's streams, decreasing the amount of Yellow Warbler habitat. Yellow Warblers lack confirmed breeding status on Vashon, as no one has seen a nest or adults feeding young. These warblers do breed in wetlands further east in King County, making a Vashon breeding record appear possible. Yellow Warblers are one of the top three birds parasitized by cowbirds (Ehrlich et al. 1988). They sometimes foil the cowbirds by covering the cowbird egg with further nesting material so that it cools and dies. The last few decades probably brought a decline in their numbers on Vashon as forest succession brought more coniferous and mature deciduous woods.

BBS (USGS 2013): 1998

Very rare Palm Warbler found by author at KVI Beach on 6 May 2013. © Ed Swan

Palm Warbler

(SS, FL, ST) Status: Very rare visitor. One record.

The author found a Palm Warbler of the western subspecies on 6 May 2013 at KVI Beach. This species breeds in boggy thicket areas in Canada, from the northeastern corner of British Columbia east. Palm Warblers appear in our area as very rare migrants, primarily in the fall, with a few spring records. King County has seventeen records, with three in the spring (Hunn 2012). Observers first found Palm Warblers in the mid-1960s in Washington and Oregon (Wahl et al. 2005, Marshall et al. 2003, 2006). It's unclear why this species was not seen before that time period. Palm Warblers hunt for bugs mostly on the ground and run along the ground more than other warblers. Typically, they show up in shoreline areas with thickets and might be seen with crowned sparrows or Savannah Sparrows. At KVI Beach, the Vashon bird foraged in trees closest to the shore, flew into the beach grass, then ran along in the sand and popped up on a drift log to better spot prey.

Yellow-rumped Warbler

(FL, DC, WC, HW, ST, DA) Status: Common spring and fall migrant, rare summer and winter resident.

Two subspecies of Yellow-rumped Warbler visit Vashon, the more common Audubon's Warbler and the less common Myrtle Warbler. Myrtle Warblers have a white throat, whereas the Audubon's is yellow. Myrtles also have a distinct white eyebrow. Audubon's Warblers show up year-round, occurring especially commonly in migration. Yellow-rumped Warblers breed in open coniferous woods in the Olympics (Sharpe 1993) and apparently bred in the south Pierce County prairies in the early 1900s (Bent 1963c). Some birds utilize Pacific Madrone woods in the San Juans, which might be a possibility on Vashon as well (Smith et al. 1997). Most Vashon sightings fail to include subspecific details of the bird in question. During the peak of spring migration in 2003, the author's observations and reports from several observers indicate that Myrtles accounted for as much as one-third to one-half of the Yellow-rumps passing through in the latter half of April.

Most records for either subspecies occur in migration. While they utilize many habitats, Yellow-rumps on Vashon can be seen most commonly in hardwood forest. Apart from migrants, one Yellow-rump was seen by Dan Willsie on 11 July 2002 at the Old Mill Road pond. Carole Elder found one on her June 2004 Breeding Bird Survey, for another summer record. Others show up occasionally on the Christmas Bird Counts.The summer sightings indicate the possibility of a rare local breeder. It would be nice to verify if breeding actually takes place on the Island.

BBS (USGS 2013): 2004

CBC by area (Trevathan 1999-2013):
Vashon North: 2008, 2012-2013
Maury Island-Tramp Harbor: 2007-2011, 2013
Vashon South: 2002, 2004

Black-throated Gray Warbler

(DC, WC, HW, DA) Status: Fairly common spring through fall. Breeds.

Black-throated Gray Warblers inhabit second-growth woods that provide a mixed forest with large hardwood trees (Smith et al. 1997). As Vashon converted to that habitat type through logging followed by forest regrowth, Black-throated Gray numbers undoubtedly increased. Their *zee-a zee-a zee* song provides the easiest way to find them. Paradise Valley and areas along Westside Highway make the best places to listen for their song. In the spring of 2000, Sue Trevathan found one nesting, feeding its young and a young cowbird. The nest was about fifteen feet up in an alder at Point Robinson.

BBS (USGS 2013): 1995-1998, 2000-2006, 2009

Townsend's Warbler

(DC, WC, HW, DA) Status: Uncommon winter resident, rare spring through fall.

The Island's winter warbler, Townsend's often begin singing as early as February. In February and early March, few other birds actively sing and no other warblers. These bright, yellow and black-masked warblers mostly glean for bugs up high in conifers and sporadically lower in shrubs. Sometimes they add birdseed to their diet. In the winter of 2001/02, Townsend's Warblers came to sunflower seed feeders in three widely separated locations around the Island. Observers notice this type of feeding a few times each year. On 1 February 2007, Rebecca Strong actually saw one drinking from her hummingbird feeder.

Townsend's Warblers occasionally join in with mixed flocks of chickadees, kinglets, and nuthatches in winter. As the related Black-throated Gray Warbler migrates in to replace them during the breeding season, most Townsend's Warblers move north or into the mountains for nesting. Townsend's Warblers breed fairly low in nearby Kitsap County. The rare attempt at nesting should be watched for and reported on Vashon as well.

In the southern Cascades, the range of the Hermit Warbler—another close relative—overlaps with the Townsend's. The two hybridize extensively in areas where they coincide (Wahl et al. 2005). Birds in Western Washington near the contact zone usually appear a mix of the two, showing more of the plumage of one species or the other. Some birds look pure until closely examined. Both hybrids and pure Hermit Warblers visit nearby areas of King and Kitsap Counties. Rick Sanders noted a hybrid at his place on 3 February 2007 that had a face like a Townsend's but an all-white breast and minimal streaking along the sides and flanks.

BBS (USGS 2013): 1997, 2005

CBC by area (Trevathan 1999-2013):
Vashon North: 1999-2004, 2007, 2010-2013
Maury Island-Tramp Harbor: 1999-2000, 2002-2003, 2005, 2012-2013
Vashon South: 2002, 2006, cw2008, 2011

Hermit Warbler

(DC, WC, HW) Status: Very rare visitor. One record. Change in Status: New addition to the Island list after the first edition.

Hermit Warblers breed in conifer-dominated forests on the western slopes of the Cascades, the eastern slopes of the Olympics, and south down into the Willapa Hills (Chappell and Ringer 1983). They formerly bred in the dry coniferous woods and prairie complex of Pierce County as well. They otherwise tend to stick to low to mid-elevation hills and mountains. Vashon might expect to see a few in migration, but its low elevation and dominance of mixed woods make the Island an unlikely place for many sightings. Their vocalizations sound similar to the closely related Townsend's and Black-throated Gray Warblers. Hermit Warblers prefer to forage high up in conifer treetops so that finding one on the Island takes extra work. In addition, they hybridize with Townsend's Warblers (see the discussion in the Townsend's Warbler section above), requiring further care to ensure a proper identification. The author found a female in Paradise Valley on 20 September 2011 for the only Vashon record.

Wilson's Warbler

(DC, WC, HW, ST, DA) Status: Fairly common spring migrant and summer resident. Breeds.

Wilson's Warblers inhabit any forested area with brushy edges or significant small clearings with thickets (Smith et al. 1997). They also utilize forests where the canopy remains open enough to allow a varied understory. Wilson's Warblers seem particularly attracted by bird baths, coming especially to more natural ground-based water features or those carved into a large piece of wood or rock. When the migratory waves arrive in

Spotted Towhee drying off after a bath. © Doug Parrott

late April, these warblers occur widely. They scatter throughout yards and gardens with good amounts of shrubby cover, as well as the more appropriate forested edge habitat. As breeding season comes along, they continue singing into early July. Nesting takes place in more thickly wooded areas with openings for thickets. Joe Van Os has had active nests on his property on Maury Island.

BBS (USGS 2013): 1995-1998, 2000-2006, 2013

Yellow-breasted Chat

(ST, DA) Status: Very rare. Two records.

Two records of Yellow-breasted Chat exist for Vashon. Alan Richards found one at Portage on 10 May 1977 (Richards pers. com. 2005). Carole Elder spotted another on 29 May 1985 (*AB39*: 344). A few records exist for King County, but the normal range for chats lies east of the Cascades.

New World Sparrows

Spotted Towhee

(HW, ST, DA) Status: Common resident. Breeds.

Towhees abound in yards and edges of lowland woods with plenty of underbrush. They skulk along the ground, hiding behind leafy branches and scratching with both feet simultaneously to find bugs under fallen leaves and twigs. They eat seeds to a lesser extent. Observers find them most easily when they kick up the dust under a feeder looking for spilled seed.

In spring, towhees show up at the top of bushes, singing their song of six or so notes followed by a messy, buzzy trill. They have a call similar to a cat's meow, resulting in the nickname of "Catbird," though they have no relation to the bird of that name in the thrasher family. Very young birds being fed by adults appear in gardens and yards throughout the Island by mid-June. Rich Siegrist has found a number of nests at his place in the Colvos area in the brushy patches of his yard. Young birds emerge from May through July, as many pairs produce two broods.

BBS (USGS 2013): 1995-1998, 2000-2006, 2009, 2013

CBC by area (Trevathan 1999-2013) Trend: Stable.

Vashon North: 1999-2013
Maury Island-Tramp Harbor: 1999-2013
Vashon South: 1999-2013

Chipping Sparrow

(FL, DC, ST, DA) Status: Very rare spring migrant. Twelve records.

The Chipping Sparrow lives commonly in the dry, open forests east of the Cascades. The Joint Base Lewis-McChord prairies and open, dry coniferous forest there host the nearest significant population. Smaller breeding groups exist in Kitsap and San Juan Counties (Smith et al. 1997). Smith et al. list them as common in open grassy farmlands in Clark County. Chipping Sparrows may have been somewhat common in the past on Vashon, as Rathbun considered them so in the Seattle area (Rathbun 1911). These sparrows declined in much of the Puget Sound region as urban sprawl expanded over second-growth forests and remaining prairies. No published records exist for Vashon in earlier times. Island natives don't remember this particular sparrow, making it difficult to reconstruct its abundance history. Much of Vashon's dry coniferous forest remains thick, "dog hair"-like woods, so Chipping Sparrow usage probably centered primarily around clear-cuts and agricultural areas. As those phased out, this sparrow would have changed from an uncommon to common migrant and summer resident to its current very rare migrant status. Vashon's twelve records over the last 20 years are spread all over the Island without an apparent location preference.

Vesper Sparrow

(FL) Status: Very rare fall; formerly common, and possible former breeder. One modern record.

The Vesper Sparrow belongs to the grassland cohort that, over the last 80 years, lost habitat as forests reclaimed areas and residential neighborhoods

Savannah Sparrow. © Doug Parrott

grew. Larrison lists them as commonly found on Vashon back in the 1940s (Larrison 1952). Western Washington provides a significant portion of the range of the subspecies *affinis*. The *affinis* subspecies diminished throughout its range in the state over the last several decades (Smith et al. 1997, Rogers 2000). The prairies of Thurston and Pierce Counties formed the center of their abundance in Western Washington (Rogers 2000). Observers noted them regularly in a number of other Puget Sound areas, including meadows, pastures, and agricultural fields near Seattle in the early 20th century (Rathbun 1902). Some birds still inhabit the relatively nearby prairies maintained as firing grounds on Joint Base Lewis-McChord. Very rarely, a few birds still show up on Vashon. Joe Van Os had single birds visit briefly during the fall migration at his office in south Vashon Island.

Larrison's "commonly found" may refer only to migrants. Breeding might have been possible during Vashon's agricultural period. If present as a breeder, then the birds would have been of the *affinis* subspecies. Birds in migration might be *affinis* or *confinis*, the Eastern Washington subspecies (Rogers 2000).

Savannah Sparrow

(SS, FW, FL, ST) Status: Fairly common spring through fall. Breeds.

The Savannah Sparrow breeds around the Island in wet fields with tall grass. While migrants would have used the beaches before European-American settlement, the current breeding population resulted from the clearing of forests and the creation of fields by agriculture. Rich Siegrist found an adult feeding young in June 2001 for one of the more recent breeding records. Several subspecies/forms of the Savannah Sparrow move through Western Washington. The small Brooks form breeds in the Puget Sound lowlands (Smith et al. 1997). Others, such as the large Aleutian form, migrate in spring and fall (Sharpe 1993). Migrants on the Island show up very visibly at KVI Beach and Point Robinson. It would be interesting for birders to take note of the size of birds observed along the shoreline areas to see if both Brooks and Aleutian forms pass through Vashon.

Good areas to look for breeding birds include the Wax Orchard and Old Mill Road area, the wet fields adjacent to the monument on Monument Road, the fields in Paradise Valley, and the fields along Westside Highway in the Colvos and Cove area. Savannah Sparrows fare better in Western Washington than most field and open-area birds because they use relatively small patches of weedy lots to breed (Smith et al. 1997). On Vashon, this species' breeding population needs monitoring as the forest reclaims more fields and residential area sprawls.

BBS (USGS 2013): 1995-1998, 2001-2006, 2009

Fox Sparrow

(HW, ST, DA) Status: Common fall through spring.

In April and October, a song that seems to combine the music of both warbler and sparrow sometimes floats through the air. After tracking the source down, one finds a Fox Sparrow migrating through or coming to stay for the winter. Fox Sparrows also possess a loud scolding *chuck*. Hunting down the song or scold is the easiest method to find them because they often skulk in the bushes or dig through the detritus at the bottom of brambles and thickets. They seem most visible when they briefly run out to scratch through spilled mixed seed under feeders. Fox Sparrows show up in pretty much any brushy habitat or garden with plenty of shrubs around Vashon.

Ornithologists recognize more than a dozen subspecies of Fox Sparrows across the continent. Four groupings of these subspecies, each considered a "form," may eventually be split into four different species, creating a new genus (Rising 1996). Most of the United States has only one form, the Red Fox Sparrow. The Pacific Northwest hosts a great number of subspecies in two forms, the Sooty and Slate-colored. These subspecies breed from Alaska to the Olympic Peninsula. The Sooty Fox Sparrow winters west of the Cascades and breeds along the extreme outer coast

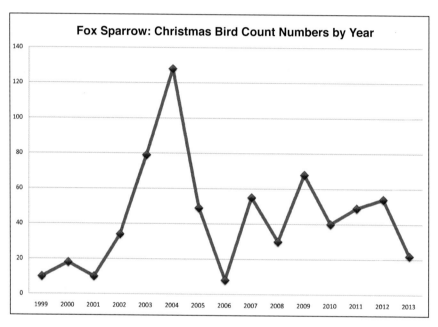

from the Olympic Peninsula to Alaska (Wahl et al. 2005, Pyle 1997). Very dark Fox Sparrows arriving in this area in winter usually consist of migrants from subspecies that breed farther north. They tend to be darker and larger the farther north they breed. The Slate-colored Fox Sparrow breeds in the Cascades, but a few move through the Puget Sound lowlands on their way back and forth from their wintering grounds in California and Arizona (Wahl et al. 2005). The reddish Fox Sparrow from the eastern United States rarely visits the Puget Sound area in winter.

CBC by area (Trevathan 1999-2009):
Vashon North: 1999, 2002-2013
Maury Island-Tramp Harbor: 1999-2013
Vashon South: 1999-2013

Song Sparrow

(SS, FW, HW, ST, DA) Status: Common resident. Breeds.

The most common sparrow of the Island, Song Sparrows utilize almost any habitat except open water. Song Sparrows inhabit brushy thickets in areas between trees and fields, as well as gardens, yards, and riparian zones. Other preferred habitat includes grass along shoreline and around beach logs. Similar to Fox Sparrows, towhees, and juncos, the Song Sparrow population expanded significantly with the clearing of forests on the Island. Song Sparrow numbers almost certainly fluctuated as clearing provided more open area, the open area changed to agriculture, and agriculture turned into brush, residential area, and forest.

Song Sparrows come to bird feeders, though they prefer the seed spilled on the ground. Song Sparrows, as goes with their name, sing year-round. On Vashon, many pairs probably produce two broods a year, with adults observed feeding young in May and June. Rich Siegrist has found many nests in the brushy areas of his yard in the Colvos area.

Experts name 31 subspecies/forms of Song Sparrows in North America. As one moves north and west across the continent, the subspecies shade darker and grow larger. The *morphna* form is the breeding subspecies in Western Washington (Smith et al. 1997). The subspecies breeding and migrating through the Puget Sound area tend to be relatively dark.

Song Sparrow. © Doug Parrott

Some appear as dark as a Sooty Fox Sparrow. Most Song Sparrows on the Island seem to be a chestnut/milk chocolate color. Every once in a while, lighter or more reddish-brown birds show up from one of the more eastern populations.

> BBS (USGS 2013): 1995-1998, 2000-2006, 2009, 2013
>
> CBC by area (Trevathan 1999-2009) Trend: Stable.
>> *Vashon North: 1999-2013*
>> *Maury Island-Tramp Harbor: 1999-2013*
>> *Vashon South: 1999-2013*

Lincoln's Sparrow

(FW, FL, HW, ST) Status: Uncommon fall through spring.

Lincoln's Sparrows prefer swampy, wet, and open shrubby areas. These sparrows probably only occurred on Vashon as spring and fall migrants prior to the clearing of coniferous forest and the creation of more thicket areas. As with many other sparrow species, a significant increase of winter sightings is apparent over the last few decades (Wahl et al. 2005). The Lincoln's Sparrow's superficial resemblance to Song Sparrows and habit of staying in the thick of a bush, even when scolding, make this species easy to miss and under-reported. While considered shy by many authorities, Island birds seem to respond well to spishing. Good fall locations include Point Robinson, Island Center Forest, and along Paradise Valley. Maury Island locations like the Marine Park produce spring records.

> CBC by area (Trevathan 1999-2013):
>> *Vashon North: cw2013*
>> *Maury Island-Tramp Harbor: 2005, 2009-2010*
>> *Vashon South: 2007, 2009, 2013*

White-throated Sparrow

(HW, ST, DA) Status: Uncommon fall through spring.

A visitor to hedgerows of blackberries and bird feeders in late fall and winter, the occasional White-throated Sparrow associates with the related Golden-crowned and White-crowned Sparrows. Flocks of these two more common species should always be checked for stray White-throated Sparrows. Bird feeders, rather than habitat, seem the main way to find this sparrow on Vashon. All but a couple of sightings took place at feeding stations, whether in more open areas or in woods. Reports for this species increased greatly in Washington since the early 1950s, when only six records existed (Wahl et al. 2005). Increased numbers appear to result from the rise in brushy habitat and bird feeding. Two morphs occur with this species: birds with either white or tan stripes on the head.

CBC by area (Trevathan 1999-2013):
Vashon North: 2003-2007, 2009-2010, cw2012
Vashon South: 2003, 2008-2009, cw2010, 2011

Harris's Sparrow

(ST, DA) Status: Very rare fall through spring. Four records.

The Harris's Sparrow breeds in the high central arctic of North America and winters predominantly in the Midwest, Kansas, and Oklahoma. A glance at the *WOSNews* sighting summaries often shows ten or so in various locations around the state in winter. Harris's Sparrows wintered on Vashon at least four times in the last decade: one stayed at the author's house in central Vashon from early October 2001 through early May 2002; another was found by Gary Shugart in the winter of 1998/99; a third was seen by Carole Elder along Cemetery Road in the mid 1990s; and Joe Van Os found one at his place on south Vashon. Harris's Sparrows should be looked for in the wintering flocks of Golden-crowned Sparrows that occur in the shrubby thickets and gardens around the Island. Reports for this species increased greatly in Washington since the early 1950s, when only five records existed (Wahl et al. 2005). The rise in numbers likely results from increased brushy habitat and observer effort.

CBC by area (Trevathan 1999-2013):
Vashon South: cw2002

White-crowned Sparrow

(FL, ST, DA) Status: Fairly common spring through fall, rare to uncommon winter. Breeds.

Spring has definitely arrived when the White-crowned Sparrow returns and begins singing on territory. Sibley renders its song as *seee zree chidle chidli chi-chi-chi teew* (Sibley 2000). Few written descriptions of birdsong really work, but that example picks up some of the essence. White-crowns also have a sharp *pink* warning note.

The singing of White-crowned Sparrows permeates our environment during spring and summer because they turn up just about everywhere but the deep woods. They hang out at Point Robinson and other shoreline areas, throughout the fields and gardens of the Island, and in the landscaping of the parking lots in town.

White-crowned Sparrow. © Doug Parrott

White-crowns begin showing up on Vashon in late March. They breed on the Island, having as many as two broods before the fall. They nest on the ground in deep brush, for the most part. Less common nest locations include out in the grass, in landscaping, and rarely up in a tree. In 2002, the author saw adults feeding young during the third week in July. An observer noted an adult giving food to a young cowbird in the first week of August. White-crowns begin to bunch up around feeders in September, as their somewhat larger relative, the Golden-crowned Sparrow, returns from the north. As October progresses, the numbers of White-crowned Sparrows decrease dramatically. It appears that most birds from our area go to central California for the winter (Bent 1968). Jewett et al. state that a bird banded on Vashon showed up in Berkeley (Jewett et al. 1953). Only a few White-crowns winter on Vashon.

Many of our wintering birds consist of the subspecies *gambelii*. They breed in the central and northern Cascades in the alpine areas and also far to the north of Washington. The subspecific composition of the winter population of Puget Sound White-crowned Sparrows appears to be changing over the last few decades from mostly *gambelii* to a higher percentage of *pugetensis*. (Wahl et al. 2005). The breeding form on Vashon consists entirely of the *pugetensis* subspecies. It appears browner overall and has a bright yellow bill.

BBS (USGS 2013): 1995-1998, 2000-2006, 2009, 2013

CBC by area (Trevathan 1999-2013) Trend: Always low numbers, stable.
  Vashon North: 1999, 2002-2003, 2007-2009, *cw2013*
  Maury Island-Tramp Harbor: 2003-2004, 2006-2009, *cw2010*, 2011-2013
  Vashon South: 2003-2005

Golden-crowned Sparrow

(FL, ST, DA) Status: Fairly common fall through early spring.

This sparrow inhabits the edges of fields with blackberry or other hedgerows. Golden-crowns like bird-feeding stations, especially when the seed is spread on the ground. They sing their *oh dear me* throughout the winter

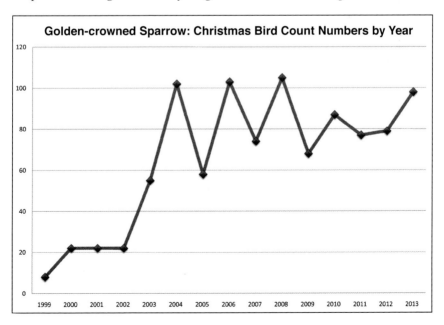

wherever they gather. Small winter flocks usually congregate at Raab's Lagoon, the bend in the road where 220th turns into Lisabeula Road, the hedgerows around central Vashon, and the horse pastures along the highway. The flocks of Golden-crowned Sparrows should be checked in winter for the less common White-crowned Sparrow, the uncommon White-throated Sparrow, and the rare Harris's Sparrow. Like several other sparrow species, winter numbers of Golden-crowned Sparrows were probably low or nonexistent before human alteration of the forested landscape opened up Vashon and increased appropriate habitat.

CBC by area (Trevathan 1999-2013) Trend: Increase over first five years of the count, followed by stability at the higher level.
Vashon North: 2001, 2003-2013
Vashon South: 1999-2013
Maury Island-Tramp Harbor: 1999-2013

Dark-eyed Junco

(FL, DC, WC, HW, ST, DA) Status: Common Resident. Breeds.

Juncos utilize just about every habitat from the coast line to high in the mountains and from forest to field. They prefer forest edge and mixed brush. Undoubtedly, their numbers on Vashon grew after the clearing of forests created many more brushy areas. Those numbers probably dipped again as agriculture covered much of the landscape. A rebound occurred as the fields grew over with early successional growth. The increased rural residential areas provide good habitat when shrubs and trees remain. The junco's diet consists mostly of seeds and the occasional insect. Caterpillars make a favorite food to feed their young. Many records exist of nesting sites for Vashon in roadside ditches, flower pots, flower beds, and other locations. Juncos may have more than one brood in a given year. Even though they start one nest in mid-April, they may still have nests or young on into July. One year, Moria Robinson on Maury Island found a junco nest with five eggs in the second week of June. About the same time, the author noticed a juvenile looking for seeds around a feeder.

In the breeding season, juncos make themselves extremely noticeable by singing/trilling from atop a tall tree. Just to confuse things, that trill sometimes takes on the similar but insect-like or metallic sound of the Chipping Sparrow, common in dry forests east of the Cascades and some spots in Western Washington. A few others call out songs sounding somewhat like a MacGillivray's Warbler. The author has run into both of these variations on Vashon and spent considerable time trying to find that rare Chipping Sparrow or unfamiliar warbler, only to have a junco finally become visible on a high branch, singing away. During the winter, flocks of up to 80 birds associating with other sparrows might congregate around a bird feeder.

The local junco species was formerly known as the Oregon Junco before the American Ornithological Union lumped it together with several other species to create the Dark-eyed Junco. During the winter, one or two of the Slate-colored Junco subspecies show up mixed in with a flock of Oregon Juncos. This subspecies was one of the former species lumped together to form the Dark-eyed Junco. Its usual range lies east of the Rockies. Male Slate-colored Juncos continue the dark slate-gray of the Oregon Junco hood all the way down the back and sides without any of the brown that appears on the Oregon form's back and sides. Females look the same in a lighter gray.

Dark-eyed Junco. © Gregg Thompson

BBS (USGS 2013): 1995-1998, 2000-2006, 2009, 2013

CBC by area (Trevathan 1999-2013) Trend: increase over first five years followed by stability at the higher level.

Vashon North: 1999-2013
Vashon South: 1999-2013
Maury Island-Tramp Harbor: 1999-2013

Tanagers

Western Tanager

(DC, WC, HW, DA) Status: Fairly common spring through fall. Breeds.

During the summer, Western Tanagers sing from the tops of conifers around the Island. They like to forage for insects at the very tops of tall conifers, making them hard to see. They are an "edge" species, often utilizing the boundaries of clear-cuts and other breaks in the canopy (Smith et al. 1997). Sharpe found them common in the Olympics in mixed forests below 700 feet, much like the Black-headed Grosbeak (Sharpe 1993). In migration, especially during the fall, they come down low to flit through brush, eating elderberries and other fruit and gleaning for insects. Joe Van Os has had active nests on his property on Maury Island.

BBS (USGS 2013): 1995-1998, 2000-2004, 2006, 2009, 2013

Grosbeak and Bunting

Black-headed Grosbeak

(HW, ST, DA) Status: Fairly common spring and summer resident. Breeds. One winter record.

These large finches have a robin-like song, heard from mixed deciduous and conifer wood stands around the Island in summer. Their *spik* locator calls keep them in contact with each other and aid the observer in finding them as well. Their bright orange and black plumage makes them very visible at sunflower seed feeders set out in spring and summer.

Black-headed Grosbeaks prefer mixed forests. They utilize evenly mixed forests, coniferous woods harboring deciduous trees in small patches, and riparian corridors of hardwood trees through coniferous woods (Smith et al. 1997). Grosbeaks increased in population regionally in the last 150 years. Jewett et al. wrote of them as not being common anywhere but regular in the right habitat (Jewett et al. 1953). On the present Vashon, the logging and the regrowth of the forests resulted in the vast majority of the woods coming back as mixed coniferous and deciduous in nature. The large number of riparian corridors provided by the many Vashon streams creates much appropriate Black-headed Grosbeak habitat.

July brings a large number of juveniles to local feeders. Other young still being fed by adults indicate that Black-headed Grosbeaks breed extensively across Vashon. Joe Van Os has had active nests on his property on Maury Island. One winter record exists. James Clark photographed a first-year bird visiting a feeder just north of Tahlequah in the south part of Vashon from about mid-December 2009 to mid-January 2010.

BBS (USGS 2013): 1995-1998, 2000-2006, 2009, 2013

CBC by area (Trevathan 1999-2013):
Vashon South: 2010

Lazuli Bunting

(FL, ST) Status: Rare spring migrant.

Lazuli Buntings take their name from the brilliant blue of their head, back, and wings, all of which flash brightly in the sunlight. The blue appears almost black when the light strikes their iridescent feathers wrong. Across the state, they prefer riparian areas, clear-cuts, fields, and thickets.

At the beginning of the 20th century, Rathbun found it uncommon in the Puget Sound area and growing more common than formerly (Rathbun 1902), which makes sense as clear-cuts spread across the region. By the mid-20th century, Larrison considered it rare in the Puget Sound area while still common in the prairies of southern Pierce County and the Joint Base Lewis-McChord area (Larrison 1952). That trend continues today, where some breeding occurs in remaining prairies areas and sporadically in Skagit County, Snohomish County, and south King County in the Kent Valley. No breeding records exist for Vashon.

Lazuli Buntings appear regularly for brief visits in mid-May. Sightings come Island-wide in thickets and brushy areas around fields and gardens.

Blackbirds, Orioles, and Allies

Red-winged Blackbird

(FW, FL, HW, ST, DA) Status: Fairly common spring and summer resident, uncommon fall, rare to uncommon winter. Breeds.

Red-winged Blackbirds breed in marshes with cattails and willows for nesting sites. Some of the most reliable places for them include Fisher Pond and the small marsh on the main highway just south of Wax Orchard

Road. They show up early at the tail end of winter in late February and remain into October. Often early arrivals and post-breeding birds utilize local feeders away from the marshes and wetlands. Red-winged Blackbirds stay through the winter in large numbers in other agricultural areas of Western Washington that have larger numbers of cattle. They sometimes appear absent in winter on Vashon, but a thorough search usually finds a few birds. Paradise Valley farm areas and ponds often attract at least a few birds through the winter.

The population of Red-winged Blackbirds surely fluctuated a number of times on Vashon over the last 150 years. Few marshes with cattails ex-

Western Meadowlark. © Doug Parrott

isted prior to European-American settlement, limiting opportunities for nesting. Then the increase in agriculture after the clearing of trees provided greater forage areas. The simultaneous creation of many ponds resulted in the development of an Island breeding population. The decline in agriculture would have lowered numbers to some extent.

BBS (USGS 2013): 1996-1998, 2000-2006, 2009

CBC by area (Trevathan 1999-2013) Trend: Erratic but stable.

Vashon North: cw2001, 2002-2005, 2007-2008, 2010-2013
Maury Island-Tramp Harbor: 2008-2009, 2013
Vashon South: 2000-2001, 2003, cw2004, 2005-2010, 2012-2013

Western Meadowlark

(SS, FL) Status: Rare spring and very rare fall migrant.

Meadowlarks would originally have been nonexistent or at most rare migrants to beaches along Vashon's shore. With the clearing of the woods and the onset of agriculture, they invaded the Island. Vashon had extensive hay fields in its agricultural "hay" day. Dan Willsie and Rich Siegrist both remember meadowlarks as common in those fields up to at least 1950.

In Western Washington as a whole, meadowlarks experienced a largely undocumented decline from the early part of the 20th century to the latter part (Rogers 2000). Observers missed commenting on the change of status from at first common to abundant in the Puget Sound region to later rare and declining. On Vashon, as the residential areas expanded and forest stands began to reclaim their former size, the farming and field areas declined radically. The meadowlark population on the Island seems to match the decrease in field habitat. Meadowlarks now visit in spring migration very rarely in fields in upland areas or rarely in grassy areas around the beaches. All but one sighting in the last decade occurred adjacent to shorelines.

Yellow-headed Blackbird

(DA) Status: Very rare spring visitor. Three records.

Uncommon in Western Washington, Yellow-headed Blackbirds appear most often from late April to late May (Wahl et al. 2005). Three records exist for Vashon. Jill Graham discovered a first-year male at her place in the Colvos area from 12 May 2002 to at least 23 May 2002. Valerie Vigesaa observed another male along 188th in the first week of May 2004. Mary Margaret Briggs photographed one at her place in the Colvos area on 9 May 2009. An unconfirmed report exists for the summer of 2001 in the Westside Highway area.

Rusty Blackbird

(FL, HW, DA) Status: Accidental. One record.

The usual range for Rusty Blackbird lies in the high north in the breeding season and east of the Mississippi in winter. One or two show up most winters in Washington State. Joe Van Os had one bird visit his place on Vashon in the early 1980s.

Brewer's Blackbird

(FL, DA) Status: Very rare visitor. Former breeder.

John Friars, a long-time resident of the Island, remembers Brewer's Blackbirds as common in the Dockton area when it consisted mainly of agricultural fields in the 1940s. Vashon almost certainly lacked any Brewer's Blackbirds until the clearing of forests. They then apparently colonized the Island in reaction to the advance of clearing and agriculture. As the forests regenerated, their numbers declined. Gary Shugart reports them as frequenting his yard along Bank Road, following his rototiller. When Augie's farm next door shut down, they disappeared. In the last few years, usually only one or two brief sightings in spring occurred around the Island. A breeding record exists with the Breeding Bird Atlas project for the 1980s (Smith et al. 1997). For the last several years, a pair visited fields to either side of where the old Vashon Highway intersects the current highway north of the Vashon Community Care Center. In April 2013, the author noted one of two pairs present gathering nesting material. A small breeding presence may still exist.

Brown-headed Cowbird

(FL, DC, WC, HW, ST, DA) Status: Fairly common spring and summer. Breeds.

The cowbird presents a challenge to other birds, as it acts as a brood parasite on other species. The female lays her eggs in the nests of other birds. The cowbird young usually grow much larger, more quickly than the host's babies do, and thus more aggressively grab the food from the host parent. They often get all of the food, and the host's young die. The author once saw a small Black-throated Gray Warbler struggling to feed a young cowbird two or three times its size and another time at Chautauqua Elementary School noted a cowbird three to four times bigger hounding a Golden-crowned Kinglet. Cowbirds prefer open areas. They also commute into forests in search of nests in which to lay their eggs, expanding the area in which they have an impact.

This Great Basin and Great Plains species followed farmers and clearing of land both west and east in North America. It reached Western Washington in 1955, and the first breeding evidence showed up in 1958 (Smith et al. 1997). Since then, the cowbird population exploded in Western Washington as forests become more fragmented. The creation of more open area provided expanded foraging habitat and greater access to the nests of forest birds. Originally not seen in forest habitats, now cowbirds can reach into forests to parasitize nests because of the creation of smaller tracts of forests. From an original base of about 50 host species, the cowbird now

Brown-headed Cowbird.© Doug Parrott

utilizes over 200 (Terborgh 1989). Terborgh notes that cowbirds especially impact neotropical migrants because they have less time to breed successfully than local, resident birds. Migrants such as vireos, thrushes, and warblers have time for only one brood. If they lose that brood to predation or parasitization, they lack the opportunity to produce young. Also, as they are relatively inexperienced with cowbirds because of the recent nest parasite's spread, many neotropical species have not evolved any defense. In Minnesota, the Kirtland's Warbler, already limited to a very specific habitat, now has such low numbers that it exists only because biologists and volunteers find their nests and remove the cowbird eggs. One should note with this example, and the situation with most lowered bird populations, that habitat loss forms the key factor. Cowbirds cause an important but secondary issue.

Cowbirds enjoy spilled grain on farms and readily come to bird feeders and cattle and horse pastures. They show up anywhere on the Island except in the large, heavily wooded tracts. They appear most abundantly visible in May and early June, the height of the local breeding season, scouring the area for nests in which to lay eggs and for opportunities to mate with each other. In late August and early September, young cowbirds look very brownish-gray, with few to no markings. They often frequent driftwood stretches along the Island beaches. Finding a very nondescript bird that doesn't really look like anything in the book probably means, if it's the right size, that one has found one of these first-year cowbirds.

BBS (USGS 2013): 1995-1998, 2000-2006, 2009, 2013

Bullock's Oriole

(FW, HW, DA) Status: Very rare spring and summer. Breeds. Change in Status: With only one sighting since 2008, the status of this species moves from rare to very rare.

Across the state in general, and in the Puget Sound lowlands in particular, the Bullock's Oriole's population increased significantly over the last quarter century (Smith et al. 1997). Where hardwoods replaced conifers or joined them along riparian corridors after the logging throughout the late 1800s and 1900s, these orioles expanded their range. On Vashon, they mainly pass through quickly and elusively as migrants in spring. Most sightings come from Point Robinson and the area around the corner of 91st and Van Olinda, where nesting occurred in some years. Two breeding records exist. One nested at Nancy Silver's house above Burton in the summer of 1997. Another nesting female was found by Carole Elder at the corner of 91st and Van Olinda on 23 May 2002. Elder saw the female take the fecal sack from a nest in an old apple tree.

Finches and Allies

Purple Finch

(DC, WC, HW, DA) Status: Fairly common resident. Breeds.

The wine-red Purple Finch inhabits forests bordered by brushy areas (Smith et al. 1997). The Purple Finch population on Vashon would have benefited from the clearing of the woods and then the patchy regrowth across the Island. Purple Finches may be declining to some extent as the forests mature and re-claim clearings and more uniformly cover the landscape. In addition, the House Finch continues to expand its range and outcompetes the Purple Finches in the growing urban and suburban areas on the Island. Residential areas now form patchy, open places near the conifer woods. Competition between the House Finch and Purple Finch occurs around these human-occupied open areas. Both finches visit bird feeders and prefer sunflower seed. Joe Van Os has had active nests on his property on Maury Island, as has Rich Siegrist on Vashon.

BBS (USGS 2013): 1995-1998, 2000-2006, 2009, 2013

CBC by area (Trevathan 1999-2013) Trend: Varible, but apparently stable.

Vashon North: 1999, 2001-2013
Maury Island-Tramp Harbor: 1999, 2003-2013
Vashon South: 1999-2012

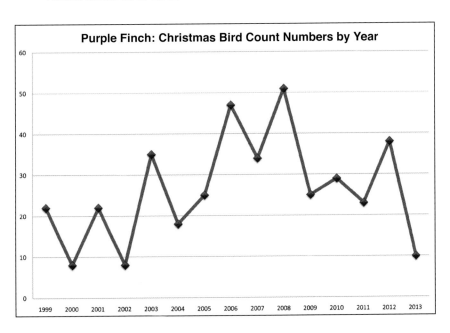

Cassin's Finch

(DC, WC, HW, DA) Status: Very rare spring migrant.

The common breeding finch of the mountains east of the Cascades, Cassin's Finch occurs as a misplaced wanderer in Western Washington. Joe Van Os banded a Cassin's passing through in spring at least twice at his place on Maury Island (Van Os pers. com. 2005). Wahl et al. note one netted from a small flock on 7 May 1984, though this may be one of the birds Joe Van Os mentions (Wahl et al. 2005).

House Finch

(SS, FL, ST, DA) Status: Fairly common resident. Breeds.

House Finches, the bright red little birds that come to any area bird feeder, invaded Western Washington from the southwestern United States in the 1950s (Sharpe 1993). Originally a bird of deserts and grasslands, this bird's

Adult House Finch feeding a fledgling. © Doug Parrott

populations now strongly correlate to the existence of urban areas and especially bird feeders (Smith et al. 1997). Besides sunflower seed at feeders, House Finches eat a variety of weed seeds and flower petals. They often replace the native Purple Finch in residential areas around Vashon. They utilize many of the open and brushy areas of the Island. Large flocks sometimes gather out on the beaches as well, especially in the grasses at KVI Beach in fall. They nest in bushes as well as structures. In the early summer of 2002, the author found an adult feeding young in a nest in a five-foot-diameter bush in town. Rich Siegrist watched a female that produced two broods within two weeks of each other in a shed in 2002.

BBS (USGS 2013): 1995-1998, 2000-2006, 2009, 2013

CBC by area (Trevathan 1999-2013) Trend: Increased over the first five years of the count to stabilize at a higher level for the last ten years.

Vashon North: 1999-2013
Maury Island-Tramp Harbor: 1999-2013
Vashon South: 1999-2002, 2004-2013

Red Crossbill

(DC, WC, DA) Status: Irregularly fairly common resident. Breeds.

All around Vashon, one might hear the *kip, kip, kip* of Red Crossbills. These birds receive their name from the way their beak's upper and lower mandibles evolved to cross each other. This adaptation allows them to pry open the cones of conifers to pluck out seeds.

Currently considered to be one species, as many as eight new species of crossbills might be split from this wandering northern finch. Each subspecies or perhaps full species is slightly different in overall size, bill size, and call note. The call note makes the best method of identifying a bird.

The different types adapted their cross-wise bill to specialize in opening the cones of a preferred conifer species. They feed on other conifer types as necessary. Six types appear in Washington, with three possible around Vashon: Type I, which prefers Western Hemlock; Type III, which prefers Western Hemlock and Sitka Spruce; and Type IV, which prefers Douglas-fir (Smith et al. 1997). Red Crossbills sometimes vary their diet and come readily to sunflower seed feeders on Vashon.

Throughout their range, crossbills tend to be quite irruptive. On Vashon, the wide range in age and type of conifer stands seems to provide forage year-round. At least a few crossbills hang out somewhere around the Island in each season, even if those numbers swing widely between highs and lows. Summer appears to attract the most birds to the Island. The crossbill population would have fluctuated widely in response to the clearing of the Island and the slow regeneration of the forests into many different types of woodlands.

Red Crossbills breed at any time of year, according to the abundance of their target cone crop (Smith et al. 1997). Joe Van Os has had active nests on his property on Maury Island. Immatures show up regularly. Rich Siegrist has seen young being fed in June near his place at Colvos.

Red Crossbill. © Gregg Thompson

BBS (USGS 2013): 1996, 1998, 2000-2006, 2013

CBC by area (Trevathan 1999-2013) Trend: Stable.

Vashon North: 2000, 2002, 2007, 2010-2013
Maury Island-Tramp Harbor: 2000, 2002-2003, cw2009, 2010-2013
Vashon South: 2000, 2002, 2004-2005, 2007, cw2008, cw2009, 2010, 2012-2013

Pine Siskin

(DC, WC, HW, ST, DA) Status: Fairly common resident. Breeds.

An irruptive northern finch, some Pine Siskins put in an appearance all year because of the many stands of conifers. Their population in any given area depends on the status of the cone crop that year. They have broader feeding habits that include a preference for weed seeds such as thistles. Siskins also come to sunflower seed bird feeders. In winter, they form large flocks of 50 to 100 birds or more, which can be heart-stopping when these finches explode upwards from a patch of weeds at one's feet. Joe Van Os observed nests at his place on Maury Island in many years.

BBS (USGS 2013): 1995, 1996, 2000-2005, 2013

CBC by area (Trevathan 1999-2013) Trend: Stable, with huge numbers in 2013.

Vashon North: 1999-2013
Maury Island-Tramp Harbor: 1999-2013
Vashon South: 2000-2005, 2007-2013

American Goldfinch

(FL, HW, ST, DA) Status: Fairly common spring through fall, uncommon to rare in winter. Breeds.

Goldfinches greatly benefited from the clearing of forests in Western Washington (Dawson and Bowles 1909, Jewett et al. 1953). Most early ornithologists in the state noted them as rare or didn't find them this side of the Cascades (Smith et al. 1997). Thickets, brushy areas, and grassland that the goldfinch favor were created with the logging of woods in the late nineteenth and early 20th centuries. Thistles, a big favorite of goldfinches and Pine Siskins, were especially adapted to growing in the disturbed areas left by all the clearing. Goldfinches multiplied with all of that seed provided for food.

Goldfinches utilize brushy areas and gardens all over Vashon. In winter, their population drops, but small groups usually stay in the neighborhood of thistle and sunflower seed feeders. Joe Van Os found nests at his place on Maury Island, and the abundance of juveniles each summer

American Goldfinch. © Doug Parrott

indicates breeding on the Island. Rich Siegrist has noted adults feeding fledged young.

BBS (USGS 2013): 1995-1998, 2000-2006, 2009, 2013

CBC by area (Trevathan 1999-2013) Trend: Erratic but stable.
Vashon North: 2002, 2004, 2006-2009, 2011-2013
Maury Island-Tramp Harbor: 2001, 2004-2012
Vashon South: 1999-2001, 2003-2004, 2006-2008, 2010, 2012

Evening Grosbeak

(DC, WC, HW, DA) Status: Rare or absent much of the year, uncommon spring and fall migrant.

Observers detect this erratic wanderer most often by its piercing one-note call as it flies overhead from one patch of woods to another. Evening Grosbeaks come to feeders and prefer sunflower seed. They like coniferous forests but also feed on various fruits and berries and on the seeds and flowers of Bigleaf Maples. Like many northern finches, Evening Grosbeaks irrupt and seem common one year or season and then rare the next. The availability of seed and fruit crops and infestations of insects such as the spruce budworm determine their variable presence in any particular area (Wahl et al. 2005). On Vashon, they show up strongly most spring migrations and then somewhat less so in the fall. No records exist outside of migration except for one count week Christmas Bird Count sighting.

Though numbers vary greatly from year to year, it appears likely that the clearing of the original old-growth forest would have resulted in a significant decline in grosbeaks (Raphael et al. 1988). The Evening Grosbeak should now have recovered with the regeneration of forests on Vashon.

BBS (USGS 2013): 2004

CBC by area (Trevathan 1999-2013):
Vashon North: cw2001

Old World Sparrows

House Sparrow

(FL, ST, DA) Status: Introduced. Fairly common resident. Breeds.
The House Sparrow was first introduced to North America in 1851 (Smith et al. 1997). It has lived with humans for ages. Its Latin name is *Passer domesticus,* a good indication that it is almost like one of our domesticated pets or livestock. House Sparrows prefer either urban areas, where they feed on garbage, seed at feeders, french fries and the like, or farming areas where they are closely associated with horses and cattle. The House Sparrow essentially followed farmers west, stealing feed grain from livestock and eating seeds out of horse dung (Sharpe 1993). They first appeared in Washington in Spokane in 1895, then Seattle in 1897, and the coast by 1916 (Smith et al. 1997). On Vashon, House Sparrows predominantly occur at bird feeders and commercial strips and around acreage with horses or cows. They remain localized in these areas and rarely visit the forested, riparian, and shoreline areas of the Island.

As anyone with a feeder using mixed seed on Vashon can attest, House Sparrows breed prolifically. Every summer, a horde of young sparrows take over any feeding station from all but the most persistent other species. Adults aggressively occupy any possible crevice or hole, out-competing other hole-nesting birds and having a dampening effect on the population of several species. Joe Van Os has had many nest at his office on south Vashon.

BBS (USGS 2013): 1995-1998, 2000, 2001, 2003-2005, 2009, 2013

CBC by area (Trevathan 1999-2009) Trend: Increase for first five count years, followed by stability at higher level.
Vashon North: 2000, 2002-2013
Maury Island-Tramp Harbor: 2001-2013
Vashon South: 1999-2013

References

Abella, S., B. Cullen, K. Higgins, G. Lucchetti, and J. Vanderhoof. 2007. "Shoreline Inventory and Characterization: Methodology and Results," *King County Shorelines Master Program Technical Appendix*, Volume 1. King County.

Acker, Jamie. Personal communication. 2005. Acker censuses owls each year on Bainbridge Island.

American Birding Association. 1999-2013. "Regional Reports." *North American Birds* 53(1)-66(3).

American Ornithologists' Union (AOU). 2012. "Fifty-third Supplement to the American Ornithologists' Union Check-list of North American Birds." *The Auk* 129(3):573-588.

Anderson, Bud. 2005. Personal communication. Anderson helped found the Falcon Research Group and has studied raptors in Washington and around the world for several decades.

Andrews, J. A. B., and K. W. Berry, eds. 2001. *The Nature of an Island*. Sand Dollar Press, Vashon Island, WA. 113 pp.

Angell, T., and K. C. Balcomb. 1982. *Marine Birds and Mammals of Puget Sound*. University of Washington Press, Seattle. 145 pp.

Angerman, Bud. Personal communication. 2009. Angerman worked at the Tacoma Game Farm from 1958 into the 1980s.

Askins, R. A. 2000. *Restoring North America's Birds: Lessons from Landscape Ecology*. Yale University, New Haven. 320 pp.

Aversa, Tom. 2005. Personal communication. Aversa compiled bird records for the Washington Ornithological Society and served on the Washington Bird Records Committee for many years.

Aycrigg, J. L., M. Anderson, G. Beauvais, M. Croft, A. Davidson, L. Duarte, J. Kagan, D. Keinath, S. Lennartz, J. Lonneker, T. Miewald, and J. Ohmann. 2013. "Ecoregional Gap Analysis of the Northwestern United States." In *Northwest Gap Analysis Project, Draft Report*. U.S. Geological Survey, Gap Analysis Program. Online at: ftp://ftp.gap.uidaho.edu/products/regional/Northwest/NWGAPDraftReportJune 2013.pdf.

Babcock, Ed. 2005. Personal communications. Babcock has resided on Vashon Island for over 70 years. As a hunter and member of the Vashon Sportmen's Club, he has been familiar with the populations and introductions of game birds on the island.

Ball, I. J., E. L. Bowhay, and C. F. Yocom. 1981. *Ecology and Management of the Western Canada Goose in Washington*. Biological Bulletin 17. Washington Department of Game. 67 pp.

Banko, W. E. 1960. *The Trumpeter Swan: Its History, Habits and Population in the United States*. North American Fauna series, Number 63. Bureau of Sport Fisheries and Wildlife, U.S. Dept. of the Interior, Washington, D.C. 214 pp.

Beaudette, Dave. 2005. Beaudette spent many years documenting King County birds in order to fill out an understanding of the bird species that were previously little documented in our state, especially those of the waters and mountains.

Bent, A. C. 1927. *Life Histories of North American Shore Birds*, Part 1. Dover, New York. 420 pp.

Bent, A. C. 1961a. *Life Histories of North American Birds of Prey*, Part 1. Dover, New York. 409 pp.

References

Bent, A. C. 1961b. *Life Histories of North American Birds of Prey,* Part 2. Dover, New York. 482 pp.

Bent, A. C. 1963a. *Life Histories of North American Diving Birds.* Dover, New York. 239 pp.

Bent, A. C. 1963b. *Life Histories of North American Gallinaceous Birds.* Dover, New York. 490 pp.

Bent, A. C. 1963c. *Life Histories of North American Wood Warblers,* Part 1. Dover, New York. 367 pp.

Bent, A. C. 1963d. *Life Histories of North American Flycatchers, Larks, Swallows, and Their Allies.* Dover, New York. 555 pp.

Bent, A. C. 1964a. *Life Histories of North American Nuthatches, Wrens, Thrashers, and Their Allies.* Dover, New York. 475 pp.

Bent, A. C. 1964b. *Life Histories of North American Thrushes, Kinglets, and Their Allies.* Dover, New York. 452 pp.

Bent, A. C. 1964c. *Life Histories of North American Jays, Crows, and Titmice.* 2 parts. Dover, New York. 495 pp.

Bent, A. C. 1964d. *Life Histories of North American Woodpeckers.* Dover, New York. 342 pp.

Bent, A. C. 1968. *Life Histories of North American Cardinals, Grosbeaks, Buntings, Towhees, Finches, Sparrows and Allies.* 3 parts. Dover, New York. 1889 pp.

Blake, J. G., and J. R. Karr. 1984. "Species Composition of Bird Communities and the Conservation Benefit of Large versus Small Forests." *Biological Conservation* 30(2):173-187.

Bock, Thais. 2008. Personal communication and records for the Tahoma Audubon Society's newletter, *Towhee.*

Brown, C. R. 1997. "Purple Martin *(Progne subis).*" In *The Birds of North America,* No. 287, edited by A. Poole and F. Gill. The Academy of Natural Sciences, Philadelphia, PA, and the American Ornithological Union, Washington, D.C. 32 pp.

Brown, P. W., and L. H. Fredrickson. 1997. "White-winged Scoter *(Melanitta fusca).*" In *The Birds of North America Online,* edited by A. Poole. Ithaca: Cornell Lab of Ornithology. Retrieved from *The Birds of North America Online:* http://bna.birds.cornell.edu/bna/species/274/articles/introduction.

Buerge, D. 1994. Curriculum Materials on Vashon-Maury Island Indians. Unpublished manuscript, Vashon branch, King County Library System. Vashon, WA.

Campbell, R. W. 1972. "The Green Heron in British Columbia." *Syesis* 5:235-247.

Campbell, R. W., N. K. Dawe, I. McTaggart-Cowan, J. M. Cooper, G. W. Kaiser, M. C. E. McNall, and G .E. J. Smith. 1990. *The Birds of British Columbia,* Volumes I-IV. Royal British Columbia Museum, Victoria, British Columbia.

Canning, D. J., and S. G. Herman. 1983. "Gadwall Breeding Range Expansion into Western Washington." *The Murrelet* 64(1):27-31.

Cannings, R. A., R. J. Cannings, and S. G. Cannings. 1987. *Birds of the Okanogan Valley, British Columbia.* Royal British Columbia Museum, Victoria, British Columbia. 420 pp.

Carey, A. B., M. M. Hardt, S. P. Horton, and B. L. Biswell. 1991. "Spring Bird Communities in the Oregon Coast Range." In *Wildlife and Vegetation of Unmanaged Douglas-Fir Forests: General Technical Report PNW-GTR-285,* edited by L. F. Ruggiero, K. B. Aubry, A. B. Carey, and M. H. Huff, pp. 123-140. USDA, Forest Service.

Carey, R. N. 1976. *Isle of the Sea Breezers.* Alderbrook Publishing Co., Seattle. 135 pp.

Carey, R. N. 1985. *Van Olinda's History of Vashon-Maury Island.* Alderbrook Publishing Co., Seattle. 84 pp.

Carey, R. N. Undated. Unpublished notebook of Vashon sightings.

Carr, J. R./Associates. 1983. *Vashon-Maury Island Water Resources Study.* King County Department of Planning and Community Development, Planning Division, Seattle.

Cassidy, K. M., C. E. Grue, M. R. Smith, and K. M. Dvornich, eds. 1997. *Washington State Gap Analysis Project-Final Report.* Volumes 1-5. Washington Cooperative Fish and Wildlife Research Unit, University of Washington, Seattle.

Chappell, C. 1997. *Washington Natural Heritage Program Site Evaluation for Point Robinson, Maury Island.* Copies available from: Washington Department of Natural Resources, Conservation, Recreation and Transactions Division, 1111 Washington Street SE, PO Box 47014, Olympia, WA 98504-7014.

Chappell, C. B., and B. J. Ringer. 1983. "Status of the Hermit Warbler in Washington." *Western Birds* 14(4):185-196.

Chu, M. 2003. "An Eerie Silence, And Fewer Birds, in the Chicago Region." *Birdscope* 17(2):1, Spring 2003. Retrieved from: http://www.birds.cornell.edu/Publications/Birdscope/Spring2003/TakingCount.html.

Churchill, Derek. 2013. Personal communications. Churchill is a member of the Vashon Forest Stewards and a forestry consultant.

Cole, C. F. 1941. *Land Utilization on Vashon Island.* Thesis (Masters). University of Washington, Seattle.

Coleman, J. S., and S. A. Temple. 1996. "On the Prowl." *Wisconsin Natural Resources Magazine,* December 1996. Wisconsin Department of Natural Resources.

Davison, M., and D. Kraege. 2002. "Marine goose research takes biologists above Arctic Circle." Washington State Department of Fish and Wildlife press release, November 5, 2002.

Dawson, W. L., and J. H. Bowles. 1909. *The Birds of Washington: A Complete Scientific and Popular Account of the 372 Species of Birds Found in the State.* 2 vols. Occidental Publishing Co., Seattle.

Dean, T., R. Holtz, J. Kuperberg, H. Meeker, J. Meeker, and F. Shipley. 1998. Vashon-Maury Island Habitats. Unpublished Manuscript. Vashon Branch of the King County Library System. 30 pp.

De Gasperi, C., E. Ferguson, and K. Stark. 2009. *Quality Assurance Project Plan for Quartermaster Harbor Nitrogen Mangagement Study.* King County Department of Natural Resources and Parks, Seattle.

De Graaf, R. M., and J. H. Rappole. 1995. *Neotropical Migratory Birds: Natural History, Distribution, and Population Change.* Cornell University Press, Ithaca, NY. 676 pp.

Donovan, H., and J. L. Bower. 2004. "Study Finds Substantial Declines in Local Marine Bird Species." *Whatcom Watch,* Vol. 13, No. 12.

Edgell, M. C. R. 1984. "Trans-Hemispheric Movements of Holarctic Anatidae: The Eurasian Wigeon *(Anas penelope L.)* in North America." *Journal of Biogeography* 11(1):27-39.

Ehrlich, P. R., D. S. Dobkin, and D. Wheye. 1988. *The Birder's Handbook: A Field Guide to the Natural History of North American Birds.* Simon & Schuster, New York. 785 pp.

Everson, Joseph. (In process). *Puget Sound Assessment and Monitoring Program Waterfowl Trends.* Washington Department of Fish and Wildlife, Puget Sound Assessment and Monitoring Program.

Ewins, Peter J., and D. V. Weseloh. 1999. "Little Gull *(Larus minutus).*" In *The Birds of North America Online,* edited by A. Poole. Ithaca: Cornell Lab of Ornithology. Retrieved from *The Birds of North America Online:* http://bna.birds.cornell.edu/bna/species/428/articles/introduction.

REFERENCES

Fahrig, Lenore. 1999. "Forest Loss and Fragmentation: Which has the Greater Effect on Persistence of Forest-dwelling Animals?" In *Forest Fragmentation: Wildlife and Management Implications,* edited by J. A. Rochelle, L. A. Lehmann, and J. Wisniewski, pp. 87-95. Brill, Leiden, The Netherlands.

Falcon Research Group. 2009. "Long-billed Hawk Syndrome." Online at http://www.frg.org/LB_synd.htm.

Forrester, Jasper. 2005. Personal communication. Forrester is a farmer and co-owner of Green Man Farm, the first biodynamic Community Supported Agriculture farm on the Island.

Franklin, J. F., and C. T. Dyrness. 1988. *Natural Vegetation of Oregon and Washington.* Oregon State University Press. 452 pp.

Friars, John. 2005. Personal communications. Friars is a master birder and has watched birds on Vashon since the 1940s.

Gaston, A. J., and S. B. Dechesne. 1996. "Rhinoceros Auklet *(Cerorhinca monocerata)*." In *The Birds of North America Online,* edited by A. Poole. Ithaca: Cornell Lab of Ornithology. Retrieved from *The Birds of North America Online:* http://bna.birds.cornell.edu/bna/species/212/articles/introduction.

Gauthier, Gilles. 1993. "Bufflehead *(Bucephala albeola)*." In *The Birds of North America Online,* edited by A. Poole. Ithaca: Cornell Lab of Ornithology. Retrieved from *The Birds of North America Online:* http://bna.birds.cornell.edu/bna/species/067/articles/introduction.

Gilbert, F. F., and R. Allwine. 1991. "Spring Bird Communities in the Oregon Cascade Range." In *Wildlife and Vegetation of Unmanaged Douglas-Fir Forests: General Technical Report PNW-GTR-285,* edited by L. F. Ruggiero, K. B. Aubry, A. B. Carey, and M. H. Huff, pp. 141-158. USDA, Forest Service.

Haulman, Bruce. 2005. Personal communications. Haulman is a history professor and member of the Vashon-Maury Island Heritage Association.

Haulman, Bruce. (In press). *A Brief History of Vashon Island.* The History Press.

Hejl, S. J. 1994. "Human-induced Changes in Bird Populations in Coniferous Forests in Western North America during the Past 100 Years," *Studies in Avian Biology* 15:232-246. In *A Century of Avifaunal Change in Western North America,* Proceedings of an International Symposium at the Centennial Meeting of the Cooper Ornithological Society, Sacramento, California, April 17, 1993. Cooper Ornithological Society.

Herlugson, C. J. 1978. "Comments on the Status and Distribution of Western and Mountain Bluebirds in Washington." *Western Birds* 9(1):21-32.

Hirsch, K. V. 1980. *Winter Ecology of Sea Ducks in the Inland Marine Waters of Washington.* Thesis (Masters). University of Washington, Seattle. 92 pp.

Holtz, Rayna. 2005. Personal communications. Holtz is a retired reference librarian and researcher of Vashon environmental issues, and a former president of Vashon-Maury Island Audubon Society.

Huff, M. H., D. A. Manuwal, and J. A. Putera. 1991. "Winter Bird Communities in the Southern Washington Cascade Range." In *Wildlife and Vegetation of Unmanaged Douglas-Fir Forests: General Technical Report PNW-GTR-285,* edited by L. F. Ruggiero, K. B. Aubry, A. B. Carey, and M. H. Huff, pp. 207-220. USDA, Forest Service.

Hunn, E. S. 1982. *Birding in Seattle and King County.* First Edition. Seattle Audubon Society, Seattle. 160 pp.

Hunn, E. S. 2012. *Birding in Seattle and King County.* Second Edition. Seattle Audubon Society, Seattle. 252 pp.

Jewett, S. G., W. P. Taylor, W. T. Shaw, and J. W. Aldrich. 1953. *Birds of Washington State.* University of Washington Press, Seattle. 768 pp.

Johnsgard, P. A. 1978. *Ducks, Geese, and Swans of the World.* University of Nebraska Press, Lincoln and London. 404 pp.

Johnsgard, P. A. 1990. *Hawks, Eagles, and Falcons of North America.* Smithsonian Institution Press, Washington and London. 403 pp.

Johnson, D. H., and T. A. O'Neil. 2001. *Wildlife-Habitat Relationships in Oregon and Washington.* Oregon State University Press, Corvallis. 736 pp.

Johnson, E. R. , and E. D. Strait. 1924. *Farming the Logged-Off Uplands in Western Washington.* Bulletin 1236, United States Department of Agriculture, Washington, D.C.

Johnston, D. 1961. *Biosystematics of American Crows.* University of Washington Press, Seattle. 119 pp.

Kessel, Brina, Deborah A. Rocque, and John S. Barclay. 2002. "Greater Scaup *(Aythya marila)*." In *The Birds of North America Online,* edited by A. Poole. Ithaca: Cornell Lab of Ornithology. Retrieved from *The Birds of North America Online:* http://bna.birds.cornell.edu/bna/species/650/articles/introduction.

King County. 1972. *Summary Shoreline Inventory: King County.* King County Department of Planning, Seattle. 142 pp.

King County. 1975. *Vashon-Maury Island Physical Characteristics and Shoreline Inventory.* Land Use Management Division, King County Department of Community Development, Seattle. 63 pp.

King County. 1986. "Land Use Map," *Vashon Community Plan Update.* King County Division of Planning. Department of Planning and Community Development, Seattle.

King County. 1995. *Vashon-Maury Island Ground Water Management Plan Supplement: Area Characterization.* Seattle-King County Department of Public Health, Environmental Health Division, Seattle.

King County. 1998. "Rural Forest Program," *Forest Monitoring 1997 Annual Report.* King County Department of Natural Resources, Seattle.

King County. 2009a. *Vashon-Maury Island 2008 Water Resources Data Report.* Prepared by E. W. Ferguson, King County Water and Land Resources Division. Seattle.

King County. 2009b. *Vashon-Maury Island Hydrologic Modeling. Technical Report.* Prepared by DHI Water and Environment. 88 pp.

King County. 2010a. *Vashon-Maury Island 2009 Water Resources Data Report.* Prepared by E. W. Ferguson, King County Water and Land Resources Division. Seattle. 101 pp.

King County. 2010b. *Initial Assessment of Nutrient Loading to Quartermaster Harbor.* Prepared by C. De Gasperi, King County Department of Natural Resources and Parks, Water and Land Resources Division. Seattle.

King County. 2012a. *Quartermaster Harbor Nearshore Freshwater Inflows Assessment.* Prepared by C. De Gasperi and E. Ferguson. King County Department of Natural Resources and Parks, Water and Land Resources Division. Seattle.

King County. 2012b. *WRIA 9 Status and Trends Monitoring Report: 2005-2010.* Prepared by the WRIA 9 Implementation Technical Committee: J. Latterell, K. Higgins, K. Lynch, K. Bergeron, T. Patterson, Elissa Ostergaard, and Matt Knox. Department of Natural Resources and Parks. Seattle.

King County. 2013a. *Current Use Taxation Programs.* "Public Benefit Rating System and Timber Lands." Department of Natural Resources and Parks. Seattle. Available online at: www.kingcounty.gov.

REFERENCES

King County. 2013b. *Current Use Taxation Programs.* "Farm and Agricultural Lands and Designated Forest Land Programs." Department of Assessments. Seattle. Available online at: www.kingcounty.gov.

Kitchin, E. A. 1925. "Maury Island, Puget Sound, Washington." *The Murrelet* 6(3):64.

Kitchin, E. A. 1934. "Recording of a Colony of Wilson's Phalarope in Western Washington." *The Murrelet* 15(2):50.

Krueger, K. L., K. B. Pierce, Jr., T. Quinn, and D. E. Penttila. 2010. "Anticipated Effects of Sea Level Rise in Puget Sound on Two Beach-Spawning Fishes." In *Puget Sound Shorelines and the Impacts of Armoring—Proceedings of a State of the Science Workshop, May 2009: U.S. Geological Survey Scientific Investigations Report 2010-5254,* edited by H. Shipman, M. N. Dethier, G. Gelfenbaum, K. L. Fresh, and R. S. Dinicola, pp. 171-178.

Larrison, E. J. 1947. *Field Guide to the Birds of King County.* Seattle Audubon Society. Seattle. 66 pp.

Larrison, E. J. 1952. *Field Guide to the Birds of Puget Sound.* Seattle Audubon Society, Seattle. 112 pp.

Larrison, E. J., and K. G. Sonnenberg. 1968. *Washington Birds: Their Location and Identification.* Seattle Audubon Society, Seattle. 258 pp.

Lewis, M. G., and F. A. Sharpe. 1987. *Birding in the San Juan Islands.* The Mountaineers, Seattle. 219 pp.

Lundquist, R. W., and J. M. Mariani. 1991. "Nesting Habitat and Abundance of Snag-Dependent Birds in the Southern Washington Cascade Range." In *Wildlife and Vegetation of Unmanaged Douglas-Fir Forests: General Technical Report PNW-GTR-285,* edited by L. F. Ruggiero, K. B. Aubry, A. B. Carey, and M. H. Huff, pp. 221-240. USDA, Forest Service.

Manuwal, D. A. 1983. "Avian Abundance and Guild Structure in Two Montana Coniferous Forests." *The Murrelet* 64(1):1-11.

Manuwal, D. A. 1986. "Characteristics of Bird Assemblages along Linear Riparian Zones in Western Montana." *The Murrelet* 67(1):10-18.

Manuwal, D. A. 1991. "Spring Bird Communities in the Southern Washington Cascade Range." In *Wildlife and Vegetation of Unmanaged Douglas-Fir Forests: General Technical Report PNW-GTR-285,* edited by L. F. Ruggiero, K. B. Aubry, A. B. Carey, and M. H. Huff, pp. 159-180. USDA, Forest Service.

Manuwal, D. A., and M. H. Huff. 1987. "Spring and Winter Bird Populations in a Douglas-Fir Forest Sere." *The Journal of Wildlife Management* 51(3):586-595.

Marra, P. P., S. Griffing, C. Caffrey, A. M. Kilpatrick, R. McLean, C. Brand, E. Saito, A. P. Dupuis, L. Kramer, and R. Novak. 2004. "West Nile Virus and Wildlife." *BioScience* 54(5):393-402.

Marshall, D. B., M. G. Hunter, and A. L. Contreras, eds. 2003, 2006. *Birds of Oregon: A General Reference.* Oregon State University Press, Corvallis, OR. 768 pp.

Marzluff, J. M., and M. Restani. 1999. "The Effects of Forest Fragmentation on Avian Nest Predation." In *Forest Fragmentation: Wildlife and Management Implications,* edited by J. A. Rochelle, L. A. Lehmann, and J. Wisniewski, pp. 155-170. Brill, Leiden, The Netherlands.

Marzluff, J. M., R. Bowman, and R. Donnelly (eds.). 2001a. *Avian Ecology and Conservation in an Urbanizing World.* Kluwer Academic Publishers, Norwell, Massachusetts. 585 pp.

Marzluff, J. M., K. J. McGowan, R. Donnelly, and R. L. Knight. 2001b. "Causes and Consequences of Expanding American Crow Populations." In *Avian Ecology and Conser-*

vation in an Urbanizing World, edited by J. M. Marzluff, R. Bowman, and R. Donnelly, pp. 331-363. Kluwer Academic Publishers, Norwell, Massachusetts.

Marzluff, John. 2013. Personal communication. Marzluff is a professor in the College of the Environment at the University of Washington and the author of many books and articles on corvids. Among birders, he is famous for showing that crows can recognize individual humans by their faces. He did this by wearing two rubber masks: one mask was "the good guy"(Vice-President Dick Cheney) and never bothered crows. The other was the "bad guy" (a Neanderthal) and banded crows. The crows remembered the bad guy and harassed him whenever he appeared but always ignored the good guy.

Matthiessen, P. 1959. *Wildlife in America.* Viking Press, New York. 304 pp.

Mattocks, P. 1988. "The October Frigatebird and Other Sightings." *Washington Ornithological Society Newsletter* 1:1-2.

Mattocks, Phil. Various years. Archival notecards for *Earthcare Northwest* bird sightings. Seattle Audubon Society.

McGarigal, K., and W. C. McComb. 1999. "Forest Fragmentation Effects on Breeding Bird Communities in the Oregon Coast Range." In *Forest Fragmentation: Wildlife and Management Implications,* edited by J. A. Rochelle, L. A. Lehmann, and J. Wisniewski, pp. 223-246. Brill, Leiden, The Netherlands.

Mlodinow, Steve. 2007. Personal communications. Mlodinow is one of the editors of *Birds of Washington.*

Moll, A. F. 1993. *Community-Integrated Forest Management Planning; the Vashon-Maury Island Project.* Thesis (Masters). University of Washington, Seattle. 29 pp.

Monson, M. A. 1956. "Nesting of Trumpeter Swan in the Lower Copper River Basin, Alaska." *Condor* 58(6):444-445.

Morrison, M. L., B. G. Marcot, and R. W. Mannan. 1992. *Wildlife-Habitat Relationships: Concepts and Applications.* University of Wisconsin Press, Madison. 343pp.

Morrison, M. L., I. C. Timossi, K. A. With, P. N. Manley. 1985. "Use of Tree Species by Forest Birds during Winter and Summer." *The Journal of Wildlife Management* 49(4):1098-1102.

Mowbray, Thomas B. 2002. "Canvasback *(Aythya valisineria)."* In *The Birds of North America Online,* edited by A. Poole. Ithaca: Cornell Lab of Ornithology. Retrieved from. *The Birds of North America Online:* http://bna.birds.cornell.edu/bna/species/659/articles/introduction.

National Audubon Society. 1947-1970. "Regional Reports," *Audubon Field Notes* (abbreviated *AFN),*Vols. 1-24.

National Audubon Society. 1971-1994. "Regional Reports,"*American Birds* (abbreviated *AB),* Vols. 25-48.

National Audubon Society. 1994-1998. "Regional Reports," *Field Notes* (abbreviated *FN)* Vols. 48-52.

NatureServe. 2009. International Ecological Classification Standard. Terrestrial Ecological Classifications. NatureServe Central Databases. Arlington, VA. Data current as of 06 February 2009. Definitions of NatureServe's ecological classifications are online at: http://www.natureserve.org/getData/vegData/nsDescriptions.pdf.

Nysewander, D. R., J. R. Evenson, B. L. Murphie, and T. A. Cyra. 2001. *Status and Trends For a Suite of Key Diving Marine Bird Species Characteristic of Greater Puget Sound, As Examined by the Marine Bird Component, Puget Sound Ambient Monitoring Program (PSAMP).* Washington Department of Fish and Wildlife.

REFERENCES

Nysewander, D. R., J. R. Evenson, B. L. Murphie and T. A. Cyra. 2003. *Trends Observed for Selected Marine Bird Species during 1993-2002 Winter Aerial Surveys, Conducted by the PSAMP Bird Component (WDFW) in the Inner Marine Waters of Washington State.* Washington Department of Fish and Wildlife.

Ohmann, J. L., and M. J. Gregory. 2002. "Predictive mapping of forest composition and structure with direct gradient analysis and nearest-neighbor imputation in coastal Oregon, USA." *Canadian Journal of Forest Research.* 32:725-741. Online at: http://www.fsl.orst.edu/lemma/export/pubs/ohmann_gregory_2002_CJFR.pdf.

Opperman, H. et al. 2003. *A Birder's Guide to Washington.* American Birding Association, Colorado Springs, CO. 635 pp.

Ostrom, C. M. 2002. "West Nile has arrived: Virus found in dead bird." *Seattle Times,* October 3, 2002.

Pacific Flyway Council. 2004. *Pacific Flyway Management Plan for Pacific Population of Brant.* Pacific Flyway Council, U.S. Fish & Wildlife Service. Portland, Oregon. 66 pp. Online at: http://pacificflyway.gov/Documents/Pb_plan.pdf.

Pacific Flyway Council. 2006. *Pacific Flyway Management Plan for the Wrangel Island Population of Lesser Snow Geese.* White Goose Subcommittee, Pacific Flyway Study Comm. [c/o USFWS], Portland, OR. Unpublished report. 20 pp. plus appendices.

Palazzi, D., M. Daily, J. Udelhoven, and P. Bloch (principal authors). 2004. *Final Supplemental Environmental Impact Statement: Maury Island Aquatic Reserve.* Washington State Department of Natural Resources, Aquatic Resources Program. Olympia, WA.

Paulsen, Ian. 2005. Personal communication. Paulsen tracks birds in Kitsap County and helps efforts to keep the county list up to date.

Paulson, D. R. 1992. "Northwest Bird Diversity: From Extravagant Past and Changing Present to Precarious Future." *The Northwest Environmental Journal* 8(1):71-118.

Paulson, D. 1993. *Shorebirds of the Pacific Northwest.* University of Washington Press in association with Seattle Audubon Society, Seattle. 406 pp.

Peale, T. R. 1848. *United States Exploring Expedition during the years 1838, 1839, 1840, 1841, 1842, Under the Command of Charles Wilkes, USN,* Vol. VIII: Mammalia and Ornithology. Printed by C. Sherman, Philadelphia. 338 pp.

Penttila, D. E. 1999. *Spawning Areas of the Pacific Herring* (Clupea), *Surf Smelt* (Hypomesus), *and the Pacific Sand Lance* (Ammodytes) *in Central Puget Sound, Washington.* Washington Department of Fish and Wildlife, Marine Resources Division.

Peterson, R. T. 1990. *A Field Guide to Western Birds.* Houghton Mifflin Company, Boston. 434 pp.

Price, K., S. Starratt, and R. Woodruff. 1999. *Final Environmental Assessment and Finding of No Significant Impact and Decision for Management of Conflicts Associated with Non-migratory (resident) Canada Geese in the Puget Sound Area.* Wildlife Services, Animal and Plant Health Inspection Service, United States Department of Agriculture, 65pp. View at http://www.aphis.usda.gov/regulations/pdfs/nepa/WA%20Resident%20Goose%20EA%201999.pdf.

Pyle, P. 1997. *Identification Guide to North American Birds.* Part I. Slate Creek Press, Bolinas, CA. 732 pp.

Ralph, C. J. 1994. "Case Histories: Evidence of Changes in Populations of the Marbled Murrelet in the Pacific Northwest." *Studies in Avian Biology* 15:286-292. In *A Century of Avifaunal Change in Western North America,* Proceedings of an International Symposium at the Centennial Meeting of the Cooper Ornithological Society, Sacramento, California, April 17, 1993. Cooper Ornithological Society.

Raphael, M. G., K. V. Rosenberg, and B. G. Marcot. 1988. "Large-scale Changes in Bird Populations of Douglas-Fir Forests, Northwestern California." *Bird Conservation* 3:63-83.

Rathbun, S. F. 1902. "A List of the Land Birds of Seattle, Washington, and Vicinity." *The Auk* 19(2):131-141.

Rathbun, S. F. 1911. "Notes on Birds of Seattle, Washington." *The Auk* 28(4):492-494.

Rathbun, S. F. 1915. "List of Water and Shore Birds of the Puget Sound Region in the Vicinity of Seattle." *The Auk* 32(4):459-465.

Reed, A., D. H. Ward, D. V. Derksen, and J. S. Sedinger. 1998. "Brant *(Branta bernicla)*." In *The Birds of North America Online,* edited by A. Poole. Ithaca: Cornell Lab of Ornithology. Retrieved from *The Birds of North America Online:* http://bna.birds.cornell.edu/bna/species/337/articles/introduction.

Richards, Alan. 2005. Personal communication. Richards has birded in Washington for many decades.

Rising, J. D. 1996. *A Guide to the Identification and Natural History of the Sparrows of the United States and Canada.* Academic Press, San Diego, CA. 365 pp.

Robinette-Ha, Renee. 2005. Personal communication. Robinette-Ha is a lecturer/research scientist at the University of Washington, specializing in animal behavior.

Robinson, S. K., F. R. Thompson III, T. M. Donovan, D. R. Whitehead, and J. Faaborg. 1995. "Regional Forest Fragmentation and the Nesting Success of Migratory Birds." *Science* 267 (March 31, 1995):1987-1990.

Rogers, R. E., Jr. 2000. *The Status and Microhabitat Selection of Streaked Horned Lark, Western Bluebird, Oregon Vesper Sparrow and Western Meadowlark in Western Washington.* Thesis submitted to Evergreen State College, Olympia, WA.

Rogers, Russell. 2009. Personal communication. Rogers is a biologist for the Washington Department of Natural Resources.

Sayer, Fred. 2005. Personal communications. Sayer is a forestry consultant and co-founder of Vashon Forest Stewards.

Schroeder, Thomas. 2013. *Witnessing the Pre-Settlement Forests of the Puget Sound Country.* Unpublished manuscript.

Sharpe, F. A. 1993. *Olympic Peninsula Birds, The Song Birds.* Unpublished draft manuscript. 206 pp.

Shugart, Gary 2013. Personal communications. Shugart is an Island resident, ornithologist, and curator at the Slater Museum of Natural History at the University of Puget Sound in Tacoma.

Sibley, D. A. 2000. *National Audubon Society The Sibley Guide to Birds.* Alfred A. Knopf, New York, 545 pp.

Sidles, Constance. 2013. Personal communication. Sidles is a master birder who birds Montlake Fill nearly every day.

Siegrist, Richard. 2013. Personal communications. Siegrist is a master birder and has watched birds on Vashon Island since the 1940s.

Slipp, J. W. 1939-1956. Unpublished field journals. Slater Museum of Natural History, University of Puget Sound, Tacoma, WA.

Slipp, J. W. 1942a. "Franklin Gull in the State of Washington: A First Record." *The Murrelet* 23(1):18.

Slipp, J. W. 1942b. "Tube-nosed Swimmers of Puget Sound. " *The Murrelet* 23(2):54-59.

Smith, M. R., P. W. Mattocks, Jr., K. M. Cassidy. 1997. "Breeding Birds of Washington

References

State. Volume 4." In *Washington State Gap Analysis-Final Report*, edited by K. M. Cassidy, C. E. Grue, M. R. Smith, and K. M. Dvornich. Seattle Audubon Society Publications in Zoology No. 1, Seattle, 538 pp.

Smith , P. W. 1987. "The Eurasian Collared-Dove Arrives in the Americas." *American Birds* 41(5):1370-79.

Stein, J. K. and L. S. Phillips, eds. 2002. *Vashon Island Archaeology: A View from Burton Acres Shell Midden.* Burke Museum of Natural History and Culture Research Report No. 8. University of Washington Press, Seattle. 151 pp.

Stick, Kurt C. 2013. Personal communication. Stick works with the Washington Department of Fish and Wildlife.

Stick, K. C., and A. Lindquist. 2009. *2008 Washington State Herring Stock Status Report.* Washington Department of Fish and Wildlife, Fish Program, Fish Management Division. 111 pp.

Stout, G. D. (ed.), R. V. Clem (illus.), P. Matthiessen (text), and R. S. Palmer (species accounts). 1967. *The Shorebirds of North America.* Viking Press, New York. 270 pp.

Suckley, G., and J. G. Cooper. 1860. "No. 3: Report upon the birds collected on the survey" in Part III-Zoological Report, in *Natural history of Washington territory and Oregon with much relating to Minnesota, Nebraska, Kansas, Utah, and California, between the thirty-sixth and forty-ninth parallels of latitude, being those parts of the final reports on the survey of the Northern Pacific railroad route, relating to the natural history of the regions explored, with full catalogues and descriptions of the plants and animals collected from 1853 to 1860.* Bailliere Brothers, New York.

Terborgh, J. 1989. *Where Have All the Birds Gone?* Princeton University Press, Princeton, NJ. 224 pp.

Terres, J. K. 1991. *The Audubon Society Encyclopedia of North American Birds.* Random House, New York. 1109 pp.

Tewksbury, J. J., S. J. Hejl, and T. E. Martin. 1998. "Breeding Productivity Does Not Decline with Increasing Fragmentation in a Western Landscape." *Ecology* 79(8):2890-2903.

Trevathan, Sue. 1999-2013. Personal communications. Vashon count circle Christmas Bird Count statistics by area. Vashon-Maury Island Audubon Society, Vashon, WA. Thanks to Sue Trevathan for acting as the CBC compiler since organizing the Vashon count.

Tweeters. 1988-2013. Online bulletin board hosted by Burke Museum, University of Washington. To subscribe: http://mailman2.u.washington.edu/mailman/listinfo/tweeters/.

USGS Patuxent Wildlife Research Center. 2013. North American Breeding Bird Survey Internet data set. Thanks to Carole Elder for collecting the data each year for the Vashon Island Breeding Bird Survey route.

Van Os, Joseph. 2013. Personal communications. Van Os is a bird bander and wildlife photo tour manager.

Vashon-Maury Island Groundwater Advisory Committee. 1998. *Vashon-Maury Island Groundwater Management Plan.* King County Department of Natural Resources, Water and Land Resources Division, Seattle.

Vashon-Maury Island Groundwater Protection Committee. 2010. *Vashon-Maury Island GWPC Overview and Comment-July 28, 2010: Vashon-Maury Island Phase II Hydrologic Model.* King County Department of Natural Resources and Parks.

Vashon-Maury Island Groundwater Protection Committee. 2011. *Assessing Our Liquid Assets: How's Our Water Doing? A Report Card to the Community.* Vashon-Maury Island Groundwater Protection Committee, Vashon.

Vashon-Maury Island Groundwater Protection Committee. 2012. *Island Stream Invertebrate Survey (ISIS) Final Report.* Prepared by Bianca Perla, Vashon Nature Center. Online at: http://www.vashonnaturecenter.org/ibi/.

Vashon-Maury Island Land Trust. 2012. *Annual Report.* Online at: http://www.vashonlandtrust.org/resources/annual-reports/.

Vashon-Maury Island Park & Recreation District. 2000. *Vashon-Maury Island Parks Map.* Available at King County Department of Natural Resources and Parks, Vashon-Maury Island Park District, or Vashon-Maury Island Land Trust.

Vashon Nature Center. 2013. *Salmon Watching 2012.* Online at http://www.vashonnaturecenter.org/salmonwatchers/.

Vermeer, K. 1981. "Food and Populations of Surf Scoters in British Columbia." *Wildfowl* 32:107-116.

Vermeer, K., and L. Rankin. 1984. "Population Trends in Nesting Double-crested and Pelagic Cormorants in Canada." *The Murrelet* 65(1): 1-9.

Wahl, T. R., and S. M. Speich. 1984. "Survey of Marine Birds in Puget Sound, Hood Canal and Waters East of Whidbey Island, Washington in Summer 1982." *Western Birds* 15(1):1-14.

Wahl, T. R. 1995. *Birds of Whatcom County.* T. R. Wahl, Bellingham, WA. 184 pp.

Wahl, T. R., and D. R. Paulson. 1991. *A Guide to Bird Finding in Washington.* T. R. Wahl, Bellingham, WA. 178 pp.

Wahl, T. R., B. Tweit, and S. G. Mlodinow (eds.) 2005. *Birds of Washington: Status and Distribution.* Oregon State University Press, Corvallis, OR. 436 pp.

WOSNews. 1994-2013. "Washington Bird Field Notes." Washington Ornithological Society.

Wild Fish Conservancy. 2002. *Vashon Island Water Type and Stream Mouth Assessment.* Website: http://wildfishconservancy.org.

White, R. 1980. *Land Use, Environment, and Social Change.* University of Washington Press, Seattle. 234 pp.

Williams, D. B. 2005. "A Little Goose Poop." *Pacific Northwest Magazine* 07/17/2005. Seattle Times.

Willsie, Dan. 2005. Personal communications. Willsie is a master birder and has watched birds on Vashon Island since the 1940s.

Willson, Mary F., and Hugh E. Kingery. 2011. "American Dipper *(Cinclus mexicanus).*" In *The Birds of North America Online,* edited by A. Poole. Ithaca: Cornell Lab of Ornithology. Retrieved from *The Birds of North America Online:* http://bna.birds.cornell.edu/bna/species/229/articles/introduction.

Wilson, U. W., and J. B. Atkinson. 1995. "Black Brant Winter and Spring Staging Use at Two Washington Coastal Areas in Relation to Eelgrass Abundance." *Condor* 97: 91-98.

Woodroffe, P. J. 2002. *Vashon Island's Agricultural Roots: Tales of the Tilth as Told by Island Farmers.* Writer's Club Press, San Jose, New York, Lincoln, Shanghai. 143 pp.

Yocom, C. F. 1961. "Recent Changes in the Canada Goose Population in Geographical Areas in Washington." *The Murrelet* 42(2):13-21.

Index

A

Aerial Space habitat. *See* Habitat Types: Aerial Space
Agren Park 77
Auklet
   Cassin's 128, 215–216
   Rhinoceros 48–49, 92, 93, 100, 101–102, 104, 128, 216

B

Bachelor Road 100–101
Bank Road 10, 19
Bates Road 49, 102–103
Blackbird
   Brewer's 16, 131, 302–311
   Red-winged 20–21, 53–54, 68, 72, 112, 131, 299–311
   Rusty 131, 302
   Yellow-headed 99, 131, 301
Bluebird
   Mountain 130, 270
   Western 16–17, 29–30, 130, 268–270
Bobwhite, Northern 21–22, 86, 125, 162
Booby, Brown 126, 172–173
Brant 29, 41, 48–49, 51, 93, 107, 108, 124, 136–137
Bufflehead 27–28, 48, 54, 92, 96, 99, 100, 103, 106, 108, 109, 110, 111, 112, 125, 155–156
Bunting
   Lazuli 16–18, 65–66, 69, 99, 112, 116, 131, 299
   Snow 130, 278–279, **279**
Burma Road 100
Burton Acres Park 74–75, 105
Bushtit 60–61, 64, 65–66, 72, 92, 106, 116, 130, 258–259

C

Camp Sealth 102–103
Canvasback 112, 125, 148
Cedarhurst Road 100
Chat, Yellow-breasted 131, 286
Chickadee
   Black-capped 18–19, 63–64, 65, 72, 105, 130, **256**, 256–257
   Chestnut-backed 60–61, 72, 99, 105, 130, 258
   Mountain 130, 257–258
Christensen Creek 55, 74
Christensen Pond Preserve 74, 103–104
Coot, American 48, 51, 111, 126, 189
Cormorant
   Brandt's 48, 51, 100, 126, 174–175
   Double-crested 26, 48, 51, 54, 100, 108, 126, 175–176
   Pelagic 48, 51, 100, 126, **176**, 176–177
Cowbird, Brown-headed 23–24, 54, 60, 64, 65, 68, 72, 83–84, 131, 302–304, **303**
Crane, Sandhill 126, 189
Creeper, Brown 60, 63–64, 94, 96, 106, 130, 260–261
Crossbill, Red 14, 60–61, 72, 94, 132, 307–309, **308**
Crow
   American 23–24, 51, 60, 64, 68, 72, 129, **246**, 247
   Northwestern 24, 129, 247–249

D

Developed Area habitat. *See* Habitat Types: Developed Area
Dipper, American 54–55, 64, 95, 130, 265–266
Dock Street 113
Dockton Forest and Natural Area 77, 84, 114
Dockton Park 48, 74–75, 77, 112–113
Douglas-fir Forest habitat. *See* Habitat Types: Douglas-fir Forest
Dove
   Eurasian Collared- 22, 68, 113, 128, 218–219
   Mourning 16, 115, 128, 219–220
Dowitcher
   Long-billed 94, 127, 199
   Short-billed 127, 198–199
Dry Douglas-fir/Madrone Forest habitat. *See* Habitat Types: Dry Douglas-fir/Madrone Forest

Duck
  Harlequin 27, 48–49, 51, 92, 109, 125, 150–151
  Long-tailed 109, 125, 155
  Ring-necked 20, 52, 54, 96, 125, 149
  Ruddy 48, 110, 111, 125, 161
  Wood 20, 25–26, 52, 54, 96, 124, 142
Dunlin 51, 107, 127, 198

E

Eagle, Bald 26–27, 48, 51, 52, 54, 64, 68, 70, 92, 96, 101, 103, 107, 111, 112, 113, 126, **180**, 182–183
Egret
  Cattle 126, 179
  Great 126, 179
Ellis Creek 61, 74
Ellisport 41, 49, 51, 108–109

F

Falcon, Peregrine 26–27, 51, 92, 107, 113, 129, 236–238
Fern Cove 39, **50**, **56**, 74, 77, 88, 93–94
Fields, Farmland, and Pasture habitat.
  See Habitat Types: Fields, Farmland, and Pasture
Finch
  Cassin's 131, 306
  House 23–24, 64, 65, 68, 72, 116, 131, **306**, 306–307
  Purple 60, 64, 71–72, 103, 131, 305
Fisher Pond 19, 39, 52, 54–55, 74, 77, 82, 88, 96–97
Flicker, Northern 18–19, 60, 64, 72, 129, 233–234, **234**
Flycatcher
  Hammond's 54, 129, 239
  Olive-sided 60, 64, 100, 107, 129, 238
  Pacific-slope 55, 60–61, 64, 72, 92, 94, 100, 104, 106, 107, 129, 240
  Willow 56, 65–66, 72, 84, 114, 129, 239
Frigatebird, Magnificent 126, 172
Fulmar, Northern 126, 171

G

Gadwall 96, 124, 142–143
Godwit, Marbled 107, 127, 194
Gold Beach 115
Goldeneye
  Barrow's 48, 93, 109, 125, 158–159
  Common 48, 81, 93, 109, 125, 156–157
Goldfinch, American 18, 64, 65, 68, 72, 116, 132, **310**
Goose
  Cackling 124, 137–139, **138**
  Canada 21–23, 48, 51, 54, 68, 72, 112, 124, 139–140
  Greater White-fronted 20–21, 51, 54, 70, 106, 124, 134–135
  Snow 70, 124, 135–136
Goshawk, Northern 11–13, 126, 186
Grebe
  Clark's 126, 170–171
  Eared 48, 125, 168–169
  Horned 27, 48, 81, 92, 100, 109, 111, 115, 125, 167–168
  Pied-billed **viii**, 20–21, 48, 52, 54, 96, 125, 167
  Red-necked 27, 48, 92, 100, 109, 111, 115, 125, 168
  Western 27–29, 48, 81, 109, **110**, 111, 112–113, 125, 169–170
Green Valley 74
Grosbeak
  Black-headed 18, 64, 72, 95, 100, 106, 116, 131, 298–299
  Evening 60, 64, 72, 132, 310–311
Grouse, Sooty 12–13, 86, 125, 164
Guillemot, Pigeon 48, 51–52, 128, 212–214
Gull
  Bonaparte's 24, 28–29, 48–49, 51, 93, 101, 104, **105**, 108, 127, 202–311
  California 48, 51, 93, 108, 127, 206–311
  Franklin's 127, 203–311
  Glaucous 100, 128, 209–311
  Glaucous-winged 48–49, 51, 68, 72, 93, 100, **101**, 108–109, 112, 128, 208–311
  Heermann's 48, 51, 100, 127, 204–311
  Herring 48, 51, 127, 207–311
  Little 127, 203
  Mew 48, 51, 93, 108, 112, 127, 204–205
  Ring-billed 127, 205–206
  Sabine's 93, 116, 127, 201–202
  Thayer's 100, **101**, 127, 208
  Western 48, 100, 127, 206

H

Habitat Types
  Aerial Space 37, 39, 69–70
  Developed Area 37, 39, 70–73, **71**, 80, 85–87

INDEX

Douglas-fir Forest 37, 39, 57–61, **58**, 80
Dry Douglas-fir/Madrone Forest 37, 39, 57, **59**, 60–61, 80
Fields, Farmland, and Pasture 37, 39, 66–69, **67**, 80, 84–85
Hardwood-Dominated Mixed Forest 37, 39, **62**, 62–64, 80
Ponds, Wetlands, and Streams 37, 39, 52–56, **53**, 80–82
Saltwater 37, 39–41, **41**, 48–49, 78–81
Saltwater Shoreline 37, 39, 49–52, **50**, 78–81
Shrubby Thicket 37, 39, 64–66, **66**, 69, 80, 84–85
Wet Coniferous Forest 37, 39, **56**, 57–59, 61, 80
Hardwood-Dominated Mixed Forest habitat. *See* Habitat Types: Hardwood-Dominated Mixed Forest
Harrier, Northern 16–17, 68, 84, 103, 126, 183–184
Hawk
  Cooper's 26, 60, 64, 65, 72, 105, 126, 185–186
  Red-tailed 15–16, 18, 60, 63–64, 68, 70, 72, 84, 101, 103, 106, 112, 126, 187–188
  Rough-legged 68, 103, 126, 188
  Sharp-shinned 26, 60, 64, 65, 72, 105, 126, **184**, 185
Heron
  Great Blue 48, 51, 54, 68, 108, 113, 126, **132**, 177–179
  Green 23–24, 51, 54, 111, 126, 180–181
Hummingbird
  Anna's 23, 61, 64, 65–66, 72, 101, 115, 116, 128, **226**, 227–228
  Costa's 128, 228–229
  Rufous 60, 64, 65, 72, 96, 116, 129, 229

I

Island Center Forest 19–20, 52–54, 74, 77, 82, 84, 88, 97–99

J

Jaeger
  Parasitic 48–49, 93, 101, 128, 211–212
  Pomarine 128, 211
Jay
  Blue 129, 245
  Steller's 60, 64, 72, 106, 129, 244–245

Western Scrub- 23–24, 113, 129, 246–247
Jensen Point 105
Judd Creek 8, 54–55, 74, 77, 82, 111
Junco, Dark-eyed 60, 64, 65, 72, 106, 131, 296–298, **297**

K

Kestrel, American 16, 68, 103, 112, 129, 235–236
Killdeer 51, 54, 68, 71–73, **88**, 96, 110, 116, 126, 190–191
Kingbird, Western 50, 107, 129, 241
Kingfisher, Belted 51–52, 54, 64, 95, 129, 229
Kinglet
  Golden-crowned 13, 60–61, 64, 72, 96, 99, 105, 130, **266**, 266–267
  Ruby-crowned 64, 65, 72, 105, 130, **267**
Kingsbury Road 112
Kittiwake, Black-legged 127, 201
KVI Beach 39, 49, 50–52, 74, 107

L

Lisabeula area 20, 52, **74**, 104
Lisabeula Park 49, 77, 104
Loon
  Common 48, 92, **99**, 109, 125, 166
  Pacific 40, 48, 100, 109, 114, 125, 165–166
  Red-throated 29, 40, 48, 109, 114, 125, 164–165
  Yellow-billed 125, 166–167
Lost Lake 19, 74
Luana Beach 74

M

Mallard 48, 51, 54, 68–69, 72, 94, 96, 99, 104, 107, 111, 112, **123**, 124, 144–311, **145**
Manzanita 48, 114–115
Marjorie R. Stanley Natural Area 74–75
Martin, Purple 29–30, 51, 70, 72, 107, 108, 129, 251–253
Maury Island Marine Park **59**, 61, 66, 76–77, 84, 116
Meadowlake 20, 53, 74, 98
Meadowlark, Western 16–17, 50, 68, 107, 131, **300**, 301
Merganser
  Common 48, 109, 125, 159–160

Hooded 20–21, 48, 52–53, 54, 96, 98, 103, 106, 109, 125, 159
Red-breasted 48, 109, 125, 160–161
Merlin 51, 68, 72, 93, 107, 112, 113, 129, 236
Mileta Creek 55, 74
Monument Road 39, 53, 69, 111–112
Mukai Pond 20, **53**, 53–54, 65, 97
Murre, Common 48–49, 100, 102, 128, 212
Murrelet
  Ancient 128, 215
  Marbled 11–14, 48, 100, 102, 128, 214–215

N

Neill Point Natural Area 101
Nighthawk, Common 29–30, 70, 128, 226
North Klahanie shore 74
Nuthatch
  Red-breasted 60, 64, 72, 103, 105, 107, 130, 259–260
  White-breasted 130, 260

O

Old Mill Road Pond 39, 103–104
Oriole, Bullock's 18, 64, 72, 131, 304
Osprey 26–27, 48, 52, 54, 70, **71**, 96, 107, 126, 181–182
Owl
  Barn 16, 68–69, 84, 96, 103, 128, 220–221
  Barred 23–24, 60, 63–64, **98**, 99, 100, 101, 106, 128, 224
  Great Horned 60, 64, 99, 100, 128, 221–223, **222**
  Long-eared 128, 225
  Northern Pygmy- 128, 223
  Northern Saw-whet 60, 64, 99, 100, 128, 225
  Short-eared 114, 128, 225
  Snowy 114, 128, 223
  Spotted 11–14, 128, 223–224
  Western Screech- 128, 221
Oystercatcher, Black 116, 126, 191

P

Paradise Cove 102–103
Paradise Ridge Park 77
Paradise Valley 10, 18, 39, 61, 66, 106–107
Paradise Valley Preserve 77

Partridge
  Chinese Bamboo- 21–22, 163
  Gray 21–22, 86, 125, 162–163
Pelican, Brown 26–27, 126, **173**, 173–174
Phalarope
  Red 116, 127, 201
  Red-necked 48–49, 93, 101, 127, 200–311
  Wilson's 127, 200
Pheasant, Ring-necked 21–22, 65, 68, 72, 103, 125, 163
Phoebe, Say's 50, 107, 129, 240–241
Pigeon
  Band-tailed 25–26, 50, 60, 64, 72, 94, 101, 107, 128, 217–218, **218**
  Rock 22, 68, 71–73, 93, 128, 216–217
Pintail, Northern 51, 52, 111, 112, 125, 147
Pipit, American 50–51, 68–69, 103, 107, 130, 276–277
Plover
  Black-bellied 107, 126, 189–190
  Semipalmated 50–51, 107, 126, 190
Point Robinson 49, 52, 66, 77, 115–116
Ponds, Wetlands, and Streams habitat. *See* Habitat Types: Ponds, Wetlands, and Streams
Portage 8, 48–49, 53, 109–110
Puffin, Tufted 128, 216

Q

Quail, California 21–22, 64, 72, 86, 125, 161–162
Quartermaster Harbor 8, 10, 19, 28, 39, 40–41, **41**, 48, 78–79, 81, 110–111

R

Raab's Lagoon 39, 52, **66**, 77, 112
Rail, Virginia 51, 53, 54, 69, 109, 111, 126, 188
Raven, Common 60, 68, 101, 103, 129, 249–250
Reddings Beach 49, 102–103
Redhead 149
Redstart, American 131, 281
Robin, American 18–19, 60, 64, 68, 71–72, 130, 273–274, **275**

S

Saltwater habitat. *See* Habitat Types: Saltwater

Saltwater Shoreline habitat. *See* Habitat Types: Saltwater Shoreline
Sanderling 49, 51, 107, 110, 111, 127, 195
Sandpiper
  Baird's 50, 107, 127, 197
  Least 26, 50–51, 54, 107, 127, 197
  Pectoral 26, 50, 51, 107, 127, 197–198
  Semipalmated 50, 107, 127, 195
  Solitary 54, 96, 127, 192
  Spotted 51, 54, 94, 102, 104, 112, 116, 126, **191**, 191–192
  Western **iii**, 25–26, 50–51, 54, 96, 107, 110, 127, 195–196
Sandy Shores 115
Sapsucker
  Red-breasted 60, 64, 101, 103, 129, 231–232
  Red-naped 129, 231
Scaup
  Greater 48, 109, 125, 149–150
  Lesser 20, 54, 125, 150
Scoter
  Black 48, 111, 114, 125, 154–155
  Surf 48, 109, 125, 151–153
  White-winged 48, 109, 125, 153–154
Shawnee 48, 51, 111
Shearwater
  Short-tailed 115, 126, 171–172
  Sooty 126, 171
Shinglemill Creek 50, 54–55, 57, 59, **62**, 63, 74, 82
Shinglemill Creek Preserve 77, 94–96
Shoveler, Northern 20, 52, 54, 96, 98, 125, 147
Shrike, Northern 129, 241
Shrubby Thicket habitat. *See* Habitat Types: Shrubby Thicket
Singer Pond 20, 39, 52–53, 106–107
Siskin, Pine 60, 64, 72, 103, 132, 309
Snipe, Wilson's 54, 68–69, 96, 99, 106, 127, 199–200
Solitaire, Townsend's 106, 130, 270–271, **271**
Sparrow
  Chipping 16–17, 131, 287
  Fox 64, 65, 72, 100, 106, 112, 131, 289–290
  Golden-crowned 16–17, 65, 68, 72, 100, 104, 106, 112, 131, 295–296
  Harris's 16–17, 65, 131, 293

House 22, 30, 68, 71–73, 132, 311
Lincoln's 54, 65–66, 68, 106, 112, 116, 131, 292
Savannah 15–17, 51, 68–69, 84, 103, 107, 112, 131, **288**, 289
Song 51, 54, 60, 64, 65, 72, 100, 112, 131, **291**, 291–292
Vesper 16, 68, 131, 287–289
White-crowned 16–17, 65, 68, 72, 104, 106, 112, 114, 116, 131, 293–295, **294**
White-throated 16–17, 65–66, 131, 292–293
Stanley Natural Area. *See* Marjorie R. Stanley Natural Area
Starling, European 22, 30, 51, 64, 68, 71–73, 93, 130, 275–276
Storm-Petrel
  Fork-tailed 126, 172
  Leach's 126, 172
Surfbird 127, 194
Swallow
  Barn 23–25, 51, 54, 68, 70, 72, 92, 96, 107, 130, 255–256
  Cliff 23–25, 51, 68, 70, 72, 112, 130, 255
  Northern Rough-winged 51–52, 70, 96, 112, 130, 254–255
  Tree 29–30, 51, 54, 64, 69, 70, 72, 96, 99, 129, **252**, 253–254
  Violet-green 54, 60, 68, 70, 72, 92, 96, 107, 130, 254
Swan
  Trumpeter 25–26, 70, 96, 124, 140–141
  Tundra 70, 124, 141
Swift
  Black 128, 227
  Vaux's 11–12, 64, 69–70, 128, 227
Sylvan Beach 49, 100

T

Tahlequah 74, 100–101
Tahlequah-Point Defiance ferry 49, 101–102
Tanager, Western 60, 64, 72, 95, 100, 106, 131, 298
Tattler, Wandering 107, 127, 192
Teal
  Blue-winged 96, 124, 146
  Cinnamon 124, 146
  Green-winged 48, 50–52, 54, 94, 96, 107, 125, 148

Tern
  Arctic 128, 211
  Caspian 23–24, 48–49, 51, 128, 209–210
  Common 28–29, 48–49, 93, 101, 128, 210–211
Thrush
  Hermit 13, 60, 102, 130, 272–273
  Swainson's 18–19, 55, 60, 64, 92, 100, 114, 116, 130, 271–272
  Varied 55–56, 60–61, 64, 71–72, 94, 100, 106, 130, 274
Towhee, Spotted 60–61, 64, 65, 72, 116, 131, **286**, 286–287
Tramp Harbor 8, 39, 49, 52, 109
Tramp Harbor Creek 74
Turnstone, Black 49, 51, **108**, 127, 194

V

Vashon Clinic area 106
Vashon-Fauntleroy ferry 49, 93
Vashon ferry dock 92–93
Vashon Lake 19, **21**
Vashon-Southworth ferry 49, 93
Vireo
  Cassin's 60, 106, 129, 242
  Hutton's 18–19, 60, 63–64, 96, 98, 101, 116, 129, 242–243
  Red-eyed 54, 129, 244
  Warbling 18, 60, 64, 65, 72, 96, 98, 106, 129, 243–244
  White-eyed 129, 242
Vulture, Turkey 70, 126, 181

W

Warbler
  Black-throated Gray 18, 60, 64, 72, 106, 131, 284
  Hermit 131, 285
  MacGillivray's 16, 64, 65, 69, 72, 112, 130, 280–281
  Nashville 54, 130, 280
  Orange-crowned 18–19, 61, 64, 65, 72, 94, 100, 106, 130, 279–280
  Palm 131, **282**, 283
  Townsend's 60, 72, 96, 99, 106, 131, 284–285

  Wilson's 11, 55, 60, 64, 65, 72, 95, 98, **102**, 106, 114, 131, 285–286
  Yellow 18, 54, 56, 64, 72, 131, 281–282
  Yellow-rumped 60, 64, 72, 100, 106, 131, 283–284
Wax Orchard Road 39, 53, 60, 68, 103–104
Waxwing, Cedar 64, 72, 104, 130, 277–278, **278**
Westside Highway 20, 39, 53, **67**, 69, 99
Wet Coniferous Forest habitat. *See* Habitat Types: Wet Coniferous Forest
Whimbrel 116, 127, 193–194
Whispering Firs Bog 20, 74, 77
Wigeon
  American 26, 48, 51, 52, 54, 69, 104, 124, 144
  Eurasian 29, 31, 48, 51, 52, 54, 69, 100, 104, 108, 124, 143–144
Woodpecker
  Downy 18, 63–64, 72–73, 103, 129, 232–233
  Hairy 12–13, 60, 129, 233
  Lewis's 12–14, 129, 230–231, **231**
  Pileated 13, 60, 64, 72, 94, **95**, 96, 103, 129, 235
Wood-Pewee, Western 60, 64, 106, 129, 238–239
Wren
  Bewick's 15–16, 18, 61, 64, 65–66, 72–73, 105, 130, 264–265
  House 16–17, 64, 65, 72, 112, 130, 261–262
  Marsh 20–21, 52–54, 98, 111, 130, 263–264
  Pacific 13, 55, 60–61, 64, 71–72, 94, 95, 96, 100, 105, 114, 130, 262–263

Y

Yellowlegs
  Greater 50–51, 54, 107, 112, **113**, 127, 192–193
  Lesser 51, 54, 127, 193
Yellowthroat, Common 15–18, 53–54, 65–66, 68–69, 72, 84, 104, 106, 112, 130, 281